CRITICAL COMPANION TO

Zora Neale Hurston

CRITICAL COMPANION TO

Zora Neale Hurston

A Literary Reference to Her Life and Work

SHARON L. JONES

le
hing

Critical Companion to Zora Neale Hurston:
A Literary Reference to Her Life and Work

Facts On File, Inc.
An imprint of Infobase Publishing
132 West 31st Street
New York NY 10001

Library of Congress Cataloging-in-Publication Data

Jones, Sharon L. (Sharon Lynette)
Critical companion to Zora Neale Hurston : a literary reference to her life and work / Sharon L. Jones.
p. cm.
Includes bibliographical references.
ISBN 978-0-8160-6885-2 (alk. paper)
1. Hurston, Zora Neale—Handbooks, manuals, etc. 2. African American authors—Biography—Handbooks, manuals, etc. 3. African Americans in literature—Handbooks, manuals, etc. I. Title.

PS3515.U789Z75 2008
813'.52—dc22 2008010052

Facts On File books are available at special discounts when purchased in bulk quantities for businesses, associations, institutions, or sales promotions. Please call our Special Sales Department in New York at (212) 967-8800 or (800) 322-8755.

You can find Facts On File on the World Wide Web at http://www.factsonfile.com

Text design by Erika K. Arroyo

Printed in the United States of America

VB Hermitage 10 9 8 7 6 5 4 3 2 1

This book is printed on acid-free paper and contains 30 percent postconsumer recycled content.

CONTENTS

ACKNOWLEDGMENTS

I wish to thank the following individuals for the support they provided me while I was researching and writing this book. Their encouragement and assistance greatly benefited me as I embarked on this experience in promoting the significance of Zora Neale Hurston as a major American author. I am grateful to my editor, Jeff Soloway, who suggested the idea of a critical companion about Zora Neale Hurston, for his devoted and careful attention to the text. I appreciate the support of my colleagues and students in the English, women's studies, and African and African-American studies programs at Wright State University. I am indebted to the Wright State University libraries and their collection of resources related to American and African-American literature. I also wish to thank Emily, Joe, and Keith Jones; Barbara McCaskill; R. Baxter Miller; Dolan Hubbard; Cheryl Collier; my mentor Mary Beth Pringle; Rose Phillips; Lillie P. Howard; and William Loudermilk. These individuals, and many others, have enabled me to help contribute to the critical discourse about Zora Neale Hurston as a significant contributor to the American literary tradition.

INTRODUCTION

When the adaptation of Zora Neale Hurston's 1937 novel *Their Eyes Were Watching God* appeared before a wide audience on network television in 2005, many Americans discovered this talented writer's work for the first time. Zora Neale Hurston passed away in 1960, poverty stricken and in bad health, but her work has enjoyed a renewed appreciation. In the past several decades, writers and scholars have helped to reintroduce students and teachers to this accomplished African-American author who made countless contributions to American literature, history, anthropology, and cultural expression. Two especially important moments in this regard occurred in the 1970s: Alice Walker's tribute to Hurston in placing a marker at her Florida grave, and the biographer Robert Hemenway's publication of his landmark *Zora Neale Hurston: A Literary Biography* (1977). While Hurston would not live to see the film version of her most popular work, the event illustrated the continued impact of her literary legacy upon American society.

Today Zora Neale Hurston's works appear on reading lists in a wide range of courses at the high school and university levels, and numerous articles, books, and conferences have contributed rich scholarly research on her life and work; passages from her writings have even been excerpted for use in standardized tests. Hurston's work has enjoyed international success, reaching audiences in

Portrait of Zora Neale Hurston, 1938 *(Library of Congress)*

countries such as Italy, Brazil, Spain, France, Germany, the Netherlands, Great Britain, and Japan. Each year, an event is held honoring Hurston in Eatonville, Florida, where she spent much of her youth. To this day, her theatrical works continue to prove relevant, with plays such as *Mule Bone* appearing on Broadway.

Born in Notasulga, Alabama, in 1891, Hurston led a life marked by migration. Although she spent her formative years in a black community in Eatonville, Florida, during much of her life she traveled between such places as Baltimore; Washington, D.C.; New York City; the Caribbean; and California. She attended Morgan Academy, Howard University, and Barnard College and was accepted into the Ph.D. program at Columbia University. Hurston published four novels: *Jonah's Gourd Vine; Their Eyes Were Watching God; Moses, Man of the Mountain;* and *Seraph on the Suwanee.* She also wrote a memoir, *Dust Tracks on a Road,* and published books about folklore and conjuring. One such book, *Mules and Men,* is considered to be a significant contribution to the field of anthropology. A dramatist as well, she wrote the plays *Color Struck* and *Mule Bone,* which was a collaboration with Langston Hughes. She also wrote numerous essays and short stories, which continue to be anthologized and read today. Her texts focus on issues of race, class, and gender in relation to the African-American experience in the United States, but Hurston proved to be a versatile writer whose themes could transcend racial boundaries. Such versatility can be seen, for example, in her novel *Seraph on the Suwanee,* which focuses primarily on white characters, with blacks taking on minor narrative roles. All told, Zora Neale Hurston composed an impressive array of works, some of which, to date, have still not been published or reissued in print, giving students and scholars potential opportunities for investigation and exploration.

Chief among her many contributions to American arts and letters was her appreciation for and celebration of the black oral tradition. By retelling black folk stories, which often focus on animals and common people, and by presenting the beauty and complexity of dialect of the black vernacular, or African-American English, Hurston was implicitly validating a literary tradition that had long been considered secondary. More than that, she presented a sense of voice and perspective in her writing that made it nuanced and memorable. Many of her literary and anthropological texts reveal her interest in promoting the oral tradition among African Americans. Hurston documented black oral folklore in her *Every Tongue Got to Confess: Negro Folk-tales from the Gulf States* and in many of her writings as a member of the depression-era Federal Writers Project (some of which are collected in the posthumous compendium *Go Gator and Muddy the Water,* which is discussed in this critical companion).

Zora Neale Hurston's life overlapped with important periods in the African-American literary scene in the 20th century, most notably the Harlem Renaissance. During this movement, there was a renewed focus on celebrating black cultural expression and the contributions of African Americans in art, literature, and music. A number of factors contributed to this flourishing of African-American expression between the years of

Langston Hughes, Charles Johnson, E. Franklin Frazier, Rudolph Fisher, and Hubert Delany near the Sugar Hill apartment of Regina Andrews and her apartment mates Louella Tucker and Ethel Nance, May 1925 *(Yale Collection of American Literature, Beinecke Rare Book and Manuscript Library)*

1900 and 1940. Among them was the Great Migration, in which many blacks migrated from the South and across the United States in search of better social and economic opportunity, which led to the expansion of concentrated black communities in the North and Midwest.

Harlem was the cultural epicenter of this rebirth dubbed the *Harlem* Renaissance, but with the new black communities throughout the United States, the movement would span a wide geographic and cultural range. Civil rights groups, such as the National Association for the Advancement of Colored People (NAACP) and the Urban League, were formed, and some of these produced journals to highlight black achievements. Two such journals were the Urban League's *Opportunity* and the NAACP's *The Crisis.* In *Opportunity,* Hurston's published pieces often won writing contests sponsored by the magazine. Patronage by wealthy individuals interested in promoting writing by black authors also facilitated literary expression during this time. For example, Zora Neale Hurston and Langston Hughes both received funding from the socialite Charlotte Osgood Mason, who was interested in supporting black culture. *The New Negro,* edited by Alain Locke and published in 1925, was a highly influential anthology at the time and featured writing by Hurston, Hughes, Jean Toomer, Countee Cullen, Claude McKay, Georgia Douglas Johnson, Anne Spencer, and Angelina Grimké. With the stock market crash of 1929 and the ensuing depression, artists and writers saw their resources and funding diminish, and the weakened economic climate brought an end to the Harlem Renaissance. Despite trying times, Hurston continued to write and to publish, a testament to her dedication to her craft. Her popularity would wane, however, and it would not be until the decades after her death in 1960 that Americans began to recognize once again the many literary treasures that Hurston left behind.

This book provides readers with extensive discussion of Hurston's life and legacy. Divided into four main parts, it covers her life history, her fiction, nonfiction, folklore, and drama, as well as people, places, and other aspects relevant to understanding Zora Neale Hurston.

Part I contains an extensive biography of Hurston's life and chronicles the major events that shaped her as a writer. This detailed discussion about Hurston's past will shed light on the social and historical context in which she lived—specifically, as an African-American female in the 20th-century United States. Her many travels and experiences influenced her writing as well as her worldview. Those interested in African-American literature, American literature generally, or women's literature will find the discussion of Hurston's life enlightening, as it reflected a variety of rich experiences during an important period in American history. She lived through major world events, such as World Wars I and II, the 1929 stock market crash and the depression of the 1930s, the Harlem Renaissance, and the emerging Civil Rights movement. The Civil Rights movement, especially, would ultimately transform the United States—and the world—as African Americans sought equal social, economic, and political rights.

Anne Spencer, contributor to the anthology *The New Negro* *(Yale Collection of American Literature, Beinecke Rare Book and Manuscript Library)*

Hurston's personal, professional, and educational experiences are often as fascinating as those of her characters in her fictional works. A master of self-representation, Hurston fashioned the narrative of her own history to present herself as the product of a rich African-American cultural heritage. The story of her life, marked by a determination to succeed as a writer despite the widespread racial and gender discrimination of the era, continues to serve as an inspiring example. The impressive amount of writing she produced is a symbol of that drive and ambition. A close examination of Hurston's life reveals that she was a complicated individual, and other interesting details about her life may come to light as scholars continue to investigate and explore it.

Part II of this book focuses primarily on Hurston's four novels: *Jonah's Gourd Vine; Their Eyes Were Watching God; Moses, Man of the Mountain;* and *Seraph on the Suwanee.* This section also addresses her other work, including short stories, plays, folklore collections—including *Mules and Men*—and her memoir, *Dust Tracks on a Road.* While Hurston's novels have been the focus of much scholarly work, her numerous short stories have received less individual attention. As a result, this book attempts to pay specific attention to these stories and contains entries on many of her most important ones. These stories present a variety of themes, often echoing those in her novels: race, class, gender, nature, marriage, migration, and religion. Within the brief space of the short story form, Hurston adeptly establishes setting and location, develops character, crafts dialogue, presents intriguing plot lines, and articulates significant themes.

Hurston follows in the tradition of American short story writing that engages in a powerful dialogue with other literature. Hurston can be read alongside other 20th-century American writers such as William Faulkner, F. Scott Fitzgerald, Eudora Welty, and Flannery O'Connor in order to assess the American experience of the epoch. However, Hurston's stories stand out because these texts emphasize African-American people and their cultural traditions. Her stories often feature African-American characters as the main focus, rather than being relegated to secondary, or even stigmatized, roles. Her characters are dynamic and complex, revealing multiple facets of their personalities or character. Readers will find in these stories that Hurston's own heritage influenced her point of view and informed her representation of the African-American experience. It is hoped that more critical attention will be paid to Hurston's sophisticated short texts, with the goal of examining them more readily within the study of American literature.

This second section also contains entries on Hurston's plays, such as *Color Struck* and *Mule Bone.* Hurston's versatility as a writer enabled her to experiment with the dramatic form, resulting in some lively and compelling pieces. *Color Struck,* which appeared in the literary magazine *Fire!!,* offers a compelling and insightful critique of intraracial relationships, a theme she would revisit in *Jonah's Gourd Vine, Their Eyes Were Watching God,* and *Moses, Man of the Mountain.* Like such Harlem Renaissance contemporaries as Jessie Fauset and Wallace Thurman, Hurston focused her texts on issues of skin color, both interracially and intraracially, particularly as viewed by blacks. Her play *Mule Bone: A Comedy of Negro Life* was a collaboration with Langston Hughes, another leading figure of the Harlem Renaissance. The play features memorable characters, humorous situations, and engaging dialogue and contains thematic and character similarities to her novel *Their Eyes Were Watching God* and her short story "The Bone of Contention." In general, the entries on Hurston's drama

Group photo with Zora Neale Hurston and Langston Hughes, 1927 *(Yale Collection of American Literature, Beinecke Rare Book and Manuscript Library)*

in this book will allow readers to draw connections between her plays and her short and long fiction. While drama was not her main literary output, Hurston's plays can be read with serious critical consideration alongside those of her contemporary dramatists Tennessee Williams, Eugene O'Neill, and Arthur Miller. As with her other work, Hurston's drama emphasizes African-American cultural expression as a medium for transmitting ideas. A careful examination of these plays will show how they, too, are crucial for understanding Hurston's literary legacy, which extends to various genres.

The entries in this section will also address Hurston's work on African-American folklore, some compilations of which were published after her death. These include *Go Gator and Muddy the Water: Writings by Zora Neale Hurston from the Federal Writers' Project* and *Every Tongue Got to Confess: Negro Folktales from the Gulf States.* These texts draw on and enrich her work in other genres, as they share common themes and ideas. Her folklore work illustrates Hurston's interest in actively collecting and preserving African-American oral traditions. These texts enable the contemporary reader to gain insight into the sophisticated and highly complex ways in which cultures have sought to understand themselves and their surrounding world, specifically through the folk creation of stories, songs, and dance. Hurston does not present these forms of popular cultural expression in patronizing or condescending terms; instead, her books show a respect and a reverence for this African-American tradition. These transcribed forms of oral works can be viewed both as examples of American literature in its own right and as cultural artifacts of the African diaspora. Hurston's dual position as both writer and anthropologist enabled her to present the material in an accessible and thoughtful manner that remains pertinent to this day.

Part II, in sum, deals with many types of writing, in multiple genres; Hurston's body of work shows that she cannot be easily categorized into one area. At the same time, these different types of literature share many thematic elements.

Part III treats people, places, films, and historical events that relate to Hurston's life and writing. This section contains entries on a wide range of topics that are useful for putting Zora Neale Hurston's life and oeuvre into historical context. There is discussion of relevant external factors relating to places where Hurston spent much of her life, such as Harlem, Jamaica, Haiti, and New Orleans, and to her educational institutions, such as Barnard College, Morgan Academy, and Howard University. Discussion of Zora Neale Hurston's relationships with other individuals includes Franz Boas, the anthropologist and professor who influenced her interest in folklore, and her patron, Charlotte Osgood Mason, who funded her research. Attention is paid as well to other important African-American writers—both Hurston's contemporaries, such as Jessie Fauset, Langston Hughes, Alain Locke, Dorothy West, and Richard Wright, and those in succeeding generations whom she influenced, such as Alice Walker and Gloria Naylor. As a means of providing a historical framework, the text includes entries on major issues including the Great Migration, Harlem, the Harlem Renaissance, and African-American journals such as *Fire!!* and *Opportunity.*

Throughout Parts I, II, and III, a variety of critical approaches and methods have been adopted in this book to present a uniform overview of the legacy of Zora Neale Hurston. It offers explication and analysis of Hurston's writings, including examination of various literary elements and strategies. Secondary sources, including literary criticism and historical information, will illuminate the critical discourse about Hurston's writings and the multiple interpretations of her works. The bibliographies at the end of each section will be useful for further reading about Zora Neale Hurston, her various publications, and related topics. Words appearing in small capital letters throughout the book are cross-references that are discussed in more depth in entries in Part III. Part IV provides a full bibliography of Hurston's works, as well as a brief chronology of her life.

In addition to serving as a reference work, this book is intended to generate interest in Zora Neale Hurston as an integral player in the American and African-American literary tradition; the book aims to reveal how Hurston's sophisticated presentation of themes such as race, class, and gender provide readers with a greater understanding of American culture and literature. Zora Neale Hurston died in relative obscurity, and her works are more widely read today than during her life; however, Hurston's contribution to American literature places her in the company of other major 20th-century writers. *Critical Companion to Zora Neale Hurston* was written with the desire and hope that others will continue to read, explore, and examine the legacy of this dynamic and enriching American writer.

Zora Neale Hurston, photograph by Carl Van Vechten. Permission granted by the Van Vechten Trust *(Yale Collection of American Literature, Beinecke Rare Book and Manuscript Library)*

BIBLIOGRAPHY

Boyd, Valerie. *Wrapped in Rainbows: The Life of Zora Neale Hurston.* New York: Scribner, 2003.

Hemenway, Robert E. *Zora Neale Hurston: A Literary Biography.* Urbana: University of Illinois Press, 1980.

Johnson, Sharon D. "All Eyes on 'Eyes': Oprah's adaptation of Zora's classic novel, starring Halle as Janie, is a historical moment for the worlds of television and literature," *Black Issues Book Review* (March–April 2005): 42–44.

Smith, Rochelle, and Sharon L. Jones, eds. *The Prentice Hall Anthology of African American Literature.* Upper Saddle River, N.J.: Prentice Hall, 2000.

PART I

Biography

Zora Neale Hurston
(1891–1960)

Although she claimed she was born in EATONVILLE, FLORIDA, Zora Neale Hurston was born in 1891 in NOTASULGA, ALABAMA, a city in the eastern part of the state, just north of Tuskegee and close to the Georgia border. Her father, JOHN HURSTON, was the son of former slaves Amy and Alfred Hurston; her mother, LUCY POTTS HURSTON, the daughter of former slaves Sarah and Richard Potts. John Hurston and Lucy Potts met at the Macedonia Baptist Church, where Lucy sang in the choir, and John was said to slip love notes into his church hymnal (Boyd 15). Lucy and John married in 1882, when Lucy was 16 and John 21. Lucy came from a more affluent family than John—the Pottses were originally from Georgia but later landowners in Alabama—and thus the Potts family objected to Lucy marrying John; her mother would not attend the wedding (Boyd 16). Hurston's novel *Jonah's Gourd Vine* was based on and inspired by the lives of her parents.

Lucy and John had several children, including John, Hezekiah Robert, Sarah Emmeline, Richard William, Joel, and Zora Lee. The family decided to move to Florida when Zora was very young. While living in Florida, Hurston's father "found opportunity, and sympathetic whites who donated land for the all-black town of Eatonville, named after one of its white benefactors" (Bordelon 5). John Hurston found a job as a minister for the Zion Hope Baptist Church, in Sanford, Florida. He purchased property in Eatonville, on which he had a home and barn built, and he would later be mayor of that town, from 1912 to 1916.

Eatonville played an important role in the development of Zora Neale Hurston, and it was Eatonville that she always considered "home" (Boyd 25), which may explain why Hurston often identified it as her birth place. Hurston scholar Valerie Boyd speculates that her parents may not have told Zora about her true birth place, or otherwise "perhaps she was told, but considered it an insignificant detail not worth repeating" (Boyd 25). At any rate, Eatonville would be the *creative* place of birth for Zora Neale Hurston, as her immersion in black cultural expression and storytelling there would inspire her writing, especially on folklore, years later. It was also where Zora would bloom as an individual, and where she would meet important black role models in government, religion, and storytelling. A store operated by Joe Clarke, where people would come to tell tales, was one source of inspiration for the folktales (Boyd 25).

From a socioeconomic perspective, the family was comfortable and their needs were met. John and Lucy's children spent a good deal of time with other children in the town, and many people were drawn by the Hurstons' hospitality to spend time in their home. Thus, the home was a type of social center for the neighbors. While the family was stable as a whole, John had a habit of getting involved with other women, and although Lucy was aware of this, it suggests his conflicted feelings toward family life (Boyd 31). In 1901, some white females from the North who were visiting her school in the South provided Zora Neale Hurston with some reading material by Jonathan Swift, Rudyard Kipling, and Robert Louis Stevenson ("Chronology" 1014), contributing to Hurston's early exposure to literature. Both parents believed in using corporal punishment on the children (Boyd 28).

According to Hurston, her mother, Lucy, had a major impact on her growing up and instilled a sense of the importance of education. Lucy was a teacher in the church; she also was good at sewing and sewed for other people in the town. She spent much time with her children, oftentimes in her room at the family home, working with them on school assignments in math or English (Boyd 27). She influenced her husband as well. Even though John was an ambitious man by nature, his wife "urged him to action" (Boyd 26). She encouraged him to preach once they moved to Eatonville, and it was with this encouragement that he eventually became a minister for the Zion Hope Baptist Church in 1893. She encouraged her children too, telling them to "jump at de sun" to spur them on (Boyd 27). Her husband, however, did not share such a positive, upbeat outlook: he believed in education but also was realistic about the racial climate.

Lucy passed away in 1904, when Zora was barely a teenager. A funeral was held in Macedonia Baptist Church, and the whole family was deeply moved by the tragedy. The passing of her caring and affectionate mother affected Zora greatly, and it precipitated "the moment her own girlhood ended" (Boyd 47).

The period following Lucy's death, from 1904 to 1917, has been little documented, according to Bordelon; however, there are some clues about the Hurston family life. Zora may have attended school in Jacksonville, while her siblings lived with their father and stepmother (Bordelon 7). Hurston's father remarried a woman named Mattie Moge, whom he met in 1905, shortly after Lucy had passed away. As a result, Zora did not like this woman. Given John's marital infidelities, some people speculated that he had been in a relationship with her while still married to Lucy (Boyd 52). During this period John joined a Baptist convention, and he served as mayor of Eatonville from 1912 to 1916. He was killed in a car accident in 1917 ("Chronology" 1015). Zora did not attend her father's funeral. Boyd suggests the passing away of Hurston's father had an important effect upon her, suggesting that it freed her emotionally and was a pivotal point in her development as an individual (Boyd 78).

In 1915 and 1916, Zora Neale Hurston worked for Gilbert and Sullivan, a musical company. She later got sick and had an operation in Baltimore that prevented her from traveling with the company. While in Baltimore, she began study at MORGAN ACADEMY, in 1917, and she earned a high school diploma in 1918. Later, she attended HOWARD UNIVERSITY, a reputable university for black students in Washington, D.C., which had been founded in 1867. Hurston, aware of Howard's reputation, took classes in Spanish, Greek, English, and public speaking there, and she worked at the same time as she studied. She graduated from Howard University with an associate degree in 1920, and continued to study there until 1924. She also met Herbert Sheen, a fellow Howard University student, whom she would later marry.

In 1921, Hurston became a member of a literary society run by ALAIN LOCKE and Montgomery Gregory. Locke was an influential scholar and writer during the HARLEM RENAISSANCE. His anthology, *The NEW NEGRO*, which was published in 1925, featured

Practice school teachers at Howard University, Washington, D.C. *(Library of Congress)*

the leading writers of the movement, including Zora Neale Hurston. Membership in this exclusive literary club was granted by writing competitions (Boyd 84). Hurston contributed to the society's publication, *The Stylus,* with such works as her poem "O Night" and her short story "John Redding Goes to Sea."

Hurston moved to New York in 1925, a year after publishing her tale "Drenched in Light" in OPPORTUNITY magazine, for which she had won a literary competition sponsored by the magazine. *Opportunity,* published by the Urban League, provided many writers of the Harlem Renaissance with national and international exposure. First published in 1923, *Opportunity* was an outlet for African-American cultural expression and advocated for civil rights issues. It provided an alternative particularly to mainstream publications aimed primarily at white audiences. The competitions it sponsored encouraged budding or aspiring writers, and celebrated the achievements of blacks within the literary world.

Other notable African-American publications at this time were *Crisis,* published by the National Association for the Advancement of Colored People (NAACP), and *Messenger,* also devoted to civil rights. LANGSTON HUGHES published in *The Crisis,* while Claude McKay appeared in *Messenger.* A crucial difference between *Opportunity* and these others, however, was that the former "reflected the Urban League's tendency toward diplomacy and gradualism" in bringing about change (Boyd 89). Eventually, *Opportunity* transformed itself by devoting its pages to the arts. At a meal honoring the winners of *Opportunity* literary awards in 1925—of which Hurston was a recipient—Hurston encountered notables such as Countee Cullen, Hughes, Annie Nathan Meyer, Carl Van Vechten, and Fannie Hurst. Annie Nathan Meyer helped Hurston attend BARNARD COLLEGE by helping her find a scholarship, while Fannie Hurst hired Hurston as an employee, even though Hurston did not type well (Bordelon 10). Huston began studies at Barnard College in 1925, at which point she was the only black American enrolled there, and she received her bachelor's degree in 1928.

In 1926, Hurston received another *Opportunity* writing award and got involved with a new literary magazine, called *FIRE!!*. This magazine tried to bring a new perspective to black publications and to "challenge the Victorian morality of the negro establishment" (Boyd 122). Ultimately, however, it would print only one issue, dated November 1926, but it published a number of literary heavyweights, and the project signaled the willingness of Hurston's generation to actively change the direction of African-American literature. The one issue of *Fire!!* cost one dollar, and there were art and literary contributions by Aaron Douglas, Richard Bruce, Wallace Thurman, Countee Cullen, Edward Silvera, Langston Hughes, Helene Johnson, Waring Cuney, Arna Bontemps, Lewis Alexander, Gwendolyn Bennett, Arthur Huff Fauset, and Zora Neale Hurston. Hurston's selections in the magazine were the play *Color Struck* and the story "Sweat."

Portrait of Countee Cullen inscribed to Carl Van Vechten, February 1925 *(Yale Collection of American Literature, Beinecke Rare Book and Manuscript Library)*

In 1927, Hurston wed Herbert Sheen, her friend from Howard and the son of a pastor, although they divorced four years later. From 1928 to 1932, Hurston's work was sponsored by the benefactor CHARLOTTE OSGOOD MASON, whom Hurston met through Langston Hughes, another recipient of her funds. According to Hurston's biographer, Mason was attracted to Hurston for her "effulgent intellect and absolute lack of pretension" (Boyd 157). Charlotte Osgood Mason was married to a wealthy doctor who had a high social status. As a benefactor, Mason was a "longtime champion of 'primitivism'" and had an interest especially in Native American culture (Boyd 157). Her notions about race and ethnicity, particularly the attitude that black and Native American cultures were "primitive," were stereotypical and backward, but her financial assistance proved invaluable for Hurston.

While Hughes eventually ended his financial relationship with Mason, Hurston continued hers, even though Mason wanted "control over every detail of Hurston's life" and to establish "power over her fieldwork"

(Bordelon 11). During this time of sponsorship, Hurston was carrying on anthropological fieldwork, observing the work environments in the lumber, turpentine, and railroad industries. While gathering information in the field, Hurston became immersed in the cultures she was observing. The economic hardships of the Great Depression affected Hurston as it did the rest of the United States. When Mason stopped giving Hurston money in 1932, Hurston relocated to Florida and began receiving money from a relative (Bordelon 12).

The fieldwork Hurston did in the South in the late 1920s was the genesis for her first novel, *Jonah's Gourd Vine.* Soon after Hurston's story "The Gilded Six-Bits" appeared in *Story,* in 1933, the publisher J.B. Lippincott contacted her about publishing a novel. Hurston claimed to have already written a book, even though she had not yet actually started composing the text (Boyd 246). Subsequently, in July 1933, she started writing the text that would become *Jonah's Gourd Vine,* and in the ensuing months "worked with monklike devotion" on the manuscript (Boyd 247). The novel contains many parallels between Hurston's own life and the fictional world depicted in the text. She based the story on the lives of her parents, John and Lucy Hurston; in fact the novel's protagonist is named John, his wife is named Lucy; and the character of Isis is a self-portrait of Hurston. Writing this autobiographical novel, Boyd suggests, may have even altered Hurston's attitude about her father, approaching something "like compassion" (247).

By the time she completed this novel, Hurston was so broke she was behind in paying her rent and had no money to pay a typist or to mail the manuscript to the publisher. Having eventually found a typist willing to be paid later, Hurston mailed the completed manuscript using borrowed funds in October 1933. Later that month, Hurston was able to earn some money by presenting a concert with performers in Sanford, Florida. She also discovered that her novel was accepted for publication and that her advance money was forthcoming from the publisher. Although she was paid, it was less money than white writers earned for similar work (Boyd 247–249).

Her first novel was published in 1934, clearing the way for *Mules and Men* to be published the following year. *Jonah's Gourd Vine* was reviewed in publications such as *Opportunity, The Crisis,* and the *New York Times Book Review.* In the review from *Opportunity,* Estelle Felton described the text as "quite easy to read and entertaining." The review points out that "few will be able to deny Miss Hurston's accomplishments in an effective use of dialogue and traditional customs." *The Crisis,* published by the NAACP, also wrote about Hurston's novel, although the critic, Andrew Burris, gave it a mixed review. He criticized the novel by asserting that Hurston "has almost completely lost sight of the equally essential elements of plot and construction, characterization and motivation." On the other hand, he noted that the novel is "a rich store of folklore" and that "there is much about the book that is fine and distinctive," including its representation of "the lusciousness and beauty of the Negro dialect."

Hurston's novel also received attention—and praise—from the mainstream press, such as Margaret Wallace's review in the *New York Times Book Review.* She wrote, "*Jonah's Gourd Vine* can be called without fear of exaggeration the most vital and original novel about the American Negro that has yet been written by a member of the Negro race." She praised the text's "authentic flavor" and its "excellent rendition of Negro dialect." In *The New Republic,* Martha Gruening described Hurston as "an insider without the insider's usual neuroses." The national attention devoted to Hurston's early effort is indicative of the merits of this first novel.

Despite sales of *Jonah's Gourd Vine,* she did not make enough money to meet her needs (Bordelon 12). In 1934 she found a teaching job at Bethune Cookman College, in Daytona Beach. The following year, Hurston returned to New York for graduate study at Columbia University, but ultimately abandoned her quest for a doctorate degree. The same year, 1935, she began working for the Federal Theatre Project. Hurston eventually earned Guggenheim grants, which enabled her to conduct research about hoodoo, a subject she had previously spent time studying.

Richard Wright, 1951 *(Library of Congress)*

Hurston spent time in the Caribbean in 1936 and 1937, during which time she composed *Their Eyes Were Watching God.* She completed the manuscript in a short amount of time while living in Haiti, in 1936, and the novel was published a year later, in 1937.

Their Eyes Were Watching God remains Hurston's most widely read, discussed, and taught novel, and it was made into a TV movie, which aired on network television in 2005. The novel chronicles the life of Janie Crawford, an African-American woman on a quest for love and identity. The granddaughter of a slave and the daughter of a mother who abandons her, Janie ends up marrying three times. Her first husband, Logan Killicks, is a very successful farmer with land and a house. The marriage is arranged by Nanny, Janie's grandmother, because she believes that Logan will provide her granddaughter with social and economic security. Janie finds herself in an unhappy marriage based not on love or passion but on economics and social status. Her second marriage is to Jody Starks, a powerful businessman, mayor, and landowner in the black town of Eatonville, Florida. Again, Janie possesses status but not happiness; their marriage is marked by Joe's violent, aggressive behavior and Janie's attempts to react against his oppressive desire for her to be subservient. After his death, Janie marries Vergible Tea Cake Woods, a younger, working-class man viewed by others as unsuitable for a woman of Janie's stature. With Woods, Janie feels a newfound sense of freedom and personal growth. After some troubling times, including a hurricane and a rabid-dog attack, Janie kills Tea Cake in self defense, thus ending with no mate at the end of the novel, but her memory of Tea Cake lingers.

This novel, like her first one, received coverage in the national press, including *New Masses, Opportunity,* and the *New York Times Book Review.* Richard Wright's famous negative review of *Their Eyes Were Watching God* depicted it as a flawed novel. Noting what he saw as a "minstrel technique" of the work, Wright claimed the characters in the novel "swing like a pendulum eternally in that safe and narrow orbit in which America likes to see the Negro." While Hurston was a protégé of Alain Locke of *Stylus,* the literary society at Howard, he too found fault with her second novel in a review for *Opportunity.* His review acknowledged Hurston's talent for "poetic phrase, for rare dialect, and folk humor" but asserted that these aspects prevent Hurston "from diving deep down either to the inner psychology of characterization or to sharp analysis of the social background." His review suggests she presents a superficial view of humanity. By contrast, Lucille Tompkins, writing in the *New York Times Book Review,* found much to praise in Hurston's novel, describing the text as "beautiful" and pointing out that "the dialect here is very easy to follow, and the images it carries are irresistible." In any case, the spirited critical reception of the novel in the 1930s—ranging from enthusiastic to highly critical—again testifies to the impact of Hurston's work. Wright's and Locke's criticism that the novel lacked depth stands in contrast to the later critical reaction to the novel as a complex analysis of race, class, and gender.

After finishing her second novel and traveling between Haiti, Florida, and New York, Hurston began working for the Federal Writers' Project in 1938, specifically to edit a book about Florida for "the American Guide series" and a book called *The Florida Negro* ("Chronology" 1024). That same year, she published *Tell My Horse* and spent time in Washington, D.C., to request more grant money, which she would need for her next significant work, *Moses, Man of the Mountain.* She had started work on this novel back in 1934 (the same year she penned "The Fire and the Cloud"), but it required more time as she was researching black folktales to incorporate into the narrative. She conducted some of that research while she was in the Caribbean in 1936, "partly in search of Moses legends" (Boyd 330). Thus Hurston's *Moses, Man of the Mountain* represents the culmination of these efforts, functioning as a retelling of the story of Moses, a figure from the Old Testament of the Bible. Hurston's interest in Moses reflects the popularity within African-American culture of the figure of Moses, a symbol of freedom and liberation for oppressed individuals. In this way, the text bears an important social and cultural significance as Hurston contributes to this tradition.

In 1939, Hurston was engaged in various pursuits, continuing her work sponsored by the federal government, recording music, tales, and other information for the Library of Congress and the Folk Arts commission of the WPA. While so employed, Hurston met and then married Albert Price III, a WPA employee. She also obtained a position at the North Carolina College for Negroes in hopes of establishing a drama program but was not happy in the environment there.

Most important, her novel *Moses, Man of the Mountain* was published that year.

The novel was reviewed in national publications such as *Saturday Review* and the *New York Times Book Review.* In *Saturday Review,* writer Louis Untermeyer considered examinations of the Bible in relationship to "psychoanalysis." In Untermeyer' view, Hurston presented Moses "as the great voodoo man of the Bible" and he saw Hurston's depiction of the protagonist as the "prime disappointment" within the novel. While he called her "approach" both "arresting" and "fresh," he contended that "the whole is less successful than the parts" and that "the total effect is that of unfulfilled expectation." As with other critics who found fault with Hurston's novel, Untermeyer still appreciated her talent for prose, noting the novel's "dramatic intensity worthy of its gifted author." Overall, the review suggests an uneven text with some innovative aspects as well as flaws in characterization and idiom. Likewise, in the *New York Times Book Review,* Percy Hutchinson wrote a mixed review. He called Hurston's "homespun" novel "an exceptionally fine piece of work far off the beaten tracks of literature" and noted particularly that the "close of the book is poetic and beautiful." But he also wrote that Hurston "reduces the dialect as she proceeds" and that as a result the text "loses something in flavor." In any case, both reviews reveal the serious attention that the literary establishment continued to devote to Hurston's publications.

In 1940, Hurston and Albert Price traveled between New York and South Carolina, where she conducted research on religion and helped to make a film about the religious practices among blacks in South Carolina (Boyd 343–345); in 1941, she moved to Los Angeles and penned the manuscript of *Dust Tracks on a Road,* and she also worked for Paramount Pictures, the film production company, "as a story consultant" ("Chronology" 1025). *Dust Tracks on a Road* remains an important text for Hurston scholars in gaining insight into how Hurston wanted to present herself to the reading public. It is in this work, which is a chronicle of her life and experiences, that Hurston says that she was born in Eatonville, Florida, even though she was actually born in Notasulga, Alabama. The book was published in 1942. The autobiography, which at times embellishes the truth about her life, may also represent Hurston's ability to create a persona for the world, constructing and reconstructing her life and experiences through a lens focusing on the complicated nature of race, class, and gender. Like Hurston's fiction, the autobiographical *Dust Tracks on a Road* also merited serious critical attention, with reviews in high-profile periodicals.

In *Saturday Review,* Phil Strong pointed out that *Dust Tracks on a Road* "is more summary than the autobiography it advertises itself as being," but he nevertheless described the work as being "delightful" and "a fine, rich autobiography" whose chapter on love was its "most amusing." Strong's review suggested that *Dust Tracks on a Road* transcended racial and ethnic lines and would be "heartening to anyone, white, black, or tan." Similarly, within her critique in the *New York Times Book Review,* Beatrice Sherman also cited the universal appeal of Hurston's autobiography. She described it as "a thumping story" and as being "live and vivid" (33). Her review praised Hurston's "gusty language" and noted her "graphic metaphors and similes that color Negro speech." Again emphasizing the accessible nature of the book, Sherman wrote that it was an "encouraging and enjoyable" book that would be appropriate "for any member of the human race."

In addition to publishing her memoir in 1942, Hurston also worked on the faculty at Florida Normal and gathered folk material in Florida. At this time, she befriended Marjorie Kinnan Rawlings, to whom she would later dedicate a novel. The following year, she joined the Florida Negro Defense Committee and divorced her husband, Albert Price.

In 1944, she became engaged to a man named James Howell Pitts, but they ultimately would not marry. She spent more time in Florida, but she returned to Harlem. She spent much of 1945 in Daytona Beach, Florida, and bought a houseboat in 1943; this proved to be significant as Hurston lived in "houseboats for the next four years" ("Chronology" 1026); she also worked on a book called *Mrs. Doctor* in 1945, but it was not published ("Chronology" 1027).

In 1947, she went to Honduras, where she composed *Seraph on the Suwanee.* Unlike most of her other published fiction, this text focuses on a white family in Florida; however, it also explores issues of race, class, and gender, just from a different perspective. *Seraph on the Suwanee* chronicles the experiences of Arvay Meserve, a white woman married to Jim Meserve, who comes from a more prominent family. Through his hard work, Jim provides adequately for the family, but the Meserves' marriage proves to be quite tumultuous. In the end, Arvay and Jim reconcile.

Hurston left Honduras in 1948, eventually landing in Harlem, and *Seraph on the Suwanee* was published later that year. The novel received reviews in publications such as the *New York Times Book Review* and the *New York Herald Tribune Weekly Book Review.* Frank Slaughter's review for the *New York Times Book Review* took a psychoanalytical approach to Hurston's text. He suggested that the character Arvay was "a textbook picture of a hysterical neurotic, right to the end of the novel." Slaughter said the novel was about "an unstable woman's search for happiness," which was "filled with ups and downs." Worth Tuttle Heddens's mixed review appeared in the *New York Herald Tribune Weekly Book Review.* "Incompatible strains in the novel mirror the complexity of the author," he wrote. Heddens praised her for the depiction of Jim Meserve, who projects "verisimilitude," and he noted that Hurston "knows every intimate detail of Arvay's physical self." While describing *Seraph on the Suwanee* as an "astonishing novel," he asserted that "you wish that Miss Hurston had used the scissors and smoothed the seams." Although *Seraph on the Suwanee* may not be as widely read as *Their Eyes Were Watching God,* it remains historically important, as it was Hurston's last published novel during her lifetime.

The year that her final novel was published, Hurston endured an allegation that she had molested a child. The episode began when her former landlord claimed that Hurston had molested her son. Hurston was "hauled into the police station, fingerprinted, and booked" on child molestation charges (Boyd 387). She was arraigned on October 11 on charges related to the accusations. Hurston "categorically denied" these charges, which her biographer characterized as "groundless" (Boyd 387). The situation was covered in the media, but the author showed that she had been in Honduras during the period when her landlord's son was supposedly molested. Hurston relocated to the Bronx. In 1949 the charges were dropped due to the child's mental state. After a stint in the Bronx during the ordeal, Hurston headed back to Florida, to Belle Glade. She started composing another book, *The Lives of Barney Turk,* which was not published. She held other employment, and became involved with a political campaign.

In 1951, Zora Neale Hurston labored on a text called "The Golden Bench of God," a short novel that she intended to turn into a play, but it was never published (Boyd 409). That summer, Hurston went to Eau Gallie, Florida, to complete *Mules and Men*; she would spend the next few years there while beginning to experience medical problems. In 1952 and 1953, she wrote about a case involving a black woman on trial for killing her white male lover, who was a doctor, for the *Pittsburgh Courier*; the trial would have generated a lot of media attention due to the interracial aspect of the crime and the romantic relationship between the accused and

Zora Neale Hurston perusing a book at the 1937 *New York Times* Book Fair *(Library of Congress)*

the doctor, given many attitudes about race in the 1950s ("Chronology" 1030–1031). In 1953, she continued working on a biographical book about the biblical figure Herod the Great, which she would continue through 1954 ("Chronology" 1031).

Responding to the landmark *Brown v. Board of Education* case, which resulted in the desegregation of schools, Hurston wrote a letter to the *Orlando Sentinel* during 1955. Within the letter, she criticizes the Supreme Court's verdict on the grounds that it implies that African-American youth are only capable of learning if they attend school with white children ("Chronology" 1031). She was evicted from her home in 1956 in Eau Gallie, Florida, since the person she was renting the house from decided to sell it; she would later relocate to Merritt Island, Florida, in 1957. She found work on a military base in 1956, but she was fired from the position the next year. In 1957, she experienced more medical problems, then moved to the city of Fort Pierce, Florida, and began writing for the *Fort Pierce Chronicle.* In 1958, she found employment at the Lincoln Park Academy, and she rented a home ("Chronology" 1030–1032). She suffered a stroke in 1959, sought aid, and eventually received food vouchers that summer. In October, she moved to the SAINT LUCIE COUNTY WELFARE HOME, where she would live out the rest of her days, silent to her friends and family elsewhere. Hurston died in 1960, and her body was buried at the Garden of Heavenly Rest in Fort Pierce.

Later, in 1973, the novelist ALICE WALKER paid a tribute to Zora Neale Hurston by placing a "marker on the grave of the novelist and anthropologist who had so inspired her own" literary career (Boyd 436). Following this memorial, Walker greatly contributed to interest in Zora Neale Hurston through an article about her trip published in *Ms.* magazine. Robert Hemenway's 1977 book about Hurston's life also promoted her legacy during the same decade. Soon after, the novel *Their Eyes Were Watching God* became a popular text to teach in classes (Boyd 437).

In her interesting and colorful life, Zora Neale Hurston experienced many of the major events of the 20th century concerning changes in race, class, and gender in America, events that would ultimately have an impact. Despite the many obstacles she faced due to her status as a black female writer in the early 20th century, Hurston produced a staggering number of texts—both published and unpublished—including short stories, novels, a memoir, drama, nonfiction essays, and folklore. As an anthropologist and creative writer, she helped to preserve important African-American oral traditions, which continue to inspire and have influence today.

BIBLIOGRAPHY

Bordelon, Pamela. "Zora Neale Hurston: A Biographical Essay." In *Go Gator and Muddy the Water: Writings By Zora Neale Hurston From the Federal Writers' Project,* edited by Pamela Bordelon, 1–49. New York: W.W. Norton & Company, 1999.

Boyd, Valerie. *Wrapped in Rainbows: The Life of Zora Neale Hurston.* New York: Scribner, 2003.

Burris, Andrew. Review of *Jonah's Gourd Vine.* In *Zora Neale Hurston: Critical Perspectives Past and Present,* edited by Henry Louis Gates, Jr., and K. A. Appiah, 6–8. New York: Amistad, 1993. (*The Crisis,* June 3, 1934)

"Chronology," in *Novels and Stories.* New York: Library of America, 1995, 1013–1032.

Felton, Estelle. Review of *Jonah's Gourd Vine.* In *Zora Neale Hurston: Critical Perspectives Past and Present,* edited by Henry Louis Gates, Jr., and K. A. Appiah, 4–5. New York: Amistad, 1993. (*Opportunity,* August 1934)

Hedden, Worth Tuttle. Review of *Seraph on the Suwanee.* In *Zora Neale Hurston: Critical Perspectives Past and Present,* edited by Henry Louis Gates, Jr., and K. A. Appiah, 35–36. New York: Amistad, 1993. (*New York Herald Tribune Weekly Book Review,* October 10, 1948)

Hutchinson, Percy. Review of *Moses, Man of the Mountain.* In *Zora Neale Hurston: Critical Perspectives Past and Present,* edited by Henry Louis Gates, Jr., and K. A. Appiah, 27–29. New York: Amistad, 1993. (*New York Times Book Review,* November 19, 1939)

Locke, Alain. Review of *Their Eyes Were Watching God.* In *Zora Neale Hurston: Critical Perspectives Past and Present,* edited by Henry Louis Gates, Jr., and K. A. Appiah, 18. New York: Amistad, 1993. (*Opportunity,* June 1, 1938)

Sherman, Beatrice. Review of *Dust Tracks on a Road.* In *Zora Neale Hurston: Critical Perspectives Past and Present,* edited by Henry Louis Gates, Jr., and K. A. Appiah, 32–33. New York: Amistad, 1993. (*New York Times Book Review,* November 29, 1942)

Slaughter, Frank G. Review of *Seraph on the Suwanee.* In *Zora Neale Hurston: Critical Perspectives Past and Present,* edited by Henry Louis Gates, Jr., and K. A. Appiah, 34–35. New York: Amistad, 1993. (*New York Times Book Review,* October 31, 1948)

Strong, Phil. Review of *Dust Tracks on a Road.* In *Zora Neale Hurston: Critical Perspectives Past and Present,* edited by Henry Louis Gates, Jr., and K. A. Appiah, 30–32. New York: Amistad, 1993. (*Saturday Review,* November 28, 1942)

Tompkins, Lucille. Review of *Their Eyes Were Watching God.* In *Zora Neale Hurston: Critical Perspectives Past and Present,* edited by Henry Louis Gates, Jr., and K. A. Appiah, 18–19. New York: Amistad, 1993. (*New York Times Book Review,* September 26, 1937)

Wallace, Margaret. Review of *Jonah's Gourd Vine.* In *Zora Neale Hurston: Critical Perspectives Past and Present,* edited by Henry Louis Gates, Jr., and K. A. Appiah, 8–9. New York: Amistad, 1993. (*New York Times Book Review,* May 6, 1934)

Wright, Richard. Review of *Their Eyes Were Watching God.* In *Zora Neale Hurston: Critical Perspectives Past and Present,* edited by Henry Louis Gates, Jr., and K. A. Appiah, 16–17. New York: Amistad, 1993. (*New Masses,* October 5, 1937)

Untermeyer, Louis. Review of *Moses, Man of the Mountain.* In *Zora Neale Hurston: Critical Perspectives Past and Present,* edited by Henry Louis Gates, Jr., and K. A. Appiah, 26–27. New York: Amistad, 1993. (*Saturday Review,* November 11, 1939)

Part II

Works A–Z

"The Bone of Contention"

This story, set in EATONVILLE, FLORIDA, presents the trial of a man accused of assaulting another man with a mule bone. The trial ultimately pits Baptists against Methodists, and portrays a power play between the mayor and a prominent minister. The mule in this story functions as an important symbol of nature, community, and identity. By focusing on the mule, Hurston reinforces the story's agrarian setting and emphasizes the significance of that animal to rural African-American folk communities in the early 20th century. Religion is also a major theme in this text, also representative of the role it played in the community. Hurston infuses this memorable tale with both humor and social commentary. This short story by Hurston served as the basis for the play *Mule Bone*; the mule in this story may also have inspired Matt Bonner's mule in *Their Eyes Were Watching God*.

"The Bone of Contention" showcases the influence that Eatonville had on Hurston, as this was a tale she would have heard during her youth in Eatonville. This story illustrates her heritage and alludes to figures that make appearances in other of Hurston's writings. The author enjoyed recounting the tale for people in social gatherings in New York (Boyd 199). The evolution of the oral tradition in African-American literature can be seen here: The story Hurston had learned as a youth would later be recounted in New York before she transformed it into a story and then a play.

SYNOPSIS

Part I

The narrator describes the town of Eatonville and the importance of Brazzle's mule to the community. According to the narrator, people talk a good deal about this mule despite its being "old, rawbony, and mean." People were happy when it died, and Eatonville residents attended the "dragging out" of the mule.

Part II

One evening, people are gathered on the porch of a shop owned by Joe Clarke. The minister Reverend Simms desires to be mayor of the town, but Clarke currently holds that position. Clarke discusses how he began the community by purchasing property and proceeds to complain about Jim Weston. Simms says the town should have prisons, and Lindsay agrees. Dave Carter comes, wanting to speak with Clarke, and the two enter the store. There, Carter says that Jim assaulted him with a mule bone and also stole his turkey. Clarke declares that a trial will take place in the Baptist church, both because the mayor's "interests lay with the other side" and because he thinks this will protect the town's animals, as Methodists are said, in the tale, to hit animals as well as people. Clarke also believes that Simms's support of Jim will hurt his "prestige" in the community.

Part III

The narrator states, "This was to be a religious and political fight." Both Baptists and Methodists attend this trial, and there is commentary on religion in the story; Dave is Baptist while Jim is Methodist. Joe Clarke begins the trial, and when a dispute arises among some women in the courtroom, Clarke demands order, asking Lum Boger to silence the women. Clarke declares to Jim what he has been accused of, and Jim admits to the action, but says "it wasnt no crime this time." Reverend Simms says a mule bone cannot be "a weepon." Elder Long, a Baptist, rises and says that the mule bone is "a weepon" because of the harm it caused Dave. He then quotes a biblical passage in which "Samson slewed" people using the "jaw-bone of a ass"; Long then pleads to the mayor that Jim be banished. Clarke announces that Jim is to be banished for a couple of years, and the trial ends.

CRITICAL COMMENTARY

The primary themes of the story include nature, religion, and race. This humorous story, illustrative of Hurston's short story composition, displays the author's complex handling of dialogue, setting, and characterization. This story anticipates the play *Mule Bone,* and some characters in this story appear in *Mule Bone* as well, including Jim Weston, Joe Clarke, Reverend Simms, and Dave Carter. The "yellow mule" anticipates Matt Bonner's mule in *Their Eyes Were Watching God.*

Race

Race functions as an important theme, as the story takes place in a black community that the narrator notes "has its colored interests." The issue of race proves especially important in the trial scene when the "white folks law" is invoked in Reverend Simms's defense of Jim. His claim is that a mule bone cannot be a weapon because "it aint in no white folks law neither," suggesting that white laws set the precedent for legal decisions in a black community. Elder Long, too, invokes the white law, saying he has "heard de white folks law" and that the real question is whether harm was caused. Simms counters by saying not to "mind bout dem white folks laws at O'landa" as this is "a colored town," ultimately deciding that white law should not be honored after all, even though it refutes his own argument. The courtroom reveals the impact that laws made by whites would have upon black communities, and Hurston's representation of this scene touches upon questions of race relations, justice, and power.

Nature

Nature is a prominent theme in Hurston's writing. In this story, Brazzle's mule symbolizes nature and represents the agrarian culture of the community. A good, compliant mule would be desirable, but Brazzle's mule proved to be problematic. Brazzle cannot sell it to anyone else due to its reputation, and when the mule passes away, people are happy. After the mule dies, it becomes an important element for the "elders," since the mule "remained with them in song and story as a simile, as a metaphor, to point a moral or adorn a tale." The mule then becomes an important aspect of the community's cultural expression and identity. The mule's legacy continues when Jim hits Dave with the mule bone. At the end of the trial, which had pitted Baptists against Methodists, Joe Clarke points out that this "mule been dead three years an' still kickin'!" Thus, the mule continues to have an impact on the town, illustrating the continued power and importance of nature.

Religion

As elsewhere in Hurston's work, religion plays a central role in this short story. "The Bone of Contention" highlights the complex relationship between Baptists and Methodists in the town and how that relates to power, justice, and identity. Valerie Boyd asserts that "before the proceedings begin, it's clear that the trial will be something of a holy war" (199). The trial about Jim assaulting Dave with a mule bone ultimately becomes a battle between Baptists and Methodists, Dave symbolizing the Baptists and Jim symbolizing the Methodists. Both Simms and Long use the Bible in their respective support or condemnation of Jim. The theme of religion also plays an important role in the rivalry between the mayor and Reverend Simms. Joe Clarke believes Reverend Simms, who wants to take the mayor position from him, will lose status in the town if he backs Jim in this trial. Thus, the trial contains important implications connecting politics and religion, as the narrator points out in saying it "was to be a religious and political fight." The mule bone then becomes a symbol of religious values and attitudes in Eatonville.

CHARACTERS

Carter, Dave Carter is a central character as he accuses Jim of assaulting him with a mule bone, leading to a trial that results in Jim being banished from the community. Carter represents the Baptists during the trial and ultimately serves as a symbol of religion and justice. Carter is also a character in *Mule Bone.*

Clarke, Joe As the town mayor and the judge, Clarke wields considerable power and uses the trial as a means of diminishing the political influence of his opponent, Simms. He is a Methodist. Clarke also appears in *Mule Bone*; he may also be a model for the character Jody Starks, mayor and business owner in *Their Eyes Were Watching God.*

Elder Long Representing the Baptist side during the trial, Long argues that the mule bone is a weapon, using the Bible story of Samson as support.

Reverend Simms A Methodist minister who also wants to be mayor, he claims that the bone of a mule cannot be a weapon because of the Bible and the "white folks law." Later, he claims that "white folks laws" should not apply, because Eatonville is a black community. Despite Simms's defense, Jim loses the trial.

Weston, Jim Jim assaults Dave with a mule bone, and admits this in court. Jim is a Methodist, and he is supported by Reverend Simms. Clarke, also a Methodist, ultimately rules against Jim, banishing him from town. Jim symbolizes the legal system, religion, and violence within the context of the story. He also appears in *Mule Bone.*

BIBLIOGRAPHY

Boyd, Valerie. *Wrapped in Rainbows: The Life of Zora Neale Hurston.* New York: Scribner, 2003.

Hurston, Zora Neale. "The Bone of Contention." In *Mule Bone: A Comedy of Negro Life* by Langston Hughes and Zora Neale Hurston, 25–39. New York: HarperPerennial, 1991.

Wall, Cheryl A. *Women of the Harlem Renaissance.* Bloomington: Indiana University Press, 1995.

"Cock Robin Beale Street" (1941)

This story, which appeared in a 1941 issue of *The Southern Literary Messenger,* functions as a morality tale and touches upon many themes: race relations, nature, marriage, adultery, violence, death, and religion. The story features a storytelling main character and most of its characters are personified animals. "Cock Robin Beale Street" contains parallels with Hurston stories involving humans, including "The Eatonville Anthology," *Jonah's Gourd Vine,* "Sweat," and "The Gilded Six-Bits"; it may be read in tandem with *Mules and Men* and *Their Eyes Were Watching God,* which also feature animals with human qualities.

SYNOPSIS

Uncle July comes home angry one day, because he has heard white people claiming that Cock Robin was a bird. His wife tries to calm him down, saying, "July, don't you come in here starting none of your foolishness wid me this day and year of our Lawd! I done told you now!" Uncle July refutes what he has heard as he tells the story of Cock Robin, who was murdered in Memphis; as A'nt Dooby hasn't heard this story, July tells it to her at length.

Cock Robin had moved to Memphis, Uncle July recounts, where he "[s]ung solo in de choir, and got round right smart wid de lady-people." Cock Robin was shot in front of a hotel: "Dere was Cock Robin laying on de sidewalk in front of de hotel wid three bullet holes in him." Later, Brother Owl assumes the role of trying to find out who was responsible for the murder in Memphis. Bull Sparrow claims to be the culprit. Bull Sparrow suspected his wife and Cock Robin of having an affair, since she used to lay white eggs but then started laying blue eggs; he assumes that Cock Robin fathered those eggs because they were blue. Another character in the story also says his wife has started laying blue eggs. Brother Owl suggests they have a funeral for Cock Robin and they begin to make funeral preparations. However, since different characters want the honor of carrying Cock Robin to the cemetery, Brother Owl cannot decide whom he should choose for that job. He then decides that those paying for the funeral should carry him. When a big feast is announced, the characters decide they want to go there instead, and Brother Owl decides to leave the burial up to the whites, since they have the power and authority.

Uncle July says he would have forgotten about his experiences in Memphis if the whites had not claimed that Cock Robin was not a person. Nonplussed, A'nt Dooby responds by saying, "Old coon for cunning; young coon for running. Now tell me whut you done wid your wages. I know you been up to something. Tell me! You and your Muckty-Duckty Beetle-Bugs!" After July's account, she believes this story is a cover and that he is actually keeping information from her about what he does with his paycheck.

CRITICAL COMMENTARY

"Cock Robin Beale Street" functions as a type of social commentary and critique about race, class, and power; it also connects with the oral storytelling tradition as Uncle July tells a tale to A'nt Dooby about Cock Robin. Hurston employs a third-person omniscient narrator with a character providing a first-person account of events and makes use of DIALECT that would be heard in the folk community.

The story suggests that the whites and blacks may share a different perception of reality and a different historical memory, while the commentary by Brother Owl about whites burying Cock Robin suggests the recognition of racial categories and the politics of power; here, even animals recognize divisions of race. Hurston's representation of this incident addresses the perception about the whites' control in Memphis. The story also suggests the idea of interracial mixing through the different colored eggs as it features a "gentle mocking of the illusion of ethnic purity" (Hemenway 290). Additionally, the story reveals a connection with the natural world through the characterization of birds as humans.

Uncle July's story about Cock Robin might also be seen as a cautionary tale against adultery and other vices, as Hurston's story reveals the consequences of the actions of infidelity at the hands of a cuckolded husband. The setting on Beale Street, a famous street in Memphis lined with blues clubs, is described as a site of deception, betrayal, and immorality; in this way, Hurston includes a theme of redemption, as Uncle July moves beyond his sinning Beale Street past and accepts a life rooted in Christian values.

CHARACTERS

A'nt Dooby An African-American woman, she functions as an important character as she is the listener to Uncle July's story about Cock Robin. The reader identifies with A'nt Dooby, as we hear the story unfolding at the same time she does. Hurston depicts A'nt Dooby as having a skeptical, assertive personality. Even after hearing the story, she remains unconvinced, demanding Uncle July tell her what he has done with his salary. Her reaction suggests she suspects the story is his way of hiding information from her.

Brother Owl Brother Owl is the mouthpiece for articulating themes of white power, privilege, and authority in the story. Like Uncle July, he makes distinctions between people along racial lines, and he rationalizes the burial plans by saying that white people want to be in control. He takes on a supervisory role and, by asking questions about the murder, incites Bull Sparrow to tell his story.

Bull Sparrow Bull Sparrow is characterized as a bird with human traits. A cuckolded character, Bull Sparrow symbolizes marriage, adultery and violence. Because Cock Robin disrupted his marriage, he shot him in a fit of anger; his reasoning implies that the shooting was justified because of what he did with his wife. Hurston's depiction of Bull Sparrow can be compared to her treatment of Joe Banks in "The Gilded Six-Bits," who is also the victim of an affair.

Cock Robin Hurston also depicts Cock Robin as a bird with human traits, but Uncle July asserts that Cock Robin was a human being and not a bird. In his story about Cock Robin, Uncle July presents him as a man who spent time on Beale Street in Memphis. Hurston characterizes Cock Robin as an adulterer, which would cause him to be shot in revenge by Bull Sparrow. The character of Cock Robin can be compared to Otis D. Slemmons in "The Gilded Six-Bits," who has an affair with Missie May, the wife of Joe Banks.

Uncle July Uncle July embodies the storytelling tradition as he relates this tale about Cock Robin and his death in Memphis in the past. Hurston presents Uncle July as a man with a dual identity: the pre-Christian self he describes during his time in Memphis and the Christian self he is said to take on. Uncle July also serves as a voice for the theme of race relations and tensions, as his story is a response to white people denying the humanity of his friend.

BIBLIOGRAPHY

Boyd, Valerie. *Wrapped in Rainbows: The Life of Zora Neale Hurston.* New York: Scribner, 2003.

Hemenway, Robert E. *Zora Neale Hurston: A Literary Biography.* Urbana: University of Illinois Press, 1980.

Hurston, Zora Neale. "Cock Robin Beale Street." In her *The Complete Stories,* 122–126. New York: HarperCollins, 1995.

Cover illustration by Aaron Douglas of Wallace Thurman's 1929 novel, *The Blacker the Berry,* Macauley Company *(Yale Collection of American Literature, Beinecke Rare Book and Manuscript Library)*

Color Struck: A Play in Four Scenes (1926)

Color Struck earned an award from a 1925 OPPORTUNITY magazine competition and later appeared in the November 1926 *FIRE!!* magazine, to which she had submitted it along with her short story "Sweat." Together, these works would form part of the "zenith of her literary output" during the New Negro movement (Boyd 136). This drama presents a conflict between the primary characters and reveals Hurston's fascination with racial issues, here dealing with intraracial color prejudice. The same subject would be dealt with in work by other African-American writers, including Wallace Thurman's novel *The Blacker the Berry,* JESSIE FAUSET's work in *Comedy: American Style,* and by Hurston herself in *Their Eyes Were Watching God.*

SYNOPSIS

Scene I

The opening scene is set in the evening on a train. Effie tells a man that Sam will not be attending the cakewalk with her. John and Emmaline arrive, with John claiming that Emma accused him of "smiling at Effie on the street car and she had to get off and wait for another one." Emma accuses him of favoring blacks with light complexions. Dinky and Ada talk about food. John and Emma kiss. The conductor approaches and says he wants someone from Jacksonville to be awarded the cake; then he leaves. Wesley plays a song on an accordion; Emma and John walk in the aisle. John praises Effie, and Emma complains. John asks Emma why she gets upset about him and light-skinned women. Emma and John discuss love, and Emma explains her jealousy.

Scene II

This scene takes place in a "weather-board hall." Dinky claims that Emma and John will win the cake and return it to the city of Jacksonville, since they are good at cakewalking. Dinky and Joe Clarke talk, and Clarke announces that people should be getting ready for the event. John tries to reassure Emma that he cares for her, saying "De darker de berry, de sweeter de taste!" Effie offers pie to Emma and John; Emma declines, but John accepts and eats it as Emma becomes more upset, claiming he likes Effie "cause she's half-white!" When it's time for the cakewalk to begin, Emma says she wants to leave, though John wants to stay. John stays; Emma leaves, and rages about blacks with white ancestry having "everything everybody else wants!" A voice announces that John and Effie will be partners.

Scene III

The scene takes place in a dance hall. The master of ceremonies gives instructions and tells people to get in position. John and Effie begin parading, and the emcee declares that Effie and John have won the cakewalk.

Scene IV

The setting is now in a home, decades later. There is a knock at the door, and Emma lets in John; the two begin to speak. John says that they haven't seen each other in years, and he journeyed there for her. He was married and living in Philadelphia, but his wife died, and now he wants to wed Emma. She expresses the regret she felt after their relationship ended, and explains she has a sick child. When John sees the girl, he realizes she is racially mixed and says that Emma's "husband musta been pretty near *white*." Emma points out she has always been single. John recommends that Emma bring the child to a doctor, but she does not want a black physician to see her child. He continues to urge her, and offers her money, which she refuses. Emma leaves the house, then returns, angry, and says, "A half white skin." John accuses her of racial self-hatred. John leaves, and then a doctor arrives. Emma talks to the doctor, who then examines her child and places a "*sheet over the face.*" Before leaving, the doctor gives Emma some medication for herself. The play ends with her crying.

CRITICAL COMMENTARY

The play presents a tragic tale of a woman named Emma whose color consciousness causes her to alienate herself from other people, including the man who loves her, John. She ultimately finds herself lonely and depressed at the end of the play. The play serves as a commentary about the consequences and dangers of interracial color prejudice. The play *Color Struck* focuses on themes present in other texts by Hurston, including colorism, race, ethnicity, identity, marriage, parent-child relations, and black cultural expression. The topic of color consciousness and intraracial color prejudice toward lighter-skinned blacks by darker-skinned blacks is a central concern in this play. Hurston also developed the theme of intraracial prejudice in her novel *Their Eyes Were Watching God,* in the character of Mrs. Turner, whose obsession with skin color affects her relationship with other people.

Race

Hurston depicts the themes of racial identity and consciousness primarily through the character Emmaline. As Lillie Howard asserts, this play examines "how one's dissatisfaction with one's color can lead to inferiority complexes which undermine one's entire life." Emmaline's obsession with skin color creates emotional and psychological damage to her as a person and affects the others around her. Early in the play, her color consciousness becomes apparent when John remarks on her preoccupation with his greeting a light-complexioned black woman. Emma then sees Effie as a rival and resents her different complexion. Her feelings about her darker skin color ultimately create conflict between her, John, and Effie. Because of her jealousy, she refuses pie and then decides to leave the cakewalk. Her complaints are framed in racial language, as she says she believes light-skinned blacks are privileged over dark-skinned blacks.

Decades later Emmaline still faces these issues. When John comes to visit, he wants them to marry, even after discovering that she has had a child out of wedlock. When he sees the child, he notes the irony of the situation, as despite her past accusations it was she who bore a child with a lighter-skinned man. When Emma sees John with her child, she gets angry, assuming he is attracted to the girl's light complexion. John accuses her of racial self-hatred and departs, symbolizing loss. When the doctor arrives, he queries about the delay in her seeking help; again, her feelings about skin color cause problems for those around her, and mostly for herself—the play ends with her in despair.

This drama is an indictment of racial self-hatred and intraracial color prejudice, and the mechanism Hurston uses to present this is irony: the person most obsessed with others' feelings about skin color is ultimately the person who is most "color struck." Howard writes that Emma "brings about her own misery and downfall" and that *Color Struck* can be seen as a "condemnation of self-deprecatory, self-defeating attitudes" (65). With Hurston's use of irony, the play functions as an insightful critique on the matter.

Marriage

Marriage is another important theme in this play, primarily through the characters of John and Effie. At the end of the play John is a widower, and Emma is a single mother who hasn't married. The two still have feelings for each other, but Emma's insecurities concerning color consciousness prevent a happy union between her and John. By the play's end, John has departed, ending the possibility of marriage between them.

Color Struck contains important social commentary and functions as a piece of protest literature by turning its focus of racial issues in on the black community. It is a cautionary narrative about the perils of racial self-hatred, or favoring people based on their skin color. Emmaline's fixation on skin color causes behavior that affects her relationships to John, her own child, and herself. Hurston's award from *Opportunity* magazine for this drama highlights the importance of its themes to the African-American community.

CHARACTERS

Effie An African-American woman with a light complexion and biracial heritage. Emmaline sees her as a foe, thinking that her boyfriend favors her light complexion. Effie and John win first place in a cakewalk after Emmaline refuses to perform and leaves.

Emmaline Emma embodies the theme of color prejudice and consciousness. Marked by insecurity and jealousy, she obsesses about skin color and accuses her lover of preferring lighter-skinned black women, an accusation that drives a wedge between the couple. Prone to tirades about light-complexioned blacks having more than darker-skinned blacks, she is, ironically, blind to her own prejudice based on skin color. Emma has a light-skinned child out of wedlock, suggesting the father was light-skinned. Her racial insecurities cause problems right up to the end, when she finally accuses John of liking her daughter's light skin. By the play's end, she is sad at having lost everything.

John John is in love with Emma, but Emma believes he prefers black women with lighter complexions. John chooses Effie as a dance partner after Emma storms out of the cakewalk, and the two win the contest. He eventually weds someone else and lives in the North. Years later he attempts to reunite with Emma and tries to help her sick child but he leaves her when she remains finally unwilling to change.

BIBLIOGRAPHY

Boyd, Valerie. *Wrapped in Rainbows: The Life of Zora Neale Hurston.* New York: Scribner, 2003.

Howard, Lillie P. *Zora Neale Hurston.* Boston: Twayne, 1980.

Hurston, Zora Neale. *Color Struck, A Play in Four Scenes. Fire!!* (November 1926): 7–14.

"Drenched in Light" (1924)

"Drenched in Light" reflects Hurston's interest in white consumption of black cultural expression during the HARLEM RENAISSANCE. During this period, African Americans often performed for all white or mostly white audiences throughout the United States. Additionally, white patrons of the arts often supported African-American artists. White patronage and audience influenced the distribution and reception of black cultural expression. While "Drenched in Light" can be read as a coming-of-age story about a young black girl learning to express herself through dance, the politics of race and class serve as an important subtext for this work of short fiction. Hurston's description of locale and her use of DIALECT add a sense of realism to the story. While "Drenched in Light" has not received as much attention as her novels, this short story reveals Hurston's sophisticated awareness about the complex relationships between blacks and whites. This story first appeared in *OPPORTUNITY* magazine and later appeared in a revised form as "Isis," which follows the same story line, but varies in word choice and dialogue.

SYNOPSIS

Isis Watts's grandmother tells her to climb down from a gate post and begin yard work. Isis has spotted Jim and George Robinson, and she wishes to greet them, a habit she often enjoys from the gate post as others pass by along the road to Sanford or Orlando. Isis plays with her friends and some dogs, and does a bit of yard work before her father, John Watts, arrives at home. As her grandmother sews, which is her daily routine, Isis climbs under the table and daydreams. Her grandmother falls asleep and Isis decides to shave her, but her brother Joel suggests they go fishing instead, for fear of getting in trouble with their father. Their grandmother wakes up and heads outside, foiling the plan. Joel goes off fishing, and Isis hides under the house. Spotting a marching band, Isis dances as she follows behind. Before long she goes back home and gets into more household mischief, wrapping herself in one of her grandmother's tablecloths.

Later, Isis is lying in the grass next to a road, worried about being whipped. She sees an automobile with some white people she had waved to earlier, and she tells them she is committing suicide. Helen, Harry, and Sewell, who are white, invite her into the car and drive her home. Helen gives her grandmother some money to buy an outfit for Isis. Enchanted, Helen asks to take Isis to a hotel so she can give a show. Grandmother agrees, and Helen exclaims, "she's drenched in light!" Isis gets back in the car with her new friends, and Helen tells her she needs Isis's joy.

CRITICAL COMMENTARY

"Drenched in Light" is set in Florida in the early 1900s, one of many of Hurston's stories set there. The story focuses specifically on themes such as childhood, identity, imagination, and self-versus-society. Isis is a young, imaginative, creative child whose desire to express herself places her in a unique position in her family and community; her interest in dance and costume alternately incites disapproval and approval in the people around her. She wants to engage in the world, and she likes to interact with other people, although she is also precocious and gets cautioned for being too mature. She attempts to acquire different identities through daydreams and storytelling. While Isis's grandmother represents practicality, Isis represents imagination and creativity. This can be seen when she wears the tablecloth: Isis uses it as adornment, while for her grandmother it is simply functional. The tablecloth episode, along with the plan to shave grandmother, create a comic tone.

Hurston's story also offers important commentary on race and class relationships. Isis interacts with a number of white people, including the Robinsons, who pass by, and the group of white people in the car, who are impressed by her. The story offers a look at the relationship between the black artists and their audience, which was often predominantly white and middle class. Helen's interest in Isis as a symbol of youth and energy portrays this relationship between black culture and white American consumers. During the Harlem Renaissance, black artists frequently performed for white audiences who functioned as consumers of black culture, and Helen's desire for Isis's performance reflects this phenomenon.

CHARACTERS

Harry A minor character, he is one of the white men in the car, along with Helen and

Sewell. He seems unsure about Helen's relationship with Isis, but he does not object to Helen's plan for having Isis perform.

Helen Helen, a white woman, gains a sense of joy when she meets Isis. She convinces the grandmother to let Isis go to the hotel to perform. Helen symbolizes power, authority, and white consumption of black art.

Grandma Potts The grandmother of Isis, she mostly disapproves of her granddaughter's desire to meet new people and act like an adult. She serves as a parental figure for her granddaughter and grandson and tries to instill a sense of discipline and structure in them. For example, she asks Isis to get off the gate post and do yard work. Grandma believes in the importance of domestic chores and she values domestic items. Though a somewhat strict woman, she allows Isis to leave with three strangers and perform at a hotel.

Robinson, Jim and George These two white men herd cattle and enjoy spending time with Isis, and they are seen in the opening scene. They symbolize the significance of race relations. Also, the cattle serve as a reminder of the agrarian context of the story.

Sewell This is the white man who drives Isis to her grandmother's house, along with Helen and Harry.

Watts, Isis An African-American child living in Florida, Isis possesses a vivid imagination and loves to daydream about new experiences. She enjoys singing, dancing, and meeting new people, and has an ability to transform the people she comes in contact with. Prone to mischief, Isis decides it would be a good idea to shave her sleeping grandmother with her brother's help. Her penchant for performance prompts her to dance and follow a marching band in a parade. As she does this, she wears her grandmother's tablecloth, transformed into a costume. This leads to tension between her creative energy and her practical grandmother, and Isis runs to a roadside after her grandmother sees her outfit. Helen considers Isis to be "drenched in light!" and in this way Isis symbolizes the black artists performing for white middle-class consumption.

Watts, Joel He goes fishing and is complicit in the plot to shave grandmother. As Isis's brother, he tries to assert his manhood.

BIBLIOGRAPHY

Baum, Rosalie Murphy. "*The Shape of Hurston's Fiction.*" In *Zora in Florida,* edited by Steve Glassman and Kathryn Lee Seidel, 94–109. Orlando: University of Central Florida Press, 1991.

Hurston, Zora Neale. "Drenched in Light." In her *The Complete Stories,* 17–25. New York: HarperCollins, 1995.

Plant, Deborah G. *Every Tub Must Sit on Its Own Bottom: The Philosophy and Politics of Zora Neale Hurston.* Chicago: University of Illinois Press, 1995.

Dust Tracks on a Road (1942)

Published in 1942, *Dust Tracks on a Road* is a memoir documenting Zora Neale Hurston's life and experiences. It chronicles her growth and development as a writer, as well as her many migrations throughout the South, the North, and the Caribbean. Hurston offers the reader a glimpse into her mindset and the multiple influences on her creativity, which include her family, her physical environments, and her relationships with other people. *Dust Tracks on a Road* is "a very informal, conversational narrative about the people and places which form the background of Hurston's life" (Howard 161). In this book, Hurston plays the role of the storyteller as in her fictional works, but here she tells the story of her own life.

While the book is autobiographical, some of the material in the text is not true. The most obvious example is in the first chapter, "My Birthplace," in which she cites EATONVILLE, FLORIDA as her place of birth despite the fact she was born in NOTASULGA, ALABAMA. She did, however, spend much of her childhood in Eatonville. It is not clear whether this misrepresentation was deliberate, but if that is the case, it could be said that Hurston rewrites her own personal history in order to create a particular persona and be able to claim as a birthright the status of being from an all-black town. Given her rise to prominence during the New Negro movement, this may not be surprising, since that movement placed a premium on cultural and ethnic origins. Originating from an all-black town would fit into the movement's ideas of black pride, consciousness, and heritage.

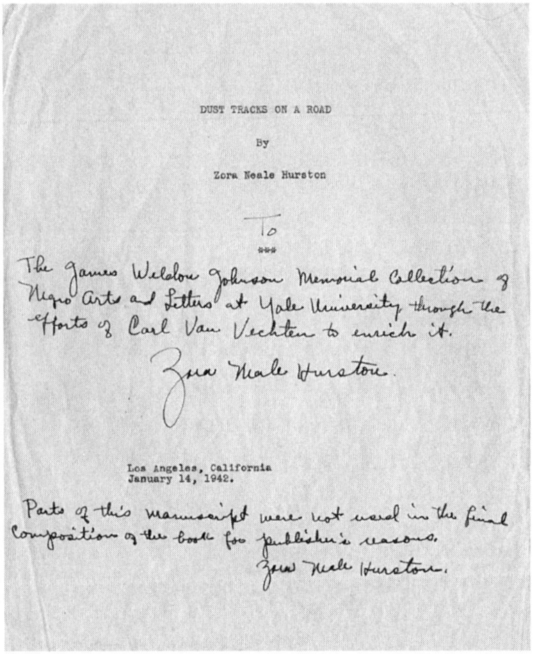
DUST TRACKS ON A ROAD

By

Zora Neale Hurston

To

***

The James Weldon Johnson Memorial Collection of Negro Arts and Letters at Yale University through the efforts of Carl Van Vechten to enrich it.

Zora Neale Hurston.

Los Angeles, California
January 14, 1942.

Parts of this manuscript were not used in the final composition of the book for publisher's reasons.

Zora Neale Hurston.

Title page of manuscript of *Dust Tracks on a Road,* 1941 *(Yale Collection of American Literature, Beinecke Rare Book and Manuscript Library)*

In any case, the inaccuracies in Hurston's text remind us that memoir or autobiography is only a construction of reality by the person writing it. In other words, writers choose to include or exclude, add or omit certain aspects of their life; plus, the point of view, which comes from the author, may represent bias and not be an objective one at all. Still, the memoir serves as an important text in giving the reader a sense of the persona Zora Neale Hurston wished to present to the rest of the world.

Also, *Dust Tracks on a Road* reveals the complicated nature of the author's relationship with the people who published or sold books, as well as the people who read them. As an African-American female, Hurston may have been constrained in what she could write, considering the obstacles she faced, and this may have had an effect on what viewpoints or perspectives she represented. Indeed, the textual history of the work points to controversy involving modifications. Cheryl Wall, in *Women of the Harlem Renaissance,* points out changes that were made between the manuscript and the published product. She cites an "incoherence" in the memoir due to a "last-minute insistence on extensive revisions, notably the deletion of an extended critique of U.S. imperialism" (198). Wall writes that this was her "most heavily edited book" and that it included editorial changes that were "rarely for the better" (198).

For this reason, readers are advised to consult the Library of America edition of *Dust Tracks on a Road* (which has been used in this *Critical Companion to Zora Neale Hurston*). The Library of America edition includes portions of her original manuscript that were left out of the 1942 edition, including four chapters left out of previous editions and one chapter that had never appeared in print. The textual history of *Dust Tracks on a Road* is an important aspect of the work, as it provides necessary context to the actual content.

Hurston composed *Dust Tracks on a Road* for the most part while living in California, where she had journeyed after being invited by a wealthy woman named Katharine Mershon. While on the West Coast, from 1941 to 1942, Hurston worked for Paramount Studios at the same time that she began composing the memoir. She continued work on the memoir in Florida, and the book was published when she was teaching at Florida Normal College, in Saint Augustine (Wall 198).

Hurston's memoir remains a well-crafted and interesting work, which features many of the themes present in her fiction, including race, class, gender, religion, nature, marriage, and identity. Read alongside Hurston's novels, *Dust Tracks on a Road* provides an especially illuminating look into the connections between her life and art. The book earned a prize from *Saturday Review* due to "its contribution to better race relations" (Howard 161).

SYNOPSIS

I
My Birthplace

Hurston opens by saying she "was born in a Negro town," or Eatonville, Florida. She emphasizes that blacks dominate the community and govern themselves, the town having distinguished itself as being an "attempt at organized self-government on the part of Negroes in America." She provides a history of the town, noting that its namesake was a man named Captain Eaton. She argues that this town carries a special status, noting that it "made history by becoming the first of its kind in America, and perhaps in the world."

II
My Folks

Hurston chronicles the lives of her parents. She writes that her father, John Hurston, was born close to Notasulga, Alabama, and explains how he met her mother, who came from a landowning family. Her mother knew that John had a lighter complexion than other black people from the area. They married, and John moved to Florida, eventually becoming mayor of Eatonville. The mother later relocated to Florida to join him. Hurston points out the complicated nature of her parents' marriage, caused especially by her father's relationships with other women. Hurston provides a description of their house and the land around her family's home, and paints a portrait of a comfortable family life. Hurston had seven siblings.

III
I Get Born

Hurston's father is not at the house when she was born; she notes, perhaps ironically, "his patience was short with me." At her birth, a white man assists in the birth by cutting her naval cord, and only later does the midwife arrive to help out. The next day, the newborn baby is given her name: Zora Neale Hurston. The white man who helped Zora's mother give birth stops by periodically afterward. Hurston begins walking only after she had an encounter with a hog. "The strangest thing about it was that once I found the use of my feet, they took to wandering," she writes. Her father, who also had a penchant for wandering, may have influenced Hurston in this respect.

IV
The Inside Search

Hurston discusses her childhood. She believed as a child that the moon was following her, a claim a childhood friend would make too. She climbs trees and notices the "horizon." She wants to travel to the horizon with her friend, but her friend declines, causing them to fight. During the holiday season, her father asks the family what they want for Christmas, and Zora wants a horse, so she can ride to that horizon. Hurston indicates her strength as a youth, with a tendency to injure other people while playing. She delights in spending time with the white man who had helped birth her. She also enjoys spending time perched on a gate post, from which she observes the "world." From that gate post, Zora would follow other travelers, often white, down the road. Her grandmother was concerned about this behavior.

Hurston also writes about some visiting white women who made an impact on her life. After reading a myth aloud about Jupiter and Persephone, Zora talks with these women; the following day, Zora visits them at a hotel. There, Zora reads from a publication provided to her; the women photograph her, and give her food and money. The women continue to send her gifts, including clothing and books. Hurston began reading the Bible when her mother would punish her, and the Bible was the only book available in the room to which she was confined. As a child, she occasionally had "visions."

V
Figure and Fancy

In this chapter, Hurston discusses the store owned by Joe Clarke. She points out that men congregated "around the store on boxes and benches" and talked, and Zora enjoyed listening to their discussions. They would tell tales about animals such as Brer Fox, Brer Rabbit, and others. Another story, which came from God, explained the origin of the different racial groups and how blacks obtained dark skin. Her father and the other ministers are great storytellers. Hurston starts creating tales too. She recalls telling her mother a story about a bird and a lake that spoke; her grandmother disapproved of the lake story.

VI
Wandering

Hurston notices her mother becoming ill as she loses weight. September 18 is an important date for Hurston. On that day, Hurston's mother says that Zora should not let anyone remove her pillow from underneath her head before her death or cover the clock or looking-glass. Later, Zora reenters, and sees someone reach for that clock and another female attempt to remove the pillow. Zora objects out loud to the removal of the pillow, given her mother's request. She also sees people cover the mirror and the clock. Her mother dies and, with her, an important part of Zora's life. "That hour began my wanderings," she writes. Hurston describes how her relatives react to the death of the mother, noting her father's sobs. Her mother's body is carried to church the following day. Later, Hurston heads for Jacksonville, where she becomes aware of her racial identity. She describes her experience at school there, and recalls catching sight of a woman who reminds her of her mother.

VII
Jacksonville and After

Hurston believes her father favors one of her sisters, Sarah. Sarah informs her that their father has wed another woman. Both Sarah and Zora have negative feelings for their stepmother, and Zora even gets in a physical altercation with her, for which the stepmother wants Hurston arrested. In Jacksonville, Zora is forced to take up cleaning to pay her bills, and wins a spelling contest at school. A school employee gives her some money so she can visit her father. When she arrives, she sees the stepmother sleeping in her own mother's bed; with a brother's support, she prevents her stepmother from sleeping there.

VIII
Back Stage and the Railroad

After leaving school in Jacksonville, Hurston moves around a lot. She attempts working, but does not have steady employment. One job is as a servant for a woman and her children, but the woman's husband does not approve of Zora and after many problems he asks her to leave. Zora concludes that this man wanted his wife to stay at home to care for their offspring. Another job is working for an ill woman, whose husband wants to leave for Canada and take Zora with him. After some other jobs and more time spent at home with her father, Zora departs to look for work elsewhere. Zora works for a doctor, then lives with her brother's family and befriends a white woman, who recommends she get a job with a singer. Zora joins the Gilbert and Sullivan music group. She has many experiences with the music group and travels with them around the country. Eventually she quits this job. During this period, she discovers Milton and reads *Paradise Lost.*

IX
School Again

Hurston comments on the necessity of funding for pursuing an education. She becomes ill and has appendix surgery. She attends school in Baltimore and then at Morgan College, which she enjoys. Hurston is encouraged to attend HOWARD UNIVERSITY, which Hurston describes as "the capstone of Negro education in the world." She moves to Washington, D.C., to work and attend that university. She learns a lot of new things, and is inspired by an instructor there to teach English. Zora was a member of a sorority, and she contributed to *The Stylus.* At this time, she corresponded with Charles S. Johnson, the legendary editor of *Opportunity* magazine, who encouraged her to send articles to him for a writing contest for the magazine. Hurston wins her first award from that magazine in 1925. Hurston moves to New York, where she gets a position with Fannie Hurst and begins attending Barnard. She meets Franz Boas, a professor of anthropology. Boas helps her get a fellowship so that she can gather folklore. For her research, she goes to Memphis, where she

Chemistry laboratory at Howard University, Washington, D.C. *(Library of Congress)*

reconnects with a brother. Zora heads next to New Orleans for research.

X
Research

Initially, Hurston does not have a good experience with her fellowship. She feels she asked questions using language that her informants find inappropriate or unexpected, and when she does get information, it is not much. She returned to New York and sobbed to Boas. A patron named CHARLOTTE OSGOOD MASON provides her with a research stipend. Hurston describes how Mason dwelled with Native Americans, and calls her "just as pagan as I."

Hurston recounts her experiences and the perilous nature of her work, commenting on evening activities such as jook joints, or clubs with music and dance. At such jook joints, fights often broke out, and Hurston recounts almost being killed at one by a woman named Lucy. Lucy does not appreciate Hurston's gathering information from Slim, "who used to be her man back up in West Florida," and tries to attack her. Hurston escapes and leaves for New Orleans. While there, she learns about hoodoo, working with Frizzly Rooster and other hoodoo experts. She studies rituals and engages in initiations with these experts. Hurston continues researching in the Bahamas, focusing specifically on the African origins of hoodoo; later, she would introduce this music when she returned to New York. While in the Bahamas, she experiences a hurricane and meets many people who impress her with their musical and folklore-telling ability. She does research on Cudjo Lewis, a man from Africa who arrived in the United States on a slave ship. She gathers folk tales in Haiti and the British West Indies, and is inspired by a female zombie, one inspiration for her book *Tell My Horse.*

XI
Books and Things

In this section, Hurston describes the beginnings of a productive period. Hurston's idea for writing *Jonah's Gourd Vine* originates with her research. In her research, she gathers many tunes, but black songwriters feel whites would not be interested in the freestyle composition. She holds an event to see how people would react, and they like it. Hurston acknowledges the effects of the Great Depression for funding research. She writes *Mules and Men* and "The Gilded Six-Bits," and begins work on *Jonah's Gourd Vine,* which she has told a publisher is already written. She says she composed *Their Eyes Were Watching God* "in seven weeks" while in Haiti, and that she wrote *Dust Tracks on a Road* while living in California.

XII
My People! My People!

Hurston discusses race issues and reflects on the black utterance "My People! My people!," noting the ways in which it is used, especially

Port-au-Prince, Haiti, ca. 1920 *(Library of Congress)*

as a means of expressing disapproval of others' actions. Hurston notes that blacks are not a monolithic group and that darker-skinned blacks, especially females, are often given trouble by other blacks.

XIII
Two Women in Particular

Hurston recounts stories about Fannie Hurst and Ethel Waters, two friends who greatly enriched her life. Hurston worked for Fannie, who was wealthy, and they traveled together. Hurston met the singer Ethel Waters at a meal honoring Hurston; she describes Waters as "gay and sombre by turns."

XIV
Love

Calling herself "such a poor picker" in romantic matters, Hurston discusses love, and what she has learned about it both in books and in real life. Hurston marries a man she met in college, but soon has second thoughts. Wanting to resume her research, Hurston urges her husband to move to Chicago, and he ends up with another woman. Later, she meets an affectionate but poor man who has an impact on her, whom she refers to as P.M.P. The two have a tumultuous relationship, as he doesn't want Zora to continue her profession. Hurston continues her travels for research, but later contacts her old lover again. In the chapter, Hurston quotes a favorite "folk-rhyme" that comments on the nature of affection.

XV
Religion

Hurston's experience with religion includes questions about God. She enjoys revivals and the preacher's behavior during these events. Hurston acknowledges that upon studying religion, she "saw that even in his religion, man carried himself along." Hurston sees purpose in religion: "People need religion because the great masses fear life and its consequences."

XVI
Looking Things Over

Hurston gives some perspective about her life and experience, commenting on history and how there is "nothing but futility in looking back over my shoulder in rebuke at the grave of some white man who has been dead too long to talk about." She reflects that her slave ancestors are no longer alive, and neither are the slave owners. She speculates that the descendants of slave owners would not feel guilty, but would distance themselves from it as it was in the past. Hurston emphasizes that she holds "no race prejudice" against others and hopes for a "a noble world" in the future.

Appendices

The appendices in this edition of the text are important. The dust jacket for this edition points out that it includes "chapters" which "represent earlier stages of Hurston's conception of the book."

My People, My People!

This is a different version of the Chapter 12 in the body text of the book. Here, Hurston notes the disparity between different classes of blacks. She defines the term "My People" as encompassing different skin tones and discusses the issue of "passing," or when blacks pretend to be white and whites pretend to be black. She suggests that the black writer James Weldon Johnson "is not a Negro." There is also discussion of various issues of interest to Hurston: blacks' inability to reach agreement and their tendency to forget the

James Weldon Johnson, NAACP officer, activist, author, and diplomat *(Yale Collection of American Literature, Beinecke Rare Book and Manuscript Library)*

past; the joys of imitating, drama, and performance; money issues and stealing; black language; stories about a monkey. The chapter ends with a story explaining the origins of black skin color.

Seeing the World As It Is

Racial and class discrimination are useless, Hurston writes; she does not view blacks as superior or inferior. Preferring to focus on individual rather than group progress, Hurston does not want to "accept responsibility for thirteen million people" and she critiques the idea of "Racial Solidarity," citing diversity. Hurston sees race consciousness and racial pride as barriers for white people as well as for black people, even if it advances group solidarity. Hurston does not believe in dwelling on history, specifically slavery, since she is part of a different generation. There is also discussion of religion and religious figures who invoke Jesus to justify violence, as well as commentary on international affairs, including Adolf Hitler. The chapter ends on this note: "tears and laughter, love and hate, make up the sum of life."

The Inside Light—Being a Salute to Friendship

This chapter focuses on the role of friends in her life, and Hurston writes that she wishes she could have been a better friend at times. Important people in her life then included Charlotte Osgood Mason, Fannie Hurst, and Carl Van Vechten, among many others. Hurston emphasizes the importance of personal relationships.

Concert

This chapter deals with the performance Hurston staged in New York in 1932 in order to expose people to authentic African-American music. During her research, Hurston gathered music material, which she passed along to Hall Johnson. Hurston gathered some dancers from the Bahamas, and asked Johnson to help organize a performance that would mix the Bahamian dancers with his musicians. Finally, Hurston put on the concert without his help, getting assistance from Charlotte Osgood Mason instead. Mason, Alain Locke, and Johnson are all present for the event, which was a success. The group did other performances, but after some frustration Hurston moved back to Florida to work on *Jonah's Gourd Vine.*

CRITICAL COMMENTARY

In this account of her life, Zora Neale Hurston meditates on race, class, gender, religion, migration, and the quest for a self. Although she positions the text as autobiography, Hurston embellishes the details of her life. She creates a persona of a Southern black woman from an all-black town steeped in African-American culture and folklore who through her own hard work and industry—and some luck—manages to achieve successes despite the obstacles in her path. The memoir offers insight into her origins, family, education, writing, and social and political beliefs. Following are thematic commentaries about the main issues exposed in the book.

Race

In *Dust Tracks on a Road,* the subject of race is prominent and directly informs Zora Neale Hurston's experience as an American.

Hurston's characterization of Eatonville as a unique type of black experiment in self-government corresponds to ideas of black power and community. Hurston emphasizes the black control of Eatonville, which suggests a type of social, political, and economic autonomy that would not have been common elsewhere in the segregated South. The setting of Eatonville affected her family in important ways, as we can see in *Dust Tracks on a Road.* Even though she wasn't born in Eatonville, she lived there for much of her childhood, and this nurturing in a black community would have an effect on her development as a black artist, as is evident throughout the work. Within this town, Hurston's mother and father possessed opportunities for social and economic advancement: John, her father, served as mayor and worked on community policy. In addition to her exposure to African-American success in politics and economics there, Hurston was exposed to the black storytelling tradition. In fact, the shop owned by Joe Clarke proved invaluable for Hurston, as the stories she heard told there would plant the seeds for her later work; this is documented in her memoir.

Questions of racial politics within Hurston's own family also play a central role in this work. Her father, for example, who had a lighter complexion in comparison to other blacks, would serve for Hurston as a personal example of an issue that was widespread among blacks. Also, it's important to note that Hurston's fictional works were often directly inspired by the events in her own life. For example, *Jonah's Gourd Vine* was inspired by her mother and father's marriage. This illustrates how the autobiographical aspects of her life and her family's life affected her creative writing, and thematic elements in her fiction and nonfiction are tightly intertwined.

In the work, Hurston presents herself as having interracial contact at a very young age. To begin with, a white male is present at her birth, and even cuts her umbilical cord; later, this man would have an influence on Hurston's life. There are also numerous white women who are mentioned in this work, many of them generous and admiring of Zora, both as a youth and as an adult. Still, these contacts with white people threw into relief Hurston's position as a minority. After her mother died and she relocated to Jacksonville, Hurston became more aware of her identification as a black person. Unlike Eatonville, Jacksonville was not a black-controlled town, and this would be Zora's adult first immersion in such an environment.

Dust Tracks on a Road also documents her work experiences and how race relations come into play in her employment. While in Florida, she finds a job as a servant for a white family. An older black female, already working there, viewed Hurston as a threat in many ways. Hurston's experience thus reveals intraracial, as well as interracial, conflicts. She also works for other white families and individuals in a variety of contexts. In another servant job, the husband takes an interest in Zora, making her feel uncomfortable. This reveals another power conflict, one based not only on race but also on gender. Her experiences being employed as a maid and a servant illustrate the limited opportunities for black women during this time period. More broadly, in her attempts to support herself, she finds many different but all short-lived jobs; her writing was the one sustaining force throughout her life.

Hurston reveals, too, that she dealt with many race issues during the time of her education. Howard symbolized the epitome of higher learning among historically black colleges, and Hurston felt privileged to attend. This would prove to be an important time in her development as an African-American writer, especially because of the people she met and the learning she attained. While in Washington, D.C., at Howard, Hurston would experience the growing civil rights movement. In the work, she reports on a black man who tries to get service at a barber shop but cannot due to the color of his skin. But the reality is complex, because Hurston herself admits she did not want him there either: It would have hindered her own economic livelihood, since it might have kept her other customers, or patrons, away. She argues that taking care of oneself would be more important than offering support or encouragement to this victim of discrimination. Her commentary reveals the many complexities of civil rights issues for the black community.

Hurston's accounts of her life in New York, especially as it relates to her formal education there, also touch on significant race issues. While in New York, she gets an award from *OPPORTUNITY*, a publication created by the Urban League, an organization that advocates for civil rights for blacks. She also worked for the famous author Fannie Hurst and attended BARNARD COLLEGE, an achievement few black women would have had the opportunity to make at that time. Her popularity while at Barnard may suggest that her white colleagues were attracted to what they saw as an exotic otherness, based on her skin color and southern origins. In effect, she becomes the racialized other amid the upper-class white women at Barnard. She shifted from being in the majority at Howard to being in the minority at Barnard College. Here, Hurston shows that she successfully navigated both the black and white worlds.

The research Hurston engages in with the help of FRANZ BOAS, an anthropology professor at Columbia University, has a major impact on Hurston. Her folklore interest offers her an opportunity to do research that connects her with black folk roots. She points out that initially she did not have much success in gathering information in the South because of the type of language she spoke with the people there, which was a more educated English than what her research subjects spoke. Back in New York, Hurston entered into a patronage relationship with Charlotte Osgood Mason, a wealthy white female with an attitude that blacks and native Americans were primitivistic and exotic. Hurston's relationship with Mason illustrates the politics of white patronage and black artistic production during the Harlem Renaissance. Often, whites with preconceived ideas about blacks funded projects; this allowed black artists to create, but this state of affairs arguably compromised some of their material out of a need to satisfy the expectations of their patrons.

Hurston's research connects with the themes of racial identity. In her research, she observes the actions of people in singing, laughing, and attending jook joints, or music clubs. She is the participant-observer as she engages in collecting information; she also spends time learning about hoodoo in New Orleans, and again becomes participant-observer by studying and participating in rituals with the experts. Hurston learns about cultural expression in the African diaspora while in the Bahamas; later, she exposes people in New York to this music from the Caribbean, one example of Hurston's efforts to diffuse African culture widely. Her research also brings her into contact with former slaves, such as Cudjo Lewis.

Hurston's memoir engages in much social and political commentary in relationship to race, across many different fields and using many devices. She talks about the politics of skin color among blacks, not just in relation to whites but also among themselves. She points out that light-skin blacks may have privileges over blacks with darker skin, and she critiques blacks who want to champion blacks but who distance themselves from black culture at the same time. She also stresses the idea that blacks are not all the same, and the reality that there is a huge diversity among blacks. She comments on history in America and the legacy of slavery, and she points out that there is no point in her making the descendents of slavery responsible for slavery. She claims that she does not have racial prejudice against other people. Hurston also explores race dynamics at the interpersonal level, notably with her friends Fannie Hurst and Ethel Waters.

Hurston's memoir presents a complicated view of race, and she seems to celebrate the connections she makes with people from different racial and ethnic backgrounds. Her analysis of the dynamics of race in relationship to the past and her own reality provide the reader with an insight into both the social climate of the day and the education of the artist.

Class

Dust Tracks on a Road treats class issues, as Hurston presents a broad range of working-, middle-, and upper-class environments in her narrative. Her memoir illustrates the dynamics of class mobility—both upward and downward—in relation to herself and those around her. Class in this work is portrayed as fluid and not static; for Hurston, it remains a complex, changing, and significant part of one's identity.

Early on in the text, Hurston describes the impact of class on her family history. Her own mother came from a landowning family, a fact that would have placed them in a privileged position over other blacks in the rural South at that time. It was also in contrast to her father's family, which was poorer. Hurston's account of her own immediate family suggests a middle-class existence, with her father in positions of power in Eatonville and a house. Elsewhere in town, Joe Clarke's store may be seen as a place encouraging the confluence of the "folk" and the bourgeois, since the middle-class store owner establishes a business functioning as a site of African-American storytelling connected with the folk traditions. Joe Clarke, like Jody Starks in *Their Eyes Were Watching God,* symbolizes the black entrepreneurial class and rise of black business in the 20th century in America.

Although Hurston's youth may have been characterized by relative privilege, she soon finds herself in a less secure financial situation once she moves to Jacksonville and has to earn money to support herself. As exposed at length in *Dust Tracks on a Road,* Hurston works as a servant for a number of white families and individuals, in which position she learns about power dynamics both among working-class workers and between the workers and their employers. When she is in the company of an older black woman already working for the family, she is resented by the other and ultimately has to leave. When she works for a woman whose husband is attracted to Zora, the narrative relates the fear of working-class black women of being viewed as sexual chattel by more powerful white males. Hurston's situation highlights the vulnerable position black female domestics were often in, as this employment was common. In her various other jobs, she again finds herself in insecure, working-class positions working for whites. The only job in which she appears to exert a degree of autonomy or freedom is her job in the theater group.

In her narrative, Hurston reveals that her social and economic situation functions as an important part of her identity. Her studies at Morgan Academy, Howard University, and Barnard College are all major achievements that few black women would have been able to experience in that era. At Howard, she must work while going to school; she finds a job at a barbershop frequented by wealthy politicians. The job would give Hurston exposure to the people who control the government and the economy. As she moves around the country, her financial situation remains fluid, her class position unfixed but precarious when compared to the upper classes. Hurston's discussion of her relationships at Barnard College, peopled with upper-class white women, especially illuminates Hurston's relation to the white bourgeoisie and elite in America. After so much time with the bourgeoisie and middle classes in New York, Hurston would immerse herself in research that would bring her back to her roots, to the other side of the class situation, as she collected folklore. In interviewing subjects, she spoke using a language and terminology she learned in college.

Hurston's class situation stands in starkest contrast to her patron, Charlotte Osgood Mason, a wealthy New York socialite. Mason, symbolizing the upper classes, had a fascination with the "lower" African-American and Native American cultures. Relationships like Hurston's with Mason were common in the Harlem Renaissance era, when wealthy whites were fascinated by the culture of underprivileged blacks, viewing it as exotic or primitive. Thus, we have the confluence of working-class cultural expression being paid for and consumed by upper-class patronage; in her research on black folklore funded by Mason, Hurston would be the mediator between the two, the researcher bridging the performer with the consumer.

Ultimately, Hurston's life as portrayed in this work illustrates social and economic fluidity. As we have seen, *Dust Tracks on a Road* paints a broad picture of how class issues affected Hurston and informed her writings; the complexities of class are explored from both an intraracial and an interracial perspective. From the differences of her two parents to her comfortable childhood, from her many menial jobs to her prestigious educational opportunities, and from her relationships with rural black folk and with wealthy New York socialites, the picture of class emerging from Hurston's memoir is a complex and dynamic one.

Charlotte Osgood Mason, the legendary and exacting patron of Zora Neale Hurston and Langston Hughes *(Yale Collection of American Literature, Beinecke Rare Book and Manuscript Library)*

Gender

In her memoir, Hurston analyzes the significance that gender roles played in her own life and in American society at large. She documents her important relationships with women and men in her life, including relatives, friends, and other acquaintances. Confronted with competing ideas about gender roles in American society, Hurston alternately accepts and rejects certain notions as she chooses her own path. Hurston's text suggests a negotiation with the complexities of gender roles in her life.

Hurston's relationships with females in her life are among the most important of her growth and development. Her mother and grandmother, clearly, are chief among them, but white women she encounters as a youth also play a role. Hurston's grandmother found her storytelling to be problematic, while her mother was not bothered by it; so she had female figures who both facilitated her growth as a storyteller and discouraged that creativity. Her mother may have contributed to Hurston's sense of trying to achieve the most in life; her mother's death left an indelible impression upon her memory. Dying when Hurston is young, her mother imparts a legacy, which may explain some of Hurston's later achievements. Before her death, Hurston observes how her mother manages her illness, how she reflects on her marriage, her nephew's death, and other matters. The reader senses that Hurston's relationship with her mother is a close one, while that with her father is distant and less close. In fact, a feminist reading of Hurston's literary legacy suggests that in her writing she tried bringing back "her mother's voice" (Wall 145).

At school in Jacksonville, Hurston's role as a woman is an important factor in her identity; this is especially apparent when she sees a woman who reminds her of her mother. At this time, Hurston's assertiveness comes to play a part in her relationship with her stepmother, with whom she does not get along. She does not accept her in a maternal role or as a figure of respect and authority. In fact, the two women engage in a physical altercation; in this way, Hurston rebels against the idea of a female being passive, demure, and submissive. Instead, she exerts strength and assertiveness.

Gender issues can be seen in the various jobs Hurston holds throughout her life, and in *Dust Tracks on a Road* these positions receive much commentary. Hurston's first employment as a servant for a white woman is terminated, and she believes that the husband wanted the wife to stay home taking care of the children. In Hurston's interpretation, then, this man desires to confine and contain his wife for fear of her behavior outside the home; he seeks to exert patriarchal power and limit his wife's freedom. Again, when working for an ill white woman, whose husband wants to run away to Canada with Hurston, we can see the vulnerable position of black females in relation to white men. This episode can be traced back to white male-black female relationships in the antebellum South, when African-American female slaves found themselves viewed as sexual property by the white male slave owners, who had positions of power and authority over them. As a performer for a troupe, Hurston experiences a greater degree of freedom and meets a wider variety of people, but that job ends when the female performer for whom Hurston worked decides to settle down and get married, following the expected pattern for women of the time period.

Hurston also uses *Dust Tracks on a Road* to explore the role of gender in her research and fieldwork. She gets money from the enabling "Godmother," Charlotte Osgood Mason, who funds her fieldwork. While engaging in her fieldwork, Hurston makes numerous observations about the behavior of males and females, and how they interact: in music and dance clubs, at work in Polk County, and so on. She also describes positive and negative female relationships of her own: for example, with Lucy, who sees her as a threat, but also with Big Sweet, a black woman with a powerful personality and presence who defends her. While doing this research, she learns much about gender dynamics in addition to the folk culture in the South.

Other women who prove to be quite influential upon Hurston include Fannie Hurst, a highly successful writer for whom she worked as a secretary, and Ethel Waters, an African-American performer whom Hurston admired very much. For her, these women symbolize friendship. In her memoir, Hurston reveals a tendency to define herself by her relationships with other people, particularly those who made an impression on her growth and development as a person. The importance of Hurston's connections with famous women is apparent, as she interacted with celebrities and high-profile talents for much of her life.

Hurston also explores the significance of males to the Eatonville community while she was growing up. Joe Clarke owned a store where men gathered to chat and tell stories, and this exposure to tales ultimately proved very important. Hurston writes that her father and other men were excellent at telling stories; Hurston herself then made up her own. In other ways, her father remains an important part of her memoir as a symbol of black manhood. He rose to the position of Eatonville mayor, and she depicts him as a patriarch who provided for his large family. However, Hurston's narrative also reveals that her father may have favored his male children over his female children. The fact that her father was not at home when she was born is a curious one, and the way Hurston frames it suggests it is not necessarily attributable just to chance. Her father as a symbol of masculinity also plays a role in the narrative. Hurston acknowledges that her father cried after her mother died but then remarried soon after. Overall, Hurston depicts the relationship with her father as problematic and complex.

Carl Van Vechten, author, photographer, and patron, photographed by Mark Lutz. Permission granted by Van Vechten Trust *(Yale Collection of American Literature, Beinecke Rare Book and Manuscript Library)*

Other men who play important roles are the anthropologist Franz Boas, who influenced her interest in collecting folklore, and Carl Van Vechten, a white patron of the Harlem Renaissance, and more significantly, her lover P.M.P. and her ex-husband. After Hurston wrote *Mules and Men* and *Jonah's Gourd Vine,* P.M.P. said he wanted to marry her, but he did not want her to continue her professional goals, evincing a somewhat traditional viewpoint about marriage for the time, in which female ambition was stifled. The relationship ended, and the novel she wrote afterward, *Their Eyes Were Watching God,* is rich with Hurston's feelings and deals with the tension between conforming to and rebelling against prescribed gender roles for women. The novel focuses on the quest for self and identity in the context of marriage, and Hurston's own experience with these failed relationships may have influenced that novel.

Ultimately, in *Dust Tracks on a Road,* Hurston offers a varied look at how gender plays a part in her relationships and her sense of self and identity. More broadly, the thematic concerns of race and class in relation to gender connect with her other, fictional works. Her memoir is a fascinating exploration of her life and provides us with a sense of what shaped Hurston as a person and artist. It is a complex account of her life as she desired her readers to perceive it. In effect, she becomes the manipulator and crafter of her life story.

BIBLIOGRAPHY

Howard, Lillie P. *Zora Neale Hurston.* Boston: Twayne, 1980.

Hurston, Zora Neale. *Dust Tracks on a Road.* In her *Folklore, Memoirs, and Other Writings,* 557–808. New York: Library of America, 1995.

Wall, Cheryl A. *Women of the Harlem Renaissance.* Bloomington: Indiana University Press, 1995.

"The Eatonville Anthology" (1926)

This short work, set in EATONVILLE, FLORIDA, consists of several vignettes about the people, places, and themes significant to this rural black community. The stories, based on Hurston's experience there and less fictional than her other works, also depict the oral tradition, as the reader gets a glimpse of its role in that community. "The Eatonville Anthology" appeared in 1926 in *The Messenger,* a civil rights magazine published by the Brotherhood of Sleeping Car Porters and one of the major publications of the HARLEM RENAISSANCE. Robert E. Hemenway comments, "The reader has the impression of sitting in a corner listening to anecdotes" (69).

SYNOPSIS

The vignettes or anecdotes that make up "The Eatonville Anthology" can be read together as a unified text or as separate stories in their own right. Strains of marriage, nature, community, and the relationship of past and present can be read throughout the tales. In part I, Mrs. Tony Roberts asks Mr. Clarke for meat because her family suffers from hunger. Clarke gives it to her but charges her husband. Part II describes Jim Merchant and his marriage. Before marrying Jim, his fiancée has "fits." Turpentine, a folk remedy, stops her fits, and the couple marry. Part III sketches the life of Becky Moore, a single mother with several children. Part IV presents Sykes Jones, who comes from a gambling family whose dog, Tippy, likes to steal food from people. Part V recounts the story of Old Man Anderson, a farmer living outside of Eatonville, who at his first sight of a train is scared and flees. In part VI, Coon Taylor is caught stealing fruit and animals, notably some cane from Joe Clarke, who banishes him from the area for several months as a punishment. In part VII, Joe Lindsay watches a physician perform an operation. In part VIII, we see Sewell moving constantly, and his chickens too become accustomed to the moving. In part IX, we get a glimpse of Mrs. Clarke, who is abused by her husband, Joe. Part X is a profile of Mrs. McDuffy, a churchgoer who is also abused by her husband. In part XI we see the tension between the past and present as the town engages in a ritual dance involving the youth and the elders. In part XII, Daisy Taylor is presented as a "vamp," flirting with other women's husbands and having an affair with Laura Crooms's husband. Mrs. Crooms confronts Daisy about this and assaults her with part of an ax. In part XIII, Cal'line Potts's husband, Mitchell, has an affair with Delphine; one day Cal'line takes up an ax and "followed in his wake." In part XIV, we get a series of animal stories. Mr. Dog and Mr. Rabbit propose to Miss Coon. Mr. Rabbit tells Mr. Dog he will help him sing well to attract Miss Coon, but it's a trick and Mr. Rabbit cuts

Mr. Dog's tongue, which explains why dogs have a slit in their tongues.

CRITICAL COMMENTARY

Hurston presents a series of anecdotes or sketches, stories about the lives of the residents of Eatonville, Florida. The stories treat a variety of themes such as marriage, family, nature, and history. While the individual tales can be read as self-contained units, there are thematic similarities bridging the tales.

Marriage, for example, is central in parts I, II, IX, X, XII, and XIII, tales focusing on the complexities of marriage. Hurston presents these marriages as problematic, rife with difficulties such as lies, deception, adultery, and domestic violence. Anticipating a namesake character in *Their Eyes Were Watching God,* Mrs. Tony Roberts in part I claims her husband does not provide for her; her title of Mrs. Tony Roberts suggests her identity is connected with that of her husband. Part II also reveals the tensions of marriage, with Mrs. Merchant's jittery condition before marrying her husband; this character can be compared to Arvay Henson Meserve, who experiences similar problems when courted in *Seraph on the Suwanee.* Violence between husband and wife characterizes parts IX and X, with Mrs. Clarke and Mrs. McDuffy the victims of beatings by their husbands; this crucial theme appears in other works in which husbands strike their wives, such as *Their Eyes Were Watching God* and *Jonah's Gourd Vine.* Adultery is addressed in the character of Daisy Taylor in part XII, as well as Cal'line Potts, her husband, Mitchell, and his amour, Delphine, in part XIII. Together, these tales expose the many problems that married people experience.

The theme of nature plays an important role in "The Eatonville Anthology," as it does in much of Hurston's fiction and folklore, such as *Mules and Men.* Here, part XIV is mainly concerned with this theme. Hurston uses nature as a parable for human actions; the stories often contain a moral. Part XIV focuses on animals rather than human beings, and Hurston uses personification for these animals. Mr. Rabbit cuts Mr. Dog's tongue in a fit of jealousy and rivalry for the affections of Miss Coon. The animals' actions symbolize the lengths people will go to for love. Hurston also employs animals as minor characters in part IV with the dog Tippy, who likes to steal, and the chickens in part VIII, who become accustomed to the many migrations of their owner, Sewell. In part VI, Coon Taylor is the protagonist; his name Coon, as a variation of "raccoon," ties him to the rural environment.

"The Eatonville Anthology" also comments on the theme of history, mostly in part XI, which focuses on cultural traditions that no longer exist in Eatonville. Hurston presents a nostalgic look at the past in this sense. The tension between past and present also serves as a context for part V, which features Old Man Anderson. Anderson symbolizes the agrarian past of Florida, invoked in his name "Old Man" and detailed in his ignorance of technology symbolized by the train. When he finally sees a train, he flees, revealing his discomfort with new technologies that change the environment and community. He clings to the past as a sort of protection against the future.

"The Eatonville Anthology" anticipates later works such as *Their Eyes Were Watching God* in emphasizing the oral tradition and the characterization of marriage and power, leading sometimes to violence. Most significantly, Eatonville serves as the setting of *Their Eyes Were Watching God,* and the stories in "The Eatonville Anthology" inform that fictional work.

CHARACTERS

Old Man Anderson Although he does not live in Eatonville, he resides near the small town. He resists technology and symbolizes the rural, agrarian past of the African-American community.

Mr. Clarke Clarke appears in several vignettes here. In part I, he gives food to Mrs. Tony Roberts, but he charges it to her husband, and in part IX, he commits violent acts against his wife. In part VI, he punishes Coon Taylor for stealing. He symbolizes violence, power, authority, and social status. A precursor of Jody Starks in *Their Eyes Were Watching God,* he illustrates the rising black entrepreneur.

Mrs. Clarke We see Mrs. Clarke in part IX as the abused wife of Joe Clarke; she symbolizes marriage and the oppression of women in this tale. She anticipates the character Janie Starks in *Their Eyes Were Watching God.*

Coon, Miss Nancy A personified animal, she is the object of desire of Mr. Dog and Mr. Rabbit.

Crooms, Laura Hurston employs this character in part XII to illustrate betrayal and deception in marriage. Like Lucy Pearson, Hattie Tyson, and Sally Lovelace in *Jonah's Gourd Vine,* Laura Crooms is married to an adulterous husband. In revolt, she attacks his mistress with part of an ax.

Jones, Sykes A gambler, Sykes bears resemblance to other characters in Hurston's fiction, like Muttsy in "Muttsy" and Tea Cake in *Their Eyes Were Watching God.* His depiction illustrates the importance of gambling to the underground economy of Eatonville.

Lindsay, Joe Joe functions to symbolize the importance of tall tales in the community. His highly unbelievable tale about a doctor suggests myths about the power of health practitioners.

McDuffy, Mrs. In part X, Mrs. Clarke suffers at the hands of an abusive husband. She is a religious woman who attends church regularly.

Merchant, Jim Jim wants to wed a woman who suffers from a jittery condition, which is treated with turpentine.

Moore, Becky In part III, Becky is a single mother with many children, suggesting her sexuality and fertility. Being single, she is different from the married women in the community.

Potts, Cal'line She suffers from an adulterous husband, who cheats on her with Delphine, leading her to follow him one day with an ax, which suggests that she may kill him.

Potts, Mitchell The husband of Cal'line Potts in part XIII, he cheats on his wife. Potts bears resemblance to characters such as John Pearson in *Jonah's Gourd Vine* and Laura Crooms's husband in part XII of "The

Eatonville Anthology" in his betrayal of wedding vows.

Roberts, Mrs. Tony She goes to the store and claims that her husband will not feed her, symbolizing the need for family, marriage, and nourishment. She anticipates Mrs. Tony Robbins in *Their Eyes Were Watching God.*

Taylor, Coon He symbolizes nature, with a name suggesting a raccoon. He steals fruit and animals, but is caught by Joe Clarke and punished.

Taylor, Daisy Daisy symbolizes sexuality and female beauty. She is a flirtatious woman and has an affair with a married man. After her husband assaults her with part of an ax, she leaves town. She anticipates Daisy Blunt in *Their Eyes Were Watching God.*

BIBLIOGRAPHY

Hemenway, Robert E. *Zora Neale Hurston: A Literary Biography.* Urbana: University of Illinois Press, 1980.

Hurston, Zora Neale. "The Eatonville Anthology." In her *The Complete Stories,* 59–72. New York: HarperCollins, 1995.

Every Tongue Got to Confess: Negro Folk-Tales from the Gulf States (2001)

The folklore Hurston collected in the 1920s would be published in various works, notably *Mules and Men,* "The Florida Negro," and *Every Tongue Got to Confess: Negro Folk-Tales from the Gulf States,* which was published posthumously. This text continues some, but not many, modifications to Hurston's original manuscript. *Every Tongue Got to Confess* is a worthy example of Hurston's work as an anthropologist dedicated to preserving and promoting the African-American folklore tradition. The text recounts stories that had been told orally and that range from the comic to the serious. These tales engage in significant social, political, and economic commentary, and should be read in connection with Hurston's other work. Some characters and versions of these tales can be found in *Mules and Men,* her landmark folklore collection. This work is divided into several categories, each discussed in the synopsis that follows.

SYNOPSIS

God Tales

These tales focus on God and the relationship between God and humanity. Tales include biblical topics such as the creation of Adam, and Christ and the disciples. The tales also discuss God's roles in relation to humans, particularly as regards relations between men and women, between blacks and whites. Also discussed are God's effect on race and power, the role of God in nature, and God's impact on people.

Preacher Tales

The tales in this section focus on ministers, the people who attend church, and the connection between religion and the community. Specific attention is given to questions of preaching as vocation, and of baptism, confession, and salvation. Also discussed are faith and sin, heaven and hell, and other issues like technology, slavery, and gambling.

Devil Tales

The devil appears as a character in these tales, showing his significance as a figure in the oral folktales. These stories deal with a variety of topics such as communion, ministers, farming, gambling, marriage, wealth, and family.

Witch and Haunt Tales

These tales illustrate the importance of witches and ghosts in oral folklore. They include tales of witches who want to eat people, women who can tell fortunes, a man who sells himself "to de high chief devil," and a "haunted house."

Heaven Tales

These stories highlight the importance of heaven, and they touch on the opposition between heaven and hell, including the actions that bring the right or wrong consequences. In one tale, a black man flies in heaven; in another, President Harding is shown as going to heaven.

John and Massa Tales

The tales feature the relationship between John, a slave, and Massa, his white owner, and the power dynamics between these two popular folk figures.

Massa and White Tales

These tales focus on slavery and race relations, particularly the relationship between master and slave.

Tall Tales

This series of short tales deals with many quotidian topics connecting the physical environment to human experience. Topics include: ugliness, meanness, height, stinginess, race, speed, animal appearance, fruit, vegetable, tree size, soil, wind, rain, drought, night, weather, and animals.

Mosquito and Gnat Tales

The relationship of people to the environment is dealt with through tales about insects.

Neatest Trick Tales

These tales deal with topics like hunting, courtship, and education.

Mistaken Identity Tales

These stories deal with issues of mistaken identity and touch upon questions of slavery, religion, race relations, death, and family dynamics.

Fool Tales

Tales in this section deal with subjects like courtship and marriage.

Women Tales

The stories focus on topics like marriage and infidelity, religion and hoodoo, lending and borrowing, the military, and fire.

School Tales

These tales center on education, and how it relates to family.

Miscellaneous Tales

The tales in this section treat a miscellany of topics, like marriage, illness, death, courtship, family, pests, the automobile, and animals.

Talking Animal Tales

In these stories, animals speak using the same language as humans.

Animal Tales

These colorful tales show the diversity and complexity of animals and the environment.

CRITICAL COMMENTARY

Hurston's *Every Tongue Got to Confess* functions as an important text within Hurston's folktale work, and it is a significant record of African-American cultural expression from the early 20th century. The stories reveal the importance of oral storytelling to African-American and southern American literature.

The numerous tales are told by various storytellers and from different points of view, touching on significant themes within the short space of the oral folk form. The themes include nature, religion, marriage, slavery, freedom, gender roles, and family, among others. Often humorous, the tales also frequently employ personification of the natural world, in which animals can talk and act like humans. While the stories may be entertaining, a social message remains clear. The variety of these tales from multiple origins is evidence of the centrality and diversity of this folk art form.

Religion

Religion functions as a prominent theme in these oral tales, and it is a subject Hurston knew well, as her father was a Baptist preacher and she grew up in a religious community. The tales in *Every Tongue Got to Confess* that deal with religion demonstrate the importance of the religious life to southern African-American communities, and the power that preachers, congregations, and churches had over them. In rendering Judeo-Christian ideas, these tales range from the serious to the comic and intertwine the spiritual with the secular; the very variety and number of the tales that take on the subject of religion attest to the power that religious representation has in Hurston's body of work.

In "Why God Made Adam Last," the story retells the biblical account of the creation of the world, saying God created Adam after the other flora and fauna because he knew Adam would take credit for these things if he had been created first—and boast about his achievement to Eve. In another tale, a minister preaches to his congregation against lying but is then accused of lying about a song, and has to leave; the story suggests the problematic relationship between preacher and congregation. Hurston also explores the connection between religion and race, such as in "Uncle Jeff and the Church." Jeff, a slave, wants to be a member of a white church. Jeff informs the white people of his desire, but the minister says he must have misunderstood what God desired for him, advising Jeff to consult with God another time. Jeff leaves the church and then returns, informing the minister he spoke with God and "He ain't never even joined here hisself." The story critiques the hypocrisy of white Christians who discriminate against black people.

"Why Negroes Have Nothing" attempts to use a religious context to explain black disenfranchisement and economic inopportunity in America. God created the world and then asked the different ethnic groups what they wanted. The black man was resting, so he couldn't make his request, but the other groups make their requests. Eventually the black man tells God he does not want anything, and thus, "Thass how come we ain't got nothin'."

The story serves as a commentary on race and ethnicity in a humorous, fatalistic way.

Stories such as these connect religion with race and illustrate the complex connection between spirituality and race as expressed in the oral tradition. They also provide important examples of social and historical commentary on American society.

Nature

The natural world plays an important role in these folktales. Due to the significance of agriculture in the South, and the large numbers of blacks working in it, the engagement between humans and their environment is of great importance in the folklore tradition. The tales often seek to explain the meaning or relevance of features of the surrounding environment. Animals, insects, and even the environment can take on human characteristics, connecting them in a unique way to the human world.

Tales demonstrate the dynamics among animals in relationship to each other, and these serve as parables for human action. In "Rooster and Fox," Brer Fox asks a rooster to fly away from the tree where he roosts, but the rooster refuses. This fox tries to trick the rooster into leaving, but when he hears the sounds of hounds, the fox realizes he is the one that needs to leave; the rooster survives. In folklore, the fox typically functions as a crafty, manipulative character who tries to conquer other animals with his wit; however, in this story, the fox ultimately is the loser. In "The Lion and the Rabbit," a lion asks a rabbit for water, with the intention of eating it. The rabbit is not tricked, and the rabbit causes the lion to be shot by a man, and ultimately the rabbit wins. The rabbit may be smaller, but he outwits the lion; here, cunning is more important than physical power.

Some tales are less moralistic but seek to explain the natural appearance of animals or other natural phenomena. For example, the rabbit who is impatient to hop to the cabbage patch has its tail snapped by a gator, explaining the rabbit's short tail. In "Why De Donkey's Ears Is Long," the donkey got his long ears because he was stubborn and a man pulled on his ears to control him. Clearly fanciful explanations, the stories have no basis in reality, but what is important is the attempt by the storyteller to explain, classify, and order the world.

Race Relations

Race relations are an important theme in these stories, particularly in the depiction of slavery versus freedom. Folktales were a powerful way for African Americans to deal with the issue of slavery in a literary context; Hurston's own grandparents were slaves, so the issue has particular resonance for her life and work. Specifically, the stories highlight the complex relationships between the slaves and the masters, the blacks and the whites. They demonstrate inequality as the legacy of slavery, and yet the stories also reveal a hope for justice, as symbolized by John in his attempts to win against his master.

Indeed, in many of these tales, John and the Master function as the symbols in the slavery-versus-freedom struggle. In more than one tale, John uses his intelligence and wit as a means of obtaining freedom. For example, in the bet between John and his master in which they fight a panther, he outsmarts his master, showing the triumph of the oppressed over the oppressor. In another tale, John is targeted by fellow slave Bill, who consults with the devil in order to overtake John. John comes out ahead; here we also see the dynamic among slaves, and the connection between religion and spirituality.

CHARACTERS

The characters in these tales are too numerous to discuss in depth here, but two important characters are addressed.

John This popular figure from African-American folklore exposes the theme of freedom versus slavery. John attempts to use his skills and abilities as a means of operating within the oppressive system, and he represents the hope and desire for liberation from enslavement. John appears in other books by Hurston, including *Mules and Men* and *Go Gator and Muddy the Water.*

The Master The slave master in the antebellum South, the master serves as the counterpoint to John, and he is the symbol of white male power, authority, and privilege. This character also appears in texts by Hurston such as *Mules and Men* and *Go Gator and Muddy the Water.*

BIBLIOGRAPHY

Boyd, Valerie. *Wrapped in Rainbows: The Life of Zora Neale Hurston.* New York: Scribner, 2003.

Howard, Lillie P. *Zora Neale Hurston.* Boston: Twayne, 1980.

Hurston, Zora Neale. *Every Tongue Got to Confess: Negro Folk-tales from the Gulf States.* New York: HarperCollins, 2001.

"The Fire and the Cloud" (1934)

This short story about Moses was published in a 1934 issue of *Challenge,* a magazine edited by Hurston's friend DOROTHY WEST that sought to recapture the earlier spirit of the HARLEM RENAISSANCE. The short story "The Fire and the Cloud" is a "synopsis of the trials and triumphs of Moses' leadership, which is at its end" (McDowell 230). Moses is a key figure in Hurston's writings, notably in *Mules and Men* and *Moses, Man of the Mountain.* Deborah G. Plant writes, "Hurston was fascinated with Moses as another representation of the ideal individual and self-made man" (127). In fact, Moses is a common figure in African-American literature as a freedom fighter or liberator; in oral stories and in song, Moses is treated as a hero, inspiring freedom from oppression.

SYNOPSIS

Moses sits at a grave overlooking Canaan, as a lizard speaks to him. Moses has been at Mt. Nebo for 30 days, and says he is "alone," and is expecting Joshua to look for him. He tells the lizard he has been a leader for many years, having gone back to the land of Egypt and conquered the pharaoh to free his people. He is upset that the people he freed revolted and were now saying bad things about him. The lizard, after awakening from sleep, comments on Moses, and asks him what the grave is. Moses explains what it is, places "his rod" on the grave structure, and strolls onward. Moses says that Joshua can get the rod.

CRITICAL COMMENTARY

Based on the story of Moses, who led the Jews out of slavery and freed them from Egyptian bondage, this story is an example of Hurston's religious retellings. In retelling the story of Moses from the Bible, she is also offering a social commentary about complex relationships between a leader and a leader's people. This short piece can be read in tandem with *Moses, Man of the Mountain.*

As a liberator, Moses assists his people in gaining freedom from slavery and oppression. Although he assumes this important role, he feels that he has been betrayed by his people, who revolted against his authority. Hurston presents him as a weary leader, tired of his followers' actions. Moses' claim that Joshua will take his rod suggests his desire to pass on leadership to another person. By portraying this major biblical figure as tired and disappointed, Hurston imbues him with qualities that make him seem like an ordinary person. Moses also holds a unique relationship with nature, for he can communicate with the animal world, as seen in his conversation with the lizard.

CHARACTERS

Moses An important figure in the Old Testament of the Bible, Moses leads the enslaved Israelites to freedom. Within the African-American oral and written tradition, he takes on particular significance. Black slaves often appropriated characters from the Bible who possessed qualities they could identity with as slaves, many of them identifying with the enslaved Israelites in the Old Testament. Moses, then, becomes a hero to many African Americans, and many longed for a Moses figure to lead them to freedom. In "The Fire and The Cloud," Moses is presented as questioning his authority and identity; by imbuing him with normal human traits, she makes him accessible to her readers.

BIBLIOGRAPHY

Boyd, Valerie. *Wrapped in Rainbows: The Life of Zora Neale Hurston.* New York: Scribner, 2003.

Hurston, Zora Neale. "The Fire and the Cloud." In her *The Complete Stories,* 117–121. New York: HarperCollins, 1995.

McDowell, Deborah E. "Lines of Descent/Dissenting Lines." In *Zora Neale Hurston: Critical Perspectives Past and Present,* edited by Henry Louis Gates and K. A. Appiah, 230–240. New York: Amistad, 1993.

Plant, Deborah G. *Every Tub Must Sit on Its Own Bottom: The Philosophy and Politics of Zora Neale Hurston.* Urbana: University of Illinois Press, 1995.

"The Gilded Six-Bits" (1933)

"The Gilded Six-Bits" was published originally in *Story* in 1933; in response to this story, Bertram Lippincott contacted Hurston and would later publish her first novel, *Jonah's Gourd Vine.* The idea of love and sexuality as an economic exchange serves as a thematic focal point of "The Gilded Six-Bits." The "gilded six-bits" refers to the duplicity of Otis D. Slemmons, who deceives Missie May into thinking he has great wealth when that is far from his reality. In the end, Missie May and her husband reunite and reconcile.

SYNOPSIS

The setting is an African-American community reliant upon a fertilizing company for money. The story begins on Saturday in a very well maintained home occupied by a black couple, Missie May and Joe. The couple have a playful ritual in which he throws money in their entranceway on Saturdays, and she picks it up. Each time she hears the money, she becomes happy and asks who would be throwing money, even though she knows it's her husband. On this particular day, Missie May prepares for her husband's arrival. He arrives home, and they engage in playful banter. She prepares a wonderful feast for them, during which he announces they will dress up and go out to an ice cream parlor opened by Otis D. Slemmons, a handsome, well-dressed man in town. Later, when Missie May meets him, she notices that he wears a lot of gold; Otis tells her he is a rich man with expensive jewelry.

One evening Joe comes home and catches his wife in the bedroom with Otis, and "could see the man's legs fighting with his breeches in his frantic desire to get them on." Otis tries to pay Joe not to murder him, but Joe assaults him and Otis runs out of the house. Joe obtains the man's "golden watch charm" and "broken chain" as a result of the fight. Missie May explains to him that Otis has wooed her with promises of money and riches, causing a rupture in the marriage; the Saturday rituals end. Missie May later realizes that the "gold" jewelry that Otis sports is fake, just gilded with a layer of gold. She sees that the stickpin is "a gilded quarter" and the watch charm "a four-bit piece."

While doing chores one day, Missie May talks with Joe about the baby she will have, and she says it will look like him. Missie has the baby several months later, and it looks like Joe. Joe travels to Orlando to go shopping. He places the "gilded half dollar on the counter" and the clerk is shocked. Joe tells the clerk the story about Otis's deception, and how he got the four bits during the fight. Joe buys candy, and the store clerk thinks that blacks have no cares in the world. He goes home, throwing money in the entranceway, restarting their earlier ritual.

CRITICAL COMMENTARY

This story contains a portrait of a marriage in a love triangle. Marriage functions as the central theme in the story, played out by the characters Missie May and Joe Banks. In this case, it is the wife, Missie May, who commits adultery. With his flashy outward appearance, his ice cream parlor, and his experience living elsewhere, Otis seems very appealing to Missie May. In fact, from the very beginning, Hurston presents Missie May as a woman who connects love and romance with money, as exemplified by their weekly ritual. There is a suggestion that, for some people, love may be a commodity that can be bought and sold for a price. But Hurston's treatment of the characters is remarkable, for "their range is more than sentimental or comic emotion" (Jones 152).

After having the affair with Otis, Missie May feels ashamed, and she tries to reconcile with her husband, even bears him a child; since the child looks like him, there is no question about who the father is. When she discovers that Otis's gold jewelry was really fake, she begins to realize the artificiality of his image and how the man duped her; she feels that she sold herself, in a way. Despite the problems she has caused, she still loves Joe and they do make up in the end.

Joe Banks plays the role of a devoted husband, trying to provide a good home and even engaging in a ritual that seems harmless but ultimately suggests a commodification of their love. Also, his last name, Banks, is a clear reference to money. Ironically, it is he who suggests they go to Otis's shop, and even comments on Otis's good looks. He too is in awe of this man, who seems so successful and who has brought a black-owned business to the town. Joe realizes the artificiality of Otis's affluence when he pulls off his gilded watch charm. He realizes that Otis is only pretending to be rich, and this makes Joe feels a greater sense of his own identity. In Orlando, when Joe uses the gilded money to buy candy for his wife and brags to the clerk about how he got it, this is a means both of ridiculing Otis D. Slemmons and of getting rid of the reminder of the adultery in his relationship. However, upon returning home, he starts up his old ritual, in effect reinforcing the connection between love and money.

Otis D. Slemmons symbolizes trickery and betrayal, and the positive image associated with class. He arrives in their community as an outsider, and people admire him because he seems wealthy and worldly. He opens an ice cream parlor, which Hurston uses as a sly metaphor for Otis himself. Like ice cream, Otis functions socially as a temporary pleasure. Otis's duplicity about his watch charm is revealed after a fight with Joe, in which Joe pulls off his charm and chain, which proved to be not gold but just a thin veneer of gilding. When Joe uses Otis's gilded coin to buy candy for his wife and brags about beating him up, Otis D. Slemmons's shame is made public.

"The Gilded Six-Bits" illustrates Hurston's interest in focusing her fiction on domestic issues, often good-heartedly. At the same time, she imbues the story with social commentary about marriage, money, and identity. The theme of troubled marriage can be seen in "Sweat," "The Eatonville Anthology," and *Jonah's Gourd Vine* as well.

CHARACTERS

Banks, Joe Joe's last name, Banks, calls to mind the theme of money, which is central to the story. In his marriage to Missie May, he throws money in their entrance when he comes home; he expects devotion from his wife and seeks to impress her by taking her to an ice cream parlor run by Otis D. Slemmons. When he catches his wife with her lover, he beats the man up and discovers that he is a fake. The discovery of this betrayal by his wife threatens him, and he stops his ritual of throwing money in their entrance. Although the two reconcile, he remembers the betrayal as symbolized by the gilded charm, which he tries to get rid of by buying candy.

Banks, Missie May Missie May begins as a naïve individual easily swayed by money and the appearance of wealth. In the beginning of the story, Hurston portrays her as the loving and dutiful wife of Joe Banks. She takes care of him and their home, and on Saturdays she anxiously awaits the money he will throw at the door, which symbolizes a type of payment for their marriage. Swayed by Otis's charms, she has an affair with him, but she is caught. When she discovers that Otis is a fake, she realizes the folly of her ways. She feels guilty and is especially affected when Joe stops throwing money at the door. She patches things up by having a baby with Joe, and she represents above all the potential for reconciliation.

Slemmons, Otis D. When he arrives in the community and opens an ice cream parlor, Otis is revered among the townspeople. People are impressed by his ability to operate a business and by his appearance, characterized by gold jewelry and fine-looking clothes. He sleeps with a married woman, Missie May, and is beaten up by Joe Banks, who thus exposes the fraud. His belief that displays of material wealth will impress others is a character trait that Hurston uses in other of her works. Hurston employs a sly metaphor by having Otis open an ice cream parlor: He too is a fleeting pleasure. Additionally, it is not just his jewelry that is gilded, but his personality as well.

BIBLIOGRAPHY

Howard, Lillie P. *Zora Neale Hurston.* Boston: Twayne Publishers, 1980.

Hurston, Zora Neale. "The Gilded Six-Bits." In her *The Complete Stories,* 86–98. New York: HarperCollins, 1995.

Jones, Gayl. "Breaking Out of the Conventions of Dialect." In *Zora Neale Hurston: Critical Perspectives Past and Present.,* edited by Henry Louis Gates, Jr., and K. A. Appiah, 141–153. New York: Amistad, 1993.

Go Gator and Muddy the Water: Writings by Zora Neale Hurston from the Federal Writers' Project (1999)

Zora Neale Hurston's work for the Federal Writer's Project helped to provide a deeper and richer understanding of African-American culture and the African diaspora. After Hurston finished *Tell My Horse,* the author joined the Federal Writer's Project, a program started in 1935 as a means of employing writers during the Great Depression. It was "the New Deal's answer to literary unemployment" (Hemenway 251), and it put authors such as Saul Bellow, John Cheever, and Conrad Aiken to work. African-American authors found this appealing because "hiring was often free of discrimination," and the program thus employed writers such as Sterling Brown, Willard Motley, Ralph Ellison, and Richard Wright (Hemenway 251). In 1938, Hurston began in the Federal Writers Project in an editorial position for "the Florida volume of the American Guide series" during 1938 (Howard 38). Hurston's work was also instrumental to the publishing of *The Florida Negro.* Hurston spent time with African Americans in the Florida Everglades documenting cultural traditions, and she also spent time in Washington to acquire funding. *The Florida Negro,* however, did not get published during her lifetime. In July 1939, the Federal Writers Project began to change and Hurston found other employment. Later, she would use the anthropological work she did at that time as a source in *Seraph on the Suwanee.*

Go Gator and Muddy the Water: Writings by Zora Neale Hurston from the Federal Writers' Project, which was published in 1999, contains writing Hurston did as part of her work for the Federal Writers Project. According to the book's foreword, "Hurston was given the lowliest" status in the Federal Writers Project in Florida and, particularly problematic, "state editors passed over much of her work and published less worthy pieces" (Bordelon ix). *Go Gator and Muddy the Water,* collects the work she did for that organization and also attests to "how great a talent the Florida FWP ignored" (Bordelon ix).

Go Gator and Muddy the Water is an important addition to Hurston's traditional corpus of works, as it prints Hurston's Federal Writers Project text, annotated with commentary. *Go Gator and Muddy the Water* sheds light on an important time in Hurston's career. While Hurston is better known for her novels and short fiction, the texts in this work will introduce readers to her nonfiction anthropological work. The work reveals the significance of African-American folklore and folkways to Florida, and to American culture. Hurston serves as both observer and participant in

Zora Neale Hurston (second from left) and Langston Hughes (third from left) with friends, 1927 *(Yale Collection of American Literature, Beinecke Rare Book and Manuscript Library)*

some of these texts, and we as readers have firsthand access to some of the rituals, traditions, beliefs, and customs of African Americans during that time period. This, in turn, provides the reader with a fuller context for better understanding the cultural milieu in which Hurston lived, researched, and wrote.

SYNOPSIS

Go Gator and Muddy the Water is a posthumous compendium edited by Hurston scholar Pamela Bordelon, and this *Critical Companion* volume will comment exclusively on the Hurston texts within it, rather than the edited work as a whole.

Proposed Recording Expedition into the Floridas

Area I

This text begins with lines from a song about a man who wants to murder a black man. The essay also describes western Florida and its territory. Some of the people there know the individuals who had historically sought "to control this area" (63). This part of

Florida contains examples of Creole cultural expression as well as folklore and songs from African Americans. The area is agricultural, containing tobacco, corn, and cotton; along the coastal area, there are people working in the fishing industries who have cultural knowledge as well. Hurston suggests making "recordings" related to "the economic and sociological setup" in western Florida (63).

Area II

This section begins with lyrics from a song about an illiterate sea captain. The essay describes northeastern Florida, which has rich multicultural diversity including people of Spanish, French, and English descent. Pap Drummond speaks about pirates and claims to have been involved "in the last recovery of pirate treasure" (64). Hurston's essay suggests interviewing people in the turpentine industry; it also notes the body of cultural expression available among the river workers, as well as prayer and sermon material.

Area III

This section begins with song lyrics about a woman and her body. The essay describes the peninsular portion of Florida, whose resources include turpentine, citrus, celery, phosphate, and lumber. Tourism is another important industry. Polk County is in this area, and contains rich material for stories and music. There is music about "road and camp," (65) and the region would be useful for recording about Big John de Conquer, a major figure in African-American folktales.

Area IV

This section begins with lyrics about a baby. The essay details southern Florida, which contains Cuban music as well as folk culture; Miami represents South American as well as Caribbean heritage. Hurston mentions a "sanctified church," and notes that Tampa contains "the largest Latin colony in the United States" (66). There are also African Americans and their cultural traditions, along with white Americans. The Everglades is an important cultural source; near Palm Beach and Key West are many Cuban and Bahamian "elements" (66).

Summary

Hurston says that Florida remains unequalled in the abundance of material for anthropological recording. Florida is the "inner melting pot of the great melting pot America," Hurston writes (67). The section closes with a hymn about God.

"Go Gator and Muddy the Water"

"Folklore," Hurston writes, "is the art of the people before they find out there is any such thing as art, and they make it out of whatever they find at hand" (70). This essay discusses the history and significance of folklore, noting that all countries possess folklore, and it is part of our shared humanity. It is manifested in the spoken word as well as in song, especially in ballads and the blues. African-American blues music is an extension of this lyrical tradition. Hurston discusses the words and music—their structure, rhythm, and rhyme—of a number of blues pieces, such as "East Coast Blues," "Halimuhfask," "Angeline," "Uncle Bud." Examples of ballads include "Delia" and "John Henry." Hurston notes that folklore continues to be developed in Florida, and it is particularly rich due to Florida's many cultures. She makes reference to Daddy Mention, a heroic figure in folklore that is "new" in the tradition and "another incarnation of Big John de Conquer" (69).

Folktales

In "Go Gator and Muddy the Water," Hurston documents black folktale examples from Florida, the two major ones being "Big John de Conquer" and "Daddy Mention." These folktales range in subject matter, but most include some meditation on the connection between the physical and spiritual worlds.

Big John de Conquer

Big John de Conquer was a mythical figure, symbolizing the desire of the powerless to possess power. John is a slave, and he can hear what his master says. John informs the other slaves that he has the ability to "tell fortunes" (79), and indeed he correctly predicts the future based on what he has overheard. John watches an animal swallow his master's ring; he goes to his master and tells him his "prediction," and the master then believes his ability to tell the future. John must yet prove himself in a bet concerning a wash pot, which he wins when he predicts there is a raccoon underneath it. John is liberated from slavery and is given some money, while the master heads to Philadelphia. John is to oversee the plantation, and throws a party, during which his master enters, disguised as poor white folk. He then reveals his identity and threatens to hang John. With the help of a friend, John devises a plan: He prays before being hanged, and asks God for a sign, which his friend provides by lighting a match. His master becomes spooked, and flees. Later, he frees the slaves. John is part of a "hero cycle yet unfinished" (83).

Daddy Mention

The following accounts center around the captive Daddy Mention, who symbolizes the desire of an individual to triumph against adversity. He, like John de Conquer, represents the underdog in society.

The first section serves as an introduction to Daddy Mention and addresses his mysterious origin. The narrator points out that Daddy Mention has been in many jails and prisons.

Daddy Mention's Escape Daddy is in jail for being a vagrant. He does not work quickly enough to suit Captain Smith, and he complains about mistreatment. The captain places him in a box for a period of time, after which he sends him to join the group chopping trees. Daddy has the ability to pick up trees and carry them without assistance. One day he uses this ability to escape, as he carries a log and passes through the gate. The narrator says he talked with Daddy Mention, who continued to carry this log but eventually sold it. With that money he was able "to ***ride*** to Tampa" (86).

Daddy Mention and the Mule In this story, Daddy Mention sells liquor to canal workers. While getting liquor from Ocala, he tells some tales to an officer, who imprisons him, and later Daddy is sentenced to prison by a judge. He decides to flee the prison in Raiford. When he does, a guard whistles, and a mule comes out. This mule and some dogs pursue Daddy Mention, and he hides in a tree. The mule tears at his clothing, and Daddy flees. The mule follows and bites him as he climbs the prison fence. The captain approaches and Daddy Mention ends up in the box.

Other Negro Folklore Influences

Cuban cultural expression occurs in the western portion of Florida; in the eastern section of Florida, there is cultural expression from the Bahamas. Additionally, the influence of the African diaspora can be seen in the folktales from Cuba and the Bahamas, as well as Haiti and the British West Indies, as the stories often share similar elements. Another enriching factor in Florida is Native American influence, and the interaction of Native and black culture.

Hurston's essay argues that the cultural expression among people from the Bahamas contains more African influences than that of the African Americans. This is because black slaves were suppressed by their masters, while Caribbean masters were less controlling. The primary forms of the Bahamian dance music are the "ring dance" and the "jumping dance" (90). The jumping dance is brief and repeats itself, while the ring dance is more elaborate. The essay documents lyrics and choreographic instructions for certain songs and dances, including "Lime, OH, Lime" and "Bone Fish."

Hurston also documents a story about the origin of skin color: God decided to give people color, and some people did not show up on time. When they finally arrive, God assigns them the color black.

The Sanctified Church

In this essay, Hurston writes about the importance of the sanctified church and its influence upon religion and music in African-American culture. She claims that the sanctified church merges black cultural and spiritual expression; people following this religious movement see themselves as distinct from the whites who worship God. The essay contains a story called "The White Man's Prayer," in which Brother John prays for rain and emphasizes in his prayer to God that he is white.

New Children's Games

This essay describes children's games, some of which had African origins and others of which were borrowed from the whites, many of these latter having origins in England. Such games include rhymes about the British government, London Bridge, and royalty. When blacks recited rhymes that they had learned from whites, they often changed words or added rhythm, dance, and clapping. The essay discusses rhymes and games such as "Little Sally Walker," "Sissy in the Barn" "Chick-Mah-Chick-Mah-Craney-Crow," and "Rabbit Dance."

Negro Mythical Places

Diddy-Wah-Diddy Diddy-Wah-Diddy is a mythical place where people don't have to work, food abounds, and the people and animals have no concerns.

Zar Zar is "farthest known point of the imagination" (108) and thus there is not much information regarding the folks from Zar.

Beluthahatchee Beluthahatchee is a place for forgiving.

Heaven The main streets are Amen Street and Hallelujah Avenue. Some people say that blacks are absent from Heaven. This was because a black person who was unwilling to "wait until Old Gabriel showed him how to fly" flies to Heaven and causes some destruction (109). As a result, Gabriel took away his wings, and ever since some people claim that blacks are not in Heaven due to caution.

West Hell This location is the hottest part of hell, and it is where the worst people end up. Big John de Conquer fights with the devil here. John conquers the devil, and is thus able to wed the devil's daughter. John also cools down portions of hell before departing, as he and his wife intend on returning for a visit with his wife's family.

Other Florida Guidebook Folktales

Jack and the Beanstalk

Some siblings plant corn, and one of the brothers sells this corn "to the angels," leaving a message for his brother (113).

How the Florida Land Turtle [Gopher Tortoise] Got Its Name

God is "sitting on Tampa Bay" creating things to put in the ocean (113). The devil claims to have the same ability, and he creates a turtle, but it will not stay in the water. God places "life" within this turtle; however, this animal will still not stay in water. The devil claims it could "go fer" since it is turtle-like, thus naming the animal (113).

Uncle Monday

Uncle Monday was an "African medicine man" (115) who fled a plantation in South Carolina or Georgia and settled in Florida. He practiced medicine and joined in the wars against the whites. He swims with alligators and considers himself part of a "crocodile clan" (115). A woman named Judy Bronson is jealous of Uncle Monday and she claims to be a better conjurer than him. One day she falls in the lake. A voice tells her to be quiet, and she sees Uncle Monday along with the alligators in the lake; then they disappear. From then on she believes in his powers.

Roy Makes a Car

Roy Tyle is a mechanical expert and invents a car that rides low, underneath vehicles. He eventually sells it, and makes a lot of money. Roy builds another vehicle with wings, and God buys it from Roy.

Two Towns

"Eatonville When You Look at It"

Hurston describes EATONVILLE, FLORIDA, in this essay. One corner is of particular interest; it is where Joe Clarke built his store long ago, and people gather there to talk. She also discusses the church, the orange grove, and the gas station, in addition to Macedonia Baptist church, a school, and someone's yard. A large alligator lives in Lake Belle in Eatonville.

"Goldsborough"

Goldsborough was a black town, incorporated in 1891, which ended in 1911. Hurston provides the history of the town and describes its people. People felt Goldsborough inhibited expansion of the adjacent town, so a senator had the legislature revoke its charter and incorporated it within the larger Stanford.

"Turpentine"

In this essay, Hurston describes her experience learning about the turpentine industry. Writing in the first person, she describes what she learned from a foreman. She stays at his home overnight, wakes up early the next day, then observes the workers as they engage in various chores, including pulling, chipping, and dipping, which involves extracting the gum from the tree. She also documents information about workers' salaries and housing and technical information about the wood and land.

The Citrus Industry

In this essay about the citrus industry, Hurston interviews a man who explains the orange industry. The harvesting season extends from September to June, when workers clip oranges and place them in a bag; the bags go in boxes, and are loaded onto a truck. During thc day, grove workers sing blues music, and talk about women and alcohol. Hurston also describes the packing of the fruit, how frosts and pest animals are dealt with, and the sale and distribution of the crop.

"Art and Such"

In this essay, Hurston examines the African-American tradition of cultural expression from the time of slavery through Reconstruction to the present. She acknowledges the importance of the oral tradition in pre–Reconstruction America, with its music and folktales. Considering the economic and social hurdles in post–Civil War America, Hurston notes that black creativity was stagnant, but that this period was nonetheless important to the history of African-American art. She points out that during the period, some African Americans emerged as leaders in their community through the use of oratory. She analyzes the role and authority of certain African-American leaders, whom she labels "Race Champions" (140), and points out that they were seen as spokespersons for all black people in America. She laments that "sufferings" is such a common theme in black artistic creativity and cultural expression throughout the United States. She then discusses the role of contemporary African-American writers and artists, such as the painter O. Richard Reid, the sculptor Augusta Savage, and the composer J. Rosamond Johnson. She also discusses writers such as James Weldon Johnson and herself, stressing that she gained the attention she did because of her "objective point of view" in writing (144). She ends this essay by hoping for a "weakening of race consciousness, impatience with Race Champions, and a growing taste for literature as such" (145).

Lift Every Voice and Sing, Augusta Savage's sculpture for the 1939 New York World's Fair. Photograph by Carl Van Vechten. Permission granted by Van Vechten Trust *(Yale Collection of American Literature, Beinecke Rare Book and Manuscript Library)*

"The Ocoee Riot"

This essay describes the Ocoee Riot, which took place on November 2, 1920. As people in Ocoee were voting without incident, a group of white people from nearby Winter Garden arrived with the intention of suppressing the black vote. Mose Norman, a black man, tried to vote in Ocoee, but was prevented from doing so. He left town to consult a lawyer, but as soon as he returned, others "set upon" him. A group of white troublemakers planned to head over to the home of July Perry, another black man, to "chastise" Mose Norman, who they'd heard was staying with Perry. Perry prepared for an attack, and Norman fled. In the confrontation with the mob, Perry fought back with a gun, and accidentally shot one of his children. The fighting ceased; some of the attackers were hurt or killed, and Perry himself was wounded. At this point, Perry, aided by his wife, made it to the "cane patch" area. The mob returned, however, and they found Perry. They put him in jail and would later murder him.

Zora Neale Hurston beating the hountar, or mama drum *(Library of Congress)*

"Fire Dance"

This essay alludes to forms of cultural expression common among Bahamas natives living in southern Florida. One example is a Bahamian dance tradition called the jumping dance, which functions as one section within the dance cycle called the Fire Dance (153). This dance cycle has origins in West Africa, and it includes other sections such as the Jumping Dance, the Ring Play, and the Crow Dance (153). The jumping dance features a heated drum played by a musician; others participate by singing, clapping hands, and dancing. The dance moves change according to the drumbeats. The Ring Play, which incorporates African as well as European cultural elements, is a dance form in which two people dance together. In the Crow Dance, as the drumming changes, a person disguised as a crow makes an appearance, then departs. For all three, Hurston's essay makes references to the types of spoken expressions heard during this dance. Hurston writes, "the movements of the dance say something about the procreation of life."

The Jacksonville Recordings

This section contains "the transcription of Hurston's interview and song material from the WPA's Jacksonville recording session in June 1939" (Bordelon 157). In this section, there are interviews about the origins and cultural significance of the songs (with lyrics included). Most of the interviews with Hurston are conducted by Herbert Halpert, a folklorist, while the interview about "The Fire Dance" is conducted by Dr. Carita Doggett Corse. Hurston answers questions posed by Halpert about songs and a chant/holler, including "Goin' to See My Long-haired Babe," "Ah, Mobile," "Shove It Over," "Mule on the Mount," "Let the Deal Go Down Boys," "Uncle Bud," "The Beaufort Boat," "Ever Been Down," "Halimuhfask," "Tampa," "Poor Boy or Poor Gal," and the chant/holler "Shack Rouser." She answers questions about "The Fire Dance" from Dr. Carita Doggett Corse regarding the background and purpose of the song.

CRITICAL COMMENTARY

The compilation *Go Gator and Muddy the Water* enriches Hurston's collective body of work as it publishes in an accessible form her writings for the Federal Writers Project. These pieces reflect Hurston's interest in folklore, history, and cultural traditions in Florida, especially relating to the African diaspora. In these pieces, Hurston is functioning not as novelist or artist but as anthropologist and chronicler of 20th-century life, and the varied material reveals the diversity of Hurston's body of work. Still, some of this material bears resemblance to her works of fiction, particularly in the themes relating to race, class, gender, nature, history, and religion. An examination of the pieces within *Go Gator and Muddy the Water* indicates the complexities of Hurston's representation of African-American experience. And by chronicling the work, song, and tales, Hurston shows her interest in understanding about not just individual communities' cultural production, but about the lives and work of the people.

Hurston's writings for the Federal Writers Project go especially far in revealing the complex nature of race relations in early 20th-century Florida. She presents Florida as a mixture of different ethnic and racial groups, of various origins, all with different cultural traditions. In the essay "Proposed Recording Expedition in the Floridas," Hurston chronicles the racial and ethnic characteristics of different areas to ascertain the value of collecting material there. She notes that the state of Florida combines many different ancestries, depending on geography: Creole, African, European, Caribbean, and South American. There is a notable presence of Caribbean and Cuban cultural dance, music, and folklore traditions, which draw on African origins to different degrees than the culture of American slaves. With this diversity of racial and ethnic groups, Florida can be seen as a microcosm.

As in her fiction, Hurston's Federal Writers Project work addresses the realities of class differences in American society. In "Proposed Recording Expedition into the Floridas," Hurston proposes sources of collecting information among the diverse working-class populations in Florida, stressing that their employment and cultural traditions vary throughout the state of Florida. The differences in lifestyle can be related to employment, which might be for the seafood industry working on the coast, for the railroad, for the turpentine industry, or other industrial or agricultural concerns. For example, Hurston explores the lives of workers in Florida within her essays "Turpentine" and "The Citrus Industry." Through these chronicles, the reader gains an inside view of the work these men and women do as Hurston provides a glimpse into the lives of working-class laborers. She shows the lives of the working classes as central rather than peripheral to the economy of Florida. Hurston wishes to examine not only the cultural production of the "folk" in Florida, but also how their work and home life may inform that.

In "Other Negro Folklore Influences," Hurston examines the ethnic makeup of Florida, with many Cubans in the west and Bahamians in the east. Hurston makes the interesting point that African influence is greater in Bahamian cultural expression than in African-American cultural expression among blacks in the United States. The point is that black cultural expression manifests itself differently based on many different factors, including geography, history, and origin; as far as culture is concerned, the African diaspora cannot be dealt with as a unified event. In this piece, Hurston also explores the role that slavery and, more generally, the results of the African diaspora have upon class structure and economics. She argues that the Bahamian cultural expression contains a higher degree of African influence than that of African Americans. This, according to Hurston, stems from the history of slavery. The slave class in America was more influenced by the master class, while in the Caribbean this was less true. The commonalities in folktales, however, such as Brer Rabbit among the various Caribbean peoples, reminds us of the common origins of the different traditions. In "New Children's Games," Hurston points to racial politics, as many of the rhymes and games have a British influence but are appropriated by the blacks, who incorporate their own elements.

Across the many different geographic and work communities, important cultural aspects remain common, especially folklore and blues music. These forms of cultural expression common in the working-class black populations express emotion and shared experience. In Polk County, for example, the popularity of the figure of Big John de Conquer can be seen as a symbol for the underclass fighting against the powerful bosses. According to Hurston's discussion, the stories about John continue to evolve, each community and generation imbuing this character with traits and stories that reflect their own experiences. The story of Daddy Mention also can be seen as a representation of the underclasses against power and authority. In "The Jacksonville Recordings," we get a glimpse at how workers often combined folktale elements with song, rhythm, chants, and shouting. Like the folktales, this music comments upon the lives and work of those who engage in it. The folktales and the songs in themselves can function as an examination and exploration of the dynamics of class within American culture.

Among these works, Hurston explores primarily two major folktales that had special resonance with African Americans. One folktale focus is John de Conquer, a humorous character who makes appearances in *Mules and Men* and *Every Tongue Got to Confess*. John, a black slave, uses his wit and intelligence to battle against and prevail over his slave owner. In claiming supernatural abilities, he eventually tricks his master and wins the freedom of himself and his fellow slaves. The figure of John thus symbolized for blacks the desire to be strong and overcome adversity. While symbolizing the plight of African-Americans slaves, in his action he also symbolizes the promise of liberation. Another focus is Daddy Mention, a legendary folklore figure, who challenged authority as a slave and represents the desire to be free. The Daddy Mention tales deal largely with questions of captivity and liberation. In these stories, which frequently vary in the details of Daddy Mention's whereabouts, the common factor is that he escapes prison and flees his captors. Both John de Conquer and Daddy Mention tales are funny, but they also provide an indictment against the powerful oppressors.

Many of the folktales deal with the connection between the physical and spiritual worlds, between blacks and whites, between heaven and hell. For Hurston, geographical space and race remain interconnected in her discussion of Goldsborough, an African-American town that was reincorporated into a larger town soon after its birth. The essay reflects on the demise of a black community and calls attention to a sad history imposed on a people. Hurston broadens her discussion to racial politics in the "The Ocoee Riot," in which she demonstrates her sensitivity to and awareness of civil rights issues. The account of this attempt to thwart blacks' democratic right to vote, and the resulting violence, testifies to the injustices blacks suffered in the post-Reconstruction South.

Hurston bridges race with religion in "The Sanctified Church," an insightful examination of religious traditions among blacks. She notes that there are still many black people who practice non-Christian forms of religion, worshiping other gods and incorporating African traditions such as shouting. Interestingly, Hurston explains, some blacks in the sanctified church view themselves as different from whites who engage in religious worship. In the story about a white man who wants God to control the behavior of blacks, we see further evidence of whites' desire to diminish the power of blacks. Her discussion of this type of church seems to suggest that "the sanctified church" movement appeals to working-class blacks connected to their African ancestry. The essay suggests that, in religion as in culture, blacks do not rely on whites.

As in Hurston's novels, *Go Gator and Muddy the Water* engages the theme of nature and environment, but this is revealed in a very different way than in her fiction. Her writings from the Federal Writers Project seek to present the reader with images of Florida, its landscape, and its wildlife. Whether she is writing about Brother John praying for rain in "The Sanctified Church" or about children mimicking animals in their games, or the role that the environment and the weather plays in the turpentine and citrus industries, Hurston brings a subtle focus to this aspect of her subjects' lives. In "Proposed Recording Expedition into the Floridas," Hurston describes the topography of the state to show how the state's natural diversity may have an effect on its people and their livelihoods. For example, those involved in citrus farming have different experiences than those involved in turpentine production, or fishing, or lumbering, and these differences may be revealed in the lives they lead and the culture they produce. Hurston's contribution showcases the interplay between nature, the environment, and culture.

The folktales themselves also reinforce the importance of the natural world to the African-American communities, many of them weaving details of the natural and animal worlds into the human narratives to enrich the stories or to teach a lesson. The complex interplay between humans and nature can be seen in tales such as "Jack and the Beanstalk," "How the Florida Land Turtle Got Its Name," or "Uncle Monday." In this last story, we see the connection especially clearly, as Uncle Monday can be both human and alligator, suggesting a tie to nature much closer than is often expressed.

In her discussion of the African-American literary tradition, Hurston argues that the period known as Reconstruction, after the end of the Civil War, was a weak period for black creativity, even as it was an important time for creation of a black identity. She notes, optimistically, that there seems to be an evolving interest in literature. The essay represents an important one as she self-consciously assesses the state of black creativity in American history, a tradition in which she herself plays a part.

Overall, Hurston's Federal Writers' Project writings prove to be an important documentary collection. In them, Hurston managed to be both descriptive and analytical in her assessment of race, culture, and identity. Her discussion of tales, songs, culture, and history relates to her in-depth analysis of how Africans constructed cultural traditions and contributed to the culture of the United States. Her emphasis on African retentions and transformations in black cultural expression testify to the dynamic nature of African-American culture. In addition, Hurston's Federal Writers' Project pieces, as presented in *Go Gator and Muddy the Water*, illustrate the range and scope of her ability as a writer. These texts provide the reader with insight into Hurston's appreciation of black cultural expression, her celebration of folkways and heritage, but most significantly, her detailed and thorough anthropological work. While Hurston may be best known for her novels and short stories, her nonfiction essays in this collection are important for the insights they bring to her work as a whole.

BIBLIOGRAPHY

Bordelon, Pamela. "Zora Neale Hurston: A Biographical Essay." In *Go Gator and Muddy the Water: Writings by Zora Neale Hurston from the Federal Writers' Project,* edited by Pamela Bordelon, 1–49. New York: Norton, 1999.

Hemenway, Robert E. *Zora Neale Hurston: A Literary Biography.* Urbana: University of Illinois Press, 1980.

Howard Lillie P. *Zora Neale Hurston.* Boston: Twayne, 1980.

Hurston, Zora Neale. *Go Gator and Muddy the Water: Writings by Zora Neale Hurston from the Federal Writers' Project.* Edited by Pamela Bordelon. New York: Norton, 1999

"How It Feels to Be Colored Me" (1928)

"How It Feels to Be Colored Me" presents Zora Neale Hurston's commentary on the early part of her life. It briefly covers a broad swath of her life, functioning more as a reflection on her blackness rather than a strict narrative account of her life. The piece can be viewed as a "meditation" about race (Wall 24). The essay was originally published in 1928 in a publication called *The World Tomorrow.*

SYNOPSIS

In this first-person narrative, Hurston describes herself as "colored," pointing out her recognition of her racial identity, and then proceeds to provide information about her life. Hurston lived in EATONVILLE, FLORIDA, a black community, until she reached age 13. While she says that Eatonville was all black, whites passed through "going to or coming from Orlando." As a child, she liked to situate herself on a "gate-post" and would converse with people traveling by; sometimes, whites would give her money for performing. Hurston later relocated to Jacksonville, which was not all black and thus she "was now a little colored girl."

She claims her slave ancestry and asserts that she does not pity herself for being black. She claims that discrimination does not cause anger in her. While there are times when she does not "feel colored," Hurston felt her blackness especially strongly when "against a sharp white background," such as when she was a student at BARNARD COLLEGE. At a cabaret once, she also felt her ethnic difference. While listening to the music, she became stirred, wanting to "dance wildly inside" as she listened, which is not how the whites around her reacted. In one passage, she writes, "He is so pale with his whiteness then and I am *so* colored." At times, she even feels raceless, as when she is in HARLEM, NEW YORK. She describes herself as a "brown bag of miscellany propped against a wall."

CRITICAL COMMENTARY

The essay should be read within the social and historical context in which Hurston wrote it, the HARLEM RENAISSANCE. The essay emphasizes the ideologies of black identity and empowerment prevalent during the Harlem Renaissance; in this essay blackness or being "colored" becomes a cause of celebration rather than shame or defeat. Hurston attempts to provide the reader with an understanding of her feelings as a black person in America. The essay affirms her sense of selfhood through specific examples drawn from her life. The primary themes in this essay remain race, ethnicity, and identity.

Hurston emphasizes the effects that growing up in an all-black community had on her, and she positions herself as a product of this all-black environment. In her social context, it may have been beneficial for her to stress this background. It is worth recalling that, while Hurston lived there for much of her childhood, she was not born there as she claims. The whites who gave her money and had her perform as a child would be the inspiration for the short story "Drenched in Light"; the anecdote reveals the reality of black performers being supported by white patronage, a principal characteristic of the period in which Hurston worked.

Hurston's essay suggests the fluidity of race and ethnic identity; she can even point to the time in her life when she first realized she had an ethnic identity. She became "colored" after moving to Jacksonville, but she emphasizes her refusal to engage in self-pity. "I am not tragically colored," she writes in an important passage, asserting her knowledge that blackness is not an affliction. And while acknowledging that her ancestors were slaves, she emphasizes that this was history, not to be dwelled upon. However, the color of her skin would play an important role in her identity, and she stresses that her sense of being "colored" arose particularly saliently in places such as Barnard College, peopled almost exclusively with wealthy white women.

It was a feeling she also had among the reserved white people at the cabaret, when she wanted to express herself the way she had among her fellow blacks. Interestingly, Hurston writes about her experience with jazz music using primitivistic language, claiming a primal connection to this music that the white people did not possess. This viewpoint leads to a problematic analysis, as it presents African-American cultural expression in essentialist and patronizing terms. Cheryl Wall stresses that this "description of the jazz performance relies on jungle metaphors, as does the description of the writer's" reaction (27–28). Hurston's representation of this cabaret is nonetheless a common depiction for writing from the time period. Why does Hurston herself employ this type of approach in discussing the music? The author may "parody the myth of exotic primitivism" while revealing this musical expression's force as "genuine" (Wall 29). Hurston's commentary here may stem from her own ideas or she may be playing to a potential readership who view African-American culture in these terms.

Hurston also explains how she feels raceless on occasion, such as in Harlem, and that she does not react angrily to discrimination. She wonders at people who would not want to be around her. Hurston's discussion of race and identity suggests that these concepts may be socially constructed and fluid; in other words, her sense of her race and ethnicity are affected by her environment. She did not consider herself as "colored" in Eatonville, yet she transforms into being "colored" in Jacksonville. Her sense of being "colored" is active in a place such as Barnard, a mostly white college, or even in the cabaret. She becomes raceless while in Harlem, an area with a large black population. Hurston's essay challenges the reader to consider race and ethnicity as fluid, evolving, and dynamic rather than static and unchanging.

BIBLIOGRAPHY

Hemenway, Robert E. *Zora Neale Hurston: A Literary Biography.* Urbana: University of Illinois Press, 1980.

Hurston, Zora Neale. "How It Feels to Be Colored Me." In her *Folklore, Memoirs, and Other Writings,* 826–829. New York: Library of America, 1995.

Wall, Cheryl A. *Women of the Harlem Renaissance.* Bloomington: Indiana University Press, 1995.

"John Redding Goes to Sea" (1921)

"John Redding Goes to Sea" focuses on an African-American man in the South, and it deals with nature, travel, marriage, and conjuring. This story is notable for Hurston's early, sensitive use of DIALECT to effect a sense of realism and local color. The use of non-standard English reflects the author's heritage (Boyd 86). This story appeared in *The Stylus*, the literary journal of HOWARD UNIVERSITY. Hurston's piece appeared while she was a student there. This story helped facilitate Hurston's career. Charles Johnson, the editor of *OPPORTUNITY*, read the issue of *The Stylus* in which her story appeared. He praised Hurston and sought "more material" (Wall 146).

SYNOPSIS

As a youth, John Redding enjoys communing with nature and fantasizing about traveling.

Charles S. Johnson *(Library of Congress)*

His mother believes someone conjured against her child, using a sort of "travel dust" to make him want to journey. John's father understands his goals in life, however, despite his wife's very different feelings about John's wanderlust. Time passes, and John goes to school. He marries Stella Kanty, to whom he reveals his desire for traveling. He later announces that he has an opportunity to join the navy; his mother becomes upset at the news.

When a white man requests assistance with the work he is doing to a bridge before an impending storm, John agrees to help. A fierce storm passes. Some men die, and John is missing. John's father heads to the bridge to look for his son, and Stella and his mother come as well. A man explains what happened to John's father, and he sees his son's body floating on wood in the water. Everyone is shocked; John's father does not want anyone to retrieve his body.

CRITICAL COMMENTARY

"John Redding Goes to Sea" demonstrates an early ability of the artist to make use of the short fiction form to present a compelling story with complex characters. The story expresses the tension between the individual and society. John functions as an outsider, whose goals in life conflict with the expectations of his family, including his wife and his mother. The emphasis on issues such as nature and travel provide the reader with a memorable story about one person's aims toward selfhood and happiness. The fulfillment of personal goals is a theme that provides a wide appeal and transcends racial, class, and gender differences.

As in Hurston's other fiction, nature operates as a central theme in this story. In his youth, John connects with the environment. The natural world stimulates his imagination. He lives near the St. John's River, in which he enjoys placing pieces of wood. As he watches the wood pieces float on the water, he imagines having the freedom to float and move around like them, and he imagines himself on a boat wandering down the river. Water functions as an important element in the story, providing adventure and life and, during the storm, death. His dead body floats upon a piece of wood; ironically, he finally gets his chance to travel. His own father understands this, and wants to let his son's body achieve in death what he had dreamed in life. In death, he travels, and reconnects with nature.

Travel, separately, is another major theme here. Throughout his life, John desires travel and adventure. As a boy he imagines travel as a means to escape his small community. His mother is against this, even thinking he had been conjured against. His own wife reacts in a similar way as his mother. The fact that his surrounding family is at odds with this goal further alienates John from the very community he seeks to escape. While when he was alive John could not fulfill his goal of traveling, he gets to travel in death. He perishes in the storm, and his body floats along the water on wood.

Marriage is another central theme in this story. The two marriages profiled are that of John's parents, Alfred and Matty, and that of John and Stella. In both cases, John's desires create a form of tension between husband and wife. The men see a world of experience existing outside their community, while the women see domestic life as the reality that matters. While John does marry Stella, his desire to explore does not wane, as is evident when he decides to join the navy.

While a simple story by a young writer, "John Redding Goes to Sea," is an interesting study of human nature and relationships. The main characters reveal different desires and aspirations, linked together by one central character. His outside status puts him at odds with his family and community, but his desire to live the life of an individual is admirable. The story can be viewed as an apprentice work by Hurston; within the context of her career, it demonstrates her talent and potential as a writer.

CHARACTERS

Redding, Alfred John's father, he is sympathetic to his son's ambitions to travel, a wish he shared as a youth. His request that his son's body not be retrieved from the river reveals his sensitivity to his son's needs and desires.

Redding, John The central character, John is an outsider figure. He enjoys communing with nature and imagines venturing far away, not content to spend his life in the same community. His character creates tension in his relationships with others. His decides to join the navy. He ultimately dies while helping repair a bridge in a major storm. At his father's request, his body is left to float freely down the river.

Redding, Matty Matty, John's mother, does not agree with her son's ambitions. She believes, in fact, that her son has been conjured against. These beliefs may be seen as part of her maternal, protective nature.

Redding, Stella John's wife, she expresses her dissatisfaction at John's plans to travel. At the story's end, she is a widow.

BIBLIOGRAPHY

Boyd, Valerie. *Wrapped in Rainbows: The Life of Zora Neale Hurston.* New York: Scribner, 2003.

Hurston, Zora Neale. "John Redding Goes to Sea." In her *Zora Neale Hurston: The Complete Stories,* 1–16. New York: HarperCollins, 1995.

Wall, Cheryl A. *Women of the Harlem Renaissance.* Bloomington: Indiana University Press, 1995.

Jonah's Gourd Vine (1934)

Jonah's Gourd Vine is Hurston's first novel and reflects Hurston's interest in the oral tradition, dialect, spirituality, and folk customs. Set in Alabama and Florida, the novel focuses on the protagonist, John Pearson, a minister, and his first wife, Lucy Pearson. The novel may be autobiographical, as many similarities exist between John and Lucy Pearson and Hurston's own parents. *Jonah's Gourd Vine* functions as a 20th-century morality tale about the consequences of one man's actions. Hurston started composing the novel in 1933 after publisher Bertram Lippincott expressed interest after reading her "The Gilded Six-Bits."

SYNOPSIS

Chapter I

The novel opens with a discussion between Amy and Ned Crittenden, a couple with several children living in rural NOTASULGA, ALABAMA, during the early 1900s. The couple argues about raising their children, particularly about John, a child of Amy's who was fathered by another man. Ned comments on John's racial heritage of black and white ancestry, as evidenced by his light complexion, and Ned implies that John has more opportunities than darker-skinned African Americans. Both Amy and Ned were born when slavery was legal, and slavery remains in their thoughts. Amy suggests that their children represent the next generation, and that their lives will be different from their parents because they were born free. Amy and Ned also discuss their economic situation. The family has spent a year raising cotton but will not see the profits from it; Ned left the cotton in the barn of a prominent white man who will make the profit from it. Ned leaves the house to feed the mules and returns with a whip. Upon seeing that Amy has not set out a dinner plate for him, he whips her. She fights back, and he chokes her. John hits Ned in defense of his mother, and Ned demands that he leave the house. John departs and heads over "the Big Creek" in search of more social and economic opportunity.

Chapter II

John arrives in the area "over the Creek." He spots a school, and he becomes excited about the idea of African-American children having the opportunity to learn to read. Where he comes from, the children must work on the farms, and they do not have the opportunity to get an education. He recognizes the social and economic inequalities depending on where families live and work. John asks where Alf Pearson's place is. He meets Lucy Potts, whom he will marry later on in the novel, for the first time. He also sees a train for the first time, a startling discovery. At the cotton gin, he finds Alf Pearson and introduces himself. He tells Pearson that he is "Sixteen, goin' on sebenteen" and that his mother is named Amy Crittenden, one of Pearson's slaves when slavery was legal. In fact, he says, he was born on Pearson's plantation. Pearson agrees to hire John, and John moves into Pheemy's cabin.

Pearson enlists him in chores around the farm, but he also encourages him to go to school to learn writing and reading. John enjoys attending school, and he wants to impress Lucy Potts, one of the star pupils at the school; he has developed a romantic interest in her. He also attends church, where Lucy sings in the church choir. Pearson encourages John to head back home to tell his mother that he is doing well and to recruit other people who can work on the farm. When he returns home, his mother is happy, and impressed that her son is getting an education. She tells Ned that her other children need to go to school as well. John tells his mother that Alf Pearson wants some more people to pick cotton, and this is an idea Ned likes. Ned wants some of his family to make money picking cotton for Pearson, which they will do.

After they pick cotton, they have a big party. They eat and dance to African-inspired music. John continues to study and becomes increasingly interested in Lucy. As they walk home from school, he impresses Lucy by killing a snake; this becomes a pivotal point in their relationship. The chapter ends with a description of a special ceremony to mark the end of the school term. Lucy Potts delivers a speech, and then Lucy and John sing a song together. John begins to establish a reputation as an important member of the community despite being an outsider initially.

Chapter III

Amy tells John that Ned is in trouble. Ned believes that Beasley is exploiting them by cheating them out of their cotton crop; in revenge, he kills an animal owned by Beasley for them to eat. Beasley finds out about this, and as a result Amy and Ned depart to Shelby's land, where they will work. Amy pleads for John to move back in with them, and to join them working on Shelby's land. John tells Pearson that he does not want to go to Shelby's, and Pearson assures John that even if he does end up leaving, he can always come back in the future.

Chapter IV

Ned and John work on the land owned by Shelby, performing agricultural work. Ned expresses anger and resentment toward John, feeling that John's experience at Pearson's place has changed him—and made him more assertive. John's relationship with Lucy continues to evolve as he reads a love letter from her. John becomes preoccupied with the emotions in the letter; when Ned calls his name and asks for some help, John does not hear because he is so consumed by the love letter. Ned threatens John for disrespect, but John stands up to him; he later leaves Shelby's and returns to Pheemy's to escape the turmoil of family life with Ned.

Chapter V

John returns to Alf Pearson's place, and Pearson offers John his old clothes to wear. Now that John can read and write, Pearson gives John the job of documenting the feed, fertilizer, and groceries, as Pearson has other responsibilities to do. He cautions John not to get involved with Exie, the wife of Duke. John says he has not been pursuing the woman, but that she pursued him. Later, a woman, Mehaley, professes her love to John, claiming she thought John loved her in the past. Meanwhile, John is still in love with Lucy Ann Potts, and he inscribes her name on the chimney in Pheemy's house. At church on Sunday, he continues his courtship with Lucy, and they exchange a hymn book with love notes in it. In all this, John is distracted by Lucy.

The workers have a big barbecue to celebrate that they have finished picking the cotton. During it, John and Exie spend time alone together, and when Duke finds out he threatens to stab John later, but he leaves him alone for now. John stays on and dances, but later that evening he reveals to his brother Zeke that he plans to leave the area, confessing at the same time his love for Lucy. John plans to leave town and make some money, working at a turpentine camp. He plans to write letters to Zeke that he will pass on to Lucy. He departs and travels to the town of Opelika, and then to the area of "the tie-woods on the Alabama River."

Chapter VI

John arrives at the turpentine camp, where he begins to work hard and enjoys cutting trees. He goes to town on Saturday with another worker and he meets some women, and they return the next day. John waits a couple of weeks before he sends a letter to his brother Zeke, and he begins to despair that he will not hear anything from his beloved Lucy. John becomes a strong presence at camp, with his athletic abilities and engaging storytelling of tall tales. One day Zeke comes to the camp, and he brings a letter from Lucy; Zeke stays with John at the camp. John later fights with Coon, another worker, when Coon eats the bread John made for Zeke. He wins the fight and serves his brother some more bread.

Chapter VII

Zeke and John return to Alabama. Lucy's mother gets upset when she learns that John has given Lucy a Christmas gift. She does not consider him to be suitable for Lucy, as she wants Lucy to marry Artie Mimms.

Chapter VIII

John returns to Alf Pearson, who advises John not to spend time with Duke's wife. On Sunday, John goes to church and sees Emmeline Potts, Lucy's mother. He asks if he can walk Lucy back home after church. Emmeline tells John that Lucy is too young, and that she will decide which men Lucy can spend time with. But Richard, Lucy's father, gives him permission to walk Lucy home. The affection develops between the two young lovers, and Richard invites John to dine with the family. John realizes that Lucy's family is more affluent than the other black people in the area. Lucy begins to notice physical changes in her body as she develops into a woman, and she sends John a letter saying they can have a special relationship.

Chapter IX

Emmeline demands that John keep a distance from Lucy as they leave church, as John and Lucy discuss the sermon. Later, at Lucy's home, John discusses their relationship with Lucy. Lucy acknowledges they have been dating almost one year. They go outside and sit side by side on the porch, where John confesses his love for Lucy. Emmeline comes out and sees them, and demands that Lucy move away from John, which Lucy refuses to do. Richard comes out and tells Emmeline to stop acting that way, and Emmeline returns to the parlor, where she peers at them through a curtain. She does not approve of their relationship, and she prays about it. The following day John and Lucy meet by a tree, and they kiss. John then proposes to her, and she agrees to marry him on her birthday. The evening of the wedding, her mother declares she wanted her daughter to marry Artie Mimms, a landowner, and she decides not to attend the wedding. Lucy marries John that night at the church with the support of her father. After the wedding, John tells Lucy he will be her new family.

Chapter X

Newly wed, John and Lucy relocate to the servant living space behind Alf Pearson's home. Pearson gives them generous gifts, including a bed. Lucy has their first child. Mehaley, still interested in John, continues to try to start a relationship with him. John tells Mehaley to wed Pomp Lamar, which she ends up doing; Pomp and Mehaley leave the area to explore new opportunities elsewhere. John continues to gain importance in the community, becoming foreman on Pearson's farm. One day John heads off to look at some animals for Pearson, during which time he visits with Big 'Oman, whom Pearson warns him about. On his ride home on horseback, a bridge collapses as he crosses, and John awakes to see he has been rescued after the accident.

The following day, Lucy admits that she knows about his relationship with Big 'Oman. John tells Lucy he loves her and promises not to cheat anymore; they already have three children and she is pregnant with a fourth child. At a church service, he recites a prayer, which impresses the church deacons. Despite his promise to Lucy, John gets involved with Delphine. As a result, he spends less time at church and at home. When her brother Bud comes to pick up some money he had loaned, Lucy says John is not there. Her brother tells Lucy that there are rumors involving John and Delphine. As Lucy doesn't have the money to give back, Bud decides to take their bed instead. That evening Lucy bears another child, a daughter; near morning, John arrives at the house and he sees the baby. When Lucy awakens, John is out chopping wood, and upon his return he learns that her brother took the bed in repayment for the loan. John goes to Bud's home and beats him up. Later he kills an animal so that his family will have food. Lucy fears that her brother will tell the whites that John assaulted him and that John will be put in jail.

Chapter XI

Duke tells Lucy that John has been arrested for assaulting Bud and stealing someone's animal. Lucy goes to see the justice of the peace on behalf of her husband, and then later to Alf Pearson, who is also a judge. Alf Pearson obtains John's release, and pays the owner of the hog that John killed. John is sent to another court for attacking Bud. Pearson gives John some money and advises him to leave town because of his legal troubles. John leaves his wife and family to embark on a new life.

Chapter XII

As he embarks on a new stage in his life, John heads to Florida on a train, and he meets another African-American man heading in the same direction. They ride in a train, which John enjoys, as it symbolizes power to him: "The greatest accumulation of power that he had ever seen."

Chapter XIII

John arrives in Sanford, Florida, with his fellow traveler. A white man offers them jobs working on the railroad. The following day, John begins working on the railroad, and with the money he earns he writes to Lucy and mails her money. One Sunday evening John delivers a sermon. Later John learns about EATONVILLE, FLORIDA, from a fellow worker, visits the all-black town, and plans to return. John eventually moves to Eatonville and gains employment in the town of Maitland as a tree-pruner. He continues to send money to Pearson to give to Lucy. Eventually the family reunites in Eatonville. When Lucy arrives, she says she is glad to see him, and she declares she likes the town because everyone is black. She encourages John to build houses as a carpenter, which he does. At her insistence, they buy their home from Joe Clarke.

John and Lucy discuss their marriage, and he tells her he will kill her if she ever leaves. John becomes a preacher and then, as his influence grows, pastor of his church. He begins at Ocoee and later moves on to Zion Hope, in Sanford. Later, John becomes "moderator" of a church organization in Florida. He also becomes mayor. John has another affair; meanwhile, their daughter Isis gets sick with typhoid, and John arrives late to see her after being at a religious revival. John says it is difficult for him to be around a sick child, and he leaves for Tampa, where he spends time with Hattie Tyson. John returns home eventually, and his daughter recovers. He gives Lucy clothing and fruit as token of affection upon his arrival home.

Chapter XIV

The Sanford residents tell Lucy rumors about John's relationships with women, but Lucy already knows about Hattie Tyson. The folks say he cannot have a relationship with Hattie and preach at the same time, but John denies being with Hattie. Despite a night conference at church and growing concern among the congregation about John's actions, no one brings up the matter. After the conference, a church member tells John there's a rumor he's involved with a woman in Oviedo. Lucy advises him to preach a sermon about his strengths to the congregation, and she wants him to be truthful. That Sunday he preaches, asking the people to think about whether he's done any good, and he says he will stop preaching unless people support him.

Chapter XV

A conjure woman, An' Dangie Dewoe, performs special rituals to cause changes in people's lives and habits. Hattie visits her and An' Dangie Dewoe conjures against John to break up his relationship with Lucy and make him love Hattie.

Chapter XVI

Lucy suffers an illness, and while ill, she argues with John about his relationship with Hattie. John hits Lucy in anger about her complaints. That night John goes into the bedroom and looks at his wife. He asks her if she needs something, and she tells him that she will die soon. The next morning he asks one of their daughters to check on Lucy, who reports that her condition has not improved. The following day Mattie Clarke watches over Lucy and asks her about her relationship with God. The next evening, their son John comes to visit. Lucy eventually dies. Her body is prepared for burial; there is a strong wind in the night, and her husband feels fear.

Chapter XVII

This chapter describes Lucy's funeral preparations. Lucy's body is placed in a coffin, which is transported by wagon away from the home. In the evening, the family grieves. A day later, the man who transported Lucy's dead body points out to John that it was he who brought Lucy to town by wagon years before.

Chapter XVIII

Several deacons confront John about a rumor that he has wed Hattie Tyson, and John admits that the rumor is true. After they depart John's parsonage, Hattie speaks to John about the situation, having overheard the conversation. In "her stiff back hair," she has John de Conquer root, a special type of root that provides people with power and control over others. The plant root's name derives from the legend of John the Conqueror, a black slave who outwitted his master and whose essence is said to be contained in the root. When John leaves the community for a religious event, Hattie goes to see An' Dangie Dewoe.

Chapter XIX

As time passes, stories about John circulate in the community. Some people are pleased that John no longer holds a leadership position in the church association. John starts to spend time with Zeke, who admires him. In the meantime, John's congregation at Zion Hope becomes smaller, due to his decreased popularity. John asks Hattie about their marriage, and he admits that he had not intended to marry her and that he no longer desires her. She cannot match his first wife, he says. The couple continue to quarrel, and he beats Hattie when she upsets him. He does not provide her money for goods such as shoes. One of the church members, Harris, calls John "dat Jonah's gourd vine," suggesting that he would bring down John if possible. Harris suggests that Hattie go see a conjurer for help with her problems, and he recommends a conjurer near Palatka. In the meantime, the nation faces war, which changes the social climate. After the war ends, people begin to migrate from the South to the North, as the southerners see the North as a land of promise and prosperity. Hambo expresses his concerns to John Pearson about a black exodus to the North. John Pearson notes the dilemma of blacks, and he says ministers can stay or go North with their congregations.

Chapter XX

Harris stops by the parsonage while Hattie washes; he tells her he has found a reverend from west Florida to replace John. Hattie and John's marriage problems continue, as John becomes interested in yet another woman, but it proves to be fleeting, and Hattie is relieved.

Chapter XXI

One Sunday, John is informed that another preacher, Reverend Felton Cozy, will give a sermon that evening. That evening John delivers a sermon, which the congregation enjoys. Afterward, Cozy delivers another sermon, about black pride, which is less appreciated; Harris's attempt to find a replacement preacher backfires.

Chapter XXII

Hattie and others try to topple John Pearson from his role in the community. Hambo tells John that his wife uses conjure against him, and John finds evidence after searching through the house. Hambo tells him that a conjurer can reverse the effects, and that he must beat up his wife. When Hattie returns home, John confronts her about the hoodoo; he assaults her, and Hattie leaves. She files for divorce. Hambo tells John that she can ruin his career if she shows evidence of infidelity against him.

Chapter XXIII

John and Hattie's marriage is annulled in court after testimonies and John's admission of guilt. While in court, John recalls being in trouble for criminal behavior in Alabama years before.

Chapter XXIV

The church holds a conference to decide John's fate as minister. Hattie says she wants to charge her husband, but Hambo points out that Hattie doesn't have a husband any more at that church. The meeting ends without any decision, but John now realizes that he lacks friends and status in the community. He delivers a sermon focusing on Jesus, and afterward he leaves the church. Reverend Cozy gets his old job at the church. Rumors circulate about John. He decides to leave town and heads to Plant City, where he meets a woman named Sally Lovelace, who has heard him preach in the past. A widow, Sally invites him to her home for a meal. She pays John to do work on her house and tells him that some people want him to deliver a sermon. He preaches, and Sally is delighted at his performance. She suggests they wed, and John agrees. Sally informs him that the congregation would want to make him their permanent pastor at the Pilgrim Rest Baptist Church.

Chapter XXV

The two have been newlyweds for a year, and Sally buys John a Cadillac as an anniversary gift. John drives over to Hambo's house one day in his new car, to the admiration of some women. He discovers that after he left Sanford, people were not happy. A man tells John he should preach at Zion Hope Church on Sunday because he preaches so well. John dines at Hambo's home, and Hambo tells him about one of the girls who admired his car, Ora Patton. Ora is waiting for John when he arrives at his car, and they drive away. She kisses John, and they return to a garage. He and Ora begin a relationship as they take another ride on a Friday evening.

Chapter XXVI

The final chapter begins in the town of Oviedo after a tryst between Ora and John. He leaves Ora in a room and heads out to his car. She tries to catch up with John, but he pushes Ora away. As he drives home, a train hits him and he is killed. Sally mourns his death and promises to give the railroad settlement money to John's children. Many people show up for his funeral. Zion Hope in Sanford holds a memorial for him, and the minister conducting the service delivers a piece of poetry about dying. The preacher claims that only God knew John.

CRITICAL COMMENTARY

Jonah's Gourd Vine, published in 1934, was the first of Hurston's novels and serves as a model for her later ones, *Their Eyes Were*

Watching God (1937), *Moses, Man of the Mountain* (1939), and *Seraph on the Suwanee* (1948). This first novel sets the major themes that would be addressed in her later works, such as race, class, gender, family, love, marriage, identity, conjuring, religion, nature, and migration. Hurston's narrative documents the social, emotional, physical, and psychological development of a protagonist, John, and those surrounding him. In *Jonah's Gourd Vine,* John Pearson fails to achieve a level of maturation and awareness; Hurston presents him as a flawed figure whose untimely death occurs at a moment that prohibits him from reaching self-actualization. Hurston's novel can be seen as a tragic morality tale.

Set alternately in small towns of Alabama and Florida, *Jonah's Gourd Vine* focuses on the lives of African Americans in rural, agrarian settings. The novel takes place in the post-slavery America of the late 19th and early 20th centuries. Historically, in this time period in the South, many African Americans worked as agricultural laborers on large farms owned by wealthy whites in a system called sharecropping. In exchange for a plot of land, African Americans would cultivate the land and harvest crops. A share of the profits would go to the sharecroppers and to the large landowners. Blacks often found themselves heavily in debt to the landowners because they were also expected to pay rent for housing and for farming supplies. Sharecropping proved to be a difficult livelihood, and many moved from farm to farm in search of a better situation. This forms an important part of the social context for *Jonah's Gourd Vine,* and Hurston's examination of the legacy of slavery situates it in relationship to race and class. Through the Crittenden family and Alf Pearson, Hurston probes into the complex dynamics of race and class relationships by chronicling the lives of former slaves and slave owners.

Both Ned and Amy Crittenden struggle to make a living by picking cotton, and they fail to achieve financial stability. Their tenuous economic situation causes stresses on their family relationships. John Pearson, the protagonist, increases the tension because his stepfather, Ned Crittenden, resents him. He considers John a threat to his masculinity, power, and authority in the household. As a working-class black man, Ned cannot derive a strong sense of identity outside the context of his home; he uses his home life to exert his control and create a sense of authority. His stepson, John Pearson, ultimately stands in stark contrast to Ned, because he rises above his humble roots and achieves a degree of fame, fortune, and success unequaled by anyone in his immediate family. As Alan Brown points out, he "is a metaphor of all black men living in rural Florida in the early decades of the twentieth century" (79).

John Pearson, the son of Amy Crittenden and stepson of Ned Crittenden, comes from humble roots. His family, one generation removed from slavery, is mired in poverty, which John ultimately breaks as he ascends in status. John's heritage marks him as different from others in the Crittenden family because he "is a mulatto, the product of a union between the owner of a plantation, Massa Alf Pearson, and a slave, Amy" (Brown 79). Hurston's depiction of John's heritage is based in the reality of interracial relations between blacks and whites on plantations; white male slave owners sometimes fathered children with black female slaves, resulting in offspring of dual heritage. Sometimes, the children of these unions would gain opportunities for education, social advancement, and freedom due to their father's race and status. In *Jonah's Gourd Vine,* Ned Crittenden believes that blacks with light complexions have social and economic advantages over blacks with darker skin. When John Pearson leaves the Crittenden home to escape problems with his stepfather, he does gain educational and job opportunities due to the biological connection with Alf Pearson, who hires him.

Hurston presents the area "over de Big Creek" to symbolize the distinction between people from different social classes. When John Pearson leaves his home and enters this new area, he meets people from a variety of classes and experiences new things. He is struck by the sight of a schoolhouse that black children go to, since he did not have an opportunity for education earlier; he also witnesses a train for the first time. This becomes an important formative moment for him, as it depicts his transition between the agrarian world and the more industrial world. His wonder at the train also foreshadows his later migrations via train: first, after he leaves Alabama and heads to Florida, and later when a train in Florida hits him. Hurston describes his first encounter with the train in vivid imagery. She writes,

> John stared at the panting monster for a terrified moment, then prepared to bolt. But as he wheeled about he saw everybody's eyes upon him and there was laughter on every face. He stopped and faced about. Tried to look unconcerned, but that great eye beneath the cloud-breathing smoke-stack glared and threatened. (16)

Because John has never seen a train before, he has no real frame of reference for it. From his perspective the train resembles "a monster," with the power to transport but also to destroy. The terror he feels initially is eventually borne out when a train kills him. The scene illustrates John's naiveté and ignorance about the world as he attempts to negotiate his new life away from the Crittenden home. Most significantly, his interpretation of the train represents the larger life passage that he is in the course of undergoing.

Alf Pearson, who symbolizes upper-class white society, becomes an important influence on his son John. Through Alf, John obtains housing and a job on the farm. By providing John with income and a home, Alf finally performs the parental role that he has previously neglected. When John goes to live with Pheemy, he also encounters another family member: his grandmother. His grandmother recognizes the family resemblance, and she explains that she is his grandparent, and she is a direct tie to the world of slavery—similar to the former slave owner Pearson, but in the opposite role of slave. This relationship with Pheemy allows John to reestablish familial ties. John learns more about his own heritage, but Alf Pearson also encourages John to gain a formal education, which he would not have had if he had stayed in the Crittenden home.

Learning to read and write permanently changes his life. John gains in self-confidence and becomes an even more useful employee to Alf Pearson, who eventually promotes him to an administrative position overseeing accounts. This propels him into a higher class and it gives him an even greater status among the blacks in the community, particularly women. Despite his popularity with a number of women, he courts Lucy Ann Potts; this becomes his first serious relationship. The relationship between John and Lucy also reveals the reality of class differences among blacks. Despite his wealthy, landowning father, as a disenfranchised black John's heritage reflects a poorer, working-class experience. For this reason, Lucy's mother, Emmeline, objects to their relationship. She establishes her discomfort with John early on in the text and ultimately refuses to attend the wedding of her own daughter. Emmeline instead presses her daughter to marry Àrtie Mimms, who has a middle-class background. As she argues with her daughter about marriage, she says, "You better want one dat kin feed yuh! Artie got dat farm and dem mules is paid fuh. He showed me and yo' paw de papers las' week." Emmeline Potts's objection mirrors Nanny's attitude on marriage in *Their Eyes Were Watching God* (Jones 77). Lucy Potts must choose between her own desires and her mother's aspirations; ultimately, she constructs a new notion of family and identity by marrying John Pearson. Lucy's decision to marry John despite her mother's objections reveals her willingness to assert her own identity and put her love for John above her mother's wishes.

The relationship between John and Lucy reveals particular insight into the character of John Pearson. Despite their early, affectionate courtship—which takes place in church, at Lucy's home, and on walks together—John is ultimately unable to commit to her, a pattern that will recur over and over in Hurston's novel. His early interest in Lucy, another outstanding student at the school, is marked by an affection and tenderness that he would not be able to sustain throughout the relationship. During their young courtship, John and Lucy even perform a song together, an important event in the town and a pivotal time in their emerging relationship. Hurston writes,

> Nobody cared whether the treble was treble or the bass was bass. It was the gestures that counted and everybody agreed that John was perfect as the philandering soldier of the piece and that Lucy was just right as the over-eager maid. They had to sing it over twice. John began to have a place of his own in the minds of folks, more than he realized. (36)

The characterization of John "as the philandering soldier" foreshadows his infidelity later in the novel, with characters such as Big 'Oman, Delphine, and Hattie Tyson. In turn, the description of Lucy "as the over-eager maid" suggests a blindness to his true nature at the early stages of their relationship.

Hurston also utilizes the character of Lucy to meditate on the themes of motherhood and marriage. Lucy is portrayed as the long-suffering wife of John Pearson: Throughout the marriage, her husband cheats on her and abandons her in times of need. With Big 'Oman, the first affair, she even tells John to leave her and let her raise the children alone if he does not care for her. She says, "Yeah John, and some uh yo' moves Ah seen mahself, and if you loves her de bes', John, you gimme our chillun and you go on where yo' love lie." He declares that he will be faithful, but he fails to follow through, the first of many such deceptions. Later, he has an affair with Delphine, and is not even present when Lucy gives birth to one of their children. Once in the role of husband, he continually fails to fulfill the roles of father and provider.

Lucy symbolizes the betrayed and neglected wife, as the tensions mount in their relationship. Hurston's depiction of the troubled marriage in this novel prefigure similar relationships in her other novels, such as between Janie Crawford and Jody Starks in *Their Eyes Were Watching God* (1937) and Amy and Jim Meserve in *Seraph on the Suwanee* (1948). All of these texts portray undervalued and oppressed married women struggling to find their voices in both society and marriage. Even with a sick daughter, John remains absent and abandons his wife to spend time with Hattie Tyson. Hurston writes,

> So John fled to Tampa away from God, and Lucy stayed by the bedside alone. He was gutted with grief, but when Hattie Tyson found out his whereabouts and joined him, he suffered it, and for some of his hours he forgot about the dying Isis, but when he returned a week later and found his daughter feebly recovering, he was glad. He brought Lucy a new dress and a pineapple. (101)

John's behavior reflects departure, both from family and from responsibility; to assuage his guilt, he sends his wife money. Lucy is aware of his relationships, as are others, and yet she still serves as a supportive wife, notably when she tries to give him advice about remaining pastor of their church just as the congregation starts to turn against him.

Lucy's death is a turning point in the novel. Throughout, she has functioned as a barometer of morality and becomes John's conscience. He alternately respects and fears his wife. Hurston writes,

> After that look in the late watches of the night John was afraid to be alone with Lucy. His fear of her kept him from his bed at night. He was afraid lest she should die while he was asleep and he should awake to find her spirit standing over him. He was equally afraid of her reproaches should she live, and he was troubled. More troubled than he had ever been in all his life. (112)

Nevertheless, when Lucy dies, John is relieved of an emotional burden; he believes he will no longer have to confront his flaws or his guilt. Lucy's death also signals the loss of John's earlier identity: She has served as a constant reminder of his youth, and when she dies, he loses that. But Lucy's memory continues to haunt him, when he realizes in his new marriage to Hattie Tyson that she lacks the refinement and grace of Lucy. John later divorces Hattie.

Unlike Lucy, Hattie Tyson, his second wife, proves to be a manipulative, jealous, and spiteful woman. Hurston characterizes her as one cause for John Pearson to lose his status in the community. Some church members do not approve of the relationship between John and Hattie. John, himself, begins to regret his decision to marry her, and misses the stability he had with Lucy. Hattie Tyson files for divorce in court as a means of revealing his infidelities to her, which leads to his public humiliation. During the court scene, he has no one to testify in his defense, which illustrates how alienated he has become; he is reduced to admitting to the accusations. Others feel similarly. Deacon

Harris wants to "cut down dat Jonah's gourd vine" as a means of destroying him socially. John's problems with Hattie symbolize the adverse consequences of his actions, and he becomes the "gourd vine" that gets cut down by people close to him.

Hurston portrays John as an estimable but flawed man. John fails ultimately to transcend his base desires and selfishness, and his promiscuity continues to create problems throughout his life. John's death draws together people that he has known from his early and later life. Sally Lovelace, his third wife, becomes the grieving widow, and she offers to give railroad settlement money to John's children, providing for them in a way John failed to. Ultimately, John's power proved short-lived. His inability to honor his commitments to his wives leaves behind a legacy of tainted memories. There may be an autobiographical element here, for Hurston's father, a minister, died in a car accident as well.

Religion and Conjuring

Religion is another important theme in *Jonah's Gourd Vine.* To begin with, the novel's title, like all of Hurston's four published novels, contains a biblical allusion. The "gourd vine" is an important religious symbol connected with John's rise and fall in the community. John Pearson fails to fully come to terms with his actions and the effects they would have on his family, friends, and the community. John Pearson, whose name could be seen as a variation on *Jonah,* suffers a social downfall, much in the way the gourd vine was brought down in the Bible. The church also brings John and Lucy together frequently, and they even use the church to exchange love letters in a hymnbook. John and Lucy connect with each other through their interest in religion. His later involvement with the church ultimately leads to his role as a minister, with a powerful influence on the community. His prominence as minister feeds his pride, and he desires to be in the public spotlight.

Religion proves important to John despite his flaws. At the moment of his impending death in a car accident, he thinks of God and the women in his life; his final thoughts involve Lucy and Sally. Hurston writes, "False pretender! Outside show to the world! Soon he would be in the shelter of Sally's presence. Faith and no questions asked. He had prayed for Lucy's return and God had answered with Sally. He drove on but half-seeing the railroad from looking inward." Hurston uses succinct language to describe the scene in which the train hits John. His moment of epiphany is brief, and it comes too late.

As a counterpoint to John's Christian religion, Hurston describes the traditional African spiritual tradition of conjuring. Conjuring is a folk tradition of magic, used for good or evil purposes, and it is commonly depicted in African-American literature. Conjure men and women use herbs, spices, and other natural ingredients, as well as individuals' personal belongings, to cast spells on people or to control their behavior. Hurston develops her fascination with conjuring further in *Mules and Men.* In *Jonah's Gourd Vine,* this theme is manifested primarily through Hattie Tyson, whose practices run counter to John's Judeo-Christian tradition. Hattie Tyson uses conjuring as a means of obtaining John's affections, disrupting his relationship with Lucy, and gaining power. Despite her use of conjuring to control John, Hattie's marriage proves troublesome. John cannot remain faithful to her, and he learns through Hambo that Hattie has conjured against him.

Nature and Migration

The theme of nature also functions as an important aspect of this text. John encounters and engages with the natural world frequently in the novel. As a young male, he engages in agricultural work, which ties him to the land, as does his carpentry work. The name of the city he moves to with Sally Lovelace, Plant City, is suggestive. Hurston presents Plant City as a place where John can potentially grow and start his life anew. John's association with the "gourd vine" also symbolizes his connection to nature. The snake is another nature allusion. When he and Lucy initially get to know each other, he kills a snake to protect her; later, after his marriage with Hattie ends and he leaves town, he dreams about a snake, of symbolic importance. In the dream, he slays the snake, but later encounters Alf Pearson while he carries Lucy. Alf tells him that "Distance is the only cure for certain diseases," causing John to leave with his wife. He eventually no longer sees Lucy and feels a sense of loss because they have become separated from each other. This dream represents the relationship between Lucy and John, and reveals that in his subconscious he has an attachment to her. The snake may be a symbol suggesting the evils of sin, in which John engages a lot, or it may be a phallic symbol, suggesting John's sexuality and promiscuity.

Migration is another important theme, and it can be seen in the symbols of the train and the automobile. The car that Sally Lovelace buys John symbolizes affluence, extravagance, wealth, power, and success, but it also is a means for migration, for transporting John both in the physical world and to his death. The automobile parallels the identity John presents to the world, of fleeting and movement. The car also transports John back to Sanford, and back to his bad old habits. Hurston writes, "Three girls in their late teens stood about his gleaming chariot when he emerged towards sundown to visit the new pastor of Zion Hope church. They admired it loudly and crudely hinted for rides, but John coolly drove off without taking any hints. He was used to admiration of his car now and he had his vows." John has traveled back to his pattern of promiscuity. After another affair, he tries to flee again, back to his life in Plant City, but he is killed in transit when a train crashes into his car. The train is another symbol of migration. The train also represents the industrialization of America, and the transformation of society from an agrarian to an urban society. The train is also a motif in one of John's sermons, when he says, "I heard de whistle of de damnation train." In the end the train and the car, these two symbols of high-speed movement, collide, bringing about the destruction of John.

CHARACTERS

Beasley A landowner in the rural Alabama community who Hurston suggests exploits the Crittenden family. The character represents the importance of social and economic power in the novel.

Big 'Oman John and this woman have a romantic relationship; she is one of the many women with whom John has an affair.

Clarke, Mattie She symbolizes friendship and concern as she watches over Lucy Pearson when she becomes ill. The character also reveals the importance of religion as she has concerns about Lucy's relationship with God.

Coon He works at a camp with John, and the two fight, but Coon loses.

Cozy, Felton (Reverend) A minister, he functions as John's rival. He preaches a sample sermon at John's church and eventually assumes John's position as minister. Cozy promotes black heritage and black pride in his sermons.

Crittenden, Amy As the mother of John Pearson, Amy plays an important role in the early chapters of the novel. Born a slave, Amy makes the transition from slave to free woman. However, her experiences on the plantation of Alf Pearson influence and affect her life. With Alf Pearson, she becomes pregnant and bears his child, John Pearson. In this way, Hurston's characterization of Amy reveals the legacy of slavery and black women treated as sexual chattel on slave plantations. Her story has a resemblance to that of the character Nanny in *Their Eyes Were Watching God,* who bears a child by her white owner.

With Ned Crittenden, Amy lives on a meager income from their ventures as sharecroppers in rural Alabama. Amy's relationship with Ned is an abusive one, and Ned resents her son's lighter skin. She states to her husband, "Naw Ned, Ah don't want mine tuh come lak yuh come nor neither lak me, and Ahm uh whole heap younger'n you, You growed up in slavery time." Her comments suggest the intergenerational tension in her family, where one generation comes from slavery and the other generation symbolizes freedom. The Crittenden family then symbolizes the transition from slavery to freedom.

The presentation of Amy Crittenden reflects the centrality of mother-son relationships in this novel. As a mother, she tries to instill morals in her children and provide for them, but her financial instability makes this particularly difficult. When John leaves, Amy is saddened but excited about the opportunities that lay ahead for him. She desires her children to have a better life than she has had. Proud of her son, she encourages him to develop to his full potential. The characterization of Amy stands in stark contrast to Emmeline, the middle-class black woman who is the mother of John's wife, Lucy.

Crittenden, Ned A working-class black man and agricultural laborer, Ned is John's stepfather and Amy's husband. As a former slave, he still bears anger and resentment toward the slave-holding class; the psychological and emotional trauma still affects him years later, and impacts his actions with his wife and children. Hurston may be using Ned Crittenden to comment on the ugly legacy of slavery, which emasculated men and caused many to assert their authority and power in the domestic space as a means of reestablishing their identity. Ned Crittenden, as an early authority figure, shapes John Pearson's ideals about manliness in the novel.

Through the character of Ned Crittenden, Hurston explores the dynamics of domestic violence and abuse. In one crucial scene, Ned attacks Amy because she has not set out a dinner plate for him. The verbal and physical abuse heaped on other members of the household by Ned reflects Hurston's complex portrayal of marriage. He abuses his wife and does not treat his children well. He resents John's lighter skin color. He has a troubled relationship with John, and he serves as an impetus for John leaving home and going to work on Alf Pearson's land and property. In an argument with Amy about child rearing, he states, "John is de house-nigger. Ole Marsa always kep' de yaller niggers in de house and give 'em uh job totin' silver dishes and goblets tuh de table. Us black niggers is de ones s'posed tuh ketch de wind and de weather."

Dewoe, An' Dangie A conjure woman, she tries to help Hattie Tyson gain John Pearson's love and affection.

Delphine She has an extramarital relationship with John.

Duke Duke, like many of the other characters, does not trust John because of his promiscuity. He believes that John has an inappropriate relationship with Duke's wife.

Exie Alf Pearson believes that John may have an inappropriate relationship with this woman.

Hambo A good friend to John, Hambo warns John about Hattie Tyson. He remains friends with John throughout his life, and John goes to visit him at the end of the novel.

Harris Deacon Harris betrays John by conspiring with Hattie Tyson to bring about John's downfall as a prominent minister. He symbolizes betrayal, duplicity, and manipulation in the novel. Harris also functions to represent the significance of the church in the rural African-American community.

Lamar, M'haley (Mehaley) She desires John but marries another man, as John is not interested.

Lamar, Pomp This man marries Mehaley.

Mimms, Artie Emmeline Potts wanted Lucy to marry Artie. He has more social and economic status than John at the time.

Patton, Ora Ora has an affair with John during his marriage to Sally. After he spends an evening with her, he is killed in the car accident.

Pearson, Alf A prominent white man, Alf Pearson owns a large amount of land. He symbolizes upper-class white society in the novel. More significantly, he symbolizes the legacy of slavery and white power and privilege in antebellum America. After slavery, he employed blacks as workers and sharecroppers on his land; thus, he still maintained a labor force composed of blacks that rely on him heavily for their income. In contrast to Ned Crittenden, Alf Pearson's sense of self comes from his status as a wealthy and powerful man. Although he has another, white, son, he takes a parental interest in John, whom he fathered with Amy Crittenden. He becomes a source of social and economic security for John by providing him with housing, clothes, food, an education, and money. Alf proves to be a continual influence in the life of John, frequently coming to his aid. As a paternalistic man, he allows John and Lucy, after their wedding, to live in a home behind his house, and he even gives them a bed as a wedding gift. His early concern about John's relationships with women proves prophetic. While whites figure as minor characters in this novel, Alf Pearson plays a major role.

Pearson, Hattie (Tyson) A deceitful, manipulative woman, she commits adultery with John while he is married to Lucy and later marries him. Once married to her, John taunts Hattie by telling her that Lucy was a better woman; her resulting frustration leads her to consult with Deacon Harris, and the two eventually plot against John to divest him of power in the church. In a desperate bid to keep John, she consults a conjurer. Her association with An' Dangie Dewoe reveals important elements in her character. She follows the conjure woman's advice to make John desire her and to win his affections. She eventually divorces him and brings to light his unfaithfulness to her in court. In the courtroom, Hurston describes Hattie in this way: "Hattie was a goddess for the moment. She sat between the Cherubim on the altar of destruction. She chewed her gum and gloated." After John's death, Hattie returns to Sanford and attends his memorial, even attempting to sit in the space reserved for John's current wife. Since she has failed to realize her own complicity in the doomed marriage with John, her trip to Sanford may symbolize guilt or a sense of triumph that she outlived a man who beat and cheated on her.

Pearson, John The son of Amy Crittenden and the stepson of Ned Crittenden, John grows up in a working-class, African-American family. Born on a plantation owned by Alf Pearson, he has a mixed racial background and heritage. While growing up in a sharecropping family struggling to make a living, he initially does not have opportunities for education or upward mobility. His family life, framed by domestic violence, is difficult for John, who endures the anger and hatred of his stepfather, Ned Crittenden. When John enters his late teens, the tensions mount and he must migrate to another area, over "the Big Creek," to find his place in the world.

John's identity radically changes upon meeting his biological father, Alf Pearson, a wealthy white man who owned John's mother and grandmother Pheemy. Through Alf, John gains money, an education, and the tools to rise up in the world. John's good looks, intelligence, and forceful personality make him popular with women; his promiscuity leads to his downfall. He marries three times in the novel, to Lucy, Hattie, and Sally. He proves to be an unfaithful man, and while he shows some guilt, he continues to engage in these affairs, neglecting his family. He rises in stature as a carpenter, minister, and mayor, and as he does, he gains pride and self-confidence. He is killed by a train.

Throughout the novel, Hurston associates John with both biblical and natural imagery. Like the "gourd vine" in the Bible, John is cut down. His name, John, calls to mind Jonah from the Bible. As a character John grows socially and economically, if not emotionally. Through John, Hurston illustrates how tenuous power and authority can be in American society.

Pearson, Lucy Ann (Potts) A bright, energetic, and beautiful woman, Lucy grows up in a landowning family and represents the black middle class. She also shares the same name as Hurston's mother, which suggests that there may be an autobiographical element in her characterization. Lucy wields an important influence on John Pearson. Her influence inspires him to study in school, become actively involved with the church, and establish himself. While Lucy is dutiful, she is also independent and strong-willed. By marrying John, she defies her mother's wishes, and she even confronts John about his adultery. Through the characterization of Lucy, Hurston manages to present a realistic character who deals with many challenges relating to race, class, gender, and marriage.

As the often-betrayed wife, Lucy must endure the hardships of performing the main parental functions in the household. She establishes, as a result, close relationships with her children. She is a respected member of the community, and people value her sense of strength and propriety. She helps John in his many roles; she encourages him and gives him advice, especially on how to handle his congregation as a successful preacher. She functions as his moral center and conscience, reminding him of wrongdoing. Her death has a dramatic impact on the community and on John. Her strong influence on him makes him relieved when she dies, yet he can still sense her presence: He thinks of her throughout his life, during his second and third marriages, in a dream, and right before he dies.

Pearson, Sally (Lovelace) John's third and final wife, Sally Lovelace reflects love, devotion, and care. Her last name may be symbolic of her love. A wealthy woman, she provides John with work and food and helps him get a job as a preacher at Pilgrim Rest Baptist Church. She is a 48-year-old woman, and sees John as her first true love, which gives her a sense of identity. A patient and loving woman, her optimistic attitude makes her willing to marry a man with a troubled past. Sally depicts the possibility of redemption and salvation for John.

Sally delights in his claims that he will not betray her in the relationship and that he does not want to spend time away from her. Hurston writes, "Sally exulted in her power and sipped honey from his lips, but she made him go, seeing the pain in John's face at the separation. It was worth her own suffering ten times over to see him that way for her." When John dies, Sally is grief-stricken and offers to give the money from the settlement to his children. She also wants to be buried next to John. She maintains that John never cheated on her and was not unfaithful, showing she was blinded by love. She claims "He wuz true to me." Sally gives John the Cadillac that he is driving when struck and killed by a train.

Pearson, Zeke As John's brother, he admires John and looks up to him as he rises in prominence. He carries communication between Lucy and John early in their relationship. He symbolizes brotherly love, affection, and admiration.

Pheemy A former slave, she is Amy Crittenden's mother and John's grandmother. She lives on Alf Pearson's farm in a cabin. John resides with her for a while. She serves as a bridge between the past and the present for the characters in the text. She also establishes a maternal link for John after he has left home.

Potts, Bud He is the brother of Lucy, and he despises John. He is assaulted by John, leading to John's departure from Alabama.

Potts, Emmeline Lucy's mother, she does not want her daughter to wed John, even refusing to attend the wedding. She considers John to be beneath their social class. Her social and economic status place her above many of the other people in their rural Alabama town. A religious woman, she prays about her daughter's relationship.

Potts, Richard The loving and supportive father of Lucy, he accepts his daughter's marriage to John and attends the wedding.

Shelby A man who owns land that John's family works on for a while.

BIBLIOGRAPHY

Brown, Alan. "'De Beast' Within: The Role of Nature in Jonah's Gourd Vine." In *Zora in Florida,* edited by Steve Glassman and Kathryn Lee Seidel, 76–85. Orlando: University of Central Florida Press, 1991.

Gates, Henry Louis, Jr., and K. A. Appiah, eds. *Zora Neale Hurston: Critical Perspectives Past and Present.* New York: Amistad, 1993.

Hurston, Zora Neale. *Jonah's Gourd Vine.* In her *Novels and Stories,* 1–171. New York: Library of America, 1995.

Jones, Sharon Lynette. *Rereading the Harlem Renaissance: Race, Class, and Gender in the Fiction of Jessie Fauset, Zora Neale Hurston, and Dorothy West.* Westport, Conn.: Greenwood Press, 2002.

Stanford, Ann Folwell. "Dynamics of Change: Men and Co-Feeling in the Fiction of Zora Neale Hurston and Alice Walker," in *Alice Walker and Zora Neale Hurston: The Common Bond,* edited by Lillie P. Howard, 109–119. Westport, Conn.: Greenwood Press, 1993.

Wall, Cheryl A. *Women of the Harlem Renaissance.* Bloomington: Indiana University Press, 1995.

"Magnolia Flower" (1925)

This short story appeared in an issue of *The Spokesman,* and it illustrates the themes of nature, love, and parent-child relationships. Hurston makes notable use of personification in her depiction of the river and the brook in this story. Although the story has received little critical attention, it deserves discussion as it deals with many of the same themes in Hurston's novels, specifically in its treatment of nature and love as shaping forces.

SYNOPSIS

Two of the protagonists in this story happen to be natural phenomena: a river and a brook. The river asks the brook why it sings and hurries; the brook claims it behaves this way due to youth and the presence of people in love, who transform the environment. The river reveals to the brook more information about the people in love who have changed the area. The river recounts the story of a black slave, Bentley, who weds a Native American woman, Swift Deer. They eventually have a child whom they name Magnolia Flower, a name that represents her beauty and connection with nature. The Civil War ends, and slaves are emancipated. Bentley builds a big house. He wants Magnolia Flower to marry a dark man because he has dark skin himself. John, a schoolteacher, falls in love with Magnolia Flower and proposes, but she knows her father wants her to be with a dark man.

Bentley gets angry when he finds out John wants to wed Magnolia Flower. He plans to hang him and make Magnolia Flower marry Joe. He orders Magnolia and John to be confined and locked in separate rooms in his house. Magnolia Flower manages to be freed from her room, and she releases John from his room as well. They flee. The next day, Bentley discovers that Magnolia Flower and John are gone. Swift Deer dies eventually, and the house falls apart. Years later, Magnolia Flower and John look for a special place in nature. Magnolia Flower does not regret being with him. Magnolia Flower hears the river and John thinks it welcomes them.

CRITICAL COMMENTARY

The text centers on "a school girl who loves her light-skinned teacher despite her father's opposition" (Hemenway 88). The exploration of color prejudice in the story reveals an important thematic concern in Hurston's writing. Bentley's insistence on Magnolia Flower marrying a dark man may come from his desire for his daughter to embrace her black heritage and carry on his legacy; his past as a slave still affects his beliefs, behavior, and values. As Valerie Boyd stresses, Hurston "again addressed the theme she'd begun to explore in her play *Color Struck*: the self-destructiveness that results from color-based prejudice among black people" (Boyd 103).

Like Ned Crittenden in *Jonah's Gourd Vine,* Bentley carries a prejudice against light-skinned blacks. The fact that he wants to hang John suggests that his feelings on the issue are quite strong and passionate. While clearly devoted to Magnolia Flower, he finds himself reluctant to let her assert her own independence and identity. He tries to exert authority over his daughter by having her and her lover locked up in the house; he treats them as captives and tries to make them serve his will.

Swift Deer finds herself caught between the desires of her daughter and her husband. She plays the loving wife and mother, but she has very little agency in the story. In contrast, Magnolia Flower, the daughter, exhibits much female agency, independence, and resistance in the story. After falling in love with John, the schoolteacher, Magnolia Flower defies her father. She is open to people of different ethnic backgrounds, and she does not place as much focus on color as her father. Magnolia Flower herself reflects bicultural heritages, as she is of both African-American and Native American ancestry. John's role as a schoolteacher emphasizes the importance of black education, and his insistence on being with Magnolia Flower despite her father's objections symbolizes a defiance of authority. The ending of the story illustrates the lasting love between him and his wife.

By making the river and the brook characters in this story, Hurston emphasizes the importance of nature and its interconnectedness with the lives of humans. The river and brook are aware of and affected by the lives of this family. When Magnolia Flower and her husband hear the river at the end of the story, they form part of a unified natural world. The river and the brook serve as the primary narrators, imbuing the story with a sense of the surreal; it also makes reference to Native American folklore. By emphasizing the communion of humans with nature, Hurston is harking back to elements that many romantic movement writers employed in reaction against the previous obsession with rationalism. The story reveals Hurston's emerging talent as a writer and a chronicler of the relationship between humans and the natural world.

CHARACTERS

Bentley Bentley is a black former slave who weds Swift Deer after the slaves have been freed. He fathers Magnolia Flower. He symbolizes the history of slavery and its legacy for African Americans, though he is an upwardly mobile man, and builds a big house for his family. While he desires for his daughter to get an education, he becomes angry when she falls in love with her teacher John.

The Brook The brook is one of the primary narrators of this story; however, as the river recounts most of the romance between Magnolia Flower and John, the brook serves as the listener to the tale.

John A light-skinned black man and schoolteacher, he illustrates the quest for education by blacks after slavery. He falls in love with Magnolia Flower as her teacher. He is locked up by Bentley, but he and Magnolia manage to escape and start a life together.

Magnolia Flower The daughter of Swift Deer and Bentley, she loves both her parents but finds herself in the situation of having to defy her father's expectations. She is of dual racial and ethnic heritage, having a black father and a Native American mother. Her name symbolizes her tie to nature. A defiant young woman, she refuses to marry Joe, the man her father wants her to wed. She finds love in John, and they end up together in happiness.

The River The river narrates the story of Magnolia Flower and John, as the brook listens. The river possesses a special relationship with the lovers of this story, for when they hear the river, John thinks it welcomes the lovers.

Swift Deer A Native American and closely linked to nature, she weds Bentley and bears a child named Magnolia Flower. She loves both her husband and daughter, but finds herself caught between their differing desires. She dies after their escape.

BIBLIOGRAPHY

Boyd, Valerie. *Wrapped in Rainbows: The Life of Zora Neale Hurston.* New York: Scribner, 2003.

Hemenway, Robert E. *Zora Neale Hurston: A Literary Biography.* Urbana: University of Illinois Press, 1980.

Hurston, Zora Neale. "Magnolia Flower." In her *The Complete Stories,* 33–40. New York: HarperCollins, 1995.

Moses, Man of the Mountain (1939)

In *Moses, Man of the Mountain,* Hurston retells the Old Testament story of Moses, chronicling his quest to lead the Israelites out of slavery under the Egyptians and to freedom. Clearly, the Israelites' struggle out of slavery is used to parallel and analogize the same struggle faced by black slaves in the United States. The novel is thus a commentary on the nature of oppression and the struggle for freedom and equality. Whereas in her other novels Hurston employs ample use of biblical allusion to enrich her narratives, *Moses, Man of the Mountain* is primarily a Bible narrative that is retold from a modern perspective. Hurston's powerful version of this tale of Moses and the Exodus "gives the biblical story a compelling immediacy" (Howard 115). This text was inspired by Hurston's short story "The Fire and the Cloud," and in fact important aspects "of the novel's last chapter were created here" (Lowe 210). She composed the novel in 1938, and it was published the following year.

As the daughter of a minister, Hurston was influenced by religion from an early age, and religious references form an important basis in her oeuvre, including this novel. But Hurston's focus on Moses also falls squarely in the African-American tradition. Valerie Boyd writes that Moses was "a figure of unparalleled splendor in black folklore" (330). In folktales and in song, blacks had a long tradition of referring to the plight of the Israelites as a means of contextualizing their own. In such allusions, Moses functions as a heroic figure, a symbol of freedom and emancipation. For many African Americans, then, the figure of Moses served as the model for emancipation as they charted their course from bondage to freedom.

SYNOPSIS

Introduction

In the introduction to this novel, Moses is described as a wise elder and lawgiver, a leader in the conflict against Pharaoh. In the Bible story, Moses was buried at Mount Nebo, but the figure of Moses has lived on in popular memory, and others have included him in other stories. In Africa, Moses "is worshipped as a god," and throughout the African diaspora people hold Moses in similarly high regard.

I

The novel begins prior to the birth of Moses. Pharaoh banned the birth of Hebrew men in the area; those born would be killed. As a result, women giving birth tried to do so privately, in Goshen. The Hebrews were made slaves and other oppressive laws were declared against them: For example, they were limited by the amount they could sleep, and they were punished for not working fast enough. The Israelites cried.

II

Amram, a slave, mentions to another slave, Caleb, that his wife will be giving birth to a child. He wants his wife to give birth privately, without "secret police" knowing about it. He intends to have his children, Miriam and Aaron, assist by keeping watch. Amram tells Caleb that in the future Pharaoh may encounter someone who can stand up to him, and he hopes for a son who will assert his manhood.

III

Caleb and Amram leave their work area and head home. When Amram arrives home, his wife, Jochebed, is in the process of giving birth. A woman named Puah assists her as Amram says that he does not feel manly. As Amram eats, Jochebed noisily continues her labor and Puah continues helping, fearing the noise will betray her childbirth to the authorities. The children, Aaron and Miriam, arrive and remain on the lookout for others. Aaron announces to his parents and Puah that Jacob, his wife, and their newborn male child were all killed due to the restrictions. Amram fears that some of the town midwives may also be informants. Jochebed gives birth to the child, and Puah announces it is male.

IV

Because of the Egyptian policy, Amram believes it would be preferable for him to kill his son himself. Jochebed disagrees. Instead, Amram decides to hide their child rather than let him die. Jochebed hopes the policy will be changed, but she still fears for his safety. The following day there is a meeting between Pharaoh and the Hebrews, at which Pharaoh accuses the Hebrews of not working hard enough, and he says that slow workers will be punished and even stricter work laws introduced. He informs them that they are not free to depart Egypt, and that the midwives have been informing the authorities about male babies. Amram goes home and tells his wife what transpired. Jochebed decides to make a basket for the baby. The entire family goes to the Nile River, where Jochebed puts their baby in the basket and places him in the river. Jochebed asks Miriam to watch the basket as it floats away.

V

Miriam sits watching, then dozes and later awakes. She has lost sight of her baby brother, but she does notice some women bathing another woman, and she sees that it is Pharaoh's daughter, whose husband died. The pharaoh's daughter goes ashore after the bath and then dresses. She spots the basket in the river, and retrieves it; she also sees Miriam, but they do not interact. Everyone returns home. Miriam's mother is crying and asks about the baby boy. Miriam tells her mother that the pharaoh's daughter brought her baby "to the palace"; she also lies and claims she was almost murdered with a sword. Miriam says the princess is friendly and Jochebed believes that the pharaoh's daughter would naturally love her child. Amram returns later and tells Jochebed that people in Goshen have been talking about the princess adopting the child. Amram expresses concern that this is really their child and he thinks they should inquire. The following day, Jochebed tries to find a job taking care of the baby, but she is not allowed to approach the palace.

VI

Pharaoh's son, Ta-Phar, has a great wish to replace his father as pharaoh one day. Pharaoh's daughter, the princess, is obligated to give birth to a male child. Moses, the princess's son, is "second in line for the throne of Egypt." People think that Moses is a good-looking boy. Moses has a mentor, Mentu, who talks with him and teaches him about the world. On one occasion, Mentu and Moses go on a search for birds, and Moses sees a lizard. Moses points out that he often sees the lizard, and Mentu explains the lizard to Moses. Moses feeds the lizard; he also frequently gives Mentu food that he has taken from the palace. Moses begins to observe holy men to learn more about their activities and requests to study what they study.

VII

Soldiers like Moses and are impressed with his war skills. Ta-Phar, brother of the princess and in line to be pharaoh, wants to make sure he succeeds in obtaining power. He considers more restrictions on Hebrews. On a battle day, Ta-Phar wants to impress people with his skill, but it is Moses who proves his skill and wins the trophy. Mentu later tells Moses that he did not have a high enough rank to participate but that he, Ta-Phar, wanted to see him in the contest. Mentu tells Moses about a special book, and reveals its location in a certain river. Moses plans to find this book.

VIII

Because of his victory, Moses becomes leader of the military, as Pharaoh wants to beat other countries at war. Egypt expands its power by defeating other countries. Meanwhile, Moses' uncle Ta-Phar dislikes him, and Moses continues to want to find that book. Mentu dies, and Moses plans a nice funeral for him. Moses takes up his religious study once again, working with holy men as in the past. Moses' real desire is to gain information that will allow him to find the book. Moses' mother dies. Moses is married to a woman from Ethiopia; he does not care about her, but is courteous to her. Moses wants Hebrews to be allowed to join the military, and as a result they are grateful to him.

IX

Moses murders an Egyptian, speaks to Pharaoh, and returns home, telling his wife he is headed off to war. His wife accuses him of being Hebrew, saying others, including Ta-Phar, believe that too; he denies that he is Hebrew. She explains to Moses that the princess's real son died, and so she claimed that Moses was her son. She also says that a woman who claims to be his sister came to the palace. The conversation makes Moses upset, and he leaves. Moses watches a foreman being cruel to a Hebrew man, and Moses retaliates by confiscating the foreman's whip. Moses then assaults him, and the foreman dies. Moses instructs that he be buried, and no one speaks further about the matter. Moses later visits Pharaoh to postpone the battle. Later, he visits the tomb of the foreman, as well as the place where he killed him; he feels lonely but not remorseful.

Another Hebrew foreman now works there, who tells Moses his laborers want to stop working so they can attend a meeting. Moses instructs them to continue working, but then discovers that his efforts are not understood. He informs a steward of his plans to leave; this steward announces his defection and that he should be considered an enemy of Egypt. Moses makes his preparations to leave.

X

Moses journeys at night, dreaming of a land of social and economic equality. One evening, he sees some chickens, and contemplates nature. Moses later finds himself by the Red Sea, where he wants a boat to take him to Asia. Moses speaks to an elderly man, who tells Moses that some other men want him to pay a lot of money for the boat. Moses gives the man money, and he tells Moses that the water level will lower with the tide, and then Moses can walk across the sea floor. Moses follows this advice and crosses the sea successfully.

XI

Moses is unsure about his destination, but he journeys onward. One evening, he arrives in a place where he observes a buzz of activity, with people from different backgrounds. He hears Sudanese music, witnesses an argument, and sees caravans around him. He speaks with a local man, and the next day he travels in a caravan with him. Moses leaves this caravan and catches sight of a mountain that impresses him. He believes it symbolizes divinity. Someone tells Moses this mountain is called Horeb and Sinai. Moses dismounts from his horse and heads in the direction of this mountain.

XII

Moses contemplates his situation, and he wants to go up the mountain the following day. Moses sees young women being harassed by some men, and he tries to help. The women are grateful for his help, and one of them invites Moses to "follow her home" when she finds out Moses does not have a place to stay for the night. Moses meets her distinguished-looking father, Jethro, also called Ruel, who thanks Moses for his assistance. Jethro expresses frustration at not having any male children and informs Moses that in their kingdom people are treated badly. Moses and Jethro are served dinner by the women; Jethro tells Moses about his eldest child, Zipporah, and Moses desires to see her. He adjusts to life in Midian, even speaking their dialect well. Moses aids Jethro with his livestock.

XIII

Several days later, Jethro accuses some former servants of attempting to take his animals, but Moses convinces him to employ them on his land again. Moses shares knowledge with Jethro, teaching him what he learned with the priests in Egypt. He believes Jethro will eventually bring him to that mountain. Jethro encourages Moses to attend an event one evening, following which Moses speaks with Zipporah, then grabs her and kisses her "with as much energy as he needed for a cavalry charge." Zipporah heads into their tent; Moses follows. Jethro declares that Moses and Zipporah will get married. Zipporah cries and Moses tells Jethro that he will be good to her. Moses leaves to go to his own tent, and Zipporah follows.

XIV

One morning Moses expresses his feelings for Zipporah, who has dark eyes and coarse hair, to Jethro. Jethro questions Moses about the special book in the river in Koptos and tells him he should be a leader. He tells Moses he will take him to Mount Horeb, but that Moses is "not ready" for this yet. "You are the son of the mountain," he tells Moses, and has him study nature. Then Jethro goes home, where he talks to his wife about Chief Zeppo, who is coming to visit. For the visit, Zipporah tells Moses that he should wear his nice clothing and not the herder's outfit. Jethro claims it's because his daughter wants other women to be jealous. The following evening Moses tells them about his past. Jethro comforts Moses; Zipporah realizes that Moses is royalty, but others are not aware of it. She says she wants to go to Egypt with him. Moses says he did not care about his wife back in Egypt, and in fact he thinks he would be killed if he returned for good. He is happy in Midian, but he asks Jethro to accompany him to Egypt to visit the gravesites of Mentu and his mother.

XV

Much time has passed. Moses loves Zipporah and his sons, and he enjoys tending to the animals and working on the land. Zipporah, still desiring to see Egypt, realizes that Moses continues to have a strong connection with her father. With Moses's assistance, Jethro becomes wealthy. He grants Moses special powers; with this power, Moses causes frogs to appear, scaring Zeppo and his kin into leaving. Zeppo complains in a letter to Jethro, but Jethro describes Moses as "the finest hoodoo man in the world." Meanwhile, Pharaoh dies and Moses heads to Egypt.

XVI

Moses returns and speaks with Jethro about his journey to Koptos. While there, Moses discovered a box and battled a snake. Moses had retrieved a book from this box, which enabled him to have power over nature. He transcribed text from this book onto papyrus, soaked the document in beer, and drank the beer so he would retain the information. Moses placed this book within the box, placed the box among other boxes on the river floor, and made the snake "guard it until he should come again." After doing all that, he returned to Midian. Moses tells Jethro about the plight of Hebrews, and Jethro reveals to Moses a monumental project for them to undertake: They should tell people about the real God. Jethro tells Moses to head to Egypt and lead the Hebrews to freedom. Moses had begun herding livestock again, and he looks to nature to help him decide what to do. One night Moses says he does not want to lead the Hebrews, and Zipporah laments his lost potential as king.

XVII

Moses climbs up the mountain and views a burning bush. He hears a voice commanding him to remove his shoes as he walks on the divine earth. He follows the orders, and the voice asks him what appears before him. Moses answers that he views a snake. The voice tells him to get the snake, which he does, and as he holds it sees it has turned into a wooden cane. The voice tells him to set it back on the ground, and it then turns back into a living snake. Moses picks it up again, and again it becomes a wooden rod. The voice commands Moses to travel to Egypt, telling him to free the individuals from the pharaoh. The voice says it will travel with him and identifies itself as "I AM WHAT I AM." It stops speaking, and the bush stops burning, but Moses is still holding the wooden rod. Moses is transformed by this experience and heads home.

XVIII

Moses explains to Jethro his concerns about leading the Hebrews. Jethro says the Hebrews want freedom and he will enlist Aaron to help him. Moses tells Jethro he will venture in the wilderness.

XIX

Moses heads to Egypt.

XX

Moses has arrived in Egypt, and people in Goshen are aware of his presence. Upon arriving in Goshen, Moses asks Aaron to have elders and other important people come to see him. One of these visitors is Miriam, his sister who has the gift of prophecy. Aaron says, "She can hit a straight lick with a crooked stick, just the same as you can do." Moses claims to be a messenger on a mission from God. The elders leave the meeting and instruct others to gather with Moses at a grove. At this grove, Moses performs a sacrifice and builds an altar. He tells the people that God favors justice, and that he does not want them to eat the meat of a pig. Moses declares they will eventually gain freedom.

XXI

Along with Aaron, Moses goes to visit the pharaoh, Ta-Phar. At the pharaoh's palace, Moses discovers that his own wife is now the queen. The pharaoh speaks with Moses and Aaron, and reacts with contempt to Moses and his special powers. Moses claims that his powers are superior; Ta-Phar says that Moses simply wants to be king and does not care about the Hebrews. Moses demonstrates that he can turn the snake into the rod. Moses instructs Aaron to put down the rod, thus turning it back into a snake. Moses then asks the pharaoh to free the Hebrews based on his power. The pharaoh refuses. Moses insists on freedom and leaves the palace.

XXII

People in Goshen discuss what transpired between the pharaoh and Moses. Moses tells Aaron that he has the power to conquer the pharaoh. Aaron departs and Moses appreciates the solitude, which allows him to reflect on his life in Midian. A man approaches, claiming to be Joshua and saying he wishes to serve Moses. Moses tells Joshua to gather his belongings and go to the house where he is staying. Joshua departs, and Moses is impressed by his manliness.

XXIII

Moses, accompanied by Aaron, visits the pharaoh again. Moses again demands that the Hebrews be freed, and Pharaoh again declines to free them. Moses raises a hand repeatedly, which turns water into blood. Pharaoh claims he will trick Moses into transforming this blood back into water. The pharaoh instructs his priests that they should demonstrate their power by claiming that they too can turn the water into blood, and then back into water again. The following day, the priests hold a ceremony at a palace well, claiming they have turned the water into blood. Moses and Aaron are present for this event, and Aaron believes the priests possess the power too. Later, during another visit to the palace, Moses repeats to the pharaoh that God wishes the Hebrews to be free. Moses shows his power by making frogs emerge from a pond.

Moses returns the following day and talks to the pharaoh about the frogs. Moses causes the frogs to head to the Nile River. Moses goes home, but is summoned back to the palace the following day by a messenger. The pharaoh says his priests can do a similar trick. Frogs appear, but his priest cannot control the frogs, so Moses uses his power to send these frogs to the river as well. Once again, Moses visits the palace and tells the pharaoh that the Hebrews should be free; the pharaoh also says he does not want to see any more frogs. Judges and counselors are summoned, and before them Moses causes lice to appear in Egypt. Moses departs, and the pharaoh grows concerned; he considers expelling the Hebrews from Egypt. His advisers, however, do not want the Hebrews expelled, as they are valuable as slaves. The pharaoh says that the Egyptians have been the cause of the lice, as the gods are angry and are punishing them.

XXIV

A month goes by during which Moses and the pharaoh do not see each other. Moses helps Joshua develop important skills and eventually reveals to Joshua it is almost time to visit the pharaoh. Joshua is looking forward to this visit.

XXV

Moses tells the pharaoh that the Hebrews should be freed and then causes flies to appear. He and Aaron leave the palace, and the people in Goshen hear about the flies. On the following day the pharaoh asks what Moses wants for the Hebrews. Moses says they want to leave Egypt and to practice their religion in freedom. The pharaoh agrees to let them leave if Moses makes the flies disappear. Moses promises to get rid of the flies and the pharaoh says that the next day Moses will be informed about when the Hebrews can leave. Moses goes home, and the flies disappear. After a week, Moses still has not received word from the pharaoh. He visits the pharaoh, and says he will punish the pharaoh by causing cattle to die throughout Egypt. Moses leaves, and the pharaoh wants to kill him. The pharaoh agrees to free the Hebrews as long as Moses stops the killing of the cattle, but then the pharaoh does not keep his promise. Moses explains how God is not pleased with the pharaoh's behavior, and promises another plague; this time he causes boils.

The pharaoh again agrees to free the Hebrews, but Moses notes that the pharaoh has not kept his promise to do so. They agree to meet at a battle site the following day, and it hails as a result of Moses' powers. Then locusts appear as well. Eventually the pharaoh says the Hebrews may practice their religion elsewhere, but he does not want them all to leave; Moses explains that God wants them all to leave. Moses provides details about the Hebrew exodus, and the pharaoh changes his mind. Moses then visits the pharaoh and reveals that he can sense the pharaoh's fear; he says that darkness will descend upon Egypt, which Moses then causes. Moses has instructed the Hebrews to obtain oil lamps to get through this period, and the darkness begins to lift several days later. Finally the pharaoh summons Moses to indicate his agreement that the Hebrews may leave; however, the animals must stay, he says. Moses leaves.

XXVI

The doors of the Goshen households have been marked with blood, a sign for God. Moses causes the first-born child of Egyptians to die, and this includes the pharaoh's own child. As a result, the pharaoh finally decides that he wants Moses, Moses' god, and the Hebrews to leave Egypt. The pharaoh summons Moses, but he does not come, so he sends Moses a message. Moses informs the Hebrews that they may leave Egypt.

XXVII

Joshua reminds the Hebrews that Moses has secured their freedom. Moses advises the Hebrews to quickly prepare for their departure. Moses asks for Joseph's bones to be prepared so they can take them with them. Moses guides the Hebrews away from Goshen. On the journey, Nun and Aaron see a fire, and Aaron asks Moses about it. Moses explains that it is a sign from "the Presence." The journey continues and the following day they set up camp by the Red Sea. Moses looks out over the sea.

XXVIII

Pharaoh notices that work has not been getting done, so he asks a servant about it. The servant says that the Hebrews have not been seen recently. Pharaoh finds out that they left Egypt. He is upset, realizing that Moses has made him look foolish, and he says that it was his grief that caused him to allow them to leave. Pharaoh says he will pursue them and make them return, and he will kill Moses. He prepares for war with Moses and the Hebrews, and sets out to find them.

XXIX

As Moses looks out at the Red Sea, Joshua yells that the Egyptians are heading toward them. Moses tries to calm his people, telling them not to fear the pharaoh or the Egyptian army. God will help them, he says, and they are comforted. A cloud hovers over the sea, and the pharaoh has planned an attack for the next day. Moses then divides the sea in two, leaving dry land for the Hebrews to walk across. The Egyptians watch in wonder and chase after them, but Moses closes the sea up again, protecting them. A man sings about the death of the pharaoh; Moses sits on a rock and speaks to God.

XXX

The following morning, people surround the tent of Moses. Joshua informs them that Moses is not sleeping but speaking with God. People return to the camp. However, Moses was not speaking with God, but rather looking out at the sea. He sees corpses, including Ta-Phar's. He removes a ring from Ta-Phar's hand, and throws it into the sea. Moses leads the Hebrews to Mount Sinai. People complain about the water; Moses drinks it, then heads into the woods to speak with God. In the woods, he has trees chopped down, which makes the water taste better, and people are happy with the water. Moses contemplates his position as leader for the Hebrews.

XXXI

The next day, Moses marches, leading his people. Moses misses Jethro and his wife; he thinks about Midian. Moses designates someone to inform Jethro of the news. Joshua is upset that he is not chosen, but Moses explains that he needs him to fight. Moses heads in the direction of Mount Sinai, thinking the people will have faith in God and will realize their freedom upon seeing this mountain. Moses leads the Hebrews across Sinai. Joshua informs Moses that people are hungry, and Moses wishes to see them. Moses seeks counsel from Aaron about people being unhappy, and at this point Moses thinks Aaron resembles Ta-Phar. The group of unhappy people approach Moses and Aaron, explaining they would have preferred to die in Egypt. Moses fixes their hunger, providing them with quail that night, then manna the following morning. Suddenly Moses feels very lonely; he misses Jethro and his family. In Rephidim, people continue to complain about a lack of water. Moses tells them that God wanted him to deliver them from Egypt, and he suggests they may be punished. Moses speaks with God, and he produces water.

Joshua gives Moses a message that the Amalekites want to fight the Hebrews. Moses says they will fight, with assistance from the power of his rod. Moses raises his arms to signal the power of Mount Sinai during the fighting of the Hebrews and the Amalekites. As his arms start to fall, the Amalekites begin to fight better; he regains strength and utilizes the rod to give his men power to fight. This pattern continues, and Moses can see the fate of his people. Hur and Aaron position a rock for him to sit on; he sits there and instructs the men to not allow his hands to lower. The Israelites win the fight. Joshua and Moses acknowledge each other's work and shake hands. Moses says the Hebrews should move to Sinai.

XXXII

Moses divides up the items that belonged to the Amalekites. The Hebrews head for Mount Sinai and set up camp there. Aaron and Miriam visit Moses and complain how badly they have been treated. Later Jethro appears, having been called by Moses. Moses kneels to show his respect for him; Jethro tells him to stand up and informs Moses that his family has accompanied him. Moses approaches Zipporah, and the two go to Moses' tent, where he explains his role as leader of the Hebrews. Miriam comes, but she does not like seeing Zipporah because she is jealous. Zipporah is given her own tent, and Miriam continues to notice how people pay more attention to Zipporah than to her. When Jethro arrives at the tent the next morning, Moses is not there as he is hearing legal cases. Jethro informs him that he cannot hear every case; he should entrust others to hear the cases as well. Jethro returns home.

XXXIII

Moses heads up a mountain, "the altar of the world." From this mountain, God speaks to Moses. God tells Moses that his people should wash, and he will eventually appear. Moses follows God's orders. Days later, people hear a sound coming from the mountain and see a cloud falling over it. Moses says God desires to speak with them. God tells Moses to come to the mountain and speak with him. Moses goes there, followed by Joshua, who is amazed. He sees Moses with the rod, responding to the voice.

XXXIV

Moses stays on the mountain for a long time, with Joshua still observing. He transforms God's words into laws, or commandments. He goes down the mountain, and Joshua follows him. Aaron creates a calf made of gold, which the people worship using song and dance.

XXXV

Moses sits on a stone, telling Joshua about the laws. He hears a noise, which Joshua hears too. Joshua says it sounds like songs for a god. He stands and walks back up the mountain, but the voice tells him to go back, that people are worshiping the calf as if it had been responsible for their liberation. Moses heads down the mountain and goes to the place where the people are worshiping the calf. He stands before the altar with the calf. Moses repeats Aaron's name and throws the tablets; ultimately the golden calf breaks. Moses questions Aaron about the ceremony, and Aaron explains, but Moses disapproves. Moses leaves and returns to the camp, asking who favors the God that freed them. Moses tells them to kill those involved in the calf ceremony. Some of Aaron's children are killed. Aaron sobs, then sings, desiring revenge. Moses creates a tabernacle, and enters it. People hear Moses speaking with God: God tells Moses to obtain a stone, to carry it to the mountain top, and to write on the stone the laws God will give him there. The following morning Moses goes to the mountain with the stones, spends time with God there, and returns with the laws in his hands. Trailed by a cloud, Moses carries the tablets into the tabernacle.

XXXVI

Miriam complains about Zipporah, remarking upon her dark complexion. Women gather around Moses' tent; Miriam and Aaron tell Moses that people are unhappy about Zipporah, but Moses says that Miriam is jealous of her. Moses tells Aaron he cannot lead, and he instructs the two of them to come to the tabernacle. They go there and others follow them. A voice from the cloud expresses anger at Aaron and Miriam. As punishment, Miriam is turned into a leper and has to leave the camp for a week, but she recovers.

XXXVII

Moses and Zipporah change, and Zipporah returns to be with Jethro. Moses continues to be leader of the Hebrews, and Joshua a follower of Moses. Joshua encounters some people who are hungry and unhappy; Joshua replies to Aaron that Moses does not have special food and that he consumes what they consume. Joshua returns to Moses, expressing the people's discontent. Moses listens to them, but he says they are only there to criticize, not to help. They leave, but Aaron stays, and Moses chastises him for not giving him proper support. Moses tells Joshua that the elders should meet and that he will have spies view Canaan, the Promised Land.

XXXVIII

Moses looks forward to a home for the Hebrews. Spies return from Canaan, but the people will have to fight for that land, which they do not want to do. Moses understands the situation and the attitude of his people, but also that Aaron has an opportunity to challenge him. Moses goes to the tabernacle and invites elders and princes to come in. He speaks with God about his frightened people; the Hebrews consider his words and later agree to fight for Canaan. Moses says God will not assist them. The following day Moses makes the Hebrews return to the wilderness, where they will stay for four decades. Moses feels unhappy about the situation.

XXXIX

The people journey to the wilderness, and go to a place called Kadesh. They have children; they rebel; they pass away. Miriam asks Moses to allow her to pass away, acknowledging his power. She admits that she used to be a prophet in Egypt, but she knows that Moses has more power than she. Moses feels sorry for her, and she departs. That night she dies, and her body is found the next morning. Moses buries her, has a tomb built, and ponders her role in the Exodus. Moses learns from a messenger that Jethro is ill, and he goes back to Midian to visit. They speak about Moses' life, and then Jethro dies. Moses buries him, then heads back to camp. Joshua proves to be a forceful leader in war. People want Moses to be crowned for his role in liberating them from slavery. Moses expresses gratitude, but he wants the Hebrews to be a free people.

Later, the Hebrews camp near Mount Hor. Some people complain to Moses about what he has done as a leader, and Moses knows that these words come from someone else. He calls for Aaron, and they speak. Moses asks Aaron if he wants to journey up the mountain with him when he goes to speak with God. Moses, Aaron, and Aaron's son go up the mountain, but Aaron and Moses continue higher than the son. Aaron tells Moses he plans to make it to the Promised Land, saying he could lead the people better than Moses. Aaron complains about Moses' murdering his sons and asks to be a high-ranking priest in the Promised Land. Moses instructs Aaron to disrobe, and Aaron eventually disrobes. Moses kills Aaron; he cries and buries him. Moses heads down the mountain, giving the robes to Aaron's son and making him the priest of high rank. Aaron's son puts on his father's clothes, and he goes down the mountain with Moses. Moses informs the people they should prepare a tomb for Aaron and mourn for him.

XL

The Israelites engage in fighting and win, and they move toward Canaan. Moses leads them. In his journal, Moses chronicles their journey. Moses tells Joshua about aging, advising him and explaining about his talks with God at Mount Sinai. He reveals to Joshua his plans to head up Mount Nebo, where he will speak with God. Moses goes up Mount Nebo with his rod and sits down; in the distance, he sees the Hebrew tents. Moses recognizes that he has not liberated a people: Liberation is something people must feel within themselves, he now sees.

From Mount Nebo, Moses looks down at Israel and the Promised Land as he considers the Hebrews' future and his own past. Moses did not want to be the ruler, but that was his role in life. How would the Israelites view him for departing? he wonders. Moses prepares his own tomb and speaks with a lizard, who claims that it has descended from those who created the world. The lizard tells Moses about another lizard that knows about the past, and he tells Moses where he can find it. Moses says he will sleep and then find the other lizard on Mount Sinai in the morning. Moses sits there, picks up his rod and raises it, causing the mountain to tremble. He hears the "voice of the thunder," and he says goodbye. Moses then travels down the mountain's "other side."

CRITICAL COMMENTARY

Moses, Man of the Mountain is quite distinct in comparison to Hurston's other works of long fiction in that it retells the story of Moses from the Old Testament of the Bible; however, Hurston uses this biblical framework as a means of treating many of the themes present in her other novels, including religion, gender, class, freedom, and nature. Hurston's text was a product of the early 20th century, and in dealing with issues relevant to African Americans post-slavery, this text uses biblical events as a parable for current events. In fact, Hurston was following in a long tradition of appropriating Bible stories to comment on current social and political woes. The Hebrews in the novel parallel the plight of the African Americans; the Egyptians parallel Euro-American slave owners in the United States before abolition. Canaan symbolizes freedom, not just a geographic area where a free people live, but also a state of mind. Framed by the story of Moses and the Egyptians, the novel then speaks to the struggle for freedom faced by African Americans, and their search for a newfound identity as a liberated people.

Religion and Freedom

Religion functions as the primary narrative framework, which allows Hurston to treat various other themes in the novel. The tensions between the Hebrews (or Israelites) and the Egyptians derives from the central question of religion and power. In the novel's opening pages, Pharaoh decrees a ban on male children and sets a number of other laws meant to oppress the Hebrew people, viewing the Hebrews as a threat to his power and authority. The pharaoh views the Hebrews as inferior and their worth as people is defined solely by the work they do as slaves—and even the work, according to the pharaoh, is not sufficient, as he complains about them working too slowly or not enough. But Hurston presents the Hebrews as resistors to these forms of oppression through the characters of Amram and his wife, who have a child and hide him to save his life. This child, Moses, was the product of resistance against the oppressive laws, and it is thus fitting that he is the ultimate victor over the pharaoh. Moses himself comes from a slave family; yet his slave father, Amram, holds high hopes for a son who could achieve manhood and power. Moses' ascendance in society is permitted because he grows up a free man, raised as an Egyptian by the pharaoh's daughter who claims him as her own. He thus gains opportunities that he would not have had otherwise.

Hurston characterizes Moses as a leading religious figure with mental, physical, and spiritual prowess. Although he is raised in the pharaoh's household by the pharaoh's daughter, who claims he is her own son, he will ultimately break free from the royal household after devoting himself to study and gaining much experience. While living in the pharaoh's household, Moses engages in spiritual and intellectual pursuits that will later lead to an enlightenment and the knowledge of how he is to lead. While viewed as a person of royal lineage in Egypt, Moses's actual ethnic background is hinted at, particularly when his wife accuses him of being Hebrew after hearing rumors. Moses also finds himself responsible for killing an Egyptian foreman who was taunting a Hebrew man; this symbolizes his early empathy toward the Hebrew people. In fact, the event with the foreman becomes a catalyst in his life, the turning point at which he begins to realize his fate as the leader of the Hebrews. The animosity toward Moses propels him to leave Egypt, and thus begin his important spiritual and religious journey. During his travels, Moses sees Mount Sinai (or Horeb), which symbolizes divinity, and the relation between man, nature, and divinity. Sinai functions as a religious site in the novel, and important revelations and battles occur there.

Moses' encounter with Jethro and his family in Midian becomes a pivotal moment in his spiritual odyssey. Moses gains the favor of Jethro and his family after he helps them retrieve some missing livestock. Jethro and Moses share knowledge and experience, most notably about religion. Jethro eventually transforms Moses into a priest figure, granting him special powers that enable him to transform the world. For example, he causes frogs to appear to encourage Zeppo and his family to leave Jethro's household. Here, especially, we see a connection between this novel and the conjuring stories that Hurston tells elsewhere. Jethro himself acknowledges Moses's conjuring power, calling him "the finest hoodoo man in the world." These powers continue after a journey to Koptos, in which Moses retrieves the book from the river and internalizes its contents by copying the ideas onto paper, soaking the paper in beer, and drinking the beer. Later, after returning to Midian, Jethro informs Moses of the journey he will have to take. He must free the Hebrews, and inform them of the real God. Through his evolving powers over nature, Moses becomes a conduit between the people and God.

There are many scenes in this novel where Hurston presents a connection between nature and religion; the spiritual often reveals itself to humans through the natural world. Most dramatic is perhaps the episode in which Moses travels up the mountain and sees the burning bush. There, a divine voice speaks to Moses. It tells him that he walks on divine earth and instructs him to go to Egypt and free the people there. Moses also obtains the rod, which enables him to utilize his powers. This experience changes Moses, causing him to realize that he must take on the role of leader. The event propels Moses forward in his resolve. He returns to Egypt and informs Israeli elders that he comes as a messenger from God, trying to establish his leadership role. He meets some people at a grove, revealing to them the truth about God and laying down rules, such as the rule against eating pork.

Hurston's depiction of Ta-Phar, later Pharaoh, and his priests stands in contrast to that of Moses. Hurston emphasizes the struggle between slavery and freedom in the interaction between Moses and Ta-Phar, the new pharaoh. Ta-Phar symbolizes captivity and oppression, and as a character he is portrayed as being deceitful, power-hungry, and contemptuous. Moses must illustrate to the Egyptians that he possesses special power that surpasses that of the priests. As pharaoh, Ta-Phar is shown as contemptuous, refusing to believe in Moses' powers. When Moses shows him the power of his rod, Ta-Phar is fearful and devises many plans to try to trick Moses into thinking he has the same abilities. The charade continues, with Ta-Phar pretending he too can turn water into blood. At this point, Moses begins a series of plagues to harm the people of Egypt. The plagues include frogs, lice, flies, boils, locusts, dying cattle, and darkness. Ta-Phar is revealed to be a deceitful man, as he continues to promise to free the Hebrews just to have Moses' plagues end but then does not free them. Only at the last plague, darkness, does the pharaoh agree to free the Hebrews, but even then their freedom does not come without a fight.

Moses can finally lead the Exodus of Hebrews out of Egypt and to newfound freedom. The pharaoh decides that he wants the Hebrews to come back, and he wages war, but Moses overcomes him with his powers. Moses performs the miracle of dividing the Red Sea so that his people can march through it, and then he closes it up again when the Egyptians follow, defeating and killing them. Finally, Moses uses his special powers, specifically the rod, to help the Hebrews to win in the battle against the Amalekites. Once they have won, Moses tells Joshua they should head toward Sinai. He leads his people to the divine Mount Sinai, and he produces food and water for his people to survive on. Moses' special powers and his message to the people about the importance of God all reinforce his stature as a natural leader for a people being liberated, physically and spiritually. In fact, Moses' journeys throughout the novel represent his movement toward a closer relationship with God. More generally, the Exodus of the Hebrews, an important event in the Old Testament of the Bible, represents the journey from slavery to freedom.

Hurston's novel suggests the struggle of the Hebrews to accept their new identity. Moses' devotion to God and the people's devotion to their previous religious traditions prove to be in conflict. Upon returning from Sinai, Moses discovers that the Hebrews are worshiping a calf as an idol, suggesting that they still are attached to their old pagan ways. They view the calf and the pagan gods, rather than Moses and God, as responsible for their liberation. This illustrates the tension between the old and new ways of worship. Despite Moses's feats and his delivering them from Egyptian rule, they still cling to old religious habits. Moses instructs others to kill those who are involved in the calf worship, including some of Aaron's children, which would lead to further rivalry between the two. Then, to establish a place for worshiping God, Moses creates a tabernacle, where he converses with God. God instructs him to take stone tablets to the top of Mount Sinai, where his laws will be set in stone. Moses places them in the tabernacle for the people to see, showing his function both as a spiritual leader for the Hebrews but also as a follower of God. One of Moses' chief struggles remains his desire to promote a theology for the Hebrews despite their resistance.

The tension between Moses and the Hebrews is a defining factor in the novel, as Moses must constantly deal with people who, despite having been liberated, are dissatisfied still. "The Israelites are constantly faced with a choice as well; obedience to God's laws and commandments, as expressed by Moses, his agent and their leader, or personal, independent action that could be described as creative rather than merely rebellious" (Lowe 206). Hurston presents numerous examples of people resisting Moses or lacking confidence in him. For example, the elders become upset about the lack of food, and many are unwilling to fight to enter the Promised Land. Because of this, Moses makes the people return to the wilderness for four decades until he feels they are ready to live in the Promised Land. Hurston thus illustrates that the journey from slavery to freedom is a complicated one. Instead of transforming to lives of comfort and bliss following their liberation from the Egyptians, many of the hostile, doubtful, or unappreciative Hebrews do not value the struggle. They complain about not having adequate water or food. Because of their unfitness to reach the Promised Land, Moses exiles them into the wilderness for many decades, demonstrating that liberation from slavery does not necessarily equate to freedom in a fuller sense.

The voyage to the Promised Land proves to be a monumental struggle for Moses and the Hebrews, especially because of personal conflicts with Miriam and Aaron. Aaron has spent much of his life attempting to thwart Moses, and he ultimately tries to undermine

Moses' role as a leader of the Exodus; in fact, on Mount Sinai, he argues that he could be a better leader than Moses, and so he wants to be a high priest. Moses kills Aaron, then bestows the title of high priest upon his son. At the end of the novel, Moses speaks with Joshua about his experience on Mount Sinai when God passed down the laws to him, and he reflects upon the new religion versus the old pagan ways. From the vantage of Nebo, Moses looks upon Canaan and considers his life and his role as leader of the Hebrews, but he experiences disappointment. It is only at the end, while on Mount Nebo, that Moses realizes he did not achieve liberation for the Hebrew people: Individuals cannot be free until they feel free inside themselves, he realizes. And yet he knows that the Israelites possess law, military power, and God.

Moses and the story of the Hebrews resonate in the African-American literary tradition, due to the parallels between the enslaved Egyptians and the enslaved blacks. African Americans appropriated the figure of Moses to symbolize their hope for emancipation from slavery since, in this particular novel, "Moses leads his people from bondage and slavery into the land of Canaan, a land of new promise and freedom" (Stanford 115). There are thus many connections between the story of Moses as told here and the story of blacks in America. There is the sense that freedom may involve a mental, emotional, and psychological dimension that accompanies the physical state of liberation. The move from oppression and captivity to freedom requires more than the geographical space in which to act freely; the novel thus suggests that freedom for the Hebrews—and by extension for African Americans—is a spiritual as well as physical journey.

Gender

As in other Hurston novels, gender roles play an important part in *Moses, Man of the Mountain.* Notions of masculinity and femininity are important determiners for the characters' actions, as Hurston positions characters in relation to their acceptance or rejection of traditional gender roles. Manliness can be seen as representing strength, bravery, courage, and leadership; the roles of father, husband, and leader are the sources of power. Femininity is defined less on its own terms than in relation to the men—itself a revealing fact—and women are often seen as subservient or simply relying upon the actions and strengths of men.

Manhood, or manliness, serves as an important characteristic in the novel, especially in Hurston's portrayal of Moses himself. Moses is characterized by opposition to the pharaoh, who, while strong, practices the illegitimate form of authority of dictators. The pharaoh possesses social, political, and economic control over the Egyptians and the Hebrews. He is threatened by the idea of Hebrew manhood as a direct challenge to his authority, so he decrees that all newborn males will be killed. Female children, on the other hand, are not perceived as being a threat to his power.

Moses represents the greatest individual challenge to the pharaoh, and while he is portrayed as a strong, brave man, that is not the only way in which he challenges the pharaoh's authority; it is also his spiritual powers, his relation to God, that ultimately triumphs over the pharaoh. While the pharaoh exerts power in economic, social, and political ways, he cannot compete with Moses's connection to a higher religious power. This is ultimately what distinguishes the two men: Moses leads using strength and compassion, while Pharaoh leads with terror.

Moses assumes his manliness through his military knowledge and skill. He illustrates this by winning a trophy at a military contest and proving to be more adept than Ta-Phar. As a tribute to his skill, Moses later becomes head of the military; later, he would practice a subtler but more powerful leadership role as liberator of the Hebrews. Hurston also presents Moses as a wise man in his roles as judge and as lawgiver. Hurston depicts Moses' journeys after leaving Egypt initially as a quest toward manhood and identity formation. When he sees the young women in trouble, Moses comes to the rescue, and ultimately ends up marrying one of them, Zipporah. Her father, Jethro, is also a strong symbol of masculine power and patriarchy; in Jethro's household, the women serve food to the men, clearly showing that gender roles are upheld in the family. Jethro even regrets that he does not have other male offspring, which may explain his very close relationship with Moses. He is a mentor to Moses, and Moses his student. More significantly, he "becomes a father to Moses and teaches him everything he knows, just as the old stableman Mentu had done during Moses's youth" (Boyd 333).

Moses expresses affection toward his wife, but his ultimate devotion to his leadership, spiritual, and military pursuits suggests a strain in their relationship and that she serves as a secondary figure in Moses' life. Moses spends much time with Jethro, and it is often Jethro who he misses when he is far away. The relationship between Moses and Jethro reflects male bonding. Another form of male bonding is that between Moses and Joshua. Moses acts as a mentor for Joshua; he teaches him and tries to help him develop and grow as a person. Joshua is a trustworthy friend who admires and respects Moses, and he desires to follow in Moses' path.

Moses' principal relationships in the novel, then, are with other men. While Hurston depicts some of his attempts to function as a good husband and father to his sons, his most important interactions are with other men: notably Jethro, Joshua, Aaron, and Pharaoh, and to a lesser extent Mentu and Amram. In the case of Jethro and Joshua, the relationships are positive since the men's personalities are complementary and noncompetitive with Moses; with rivals Aaron and Pharaoh, on the other hand, the interactions are competitive and lead to violence. The two patriarchal powers clash, and the result is violence on the battlefield or between men. The importance of patriarchy and of male roles is seen when Moses kills Aaron and bestows priesthood on Aaron's son. In doing so, he is usurping the father role from Aaron to give power to the son. Even if not seen between Moses and his own son, the father-son relationship is important. In the various male-male clashes, Moses usually wins, of course, but again we can see that Hurston presents violence between men as the result of a conflict of power, and uniquely a masculine domain.

Hurston depicts Moses's manhood as ultimately complex. He is a brave, wise, and mighty leader, but in leading he is also nurturing to his people, a more feminine quality. He tries to play, perhaps, too many roles, both male and female. He is a conduit to God, but he is not God. As a result, he can liberate the Hebrews physically, and he can try to nurture them, but they will achieve freedom only when they are ready as individuals.

While masculinity is emphasized in this novel, femininity also play an important role. The women tend to take on traditional gender roles as wife, mother, daughter, and caregiver. Women's social, political, and economic power remains less than that of men. They are expected to be a part of the domestic rather than the public sphere. Although class affords some women more power than others, they still lack the patriarchal privilege and power of the male characters in the novel. Their identities remains linked and connected with men who function as spouse, child, or sibling.

Moses' fate is, in a sense, determined by the social expectations that are related to gender. The pharaoh's daughter, obligated to provide a male heir to the throne, needs to fulfill that role once again since her husband died. Thus, her saving of Moses is actually a self-saving act that allows her to fulfill her role as woman and mother in the royal family. Jochebed, Moses' mother, symbolizes maternal love and affection. Moses' sister, Miriam, possesses the gift of prophecy, which gives her a similar power as Moses, and this creates conflict. Miriam's access to power lay in her role as prophetess, which is compromised by Moses' rise to power and his own greater gifts of prophecy. Zipporah, Moses's second wife, is an important female character, and she frequently emphasizes her desire to be admired by other people for having a husband with high status. Overall, Jochebed and Puah are portrayed as nurturing females, while Miriam and Zipporah are portrayed as manipulative and petty females.

Social Class

Moses, Man of the Mountain also serves as a commentary on social class distinctions and how they affect or relate to individuals' actions. In the novel, Hurston comments on the question of upward mobility through Moses. He has achieved his status in the royal family by accident; if he had remained a slave, he would not have had the same opportunities.

Despite being raised in Pharaoh's home, Moses aligns himself with the lower classes in choosing to defend the Hebrews. Moses' relationship with his mentor Mentu, a lower-class man, reveals his empathy for the lower classes. Mentu helps him and earns great respect from Moses. Mentu understands his own low status, indicating that he should not have viewed Moses in the military contest, but he wanted to see Moses in action. When Mentu dies, Moses ensures that he receives a proper funeral. Before he leads them, he believes Hebrews should have equal rights as Egyptians, such as enlisting in the military and becoming citizens. His killing of an Egyptian who was taunting a Hebrew is such an example. The irony is that Moses himself came from a lowly slave family; unbeknownst to him, he remains close to his roots. He "repudiates his position of power in Pharaoh's court and chooses to side with his people, the oppressed Hebrews, because he feels compassion for their plight" (Stanford 114–115). Later, as leader of the Hebrews, he resists the opportunity to fully capitalize on the status accorded him by his people. When the people desire him to have a crown, he refuses.

Hurston reveals the reliance of the upper class on the lower classes. Hurston depicts

Ta-Phar's resistance to freeing the Hebrews as mostly economic: What he cares about most is having the Hebrews there to do work for him. In fact, his status as a rule rests entirely on his power over a subjugated people, as he is shown to be politically and militarily weak in the face of his enemies. In Midian, the social structure is far different, as there is no slave class. Leaders and common people are part of the same society, even if there are still class distinctions—as evidenced by the fact that Jethro possesses servants. Zipporah often talks about class, wealth, and image. For example, Zipporah instructs Moses to don fine clothes to impress others; Jethro says she does this because she wants other women to envy her. Her desire to travel to Egypt is rooted in the same obsession with status, as she wants to experience his royal background there. Otherwise, Zipporah's interactions with Miriam are fraught with class and status tensions. Miriam, insecure about her own position, dislikes Zipporah and remarks upon the differences in class between the two of them. Since she is so obsessed with status, Moses teaches her a lesson by temporarily transforming her into a leper and banishing her from the camp.

Nature

Hurston presents the connection between the natural world and the spiritual world as an integral part of this retelling of the Moses story from the Bible. In this novel, nature—in the form of animals, insects, water, and mountains—plays an important role. It serves as a source of spirituality, life, and death; it is where humans and God connect.

The novel's title, *Moses, Man of the Mountain,* indicates that the mountain is a very important aspect of this story. The mountain functions as a symbol of God and God's power over humanity; the mountain is where Moses goes to communicate with God, and also for solitude and reflection. Some of the most important scenes of the book occur on the mountain, such as when Moses gets the rod, when he writes down the commandments from God, and when he reflects upon his life at the end of the story. Moses, through his engagement with nature, proves to be an important bridge between the natural world and the spiritual world, ultimately making use of the natural world to lead his people in spiritual development. Moses also possesses the ability to manipulate, control, or transform the natural world using what amounts to conjuring.

Hurston presents Moses as being connected with nature early on, when he is placed in the basket to drift in the Nile River. The suggestion is that Moses's fate is being left to nature to decide. The Nile River thus becomes a source of life for young Moses, for it is here that he is rescued. Growing up in the pharaoh's household, he seeks to learn more about the natural world though his mentor Mentu. Mentu teaches Moses about lizards, for example, and also about horses, which gives Moses an edge in his later military activities. It is also Mentu who reveals the secret about the book buried in the river, which becomes a central quest of Moses' life. In his travels to Koptos, he finds the box in the river and battles a snake, further suggesting his power over nature.

Hurston illustrates Moses' special relationship with nature throughout the novel, but he really begins to commune with nature once he leaves Egypt. Jethro believes that

Moses is "the son of the mountain," and he will introduce Moses to the mountain, but only when he is ready. With Jethro, Moses also studies to be a priest and develops a mastery over nature: he can cause animals and insects to appear and he can produce changes in weather conditions. Once he does travel up the mountain, he witnesses the burning bush and hears a voice from the heavens. The voice, which represents God, tells him to free the Hebrews and informs him that it will join him during his journey. He also obtains his wooden rod, which can turn into a snake and which he uses to wield God's power. Moses uses his special powers to control or produce natural events in his dealings with Ta-Phar. First he turns water to blood and makes his rod turn into a snake. And each time Ta-Phar refuses to free the Hebrews, Moses produces a plague, including frogs, lice, flies, hail, and darkness. These natural events affect the land and people, and Pharaoh says they can leave. During the journey, they see a fire, which Moses says represents God. Most significantly, Moses divides the Red Sea so they can walk across it. Here again, water is a force for life, but it also brings death.

Moses believes that Mount Sinai demonstrates the power of God and that the mountain will inspire people to have faith in God. Hurston writes that the mountain is "the altar of the world." God communicates with Moses from the mountaintop, giving him orders and the commandments to bring to his people. The commandments themselves are inscribed on stone tablets, themselves evoking the nature theme, as the word of God is written on the natural material. In the episode with the calf worship, the calf is actually not a real calf, but an artificial calf; this is crucial, because the people are thus not worshiping a product of God, but a product of man. The Hebrews must also interact with nature when Moses casts them into the wilderness after realizing they are not ready for life in Canaan, or the Promised Land. Hurston presents Moses's final engagement with nature when he heads up Mount Nebo with his rod. He contemplates his life as he looks out over the landscape, and he communicates with a lizard. He raises his rod, causing the mountain to tremble and thunder to burst out. While on the mountain, however, he also constructs his own tomb, where he will return to the earth: while he has special connection to God and to nature, in the end he is a man, not a God, and thus is mortal like all other men.

CHARACTERS

Aaron As the brother of Moses, he serves as a foil to Moses' power. At Moses' birth, he stands watch, along with his sister, for the authorities, but later he proves to be Moses' nemesis. Jealous at his brother's power, he believes that Moses does not respect him. At the end, on the mountain, he tells Moses that he would be a better leader for the Hebrews than Moses, and Moses kills him, conferring priestly duties on Aaron's son instead. Aaron serves as a cautionary example of one of the unconverted, still challenging Moses' role and unfit for Canaan.

Amram Amram is the father of Moses, Miriam, and Aaron. He is a Hebrew slave who represents defiance of his oppressors, as they hide their son instead of allowing him to be killed by the authorities. He even hopes for a male child who will assert himself. Amram's decision to let his son live allows Moses to lead the people out of slavery.

Caleb He is another slave and a friend of Amram's. The two speak about their oppression as slaves.

Jethro Jethro, also known as Ruel, is the father of Zipporah, whom Moses marries. As father-in-law, he maintains a very close relationship with Moses, teaching him about nature and power. Jethro confers powers on Moses and calls Moses "the finest hoodoo man in the world." As Moses leads his people, Jethro stands beside him and offers encouragement and advice. He is characterized as a patriarch and a leader who is fair, understanding, and wise. He and his family live in Midian.

Jochebed Jochebed is Moses' mother, a Hebrew slave and the wife of Amram. By hiding her male son, she shows defiance against the tyrannical authority of the pharaoh. She places her child in a basket to float in the Nile River, saving his life and sealing his fate.

Joshua Joshua is a main follower and protégé of Moses. He respects him and desires to serve him.

He is an able military man, who plays a major role in the defeat of the Amalekites. Joshua accompanies Moses to the mountain when God gives him the commandments. He is impressed by the power of what Moses does on the mountain. Hurston portrays Joshua as a positive and heroic figure who demonstrates courage and manhood.

Mentu Mentu teaches Moses about nature and animals, especially horses, and helps him become skilled at military affairs. Mentu informs Moses of the special book in the river. He is a low-ranking servant, but Moses respects him deeply; when Mentu dies, Moses assures that he gets a proper burial.

Miriam Moses's sister, Miriam kept watch at his birth and observes him being rescued from the river by the pharaoh's daughter. Later on, she causes problems for Moses upon his return to Egypt. She and her brother Aaron grow to resent Moses and his influence upon the Hebrews. She too is a prophetess, but her powers are no match for Moses', and she becomes jealous. She is also jealous of Moses' wife, Zipporah, for her beauty and the attention she gets from others. To punish her, Moses temporarily turns Miriam into a leper, and she later comes to understand Moses' power.

Moses The main character in the novel, he is the biblical figure who leads the Hebrews to freedom from the Egyptians. He is a unifying figure, linking men with nature, lower classes with upper classes, Hebrews with Egyptians, and people with God. Moses has a unique relationship with the environment, and has powers allowing him to alter the physical world. He is portrayed as a wise, strong leader who cares about his people but is also willing to use force and violence to achieve his goals. The figure of Moses has historically been used by many African Americans to represent the journey from slavery to freedom for blacks in America. Moses was thus viewed as a liberator of the oppressed, and his character was used as an invocation of hope against hardship.

Moses is born to a Hebrew at a time when male Hebrew children were killed by Egyptian authorities. His parents place him in a basket into the Nile River, where he is rescued by the daughter of the pharaoh, who uses him to provide the kingdom with a male heir. In the royal household, Moses learns about military activities and becomes skilled. Even growing up among the Egyptians, Moses wants Hebrews to be citizens and be treated fairly. He kills an Egyptian foreman in defense of a Hebrew, an event that leads him to Midian, where he meets his wife, Zipporah, and her father, Jethro. He studies divinity and nature and ultimately is called by God to lead the Hebrews to freedom.

Moses possesses a direct connection to God, with whom he is able to communicate. He speaks with God on Mount Sinai, where he is given a powerful rod that allows him to manipulate the natural world. He fights against Ta-Phar, the pharaoh, by releasing plagues in order to convince him to free the Hebrews. He parts the Red Sea, defeats the Egyptians, and leads his people toward the Promised Land, or Canaan. His people want to crown him king, but he refuses. Moses kills his brother, Aaron, on Mount Sinai and bestows priestly duties on Aaron's son. Before the Hebrews reach Canaan, Moses makes them wander in the wilderness for four decades, to prove their fitness. At the end, Moses is weary and disappointed, realizing that freedom is a state of mind that each individual must possess. He prepares his tomb on Mount Nebo and speaks with a lizard.

Pharaoh Pharaoh is the father of Ta-Phar and of the woman who raises Moses as her son; he is the tyrannical ruler of Egypt. He is responsible for the ban on male Hebrew births and other oppressive measures.

Puah Puah is the midwife who aids in the birth of Moses. Like other midwives, she is suspected of being an informant to the authorities, but that is not substantiated.

Ta-Phar Ta-Phar is the son of Pharaoh, and he later becomes the new pharaoh. Moses defeats him in a military contest and becomes leader of the army, making Ta-Phar jealous. As pharaoh, he is the chief enemy of Moses, refusing to free the Hebrews despite Moses' many plagues. After his son dies, he agrees to let the Hebrews leave, but then changes his mind. He dies when Moses closes the Red Sea on him and the Egyptians, drowning them all.

Zeppo Zeppo is a relative of Jethro's who overstays his welcome in Jethro's house. To get rid of him, Moses conjures frogs, which sends Zeppo out of the house, but he is angered by the plot to drive him out and writes a letter of complaint to Jethro.

Zipporah She is the second wife of Moses and the daughter of Jethro. Moses comes to her aid when she is being harassed by other men. Due to her father's role as a leader in Midian, she maintains a position of privilege, and she is preoccupied by image and prestige. She wants to go to Egypt with Moses so that she can experience royal life, and possibly so that he can become king. Zipporah presents a threat to Miriam, and they have some disagreements. She also has dark skin, a source of prejudice for Miriam and others. Hurston includes the details about her dark skin as a subtle but significant comment on racism and to draw a further connection to the situation of African Americans.

BIBLIOGRAPHY

Boyd, Valerie. *Wrapped in Rainbows: The Life of Zora Neale Hurston.* New York: Scribner, 2003.

Howard, Lillie P. *Zora Neale Hurston.* Boston: Twayne, 1980.

Hurston, Zora Neale. *Moses, Man of the Mountain.* In her *Novels and Stories,* 335–595. New York: Library of America, 1995.

Jones, Sharon L. *Rereading the Harlem Renaissance: Race, Class, and Gender in the Fiction of Jessie Fauset, Zora Neale Hurston, and Dorothy West.* Westport, Conn.: Greenwood Press, 2002.

Lowe, John. *Jump at the Sun: Zora Neale Hurston's Cosmic Comedy.* Urbana: University of Illinois Press, 1994.

Stanford, Ann Folwell. "Dynamics of Change: Men and Co-Feeling in the Fiction of Zora Neale Hurston and Alice Walker." In *Alice Walker and Zora Neale Hurston: The Common Bond,* edited by Lillie P. Howard, 109–119. Westport, Conn.: Greenwood Press, 1993.

"Mother Catherine" (1934)

"Mother Catherine" is a nonfiction profile of a woman by that name who practices a synthesis of religious forms. The story reflects Hurston's interest in religion. The text illustrates the pantheistic nature of some religious traditions in which people blend theologies from different denominations in their worship. This story, along with "Uncle Monday," appeared in *Negro: An Anthology* (1934), edited by Nancy Cunard, a landmark anthology devoted to publishing black cultural expression. In the anthology, she "emphasized the originality and artfulness of black expression, from dancing to dialect, from lovemaking to prayer" (Boyd 254). Alongside Alain Locke's 1925 *The New Negro, Negro: An Anthology* functions as an important record of Harlem Renaissance literature.

SYNOPSIS

Hurston describes the chapel of Mother Catherine, or Mother Seal, featuring white, blue, and red hues, with an African-inspired snake picture, and a tent. Mother Catherine's "compound is called the Manger." Hurston tells Mother Catherine she wants to learn more about her and her teachings, so she observes Mother Catherine for a couple of weeks. Mother Catherine prizes being original, and she values the animal world. She holds a pantheistic service, blending together different religions. Her theology centers on matriarchy, and childbirth is important. Mother Catherine also performs healing on people. According to Hurston, Mother Catherine felt the need to be a religious figure and led a chaste life for purity; she also stopped eating at times. She did have a husband, but he left her. Mother Catherine's congregation grew, which made her ministry expand to the current place.

Women devotees wear a veil, and men followers wear a band on one arm.

CRITICAL COMMENTARY

In this text Hurston chronicles her experiences with Mother Catherine, a matriarch who promotes her own version of syncretism, or a blending of religious practices, embracing ideas from different denominations. In a way, it valorizes other religions by borrowing from their belief systems. Hurston's presentation of "Mother Catherine" elevates the ideas of motherhood, which is an important theme throughout Hurston's fiction. As a maternal figure, she nurtures, heals, and cares for her congregation. She even centers her theology on the ideas of the matriarchy, which challenges patriarchal notions of religion in which men are the leaders in the church. She puts value on childbirth as a sacred act; women function as life givers, important to sustaining the human race. Mother Catherine's theology also focuses on life-giving properties, such as bearing children and healing people. She functions as a healer, using spirituality to cure people; this is an alternative to Western medical beliefs. The text reveals the ways in which Afrocentric cultural ideas blend with other traditions to produce a theology, and more largely the significance of spirituality and religion to the African-American experience.

BIBLIOGRAPHY

Boyd, Valerie. *Wrapped in Rainbows: The Life of Zora Neale Hurston.* New York: Scribner, 2003.

Howard, Lillie P. *Zora Neale Hurston.* Boston: Twayne Publishers, 1980.

Hurston, Zora Neale. "Mother Catherine." In her *The Complete Stories,* 99–105. New York: HarperCollins, 1995.

Mule Bone: A Comedy of Negro Life (1931)

This play is about a crime committed in an African-American community in the South. It was coauthored with fellow HARLEM RENAISSANCE writer LANGSTON HUGHES in the 1930s. The play, which was influenced by Hurston's story "The Bone of Contention," is a comical look at life in the community of EATONVILLE, FLORIDA. Although Hurston was known primarily as a novelist, *Mule Bone* reveals her interest in playwriting and her desire to represent the black experience on stage. Although this play was not staged while Hughes or Hurston was alive, it has subsequently been produced on stage, and the text itself enables the reader to experience Hurston's work in a theatrical collaboration. The play also reveals the continuing importance of Hurston's time spent in Eatonville, and how that would contribute to her work. Details "sprang from Hurston's memories of Eatonville" and Hurston placed these recollections from Eatonville "onstage to fulfill a new concept of drama, which she and Hughes were developing in tandem" (Wall 155).

Many different people were involved in the composing of this play. While neither Hughes nor Hurston initially revealed to their patron, CHARLOTTE OSGOOD MASON, that they were working on this together, they eventually did when they needed money to pay their typist

Langston Hughes and Arna Bontemps. Photograph by Griffith Davis *(Yale Collection of American Literature, Beinecke Rare Book and Manuscript Library)*

(Boyd 197, 201). Hughes wanted to make sure that there be a principal female role, and that the final scene be set by the rail tracks, while Hurston contributed the Eatonville setting. As the two composed the manuscript, Hurston would speak the characters' parts, altering "her voice to suit each character" (Boyd 200).

Conflicts about the play between Hurston and Hughes—most of them involving production, payment, and copyright credit—caused a rift in their relationship.

SYNOPSIS

Act One

The play begins at the store owned by Joe Clarke, a powerful businessman and politician in Eatonville. People speak to each other. Mrs. Roberts arrives, and she tells Joe Clarke that she doesn't have enough food, saying "me and my poor chillun is starvin'." He gives her some meat and she walks away. Men discuss Mrs. Roberts, disgusted at her behavior. Joe Lindsay approaches, carrying a mule bone, from the mule owned by Brazzle. He speaks about that mule's death, and how, when it died, it was dragged "to de swamp," a well-attended event. Senator Bailey asks Clarke about Daisy, then leaves as the other men discuss where Daisy could be. Bootsie and Teets appear, talk, and then depart throughout the scene. Daisy approaches and tells Clarke that her mother asked her to get food. Walter asks her who she prefers between Dave and Jim and says that if two men are attracted to a woman, then the friendship between those two men will end.

Mrs. Clarke tells her husband someone wants a stamp. Brazzle tells Hambo he did not see him at the picnic, and he says he did not go to it. Walter then criticizes the Baptist picnic. Lige tells a story about a Baptist man. Joe Clarke plays a game of checkers, then requests that the marshal get the children to leave. Lum has an exchange with a child about moving. Hambo apparently beats the mayor at checkers. Clarke comments on the loss; he goes back in his store. Mrs. Clarke calls to Lum as the mayor wants him to "tie up old lady Jackson's mule." Joe Clarke calls to his wife, and she goes within the store. Someone mentions that Elder Simms is approaching, so Frank gathers his cards and hides them. Lige tells a story about a snake, and Frank and Simms proceed to comment on snakes. Simms then changes the subject and he suggests changes for the town, saying it should have a prison. Mattie tells Joe about someone wanting something, and then he complains about ministers and women.

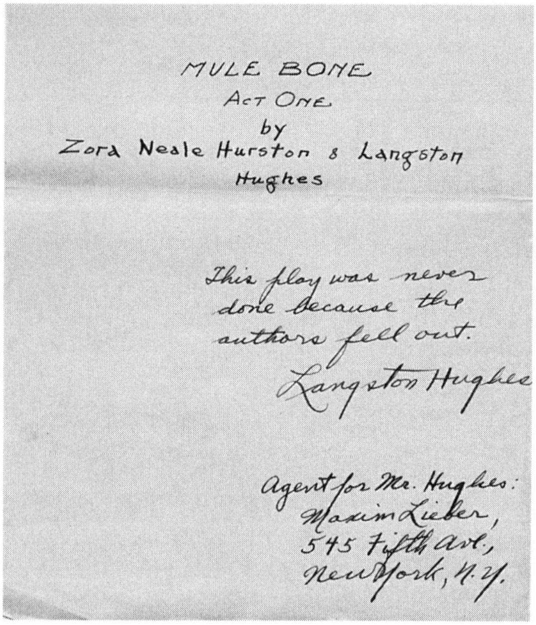

Draft of *Mule Bone: A Comedy of Negro Life in Three Acts,* 1930 *(Yale Collection of American Literature, Beinecke Rare Book and Manuscript Library)*

Jim and Dave approach, talking about Daisy. Bootsie and Teets come and go.

Jim says he is not ready to marry. Daisy approaches Jim and Dave, and she compliments them. Daisy says she wants some chewing gum. Dave offers to buy some gum for her from the store, which he does and then comes out to give it to her. But Jim has already given her some gum. Clarke comes out of his store and tells Lum to light the lamp for their community. Jim and Dave begin singing; people seem to enjoy this performance, and Daisy dances with Dave. Jim stops singing when he sees Daisy and Dave dancing. The men proceed to criticize each other and argue. Daisy claims she needs to return to the white people she works for. Dave offers to get Daisy something, and she asks for a soda. They go in the store and return with soda. However, Jim causes Dave to splatter his drink on his clothing. Daisy wants to leave and tells them not to fight. They fight anyway, and finally Jim hits Dave with the mule bone. Clarke tells him that he will be arrested for this, and Lum arrests him. Clarke declares there will be a trial in the Baptist church. Daisy is concerned about getting home.

Act Two
Scene 1
The scene takes place on the street. Sister Thomas and Sister Taylor converse, with Sister Thomas reading information about the trial for Jim being held in the church. Sister Thomas criticizes Baptists and Sister Taylor suggests that Joe Clarke be expelled from the Methodist church. Sister Jones approaches; she says she plans to attend the meeting. Elder Simms approaches and says he wants to speak with Jim prior to the trial. Clarke speaks to the two sisters, and Sister Taylor expresses her concern about Clarke judging Jim in a Baptist church, since he is a Methodist. Clarke claims that he ultimately cares about justice. Clarke tells Lum to find Dave and the mule bone. Mrs. Taylor and Lindsay insult each other. The children discuss Baptists and Methodists.

Scene II
The scene takes place in the Macedonia Baptist Church. Reverend Simms, Lum, and Jim approach as the crowd chatters. Reverend Childers and Dave follow. There is much commotion. Sister Lewis and Sister Taylor insult each other, nearly ending in a fight. Joe Clarke enters and requests his gavel, then declares that women should be quiet. Lum returns with the gavel and mule bone. Clarke

begins the trial with a prayer, and then says, "This town is bout to be tore up by backbiting and malice and mouthy women." Clarke counts the witnesses. Lindsay says he doesn't want anyone insulting his wife. Mrs. Nixon says he does not follow words with action; Clarke tells Mrs. Nixon to be quiet, and she counters with the claim that Clarke abuses his wife. Clarke says she will not be able to get free food from his store anymore. Reverend Simms decries the location of the trial in the Baptist church, and Clarke defends it. Children talk and sing about religion, and Clarke tells them to be quiet.

Dave and Jim comment on their fight. Daisy's mother claims that her daughter was headed to her white employer during that event, and Sister Anderson comments on Daisy's behavior. Her mom defends her by claiming that she is "a lady" and that "mens get stuck on her." Lum reads a list of people who claim to have witnessed the event, although not all of them did. Clarke eventually says they will proceed with the trial and asks Lum for testimony. Lum says he did not see much because he was dealing with his mule. Clarke questions Hambo, who says he is not certain what happened. He says there was a dispute and that a person "hit this boy in de head with a mule bone." Sister Pitts testifies that she did not see it; however, she claims that Dave is not capable of harming others, and she criticizes Jim. Dave gives his testimony, saying Jim caused his drink to spill on his clothing. He says he hit Jim, and later Jim assaulted him using the mule bone. Jim admits to the assault, but claims it was "no crime."

Simms later says that Jim did not commit any criminal act. He claims that the bone of a mule is not actually a weapon. Childers disagrees, claiming that Jim caused harm to Dave. Childers reads from a biblical passage about Samson killing Philistines using a bone from an ass. Simms counters that the bone in this case came from a mule. Childers and Simms argue, and Childers maintains that Jim should have to leave their community. Clarke tells Jim that he must leave Eatonville for a certain time period. The court session ends.

Act Three

The scene is in a forest. Jim approaches with a guitar, claiming he does not want to return to the town. Jim plays his guitar as he comments. He claims Dave knows he didn't intend to do him much harm. Daisy approaches and speaks. Jim says it was both Daisy's and Dave's fault that he was sent out of town, and he says he was friends with Dave before Daisy intervened. Dave approaches. Jim claims to have affection for Daisy. Dave asks which of them Daisy has more affection for. She eventually says she wishes to wed Jim, but then expresses concern about their future. She says he can gain employment doing chores instead of his music, but he is not interested in that kind of work. She proposes the same to Dave, but he feels the same as Jim. He tells her to wed Jim. Daisy ultimately says, "Neither one of y'all don't have to have me." She leaves, and Dave and Jim converse. Dave insists that Jim return to Eatonville, and Jim agrees. The play ends with Dave and Jim performing.

CRITICAL COMMENTARY

Hurston and Hughes's *Mule Bone* presents a provocative exploration of the intricacies and complexities of life in this black southern town, and it does so in the framework of a minimal story line; as Cheryl Wall, in *Women of the Harlem Renaissance,* writes, the play has "a whisper of a plot" (156).

In this play, the divide between men and women remains very significant, and it is seen in marriage and romantic relationships. Daisy is the object of desire for Jim and Dave, and each tries to impress her with his manliness and valor, such as when they compete to give her some gum. The two men compete for the affections of Daisy, who becomes a type of sexual object for them. The rivalry leads to a fight, when Jim hits Dave with the mule bone. Later, during the court scene, Mrs. Nixon points out that Joe Clarke abuses his wife when he tells her to be quiet. In the same scene, Clarke's attitudes toward women are revealed when he complains about "mouthy women" in his opening prayer.

Ironically, Daisy, who contributed to the episode leading to the crime, is not present at the trial, although she is talked about there. Her mother says that her daughter was headed to her work and thus could not attend. Sister Anderson comments on the behavior of Daisy, and her mother argues that Daisy is "a lady" and that "mens get stuck on her," suggesting that Daisy played no deliberate role in the drama that unfolded. At the end of the play, when Daisy speaks to Jim and Dave, she says she wants to wed Jim, but she has specific demands about his employment, which do not include his music. Neither Dave nor Jim wants to comply, and then Daisy wants neither of them. Jim and Dave are friends again at the end and ultimately do not allow Daisy to come between them. While Daisy and other minor female characters are presented as objects of desire for the men, these characters also possess agency.

In addition, Daisy symbolizes the working class, as she is employed by whites and dependent on them for her economic livelihood. She worries about money, and while she claims she wants to wed Jim, she worries about what will happen to them in the future. She wants him to get a job doing chores and to abandon his music career. Neither Jim nor Dave wants to do what Daisy wants, and Daisy abandons them both. Thus, marriage, economics, and class remain intertwined in the drama. For Daisy, marriage suggests a social and an economic arrangement, which is why she suggests that Jim "come live on de white folks' place wid me after we git married." The comment also suggests the idea of blacks being dependent on whites for economic means and sustenance.

Joe Clarke, on the other hand, is an example of an African-American entrepreneur. He wields control over others in the town socially, economically, and politically. In his role as a judge, he determines the fates of individuals through legal means. His store also functions as the center of the community; it is where people congregate and converse. The store symbolizes the cultural and social fabric of the town. When Jim assaults Dave with the mule bone, Clarke decides he must be arrested and that the trial will take place in the Baptist church. During the trial at Macedonia Baptist Church, Clarke asserts himself as the judge and tries to control the outcome of the trial. Clarke in effect has the power to run the trial and, in the end, to banish the accused. His authority is vested in him as a judge, but his influence derives from his position in the community as well.

Religion is important to the residents of Eatonville in *Mule Bone,* with the Baptists and Methodists serving as the two main denominations in the play. Characters emphasize perceived differences between Baptists and Methodists, and the affiliation of individuals in the town remains a vital part of their identities. When Joe Clarke determines that the mule bone trial will take place in a Baptist church, a controversy stirs; however, Clarke claims that he is more interested in justice than in the religious arguments. And yet the trial's setting in the church reflects the connection between justice and religion; Clarke even begins this trial by praying. During a discussion about whether a mule bone is a weapon, Childers cites the Samson story from the Bible, which is an attempt to use the Bible as a basis for an argument in a legal case. Even the children discuss the topic of Baptists and Methodists, suggesting at an early age they are aware of the religious attitudes in the town and have adopted this ideology; during the court hearing, they even sing about religion.

Mules play an important role in the works of Zora Neale Hurston, in this drama as well as in texts such as *Mules and Men* and *Their Eyes Were Watching God.* In *Mule Bone,* Brazzle's mule is at the center of the controversy. When Jim hits Dave with the mule bone, he gets arrested and is punished. The mule bone ultimately symbolizes nature, justice, violence, and power within the context of the play, but it represents different things to different people. For Simms, the mule bone is not really a weapon, while the ultimate ruling shows that it is.

CHARACTERS

Carter, Dave A Baptist, Dave seeks the affections of Daisy. His desire to win Daisy illustrates his masculinity. He is also an entertainer, and he performs with his friend Jim. Dave is assaulted by Jim using a mule bone, but they reconcile at the end.

Clarke, Joe As a politician, business owner, and judge, he wields considerable power. He is a black entrepreneur. A Methodist, he presides over a trial in a Baptist church and chooses Jim's punishment. During the trial, it is said that Clarke abuses his wife.

Taylor, Daisy She is a working-class Methodist woman being wooed by Jim and Dave. She seems to revel in their attentions and serves as a romantic object for them, although she rejects them both at the end. When Jim hits Dave with the mule bone, Daisy goes home; although she helped to instigate this situation, she does not appear at the trial. Within an earlier version of this play, it's important to note that in Act II, Scene II, the character Daisy Taylor is referred to as Daisy Blunt. The character Daisy Blunt in *Their Eyes Were Watching God* is sought after by Jim and Dave, which suggests carry-over among Hurston's work.

Weston, Jim Jim is a Methodist who plays the guitar and works as an entertainer. Jim hits his friend Dave with a mule bone as they fight over the attention of Daisy. After being convicted of assault, he is banished from town.

BIBLIOGRAPHY

Boyd, Valerie. *Wrapped in Rainbows: The Life of Zora Neale Hurston.* New York: Scribner, 2003.

Hurston, Zora Neale, and Langston Hughes. *Mule Bone: A Comedy of Negro Life.* New York: HarperPerennial, 1991.

Wall, Cheryl A. *Women of the Harlem Renaissance.* Bloomington: Indiana University Press, 1995.

Mules and Men (1935)

Published in 1935, *Mules and Men* is Hurston's important anthropological work documenting African-American folklore and containing folktales and songs. Functioning as an observer-participant, Hurston presents a blend of anthropology, fiction, and autobiography in this text. The text is especially important as it is the "first book of folklore" published by an African-American person (Wall 159), and it features a foreword by FRANZ BOAS, the 20th-century anthropologist who influenced Hurston's interest in documenting these oral histories.

The text is divided into two parts. The first part chronicles Hurston's experiences traveling around Florida collecting stories from rural blacks, while the second part focuses on the author's experiences in Louisiana studying hoodoo, or conjuring. Hurston uses the same techniques as in her fiction to enrich the stories she tells here and she "devises a unifying narrative that provides a context for the tales and allows her to present a range of Southern verbal art" (Wall 159). Much of the research Hurston conducted for this work was funded by CHARLOTTE OSGOOD MASON, her wealthy white patron from New York.

SYNOPSIS

Introduction

Hurston introduces her reasons for and enthusiasm about gathering folklore, setting out her motivations and intentions. She explains the background leading up to the publication of the book, noting she was raised on folklore while growing up in EATONVILLE, FLORIDA. Later, in college, she studied anthropology, and her adviser, Franz Boas, encouraged her and helped her obtain a grant. She chose to document stories in Eatonville because of its rich folklore tradition. She reflects on the stories, involving John (or Jack), animal figures, and especially appropriation of characters and themes from the Bible. In a nod to her patron, she thanks Charlotte Osgood Mason for financing the trip in which she will collect the folktales, songs, stories, recipes, and rituals.

Part One: Folktales

I

Writing in the first person, Hurston performs as the observer and participant, thereby sharing in the learning experience with the reader, as she introduces the folklore documentation she is about to narrate. She arrives in the Maitland-Eatonville area of Florida, a sure source of information, and she observes people engaged in their daily activities: People play card games on the porch and chat. She greets the people, explaining that she has come to gather folklore. She finds a place to stay in the community so that she can become integrated into their society. Hurston stays at the home of Armetta, a woman who lives in the area, after making people promise to supply her with information for her book.

Some men show up to talk to Hurston while she is at Armetta's home and tell her they are going to a "toe-party." Before heading to the party, Hurston gets the opportunity to hear a story about a frog and the folk hero John the Conqueror (Big John de Conquer),

Anthropologist Franz Boas *(Library of Congress)*

a slave who constantly battled his master for freedom. Calvin, the storyteller, recounts that the master sends John to obtain some water. As a dutiful slave, John goes to the lake to retrieve the water. A frog jumps after being disturbed by John's actions, frightening John. A superstitious man, John mistakes the frog for a "booger," which is a variation of "bogey man." John tells his master what he saw.

In an effort to compete with the previous story, another man tells Hurston a tale in which a black man travels to heaven after his hometown of Johnstown floods. There, in heaven, he explains about the natural disaster taking place back home. Traumatized by his earlier experience, John, the black man, queries Peter to see if heaven is dry. Peter has Gabriel provide the man with dry clothing and other items. He tries to tell the angels about the flooding, but the angels seem uninterested. John complains to Peter about some man who was not impressed with his story, and Peter says it was Noah, the biblical figure in the Old Testament who survived the flooding by building an ark.

After hearing the two tales and having her appetite partly fulfilled, Hurston travels to the toe-party, an important communal event. Because she has never attended one before, another person advises her on how to behave at the event. She is told that women display their feet, and men purchase them; later, the men behave kindly to the women. This is a courtship ritual. Hurston displays her toes and she gets purchased. Later, she heads to another area, where the atmosphere is quite lively and Hurston has some alcohol. Eventually, she gets into the car bound for Eatonville, and she arrives back at Armetta's home.

II

In this section, Hurston describes the store porch as the center of activity. People tell stories, often with a focus on specific ethnic and religious groups, such as Jewish and Irish people, that have also been marginalized. According to Hurston, the popular tales in the African-American oral tradition make use of European elements as well. In this section of the book, people tell stories to Zora and to each other. There is a competition to tell the best story, which motivates the storytellers.

Ellis tells a story focusing on two siblings. One brother is a clergyman, and the other is not, though he is trying to find an identity for himself in the world. He asks God to let him know if he has a vocation to be a minister, and indeed he hears a comment telling him to preach. But his dream of becoming a preacher never comes true. After missing a chance to preach at a big religious institution, he eventually asks God again. He hears a voice again saying he should "preach." Then he sees a mule and realizes who made the comment. Convinced he should not preach, he becomes a farmer and plows for a living, thus abandoning his earlier plans and using the mule.

Ellis continues with another story, about a minister. A frustrated preacher tries to inspire the congregation at a church, and he decides that exposing his church members to a new minister might stimulate renewed interest in religion and spirituality. One night, the new minister hopes to trap the congregation so that they will listen to his sermon, so he demands that the church doors be locked. He reveals a gun and points it at the members, threatening them. He tells them "to bow" and uses the gun to force them to give in to his demands. No one is exempt; he even makes the "peg-leg" bow before him. The congregation fears the minister so much that they transport the church a long way away.

Charlie tells a story about how the church came to be divided into so many denominations and factions. He provides his own version of a New Testament story about Jesus Christ and his disciples. He says that Christ talked with his disciples and demanded they gather rocks. Peter initially gets a small rock. When he sees Christ transform the rocks into bread, Peter regrets his choice of rock, and he decides he no longer wants to be left with just a small portion of food. Christ tells the disciples to gather more rocks again and Peter gets "half a mountain," thinking that this means he will have a huge piece of bread. Christ views all of the rocks and tells Peter he's constructing a church on that particular rock because of its immense size. The defiant Peter tells Christ that instead he should make the rock into bread. Christ follows Peter's advice and makes the mountain into bread, which feeds many people. Christ then makes a church by combining other rocks. The church became split because it was built on more than one rock.

The storytelling competition continues with another story about religion. The story explains why African Americans possess darker skin. In this humorous tale, God creates human beings and decides to provide colors to add variety to the human race. The blacks show up late when God is handing out colors, and he shouts "Git back!" The blacks think he's saying "black," and their skin becomes dark.

Next, Mathilda tells a story in which God put a female and a male in a home, and they battle to see who will have power over the other. The husband requests "strength" from God to control and dominate the wife. God grants this wish, making the husband the powerful one in the relationship. Feeling oppressed, the female desperately attempts to counter her husband's dominion over her. She goes to God and requests "strength" over the husband, and God will not grant her wish. Determined to win at all costs, she heads to the devil, who tells her to go to God and ask for some keys, which will give her power. She follows the advice of the devil, and gets the keys. The devil says these keys control the kitchen, the bedroom, and the cradle. This strategy works, for she ends up controlling the domestic life. The man is unable to open doors; he is kept away from the food in the kitchen and deprived of sex in the bedroom, and he cannot exert influence over the children. When he goes to God, God tell him he cannot help him overturn his wife's power, and woman conquers man with the assistance of both God and the devil. Jack tells a "Song Poem," about women, and Shug tells a story as well.

III

Shug tells a story about men competing to gain the affections of a woman. Three males compete to see who is worthy of a lovely lady as his bride. The father of the woman devises challenging tasks for them to complete. They must demonstrate their prowess in agriculture, gathering water, and killing animals to show they can provide for his daughter. The first two show they can complete the tasks successfully, but the third man so masterfully shoots a deer that he impresses the father and wins the woman as his bride.

In another story told to the group by Robert Williams, a man asks his daughter to pen a letter to his sibling. As he may be illiterate, his daughter writes as he dictates. However, the oral utterance can be more effective than the written word, and some things cannot be translated onto paper. He clucks and expects his daughter to write that down. She fails. In another story, Henry recounts a tale about his father's fast horse.

This chapter also features famous stories about Big John de Conquer and his master. Julius tells a story about John and the master, in which John assaults the master's horse, a grave show of disrespect to the slave master. The master kills John's horse even though he gave this animal to John, just to show his power. John takes the horse's skin and tells a man that this special skin can tell the future. John tells him twice about a man being in his home with his wife. The story proves to be very true both times, and John wins a reputation as a fortuneteller. The man gives John animals and money, which makes John a wealthy and prosperous slave.

John develops an impressive track record. John then tells his master to kill his own horse. The master agrees to do this, hoping to get some money. He kills his horse, but this brings him no fortune, so he must replace the old horse with a new one. John accumulates more possessions, and eventually tricks his master into drowning himself in the river. After this magnificent story, Julius tells a brief story about how a man drops a pill and it causes the earth to burn.

John French tells an allegorical story about good and evil. Jim, the good sibling, buys land and animals and leads an agrarian lifestyle. Jack, on the other hand, gambles and engages in sinful activity. In the story, Jack travels to hell by riding an eagle and goes to

Zora Neale Hurston, studio portrait by Carl Van Vechten, 1940 *(Yale Collection of American Literature, Beinecke Rare Book and Manuscript Library)*

the devil's home. The devil demands that he perform certain tasks. These tasks involve great physical labor, which Jack is not used to as he has lived a lazy life. The devil tells him to clear ground, but the daughter of the devil, who wants to marry Jack, lets Jack snooze while she performs the task herself. When he awakes, all of the ground has been cleared very well. The devil's second task involves retrieving water from a well. Again, the daughter performs this task while Jack sleeps. The impressed devil says Jack can now wed his daughter if he completes one more task successfully. Again, she completes the task while he sleeps. Jack marries the daughter of the devil, but the two do not have an easy life. She says her dad wants to kill Jack and they must flee hell. The husband and wife successfully escape because Jack says, "O Lawd, have mercy" while hiding out in a log, and clearly the devil fears God.

The storytelling leaves an impression upon Hurston. The following day she sees children singing and performing games, which she finds fascinating. Charlie Jones assists Hurston in her search by directing her to Polk County, where she will find more folklore. Charlie teaches Hurston a song about John Henry, a strong railroad worker who tried to hammer nails onto the railroad faster than the steam engine. Stories and songs about this legendary character abound. Hurston leaves for Polk County to continue in her quest for material.

IV

Hurston arrives in Polk County, Florida. Babe Hill tells her that her mother will provide lodging and board for Hurston, so she can live in the community as she researches. Hurston later discovers that Babe has committed murder. Some people find Hurston's appearance in their town troubling, and they are suspicious about her. Even though Hurston has a black southern heritage, some still see her as a potential threat to their community as they question her motivations. Cliffert Ulmer informs her that people think that she is an "officer or a detective" in the area. They assume she wants to arrest them or find information to use against them. Once Hurston claims that she is "a fugitive" from the law, people warm up to her and tell her stories. She accompanies Cliffert to a dance in the community, where she meets the other residents and is asked to dance. She feels uncomfortable about wearing her expensive clothes from New York, which singles her out from the others in their cheaper or homemade attire.

A contest for telling tales is advertised. This gives people an opportunity to trade stories, and Hurston an occasion to learn tales that may differ from the ones she learned earlier in Maitland and Eatonville. One day, Hurston and others go to see "the swamp-gang," a group of laborers who cut down trees in rural Florida for a living. She hears another tale about John and his master from a man named Good Black. The men, who were ready to work, are later told they will not have to log in that area or cut down trees, so they head to the mill and tell stories to each other.

The stories about John and his master, or "Ole Massa," continue as Cliff tells one to rival the one told by Good Black. According to this story, John likes to pray to God, and Ole Massa hears him praying and decides to play a trick on him. Massa pretends to be God and disguises himself with "a bed sheet" to fool his slave. Liza, John's wife, claims John is not at home when the master, disguised as

God, comes to his home. When John finally faces the master, he makes up excuses for not coming away with God immediately. John says he needs to put on something more suitable. John asks God to "stand back" and then runs very fast to get a head start on his master.

A man tells another story about Massa's corn being taken from his property. Since his wealth is based on land and slaves, he becomes quite concerned about the disappearance of his crop. He asks John to find out who took the corn, and John tries to find out. He finds that it is actually a bear eating the crop, but John does not kill the bear. The master holds the bear while John is supposed to get assistance. John does not do this, and he claims he was trying to let the bear go anyway.

Jim Allen tells a story about a black woman who opens a box, and the box contains work. This is why black women have so much work. John Presley offers a story in which a black man and a white man open bundles. Although the black man has the larger bundle, it contains tools for farming. In contrast, the white man's bundle contains "a writin'-pen and ink." The distinction shows the different types of work the two men will do. The chapter ends with a story from Will Richardson about Ole Massa. Massa tells a black man to kill a deer. The slave resists and claims he did not see a deer, but only a white male with "chairs on his head."

V

In this chapter, the stories continue to focus on the issue of slavery. Joe tells a tall tale. One slave claims he cursed the master and boasts how defiant he can be. The very act impresses another slave who wants to exert some sort of power and authority over his master. This slave curses the master too, hoping to get away with it like the other slave, but he ends up getting whipped by the master. When confronted, the other slave admits he did not curse the master to his face, and that he did it when the master could not hear him or see him. He then claims he looked at the underwear of the master's wife to show his defiance to the master. The other slave gullibly does this to the master's wife, and the master whips him again. Again, the slave admits to the whipped slave that the mistress's clothes were hanging to dry when he looked at the clothing.

Black Baby tells a story about the legendary John, who constantly fought against slavery. Black Baby says John came to the United States as a black man and was bought by a white master. John is introduced to things by the master because he does not know the correct words in English. Later John smokes and a fire occurs on the plantation. He tells the master about the fire using his old words, but the master does not understand. Then John uses the right terms in English to convey the severity of the situation. Gene Oliver tells a story about livestock. A man is on trial for stealing a goat. Another man knows a black male who smells worse than the goat. The man and his goat appear in court. The judge passes out from the smelly goat and the goat passes out from the smelly black man.

Joe Wiley tells a story about John and his master, a variation on the earlier one about fortune-telling. John claims that he can read people's fortunes, Massa wants to make money from John's abilities. The two place a wager on whether John can successfully tell the future. To test John, a man gets a raccoon and hides it under something. John says, "Well, you got de ole coon at last." Master wins because the man does not understand the play on words. *Coon* can mean the animal but also can be a pejorative term for African Americans. When John says this, he means that he cannot figure out what is under the object, but the man thinks he refers to a raccoon. After winning money from John's abilities, the master claims he is leaving town, but he really does not go anywhere. He intends to trick John by returning to the plantation to see what John will do while he is away. John holds a party on the plantation and invites many guests. Massa and his wife show up in disguise. The master decides to punish his slave for this by hanging him, but John tricks master once again. Just before he is hanged, John prays to God, but beforehand he arranges for a friend to come and pretend to be God delivering a sign for him. John's friend strikes a match when John asks for a sign, and the master is frightened as another match is lit. The master leaves, freeing his slaves.

Cliff then recounts a story in which a black male discovers a gold watch and chain, but a white man asks for the watch and keeps it. He tells the black man to sell any item he finds. The man later discovers a turtle, attaches string to it, and tells a black male the time of day by it.

Larkins White tells another story about Jack and the master; *Jack* is a variant of *John.* Jack hides in the woods, and his master asks another black man for help in finding Jack. In exchange for telling him of Jack's whereabouts, he promises the black man clothing. The man is enticed by the master's offer, and he betrays Jack by tricking him. While bringing him food, he promises to perform a tune. As he sings to Jack, Jack is captured. Larkins White continues with yet another tale about Jack. Jack overhears blacks in a graveyard as they speak about splitting up corn, but he tells the master that he overheard a conversation between the devil and God. The intrigued master accompanies Jack to the graveyard, but Jack leaves the master there. The frightened master gets to his house earlier than Jack as the master finds the prospect of encountering God and the devil too frightening.

Eugene tells a story that explains why whites have power over blacks. During a famine, a white man named Brother John prays to God that blacks will understand that they are subordinate. Then Larkins White tells a story that features a black man praying to God about whites. The black man prayed that God would murder whites. In retaliation, his master allows stones to be thrown at the slave while he prays. When his plan to harm whites backfires, the slave then asks God if he knows the difference between whites and blacks. Joe Wiley continues with a story about John, who tells his mistress and master that their kids are about to drown. He saves the lives of the children by rescuing them. As a reward, the master tells John he will eventually free him in thanks for saving his children. The master keeps his promise to John, freeing him. John goes to Canada, a free country.

VI

Eugene Oliver provides another tale, focusing on the issue of work. Eugene cautions his audience not to assume that whites are incapable of seeing deception in blacks. In the story, a white man employs a black man who is lazy and only pretends to work. He thinks the white employer is unaware that he has not fulfilled his obligations, but the white man, aware of the situation, refuses to pay him.

After hearing this story, Hurston and the workers head inside a mill, but there is no job for them there. They then head to "the quarters," where the African-American workers live. Bertha Allen wants them to do some yard work for her. Her grandson Cliff Ulmer says he would rather fish than do such tedious chores for her. Cliff tries to dig up bait from the yard and then he and others, including Hurston, go fishing since there is no work to do.

Big Sweet, one of the few female storytellers, provides a tale about birds. Her tale explains the absence of the "mockin' bird" on a particular day of the week. There is a thief who enjoys stealing and who is liked by birds. As punishment for stealing, the man goes to hell, but the sympathetic birds put sand in hell to quell the fire. The birds do this on Fridays. Joe Wiley responds with a story about a man who fishes on Sundays despite it being the holy day. A strong fish pulls the man into the water and the man drowns. Jim Allen responds by offering up his own animal tale to explain why snakes have venom and rattles. He says God gave the snake venom as protection from harm, but other animals complained to God. God chastises the snake for harming other animals and punishes it with a "bell" that rattles to let others know his presence as a warning.

Will House then tells a story about "a black gnat" that ate animals. The tale leads to other ones about insects and their fantastic qualities. Will House claims in a story that his dad "planted cucumbers" that grew immediately. Joe Wiley then tells an equally unbelievable story about a mule that grew tiny "jackasses." Joe Wiley counters by claiming that he and his brother grew some corn that grew quickly and sprouted huge ears of corn. Lonnie then tells a story about Noah, who tells a woodpecker not to make a hole on the ark. Noah gets angry when the bird disobeys, so he hits the bird. This accounts for the crimson color of the bird's head. The next story, by Black Baby, is about Noah too. Possums lack hair on their tails because Noah's son used a possum tail for an instrument string.

Jim Presley then tells a story about Brer Dog and Brer 'Gator, two important animal figures from folklore, both functioning as trickster figures. In this story, the two agree to give each other mouths because they both lack them. Brer 'Gator makes one for the dog, and the dog starts cutting one for the gator, but he makes it too large. This is why the gator does not like the dog. Eugene Oliver objects to this story, questioning its veracity. He claims alligators and dogs dislike each other for different reasons. In his story, Brer Dog tells Brer 'Gator there is "a big convention" and they want Brer 'Gator's "drum music." Brer Dog carries "Brer 'Gator's tongue" for use as a musical instrument to entertain people. However, he does not return the tongue, which makes the alligator angry. Big Sweet tells another story about Brer 'Gator. In this tale, Brer Rabbit "run right over Brer 'Gator" one day, causing tension between the two. Brer 'Gator asks him about it, and the rabbit leaves and sets fire to the area. Brer 'Gator gets in "de water" to avoid the situation, but turns black from the fire.

VII

The people enjoy telling stories about rabbits and dogs, and each person tries to tell a story as entertaining as the earlier ones. Joe Wiley tells another animal tale. One day, Brer Rabbit complements Brer Dog on singing well. Then the rabbit takes the tongue of the dog and pulls it from his mouth. In retaliation, the dog convinces the rabbit to accompany him home. They head off, and the rabbit hears dogs. The scared rabbit runs quickly home. Arthur Hopkins tells another funny animal story. A goat consumes a piece of his owner's clothing. His owner, in anger, puts this goat on a railroad track, but the goat uses the clothing to signal to the train, outwitting the human. Willie Roberts tells an animal story that includes John and the master. The master tells slaves to shoot deer, but John doesn't because he would cause damage to the weapon. John figures out a way to defy the master. After Roberts's story about the gun, other stories about hunting follow. Larkins tells one about a hunter who shoots turkeys and later ducks and deer. Then he places the dead animals in his wagon, but it will not roll because it's too heavy with animals. However, the following day the wagon arrives at his house.

Jim Allen tells a story about the tensions between hawks and buzzards, focusing on a hawk impaled on a tree branch. Joe Wiley tells another about an ox and a mule that talk. The mule betrays the ox by telling the master that the ox really pretends to be sick when the ox could be working hard for the master on the farm. The angry master turns over the ox to someone for slaughter. The hurt and upset ox tells the mule that he will receive his comeuppance, and he tells the mule that he will "always be war on yo' back," because part of an ox will be used as a whip for the mule. Cliff then tells a story about the origin of gophers, which followed a battle between God and the devil. The devil and God like to compete in creating animals, he says, and God makes a turtle. The devil creates a turtle from dirt, but God objects and claims it is not a real turtle. "God blowed de breath of life" in it; later he puts it in water several times, but it leaves and heads to land. This explains the origin of the gopher: It was a turtle that wouldn't stay in the water. Another man tells a story about God's creation of butterflies. Butterflies, he says, serve to provide flowers with companionship. Jim Presley provides a tale about fish and their relationship to humans. During a famine, a hungry man told his spouse they should fish. The trip proves successful, and they cook the fish. However, their cat decides to eat most of the fish while they gather water to quench their thirst. The angry man makes the cat eat the last fish, but they all die of starvation eventually. They all go to heaven, but the man tells God what happened and the cat is cast out.

Jim Allen tells a story about an obstinate cow that causes problems for the human owners. The owners decide to send their son away to school, and later his mother asks him to help them cope with the cow. The plan to control the cow does not work, and it runs away with the father. Cliff Ulmer recounts that the water and wind are mothers who enjoy boasting about their children. Each one thinks her children are superior to the other's children. Mrs. Wind tells her offspring to get water from Mrs. Water, but she drowns those children. Cliff claims that, as a result, storms symbolize the "fightin'" between the wind and the water.

VIII

Dad Boykin tells another story about Big John de Conquer. John conquers a bear. The bear and lion talk, and later the lion confronts John. John shoots the lion, who then admits defeat. After this story, the group finishes fishing and packs up. Dad Boykin tells about the best way to avoid getting cold, and they head home. Hurston cooks the fish and they consume a good meal. That evening, a minister arrives and preaches to them. They give the preacher some money, and he leaves the area.

IX

Hurston and Big Sweet head to a "jook," which is a rural nightclub. People play cards and drink alcohol. Big Sweet plays cards and wins some cash, but she gives Hurston the money. Big Sweet tells her that Lucy, a woman in the area, doesn't like Hurston's relationship with Slim, due to jealousy. A fight breaks out between Big Sweet and others, and a work supervisor tries to stop the fight. Big Sweet eventually leaves with Joe Willard. After the excitement, Hurston finds out that Box-Car Daddy served time in jail and had to work as part of his prison sentence. She hears tunes, which she likes, as this is the type of material she wants to collect from people. The following evening, Hurston heads to another social event, and Lucy wants to attack her. Big Sweet rescues Hurston from Lucy's threat, and Hurston ultimately has fun at Loughman. Cliffert tells a story focusing on the devil and Jack, in which the two debate about strength. They compete, and on the following day the devil throws a hammer and it sails for days. Jack says he will throw it to heaven.

X

Hurston goes to another area and gathers games and stories, many of which are for children. There is another story contest. Mack C. Ford tells a story about the porpoise's tail. The porpoise decides to travel around the world and race the sun to see who is quickest. God chases the porpoise and switches its tail around so it cannot run as fast. Ford tells another story about why dogs do not like cats, in which a dog and a cat buy ham together one day, but the cat eats it all. The dog gets mad and holds a grudge. Ford continues with a story about the devil, who goes to heaven to find angels to assist him. A man speaks to the devil, but the "Devil opened his mouth," signaling the angels to fly away. The devil returns for angels, but this time does not open his mouth, realizing his earlier mistake.

Ford continues with another story, on slavery. The master tells the slave to get some items and mules. Later, the master tells him to get the devil, and the slave obeys the order, getting the devil and killing him. The master gets angry, so the slave returns the devil. The slave dies, but he cannot stay in heaven, so he heads to hell. There, the devil's wife tells him to create a hell with "hot coal" because she fears anyone who can have that much power over the devil. The tale explains the origin of the jack-o'-lantern, which represents the slave. Mack Ford then explains the origin of mosquitoes and bad weather in another story. In this one, the devil sees God and says, "Christmas gift!" God tells the devil he can have the eastern region; this explains the bad weather and mosquitoes there, since it is the "Devil's property." Ford's next story is the myth of "Raw Head." The devil and Raw Head talk, and Raw Head challenges him to destroy marriages. A woman agrees to help the devil do this. She speaks with a husband and then goes to his wife to trick them both. She tells the wife to slice off her husband's mole, and she tells the husband that his wife wishes to murder him. That evening, the wife tries to slice the mole and her husband says their marriage is over, as he thinks she wanted to kill him. The devil gives the lady what she wanted in exchange for her help, but he fears her.

Horace Sharp tells a story about a farmer who marries a woman. He leads her to believe he has a lot of money, but he really does not, and has a run-down house. The materialistic woman then leaves. A.D. tells a story about a woman who wanted to get married. A man tells the master's sister that if she can get on the top of the house, he will wed her. The sister does it because she desperately wants to get married, but she dies from freezing. After her burial, she becomes an owl. A.D. continues with another story, in which a man sends his son to get a mule, who then speaks to his son. The father does not believe a mule can speak, so he goes to see the mule. He hears the mule talk, and then he sees that his dog talks too, and he is shocked. The "man is runnin' yet" at what he saw, A.D. says. A.D. then tells about a man who sells his soul up "to de high chief devil." Later, when he dies, a figure named High Walker sees the man's skull and demands it shake in response. High Walker tells another man that the skull talks, but when the man accompanies him, the skull will not speak. The man cuts off his head because it did not speak and he said it was all right to do so. Then the skull speaks, amazing the man.

Hurston heads back to Loughman, where a wedding is going on. Big Sweet tells her that some people may poison the food and drink, so she needs to be careful. Hurston goes to the "Pine Mill" and later learns folk tunes, another important part of the oral tradition. Big Sweet arrives, and Nunkie wants to dance with her. She tells Nunkie to dance with Hurston instead. Lucy, still angry at Hurston, arrives. Big Sweet and Lucy confront each other with weapons. People start fighting, and the chapter ends with Hurston fleeing to another town. Hurston's experience with the jealous Lucy, and the fights that ensue as a result between Big Sweet and Lucy, show that this work was sometimes dangerous business.

Part 2: Hoodoo

I

After spending twelve months collecting folktales, Hurston heads to Louisiana. In the second part of *Mules and Men,* Hurston documents the time she spent in Louisiana learning about conjuring. She characterizes hoodoo as a significant religious and cultural practice in the African-American community that is worthy of study. Hurston shows the connection between conjuring and the practice of magic or folk medicine. She also describes figures from the Bible as conjurers or hoodoo men and women, such as God, Moses, Jethro, and Sheba, since they possess similar abilities to control nature and people.

Hurston first consults a woman named Rachel Silas to find out where she can find "a good hoodoo doctor." Mrs. Viney White, a friend of Rachel's, gives Hurston some advice. Hurston thus visits Eulalia, a conjurer who is very knowledgeable about the practice. One lady consults Eulalia for help with love, a common area people seek assistance in from conjurers. Eulalia and Hurston head to the home of the man who is the object of the lady's desire. There, Hurston puts lemon in his land while Eulalia places "pepper into the stove." She does a "salting," or scattering, at his residence, as well. The ritual works, and the man falls in love with the woman. The woman pays Eulalia.

II

Hurston spends time in New Orleans, Louisiana, one of the conjure capitals of the United States. She requests help from a conjurer named Turner, who tells her about his teacher, Marie Laveau, a famous Louisiana conjure woman with strong powers. According to Turner, Laveau used a mixture of hoodoo and Catholicism, and so her work blended Judeo-Christian and other religious forms. He tells Hurston a story about Marie coming "out of the waters of the lake" holding a candle, which resulted in Turner eventually becoming her pupil; thus he also ranks high in the conjure community.

Turner eventually initiates Hurston as a conjurer. This initiation takes many days and requires her to have skin of snakes and "new underwear"; additional conjurers assist in this special process. She has to "lie silent and fasting" as part of the ritual for an extended period of time; she eventually gets up, and Turner is located near the front of a "Great Altar." Hurston must enter "a tub" as part of the initiation. To establish her new identity, she is renamed "Rain-Bringer." Later she says she was "dressed in the new underwear and a white veil was placed over my head." Hurston sits and is clothed, but later her finger is cut and her blood and the blood of Turner and others is combined with alcohol. They drink glasses of this mixture. Candles are lit and she must drink a glass of "blessed oil." Turner drinks it, as do the others. They eat, and then drive to an area outside, where an animal is killed. They put her "petition" inside the animal, bury the animal, and leave. Hurston studies with Turner for several months, and

Exterior, 625 Bourbon St., New Orleans, ca. 1949 *(Library of Congress)*

she impresses him as a pupil so much that he wants her to join his conjuring business; she declines the offer. By actively engaging in the conjuring activities she observes, Hurston adds to her understanding of the practice.

III

Still a participant-observer, Hurston continues to describe the rituals and practices of conjurers. After studying with Turner, she finds a new conjurer, Anatol Pierre, who will teach her. He too must initiate her as a conjurer; the practice resembles the initiation she underwent with Turner, although there are some differences. He bathes her. She and Pierre cut their fingers, creating a "blood bond," thus sealing their fates and common goals. Pierre makes sure she is dry; later, she must review the Job section of the Bible for several days, illustrating the connection between hoodoo and the Judeo-Christian experience. Her initiation allows her to reach a new level as a student. Hurston relates a story about a man named Muttsy, who thinks he is being conjured against. Anatol Pierre says it is because he is having an affair with a married woman and the cuckolded husband wants him to die. Pierre has Hurston obtain ingredients, and a ceremony is performed; the conjuring works, and the husband dies. Pierre and Hurston then conjure against a man who brags about his abilities.

IV

Zora discusses Father Watson, another conjurer with the colorful nickname of "Frizzly Rooster." She witnesses him at work and describes his flamboyant clothing, indicative of his personality. The following day she meets with him. His wife tells Hurston that "brain-coral" holds her to him. They make her do tasks for them, and she goes through a ceremony with them as she did with Turner and Pierre. Hurston cannot have sex for a certain period so that she will be pure. She must remain indoors, and she is forbidden from eating for a period of time. She enters a special place with them and some other people. Father Watson lights candles and he as well as his wife touch Hurston. She receives a special kind of candle, which she must light using other candles; she becomes the "Boss of Candles." The ceremony confers upon her a new identity. Later, she and others eat food, and she is given the candles from this ceremony. She is told she can do conjure work on her own. Her first job is to help a woman who wants to punish the man who shot at her husband. She gets counsel from Father Watson, who advises her on how to handle the situation. Hurston meets another woman, Sister Murchison, who wants her mother-in-law to leave her home; Father Watson advises her on which rituals to perform. Another task is to reduce a minister's status, for which they perform a conjure ritual.

Father Watson later tells Hurston she requires "the Black Cat Bone," which aids in invisibility, an asset to conjurers. She must not eat, but she can drink some alcohol. She is supposed to obtain a "black cat," which she then must put in a pot of boiling water and cover it. She leaves, and goes back to her residence.

V

Hurston writes about Dr. Duke, a conjurer who deals with clients having legal troubles, using rituals to help people in court. Some people, Hurston included, gather roots and herbs from swamps; "John de Conquer" is described as an important substance. One client, James Beasley, gives Dr. Duke money to help with his murder case. Dr. Duke gets "dirt" from the cemetery, a task too dangerous for Hurston since it involves the spirit world. Dr. Duke blends materials and prays during this ritual. He then gives James Beasley "underclothes" with sprinkled dirt.

Next Hurston meets Samuel Jenkins, who can tell the future. Dr. Jenkins predicts that Charles S. Johnson will be notified about a voyage, and also that a white woman would help Hurston. Both of these prove to be true. Hurston notes that, in "killing ceremonies," conjurers usually use cemeteries for material, and she provides details about dead people and the spirit world.

VI

Here Hurston recounts folklore tales highlighting conjurers' practices. In one tale, Celestine wants money from her neighbor, so the neighbor has a child give Celestine some money. A woman warns the neighbor that Celestine may have conjured against her, and that is why she wants the money. She tells her son to find out about Celestine's activities, and he leads his mother and the woman to Celestine's home, where she performs a ritual. As a result, there is a conflict between the characters.

In another story, a black woman consults with a conjurer to purchase powder to conjure against a woman named Mrs. Grant. Previously, she and Mrs. Grant "had some words" (216) with each other. Mr. Grant spits some tobacco juice when the woman dusts the powder, and Mrs. Grant sees the powder. She goes to Dr. Strong, a conjurer, and he says she must hurt the woman who sprinkled the substance. She confronts this woman and hits her with bottles, but the woman bites. She goes home and sticks her hand in a chicken as a means of neutralizing the blood she has lost from being bitten by the woman.

Hurston recounts another story in which a white man kills a black female servant with a bone. A man named Dave removes the corpse. The white man later sees Dave, who "was known to dabble in hoodoo," on his property, and as a result his wife becomes hysterical and assaults him. The man moves to South Carolina, where he thinks he spots Dave again, and chases him. He gets his gun and summons his children, but they too turn on him. The man later moves to Baltimore and fears blacks; all his problems result from his original action.

A man named Pierre Landeau tells a story about a man who switched between sanity and insanity as a result of a conjurer. A woman who takes care of him then performs a ritual to find out who caused him to be in this condition. The culprit is a man named Pere Voltaire, another conjurer. The victim eventually dies, but Voltaire's powers continue, as Landeau and his family attest.

VII

In this chapter, Hurston discusses the power of Kitty Brown, a powerful conjure woman who is known to help bring back departed loved ones. She also has a "garden" that supplies her with important ingredients. Studying with Kitty, Hurston participates in some rituals and hears about how people get their beloveds to return. Stories include those of Minnie Foster and Rachael Roe, who use her services. Rachael Roe, for example, was mad because her lover jilted her and she wants this man killed. A death ceremony is performed in which people dance. The man later leaves his spouse for Rachael, and Rachael then wants to reverse the death ceremony. It is reversed, but Hurston suspects the man went back because he knew Rachael would go to a conjurer.

Hurston ends this chapter with a story about a rat and a cat. The rat tricks the cat by telling the cat to wash itself before eating the rat. It does, and the rat gets away. The cat gets another rat, and the rat tries the same strategy, but it doesn't work. The cat eats the rat and cleans itself later. That's why cats wash after eating, Hurston says. Hurston draws an analogy between the cat and herself, suggesting she's crafty and learns from her experiences.

Appendices

In the appendices at the end of her work, Hurston includes information about both folklore and conjuring. In the glossary, she defines colorful terms, such as "woofing" (a man speaking) or "blue baby" (a dark-skinned person), as well as other important historical information related to conjuring and folklore. Hurston includes, as well, descriptions of ingredients and recipes used in conjure in

Zora Neale Hurston beating a drum *(Library of Congress)*

three sections: "Formulae of Hoodoo Doctors," "Paraphernalia of Conjure," and "Prescriptions of Root Doctors."

CRITICAL COMMENTARY

Zora Neale Hurston's *Mules and Men* provides an important description of African-American folk culture. As one of the first serious treatments of folktales and voodoo, Hurston provides the reader with an in-depth look at both the black oral storytelling tradition and the black spiritual tradition of voodoo and conjuring. In her narrative, Hurston functions as both an insider and an outsider in relation to the world she examines; although she is an African-American woman whose roots are in the South, her subsequent education in anthropology and her methodology distances her from her subjects. By being an active participant and observer in Florida and Louisiana, she straddles two worlds of experience.

Part 1 provides an understanding of how African Americans framed their world experience using these folktales. The call-and-response pattern in which storytellers engage in a dialogue, even a competitive one, is an important rhetorical aspect of the tradition, perhaps equaling the content and the style of the stories themselves. Part 2 illustrates how African Americans appropriated aspects of the Judeo-Christian religious tradition to their own concept of conjuring or voodoo as a means of expressing spirituality for practical ends. In the glossary section, Hurston documents many of the details of the black folk tradition that, without her research, would have likely been lost to history.

Hurston's *Mules and Men* is as an important contribution to the documentation of African-American oral tradition. Hurston provides her readers with a glimpse into a world they might not be particularly familiar with; at the same time, she illustrates the commonality of the human experience. In the sections that follow, specific attention is paid to several of the major themes of these stories, including race, gender, religion, nature, and conjuring.

Slavery and Freedom

In the tales themselves, the opposition between slavery and freedom is clearly one of the most important. Even though these tales were told decades after the Civil War, the memories inflicted by the terror of slavery and then the following emancipation remained a lasting legacy at the time of Hurston's research: this is evidenced by the centrality of this theme to the various folktales that Hurston is told.

Most significantly, many of these stories involve the legendary folk hero John, or John the Conqueror (Big John de Conquer), and present his antagonistic relationship with his master, frequently referred to as "Massa." In these stories, the slave John defies and defeats his master through both physical and intellectual ability, illustrating the idea that blacks are not inferior to whites. As such, the character of John and his prevalence in these tales may reflect a wish-fulfillment fantasy for the slaves who originally concocted these tales: While they may have been physically imprisoned by their masters, their minds were free to create great fantasies of escape or victory over their oppressors.

John is also a type of trickster figure, which, in the African-American oral tradition, is usually an oppressed individual who conquers the oppressor to become free, or to be put on an equal social, economic, or even intellectual level. (In many cases, specifically the animal parables, the trickster figure is represented by an animal.) These tales remain important for the African-American community because "John's trickster tales symbolized hope and faith on one level, but inspired, motivated, and provided a role model for the downtrodden on another plane" (Hemmingway 41). Indeed, examples of the trickster character are best evidenced by the tales involving John and the master. One of the first such stories recounted to Hurston in this collection is the one in which John must collect water for the master, but when he tries to retrieve it, he sees a frog, interpreted as a "bogey man." In Julius's tale about his fortune-telling abilities, John continuously outwits his master, even if the master shows initial suspicion, managing first to convince the master to kill his own grandmother and toss himself in the river and ultimately to kill the master, effectively freeing himself. His master's oppressiveness is no match ultimately for John's mental capacities.

The idea of John as a fortune-teller is recurrent in this collection and, more generally, in the African-American literary tradition. Joe Wiley's story in which John guesses, unintentionally, that there is a raccoon hidden under an object leads to complication. He throws a party, and it is then his master who gets the upper hand, catching him and deciding to hang him. While in the first case John has won against his master unintentionally, when it really comes time to prove his mettle, he wins against his master, spooking him with the match trick arranged with his friend. The result, again a wish-fulfillment fantasy, is freedom for the slaves. So, here as elsewhere, the result in many of these stories is emancipation, either for John or for all blacks. In another liberation tale told by Wiley, John is liberated and moves to Canada after he "rescues" his master's kids from drowning, even though it was John who makes the master think they will drown in the first place. Thus, John becomes an important symbol of emancipation.

Other stories about John and Massa abound, all revealing the complexity of their relationship, both using the other's tactics and achieving suspense by doing so. Many other tales continue with the same theme, such as Good Black's story about John and work, or Cliff's tale about the master tricking John, for once, by pretending to be God. Even in this latter story, we can see John's speedy departure as a bold attempt to do the seemingly impossible: to outrun God. These John and Massa stories are meant to be amusing to the people who hear them, and they are meant both to pass the time and to inspire the listeners.

Overall, as a major character in *Mules and Men,* John de Conquer symbolizes freedom, liberation, and emancipation. He refuses to see himself as a slave, and he uses his physical strength and mental capabilities to survive his condition. He frequently battles with the master, other slaves, and animals to show that he reigns supreme. On occasion, he loses battles, but for the most part he succeeds. He represents the hope for freedom of black people in America. In *Mules and Men,* the storytellers, removed from slavery, still chronicle his exploits. It should also be noted that this cultural hero is known as Jack in some of the other tales and, as Hurston explains in the glossary, the two are in fact interchangeable.

In Part II of *Mules and Men,* John plays a less pivotal role, but his influence can still be seen. In the encounter between Hurston and Dr. Duke, she learns that this conjurer values the John de Conquer root because it contains the essence of John, the folk hero. This root will give people special power and directly connects with his spirit. In another sense, this later reference also suggests John's immortality and how the legacy of his story has been passed down through the generations.

His master, by contrast, symbolizes white power, authority, and control. While he may have power over the other blacks, he consistently loses in his encounters with John. Throughout these stories, his title of "master" is ironic because John, in all respects except legally, is the master over this white man. The master, both serious and comic, functions as a stock character seen often in abolitionist literature. He is greedy, egotistical, and racist, but also vulnerable and at times easily overcome. John's challenge to the white ideology of privilege and control was still, well after the abolition of slavery, a potent metaphor for the struggles that would yet remain between blacks and whites.

Gender

In *Mules and Men,* the significance of gender roles is seen both in Hurston's first-person narrative and in the folktales themselves; numerous examples relating to the dynamics of male-female relationships are seen throughout the book. In the communities she observes, women are often portrayed as having secondary status; by contrast, her tales often reveal how women find ways to achieve a sense of selfhood and identity. As Cheryl Wall notes in *Women of the Harlem Renaissance, Mules and Men* "offers a subtle revelation of the ways in which women are relegated to subordinate roles in the culture Hurston otherwise celebrates and the means by which these women gain access to creative expression and power" (Wall 159–160). The three most important depictions of women in this work are Hurston as narrator, Big Sweet as storyteller, and Marie Laveau as practitioner of hoodoo (Wall 160).

After Hurston arrives in Florida, she attends a "toe-party," in which the roles of men and women are strictly defined. In fact, the event represents the commodification of the black female body, as men are to decide the worth of a woman based on the look of her toes alone; these men then "buy" the women. Women, in effect, become the property of the men. Hurston is among the women "purchased." Clearly, as there is no form of expression at this event by which women have the same power to commodify the men based on physical appearances, the male-female relationship here is an unequal one; while it is portrayed as a lighthearted affair, the power of gender roles is nevertheless attested to.

Some of the stories that Hurston relates in *Mules and Men* reveal the intense power relationship between men and women as well. Hurston also suggests the potential for females to acquire voice; since most of the storytellers are male, there is a suggestion that the male voice is privileged—a theme recurrent in Hurston's novels such as *Jonah's Gourd Vine* and *Their Eyes Were Watching God.* However, women have important opportunities for reacting to these men, to punctuate the male-dominated discourse, and when they do speak their voices are perhaps louder and clearer for being less present overall. And, in fact, the tales the women tell are often self-consciously addressing the male-female power divide itself. For example, Mathilda, one of the few female storytellers, relates a story about women having power, claiming that God bestowed more power on men, but that women outwitted God, and overpowered their husbands, through the use of manipulation, cunning, and trickery.

The tripartite racial, class, and gender oppression faced by black women in America also frames an important aspect of the stories here. For example, Jim Allen's story about the black woman who opened a box containing work speaks directly to the black woman's experience. During slavery and after—particularly in the South—women worked as laborers in many fields, and the contrast between the work of white women and that of black women only highlights this fact. These tales also focus on black men and issues of masculinity, serving as a counterpoint to women's issues, but also thereby calling attention to the difference between the male and female experience. Jim Presley's story about the black man and the white man opening bundles of work is an example. The black man does physical labor while the white man engages in intellectual pursuits. The story tries to explain the work inequalities between blacks and whites as being as arbitrary as opening a bundle.

Hurston characterizes the people in this work in such a way as to challenge gender roles and stereotypes. Big Sweet, a woman, defies traditional ideas of women being passive, submissive, and unassertive. A strong, powerful woman, she does not express her fear in the face of others, and she serves as a protector of Hurston, confronting those (particularly Lucy) who would give her trouble as an outsider. The juxtaposition of the words in Big Sweet's name illustrates her complex position: Big in stature and power, she also possesses charisma and charm, and the two work in tandem to create the personality that she exudes in the work.

Religion

The central theme of religion is especially important because it links the two major parts of *Mules and Men.* In part I, Hurston emphasizes the importance of religion and spirituality in the southern black folk community. The many tales about preachers, God, and religion testify to the centrality of religion to the African-American experience, and at the same time these tales present a critique of both the African-American church and Judeo-Christian ideas. For example, in the early story that Ellis tells about the preacher who threatens his congregation with a gun, the preacher's intentions are subverted by his actions, causing the exact opposite of what he wants. While the story has a comic tone, it reveals the complicated power relationship between pastors and their followers. Charlie's story about the factions within the church is based on a retelling of a biblical story. It is meant to incite humor, and puts Christ's disciples on the same level as common people, with the same vices such as greed and egotism.

Religion also serves to frame discussions of race and identity throughout the stories. One story claims that God gave blacks dark skin because of a misunderstanding; here the storyteller is revealing how trivial the color of one's skin really is, even though such significance is placed on it in society. Other tales involving the connection between race and religion are Eugene's story in which Brother John prays to God that blacks know they are subordinate to whites and Larkins White's rebuttal in which a black man asks God to murder whites. Throughout such stories, what is common is the tie between race and religion: Religion is used to explain the injustices caused by racial factors, and it is also used as a means for exerting power and racial superiority.

In many of the tales, the devil plays as integral a role as God, as he is the adversary to God. In this sense, the tales present a view of the world as in tension between two forces, between two competing powers. The stories tend to show how humans ultimately outwit and defeat the devil, who, while powerful, is only a foil to the good forces of God. The presentation of two competing forces, one for good and one for evil, is directly related to the presentation of the struggle between masters and slaves.

Conjuring

Conjuring, hoodoo, and voodoo represent rituals, beliefs, and traditions practitioners use to control people, places, and events. The terms can be used interchangeably, in this sense. Hurston frames the discussion of conjuring within the context of Judeo-Christian religious practices, showing how both African folk traditions and Christian elements combine to create a unique spiritual practice. References to God, Moses, Jethro, and Sheba suggest that these powerful figures, by extension, were conjurers too, as they possessed spiritual powers that could be used to influence the physical world. Hurston sets herself up in this section of the book as a student seeking to learn more about hoodoo. Through identification with Hurston, herself an outsider in the world of conjuring, the reader is able to more fully understand and comprehend this world she describes in this section. One can experience it vicariously through Hurston.

Hurston presents conjuring as a conduit for power: People use conjuring—both for good and for ill—to gain power over others or themselves, in the present and in the future. It employs a complex mix of spiritual powers and physical formulas to effect change in the physical world. Hurston enters the conjuring world and presents her experiences in an episodic framework, providing accounts of her own acquisition of this power and how her conjuring appears to succeed. The process of studying with conjurers and becoming one of them reinforces Hurston's role as both participant and observer. These "initiations, like those of all doctors in the founding line of conjure, occur at the hands of those who have been assured of their ability to carry power and to engage in activities akin to God's" (Baker 296). Her first teacher, Eulalia, serves as a guide, showing Hurston and, through Hurston's narrative, the reader how conjuring works. With her second teacher, Turner, Hurston discusses how the famous conjurer Marie Laveau and her protégés practice a form of conjuring that reflects some Judeo-Christian traditions by mixing hoodoo and Catholicism. This blending is reflective of the diverse methods and heritage that make up the conjuring form.

In her discussions of conjuring, Hurston explains in depth her own role in the practice, and she uses descriptive imagery to represent the initiation rituals; for example, having to purify herself by not eating and by being quiet. She also examines how becoming a conjurer can bestow a new identity, or a parallel one, upon an individual. Hurston becomes Rain-Bringer in her first experience after going through the initiation. With Anatol Pierre, Hurston also undergoes a cleansing process in preparation; with Father Watson, she must fast and abstain from sexual activity, and she is given an identity as "Boss of Candles." In her descriptions of these ceremonies, Hurston uses vivid language and focuses on the communal nature of them: Teachers and students unite in their sacred acts as they prepare for their roles. Another important point is the feminization of conjuring as Hurston depicts it in *Mules and Men.* Marie Laveau is portrayed as a legendary conjurer, and there are many other women conjurers. Even though there are also men conjurers that Hurston meets, the conjuring practice is portrayed as the domain of women.

Zora Neale Hurston posing *(Yale Collection of American Literature, Beinecke Rare Book and Manuscript Library)*

Hurston's account also draws a connection between conjuring and fortune-telling, especially in her description of Dr. Jenkins. This emphasis on fortune-telling can also be seen in the John character, in the folktales in the first part of the book, suggesting the importance of the *future* to the mind-set of the conjurer or the tale-teller. In pointing out that the fortune-tellers are often right—as is the case with Dr. Jenkins—and that the conjurers achieve their goals, Hurston suggests that this practice cannot be dismissed outright. Even if the conjurers are not the actual cause of the future event, there is at the very least evidence of a perceived connection between the narratives created by the conjurers and the observed reality. Whether or not the conjurer is affecting that reality, there is evidence of a deep spiritual connection between the conjurer characters and the natural world.

Nature

Nature serves as an important theme in the collection. A scholar has pointed out, "Florida's natural environment provided the wildlife for the animal tales in *Mules and Men*" (Hemmingway 40). The use of animals with human characteristics is immensely widespread in the African-American storytelling tradition, with Brer Rabbit, Brer Fox, and other animals playing prominent roles. In their roles mimicking humans, these animal characters shed light on truths about the relationships between human beings and expose issues relating to race, class, and gender. The animal stories often serve to highlight the idea of competition, and have an analogue in human behavior. The trickster figure, as seen in Big John de Conquer, is also an important animal character.

The tales about animals seek to explain phenomena in the natural world; for example, Big Sweet's story about why the mockingbird does not sing one day a week, or Jim Allen's tale about how a rattlesnake got its venom and rattle. In other stories, the origin of the gopher and weather phenomena are explained. Jim Presley's story about Brer Dog and Brer Gator explains their animosity toward each other. We can also see religious overtones in the attempts to explain nature, such as in the story explaining the woodpecker's color, or why possums have no tail. While fiction, these stories illustrate the importance of using tales to explain the natural world.

Certain tall tales exaggerate natural phenomena; here the humans are using far-fetched stories and humor to pretend that natural laws can be counteracted. Will House tells a story about fast-growing cucumbers, and Joe Wiley tells about a mule raising jackasses on its farm. Obviously unbelievable, these stories nevertheless suggest a close relationship between the teller and the natural world. The power of nature over humans is also represented in these tales, such as in Joe's tale about a catfish pulling a man under water while he fished, causing him to drown. The irony here is that while man tries to conquer nature, nature conquers man. So, while in some stories the natural law can be seen as shifting to please the tale-tellers, in others it remains fast.

The mule is perhaps the most important nature symbol, as it is prominently part of the title of the book. The title *Mules and Men* implies that there are two separate forces coming into play here, represented by these two entities, the mule and the man. This is not to say that the two are in constant opposition—the mule against the man—because as we have seen they often are in close relationship with one another; in fact, these two symbols are often conflated, the animals acting like men and the men acting like animals. The point is that a distinction is being made between two aspects of the natural world, even though both parts make up the integral whole.

BIBLIOGRAPHY

Baker, Houston. "Workings of the Spirit: Conjure and the Space of Black Women's Creativity." In *Zora Neale Hurston: Critical Perspectives Past and Present,* edited by Henry Louis Gates, Jr., and K. A. Appiah, 280–308. New York: Amistad, 1993.

Hemmingway, Beulah S. "*Through the Prism of Africanity: A Preliminary Investigation of Zora Neale Hurston's* Mules and Men." In *Zora in*

Florida, edited by Steve Glassman and Kathryn Lee Seidel, 38–45. Orlando: University of Central Florida Press, 1991.

Hurston, Zora Neale. *Mules and Men.* In her *Folklore, Memoirs, and Other Writings,* 1–267. New York: Library of America, 1995.

Wall, Cheryl A. *Women of the Harlem Renaissance.* Bloomington: Indiana University Press, 1995.

"Muttsy"

This short story focuses on the life of Pinkie Jones, a southern woman who migrates north in search of a better life, and documents the music, dance, and socializing of the jazz age. It reflects the GREAT MIGRATION, a gradual movement in which millions of African Americans from the South traveled north to better their lives; this migration was one of the main sources of the HARLEM RENAISSANCE as it brought new masses of people to places like HARLEM, NEW YORK. Hurston, like Pinkie Jones, migrated from the South to the North as a young woman, and her experience would have served as an inspiration for this story. The story, which won a second-place award from *OPPORTUNITY* magazine in 1926, helped to establish Hurston's literary career.

SYNOPSIS

A pianist plays on a piano owned by Mrs. Turner, the proprietress of a boardinghouse. Fewclothes tells Muttsy that a woman has arrived there to stay. Muttsy sees the woman and is interested in her. She identifies herself as Pinkie Jones, from EATONVILLE, FLORIDA, and Ma Turner leads her to her room. Pinkie returns to the parlor area, where people are gathering and drinking, as it functions as a center of the community. Muttsy arrives and Pinkie is charmed by him. Muttsy tells Pinkie to go to bed and not worry about employment. The next day Ma tells Pinkie that Muttsy finds her an attractive woman, but she also reveals Muttsy's vice, gambling. Muttsy talks to Pinkie. Pinkie goes to her bedroom after dinner, and every time Muttsy tries to see her, she is in bed. One particular night Pinkie drinks cocktails, and while she sleeps Muttsy goes upstairs, kisses her, and puts a ring on her finger. When Pinkie wakes up, Ma tells her she has on Muttsy's ring. She decides to leave the house. Muttsy later comes to see her at the house, but she is not there. Ma tells him she disapproves of gambling and reminds him that Pinkie is not from New York. Muttsy gets a job as a foreman and later encounters Pinkie again. They marry. Bluefront, an old friend, tells Muttsy he misses their fun. Muttsy starts shooting dice again and goes back to his old gambling ways.

CRITICAL COMMENTARY

The story is told by a third-person omniscient narrator and centers primarily on the theme of identity. Pinkie Jones is a vulnerable young woman new to town, hoping to obtain a good job and make a better life for herself—and carve out a new identity. Pinkie has migrated from Eatonville, Florida, where Hurston herself grew up. She tries to adjust to her new environment socially, economically, and emotionally. Hurston characterizes Pinkie as "pure, innocent, delicate," but living in Ma Turner's Harlem boardinghouse changes her (Plant 150). She is a "wide-eyed young woman who moves to Harlem from Eatonville and finds herself trapped in the lowdown life of Ma Turner's back parlor, where men and women dance, sing, drink, fight, and live 'hotly their intense lives'" (Boyd 139). The rooming house is a center of the community, where people drink alcohol, listen to jazz music, and engage in courting rituals.

The other characters in the story, including Ma and Pa, take Pinkie in and try to integrate her into the community. Despite their hospitality and warmth, they are also controlling characters, especially as Ma encourages the relationship between Muttsy and Pinkie. Ma Turner is portrayed as an alcoholic, and she may place her own desires above the best interests of her tenants. She also functions as a type of villain, comparable to "the Wolf in Red Riding Hood." Ma can sense the naiveté of Pinkie, and believes that she can take advantage of the young woman. Unlike the women in Eatonville, Ma Turner wears makeup. Pinkie has been taught that only promiscuous women wear makeup.

As this is a new environment for Pinkie, she does not immediately recognize the consequences of boarding with Ma and Pa Turner, though she slowly senses that their values are different from the ones she grew up with in the South. With them, she experiences jazz, alcohol, and predatory men who view her as an object of desire. One of these men, Muttsy, sees Pinkie's outward innocence as a challenge, and he desires her physically and emotionally. He is interested in her the moment he sees her and then pursues her aggressively. The ring he places on her finger can be seen as a means of possession; he binds her to him in a sense, which causes her to want to leave. When she finds out that the gambler Muttsy has put this ring on her finger, she decides to leave the house. When she encounters him later, he has found a real job, as a foreman, and she agrees to marry him. Still, Muttsy returns to his old behaviors, suggesting that his old habits die hard, even with Pinkie in the picture. The story ends abruptly with him gambling with his friend Bluefront, and Hurston does not reveal any more about their lives together.

CHARACTERS

Muttsy Muttsy is a gambler and an opportunist. He sets his sights on Pinkie Jones, preying on her lack of experience in the city, notably with men, sexuality, and alcohol. He places a ring on Pinkie's finger while she sleeps, causing her to leave the boardinghouse. He finds a job as a foreman and Pinkie marries him, but he returns to his old gambling habits.

Bluefront Bluefront is a friend of Muttsy's who misses their old days of gambling once Muttsy marries, and he convinces him to join him for another game of dice.

Ma Turner A shrewd woman, Ma Turner runs the boardinghouse along with her husband. She drinks alcohol, listens to jazz and the blues, and keeps the company of others enjoying the same vices. She encourages the relationship between Muttsy and Pinkie.

Pinkie Although the story is titled "Muttsy," Pinkie is arguably the central character in this story. She migrates from Eatonville, Florida, to New York in search of a job. She lives at Ma Turner's boardinghouse, where she meets many characters, who are quite different from those she knew in the South. She is the object of Muttsy's desire, and he kisses her and places a ring on her finger as she sleeps. She later marries Muttsy once he has found a stable job.

BIBLIOGRAPHY

Boyd, Valerie. *Wrapped in Rainbows: The Life of Zora Neale Hurston.* New York: Scribner, 2003.

Hurston, Zora Neale. "Muttsy." In her *The Complete Stories,* 41–56. New York: HarperCollins, 1995.

Plant, Deborah G. *Every Tub Must Sit on Its Own Bottom: The Philosophy and Politics of Zora Neale Hurston.* Urbana: University of Illinois Press, 1995.

"'Possum or Pig?" (1926)

This very short story is a folktale about John, a legendary folk hero in African-American folklore. John and the Master are two important characters described at length in *Mules and Men.* The story first appeared in an issue of *The Forum* magazine, in 1926, at the beginning of Hurston's publishing career.

SYNOPSIS

The story takes place in the South, during slavery. Master realizes that pigs are missing from his plantation and suspects John is the culprit. John is cooking a pig in his cabin, the scent drifting from his home. When his master comes to see what is going on, John invites him in. The master sits down by John's "blazing fire" and chats with John. The master says he wants to eat, but John says that his food can't compare to what he would eat back in the plantation. John says he only has possum, but his master says he wants some. John then switches his story, saying that he is cooking possum, but when he feeds his master, it may turn out to be pig. He says he is not responsible if it is in fact pig.

CRITICAL COMMENTARY

This story is one of many stories involving John and the Master, all folktales told in the African-American oral tradition. John the Conqueror, known as High John de Conquer in Hurston's tales, is a black slave who constantly outwits his master with his superior skill. In this story, too, John is revealing his defiance against the slave master by stealing and cooking the pigs. The Master, John's adversary, suspects he has taken the pigs, and he catches John cooking the pig in his cabin. John tries to outwit his master, claiming he is only cooking possum and refusing the responsibility if his master finds he is actually eating pig. This short, comic tale depicts the antagonistic relationship between John and the Master.

John John de Conquer is the folk hero of many tales, although the stories varied widely depending on who was telling them. He is a subversive trickster figure, and also a hero for defeating his Master. In some stories, he also wins his own liberation, as well as that of his fellow slaves. In this story, John steals a pig but claims it is possum.

The Master The Master is a wealthy, prominent white man, who symbolizes the power and control of the slave master. He is frequently outwitted and overpowered by his trickster slave, John. In this tale, he is upset that John has stolen his pig, but John once again gets the upper hand.

BIBLIOGRAPHY

Boyd, Valerie. *Wrapped in Rainbows: The Life of Zora Neale.* New York: Scribner, 2003.

Hemenway, Robert E. *Zora Neale Hurston: A Literary Biography.* Urbana: University of Illinois Press, 1980.

Hurston, Zora Neale. "'Possum or Pig?" In her *The Complete Stories,* 57–58. New York: HarperCollins, 1995.

Seraph on the Suwanee (1948)

Published in 1948, *Seraph on the Suwanee* was Hurston's last novel, and it deviates from her previous novels in that it primarily features white characters. The novel chronicles the lives of a white family in Florida swept up in the transition from the agrarian ways of the Old South to the industrialized New South. African-American characters play minor roles in the text, notably having to do with jazz or the blues. Still, Hurston's final work of long fiction deals with many of the same themes as her other work, such as nature, marriage, religion, gender, sexuality, race, and class. The novel appeared at a low point in Hurston's life, following a child molestation accusation in New York that ultimately proved to be groundless. While she was not convicted of wrongdoing, controversy continued to surround her at the time of the novel's publication. Hurston dedicated this novel to Marjorie Kinnan Rawlings, author of the novel *The Yearling.*

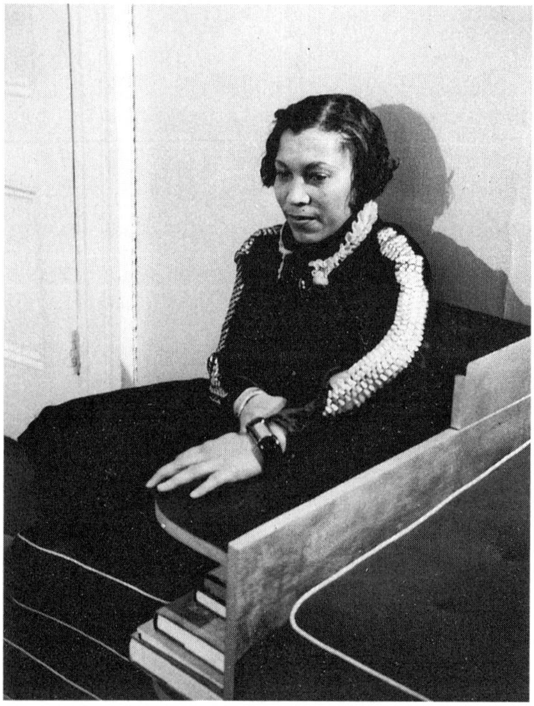

Zora Neale Hurston *(Yale Collection of American Literature, Beinecke Rare Book and Manuscript Library)*

SYNOPSIS

Chapter One

A third-person omniscient narrator begins with a description of Sawley, a town in western Florida near the Suwanee River, situated amid vast farmland. Residents are generally poor, sick, and uneducated, and many of them work in the lumber or turpentine industries. The story takes place in the early 1900s, at which point no major highways existed: "when the automobile was known as the horseless carriage, and had not exerted its tremendous influence on the roads of the nation." Prior to the arrival of whites and blacks, Native Americans dominated the area, yet "they were dead and gone." The river serves as a source of life and death: it is an important food source, but also a source of mosquitoes and malaria.

On Sunday, work at the sawmill ceases, and people go to church. For white residents, Day Spring Baptist Church is a popular place of worship. On this particular Sunday, many people attend; the topic of conversation is Arvay Henson, notoriously indifferent about romantic affairs but currently courting a handsome young man, Jim Meserve. Arvay is in her early twenties and single, unlike many of the other women in the area, who get married as teenagers. The unattached Arvay is "pretty if you liked delicate-made girls," and many people are surprised that she is not more interested in marrying and having children. The week before, Jim Meserve had accompanied Arvay to church and walked her home, and now the congregation is curious to see what will happen this week.

The narrator tells us that Arvay withdrew from society when her sister Larraine wed Carl Middleton, a pastor; she had proclaimed one Sunday "that she was through with the world and its sinful and deceitful ways." She devoted herself fully to spirituality and wanted to do missionary work, demonstrating a unique faithfulness to her religion. Many of the people in the church are happy about Arvay's decision to withdraw from society and pursue her religious studies, especially other women who see her as a role model for other females; Carl Middleton, the minister, himself admires her commitment and wishes he could do missionary work as well. Aside from her playing music at the church, which is one of her passions, Arvay otherwise seeks solitude, causing others to see her as "queer," a sort of community misfit. Her sister, Larraine, by contrast, is an outgoing and talkative person. Larraine resembles their father, Brock Henson, while Arvay resembles Maria Henson, their mother; the Henson family is poor and lives in a small, humble home. Arvay shares her mother's religious devotion as well as her predisposition to suffer seizures, an affliction others think is curable only by marriage. She has had frequent seizures after church, particularly if she is approached by men; the only way to calm her down seems to be turpentine treatment.

Jim Meserve may be the man to win Arvay's heart at last, according to the people in the town. Jim Meserve comes from a family with upper-class roots, the descendant of a plantation-owning family during slavery. His family lost their money during the Civil War, so when he arrives in Florida, he has very little money but dreams of success. With the help of Brock Henson, he finds work in the turpentine business. Jim, a brash and bold man, makes it clear that he wants to date Arvay Henson and dismisses her claims that she wants the life of a missionary instead of being a wife and mother.

The narrator then reveals background details about Arvay, noting that the townspeople know nothing about Arvay's feelings for Carl Middleton and that Larraine's popularity made Arvay lack confidence in herself. While Arvay felt intimidated by her sister's social prowess and success with men, she felt confident in her musical abilities and played the family organ daily. When Carl Middleton, the new preacher, heard her playing the organ, he became interested in Arvay and invited her to start playing at church. Arvay fell secretly in love with Carl, but soon her sister eclipsed her and gained his attention. One day, Carl walked her home from church and she announced her intention to marry him, even though their father disapproved of Middleton, thinking he should work in turpentine rather than as a preacher. Arvay was devastated at her sister's news, having thought Carl was in love with her: she "had felt wanted and warm and secure and important to someone for awhile, and it was hard for her to forget." So she had begun fantasizing about working far away as a missionary and enticing Carl to join her. But when her sister and Carl have children, Arvay loses hope and eventually has to move on.

Chapter Two

On another Sunday, Arvay, oblivious to the community's interest in her relationship with Jim, hesitates as she prepares for church. She tells her father she probably will not attend that day, and her father suggests she is avoiding Jim. Arvay's parents both want Arvay to marry and try to convince her to go to church. As she prepares, Jim comes by to take her to the church service, which is part of the courting ritual. She attempts to get to church without him, wanting to be left alone and insisting Jim wants "to make a game of me!" Jim tells her that he respects her and would not make her look foolish in front of others, wanting to provide "my good protection" in life. She will eventually see that he has her best interests at heart, he tells her. She fears other people will mock her when they see her in this courtship ritual with Jim, but she finally agrees to join him. They walk to church, along a road lined with trees and moss; eventually they are invited to ride with some others on their "buckboard," but they decline. When they arrive at the church, Arvay is shocked at how many people are at church. During the service, Arvay catches Carl taking a glimpse at her. Jim feels buoyed by the people's reaction to him; one person says, "Go, gator, and muddy the water!"

Jim touches Arvay during the service, and she feels a "common pulse." Arvay feels happy to have gained the affection of Jim, rivaling the relationship between Larraine and Carl. Jim makes a public show of their courtship by giving her money for the church collection, and she proudly walks up to place it in the collection plate—this signals to the congregation that they are a couple. Jim later walks her home as well and says he wants to marry her, praising her and likening Arvay to a natural phenomenon like "lightning." "I'd make a girl like *you* a damned fine husband," he says, but she replies that she will be a missionary, still unsure that Jim is truly interested in her.

She invites Jim into her home, and Jim notices their modest belongings. He notes his surprise that Larraine would fall in love with someone like Carl. Arvay has a seizure, and her mother tries to treat her with turpentine. As Jim assists, he accidentally lets the chemical into her eye, which causes her to scream and run around the house, shouting that he did it on purpose. Her father calms the scene, saying her seizure was over and she was not hurt, but Arvay demands that Jim leave, threatening to pour water on him. He defends himself and notes how she's been cured. Arvay begins to believe that maybe he does care about her, but her insecurity restrains this emotion; she still thinks she "was not fitten for a fine man like Jim." She leaves the room and contemplates being Jim Meserve's wife, fearing her education and poverty will get in the way, but decides to pray to God that it will work out.

She later goes outside to show Jim a mulberry tree, which is where she used to sit and think about Carl, in an effort to expiate her memories of him. Now she wants "to feel that the temple was cleansed, and that she herself was clean and worthy of what she was about to receive." During the meal, Brock Henson talks about marriage in Arkansas, alluding to *A Slow Train through Arkansas* to note that women marry young. Arvay says he's just telling stories, but Jim wants to know more. Brock says that Arkansan men first ask permission from the father to wed the daughter. Jim agrees that that is a fine method, and he reveals that he wants to marry Arvay. Brock gives him permission, and Arvay agrees, "providing you make me a promise not to drop no more teppentime in my eye."

Chapter Three

Maria Henson comments to her daughter about how much time she spends with her fiancé Jim, as her sister, Larraine, makes preparations and sews clothing for the wedding ceremony. Arvay still feels insecure about the relationship. Jim, too, is tense and uneasy about the wedding, worried about how Arvay really feels about him. One day, Jim, who is a supervisor at the turpentine camp, approaches Joe Kelsey, an African-American man, to ask Joe for advice about marriage. He respects Joe, who is married to a woman named Dessie. Joe tells Jim men need to be dominant over their wives, saying, "Take 'em and break 'em." As Jim goes to sleep, he considers Joe's advice.

Chapter Four

Joe Kelsey goes to Arvay's home to give her a message from her fiancé, which indicates that Jim will come the following day to take her on "a buggy-ride." The next day Arvay gets dressed and waits for her fiancé, who arrives dressed up in fine clothing. Her mother watches them, glad that she has the opportunity to marry a man like Jim, who she sees as a better catch than Carl, her other son-in-law. Jim tells Arvay he wants to go to the yard to "that playhouse," near the mulberry tree. There, he kisses her and tugs at her clothing, and "in a moment more, despite her struggles, Arvay knew a pain remorseless sweet." This is their first sexual encounter, in fact their first intimate act. Arvay feels a tinge of remorse, but Jim assures her he was expressing his affection. She hangs her underwear on the tree, and hugs him intently. They have another encounter here later, and she glances again at her underwear in the tree: "She took it as a kind of sign and symbol. Where this man was hurrying her off to, she had no idea, but she was going, and leaving her old life behind her."

They go into the buggy and drive off. Her parents are concerned, her mother suggesting Jim may try "to rape her" while they are gone. Jim tells Arvay that she should not pursue missionary work; she is wed, symbolized by the intimate act that took place between them. He sees her as his salvation, and she sees their sexual encounter as a means of forgetting her former love for Carl. They proceed in the carriage and get married in a civil ceremony rather than in a church. She later returns home, and spreads the news that she has married Jim; her family is happy. The couple stop over at Jim's family's house, then go to listen to some music played by Joe Kelsey and his black friends. Arvay is stirred by the music. Jim expresses his trust of Joe; Arvay sees him as a "pet Negro," assuming he is a faithful and dutiful man.

Arvay begins working at a store at camp. She is happy in marriage, but does not enjoy the visits from Larraine and Carl, worrying her sister might realize she still has feelings for Carl. Dessie, Joe's wife, reveals she is pregnant, and Arvay and Jim are happy for her.

Arvay starts having weird dreams: In one, she stabs Larraine; in another, she is outdoors and an animal attacks Larraine. As a result, she tells Jim she wants to leave the area soon. One evening as Arvay reads the Bible story of Cain and Abel, Jim makes fun of Cain and Arvay responds that that is sacrilegious.

Chapter Five

Arvay gives birth to a child, assisted by Dessie. The newborn appears to have some sort of physical deformity, resembling an uncle "who was sort of queer in his head." This concerns Arvay and Jim. Arvay promises to always love her child, and she feels that her son is the good that came of her past sinning behavior. Dessie and Arvay bake a cake, and later Arvay names the child Earl Meserve. She writes the name and date in her Bible. She prays for Earl and Jim.

Chapter Six

Jim leaves his job, and he and Arvay move to Citrabelle. There, Jim gets a position supervising fruit-picking operations. Arvay feels that people in Citrabelle have easier lives than people elsewhere, and Jim explains that people in Citrabelle earn money from the fruit harvest. Jim initially finds his job a challenge but works with the black men on the farm to try to learn more. He increases productivity on the farm by getting the men to compete with each other in their work. In their new lives, they manage to live a happy life despite their son's problems and "played music on the instrument of life." But Arvay soon grows concerned that Jim goes out and drinks alcohol. Meanwhile she continues to work on her son's physical and mental development; she lies about what Earl does when Jim is not around, but he remains doubtful. Arvay learns she's expecting another child. Jim announces one day that he has bought land by a swamp. Arvay is scared of what could be in the swampy area, but Jim assures her it is a fine, fertile, livable place. They prepare the property, and with the help of some black men in the area, he builds a house. He pays the men with wood from the property, and then replants fruit trees to bring in future income.

Chapter Seven

Arvay gives birth to another child, who resembles her sister, Larraine. Arvay is worried about this, but Jim thinks she looks like Arvay, not Larraine. Jim names their daughter Angeline in honor of his own mother's name, and he inscribes her name in their Bible. Jim spends more time with his daughter than he does with his son, upsetting Arvay. He calls her Angie and buys her a ring and a gold charm, and he boasts about how smart she is. Arvay thinks Angie has taken over the house, and that she likes Jim more. Jim disagrees, saying his daughter is a symbol of his love for her. Jim drinks alcohol out of the house, and becomes combative, getting in a fight with Hawley Pitts. Arvay asks Joe and Dessie to visit their new home, where Joe will help Jim's work.

Chapter Eight

Joe and Dessie come to Citrabelle, and Jim does not go out drinking as much while they're there. Jim gets involved with illegal liquor production. Dessie's children get along well with Angie, and Earl is upset by the attention she gets. Arvay tells Jim she is pregnant again, and he teases her, saying she must bear a son. He tells her to take it easy, and to have Earl help her carrying water and wood. Arvay becomes insecure about her relationship again, but comforts herself by placing a "hand on her abdomen" to remind her about her new child.

Arvay begins cooking and heads outside to retrieve wood without Earl's help. Outside, she prays her child will be a boy, or for God to take it away. She later admits to her husband about her prayer, and he says he'd just been teasing her about the whole thing. Jim realizes that they do not understand each other very well, and so he tries to be a more protective man for his wife. She gives birth to a son who looks like her husband, and they name him Kenny Meserve. Arvay now believes she has moved above her sister and Carl socially and economically; in fact she cannot believe she ever loved Carl, dismissing it as a youthful indiscretion. Thus she would "never be able to feel resentment toward Larraine from now on."

Chapter Nine

Kenny is an outgoing young man, similar to Jim. He likes to spend time with Belinda, the daughter of Dessie and Joe Kelsey. One day Kenny and Belinda go to look at a train, and Belinda performs gymnastics for the people aboard. People are fascinated with her display, so Kenny devises a plan to make money from the show. The train travelers give them money for her gymnastics, which makes them both happy. Jim appreciates what Kenny did, but Arvay disapproves and she punishes both of the children. Arvay blames Belinda, but Jim knows that Kenny must have been responsible for the show at the train. Jim also explains to Arvay what an asset Joe is to his business; Arvay begins to realize how much she appreciates the Kelseys, noting they "had brought her luck." Arvay slowly warms to Belinda. Jim continues to make more money, but he knows Arvay would not approve of making money through bootlegging. Arvay finds out and blames Joe Kelsey. Jim defends Joe, saying he had nothing to do with it, and Jim just wanted to improve their lives. Joe does not appreciate Arvay's complaints. Meanwhile, he buys land and a car and moves out of the Meserves' home. Arvay is glad at first, but then misses their friends; Dessie feels similarly.

Chapter Ten

Jim spends time fishing with his friends, and returns one day to announce that the Corregios will be moving to their property to work, as it is in need of more upkeep. Mrs. Corregio was from Georgia and married a Portuguese man; their two daughters, Lucy Ann and Felicia, are beautiful. Arvay feels prejudice against the family because of their Portuguese roots. One day while she prepares dinner, Arvay discovers Earl in a room yelping like an animal "trampling and running around," then speeding out of the house "like a hunting dog on the trail." Arvay is concerned about her son's strange behavior, and talks to Jim about it. Later she spots Earl spying through the windows as the Corregio family eats dinner. Arvay confronts him and brings him back home, but he hits her. Jim thinks he's dangerous and wants to send him to an institution, but Arvay refuses. Arvay blames the Corregios, suggesting that it is possibly their scent that bothers Earl. Jim believes Earl is stirred by one of the Corregio daughters, but he refuses to have them leave since they are an asset to his business.

Chapter Eleven

Jim decides to stop his bootlegging business as it may be politically risky. With the money he earned from it, he can finance another type of work. Arvay resents that Mrs. Corregio cooks for Jim, which he likes very much, and that she invites them to dine with them. She also believes Jim is attracted to their daughter, Lucy Ann, who is quite popular with young men. Arvay feels insecure and increasingly resentful in her marriage, fearing her husband does not understand her relationship with her son Earl; she feels she must grow even stronger and more forceful. Arvay considers leaving her husband, and writes to her mother about coming to visit with Earl. When she tells Jim, he gives her money but does not seem concerned about her return.

When she arrives at her old family home, the town "looked poor and shabby and mean," and she notices that her relatives do not have the same means she now has. She tries to spruce up her mother's home a bit. When her sister and brother-in-law arrive with their family, Arvay thinks they look low-class. She feels ashamed and upset about this but also proud of what she and Jim have achieved. She wonders if she could support herself if she stayed in Sawley; she sits by her favorite tree and realizes how important Jim is to her and her new way of life. She writes to her husband to tell him that she is leaving Earl in Sawley for companionship with Maria, her mother; Jim writes back agreeing to send money and saying he misses her.

Chapter Twelve

Arvay returns home to Citrabelle, but she fears she will feel like a slave; she also gets upset that no one seems to miss Earl. She later tells Jim that Earl might be in danger in Sawley, as she has had a bad dream in which Earl drowns himself in a river. Arvay returns to Sawley to retrieve Earl; upon her return, Angie and Kenny seem not to care that Earl had been away. Jim is puzzled at Arvay's behavior.

Chapter Thirteen

Kenny enjoys playing the piano, especially jazz and the blues, but Arvay doesn't appreciate it; she also says she misses Dessie and her laundering skills. Suddenly Arvay hears a noise and heads outside with an axe to investigate. Lucy Ann appears to be injured, and Mrs. Corregio tells Arvay where Earl went. The noises continue, but Arvay lays down her axe and heads back to the house. She later sees Earl in the house with the axe and advises him to flee, which he does. Jim says he and some other men will go looking for Earl. Jim tells her Earl injured Lucy Ann, but she is okay; he explains that Earl is unstable and may be a danger to others, and then he leaves. Arvay hopes Earl escapes. The next day Joe says Earl may be at Big Swamp as Hawley Pitts spotted him there. Jim comes home to update Arvay: he says Earl has his rifle, but is "surrounded" at the swamp and refuses to surrender. Jim returns to the swamp, where Earl shoots his own father, injuring him. The other men shoot and kill Earl.

Chapter Fourteen

On a Saturday, people gather for Earl's funeral. Arvay refuses to acknowledge that her son has died. Jim encourages her to face the truth, adding, "But the world ain't finished for you, honey." Arvay looks at her son's body and sees that his "weak but handsome face was unmarred and was inhabited at last by a peace and a calm." She now tells them to sound a bell for her son.

Chapter Fifteen

Arvay grieves for her dead son as Jim regrets that she no longer behaves affectionately to him. She slowly recovers and even experiences a sense of relief, noting that a "burden *had* been wrenched off her." Arvay wants to contemplate this in solitude, so she sends Kenny off to Joe's to work on his music and asks him to bring Angie with him. Arvay and Jim eat dinner, and afterward she spots Jim speaking with a woman, Mary, who has a reputation for being a flirt. Mary claims that Kenny ridiculed her. Jim finds her story amusing, but Arvay does not trust the woman's motives, wondering if she has in fact been with Jim. Arvay yells at Mary, saying she will take up the matter with her son, although she says not even God is interested in the prayer she would say about the matter. Jim laughs at their exchange, and explains he's not interested in Mary. When Angie and Kenny return, no one mentions the incident with Mary. Jim says he wants to go to the city that evening; Arvay wants him to gather Earl's belongings with Joe. Arvay begins to see her husband as "a miracle right out of the Bible" and she feels "blessed beyond all other women of this world." Jim leaves, and she saves dessert for him.

Chapter Sixteen

Angeline spends time alone, looking at her reflection in her mirror as she prepares for her graduation, in May. She combs her hair, thinking about Hatton Howland, a man she's interested in. She thinks she's pretty enough for Hatton, but knows her parents object to her dating so young. She feels women older than she will stand a better chance with him. When Arvay helps with her graduation outfit, Angie resists, thinking the dress makes her look too young. She wants a longer dress that will make her look mature. Her mother says she can dress that way after she's finished as a student in Tallahassee, but Angie balks at the idea. Arvay reminds her of the importance of a college education and says, "Boys and books don't mix, Angie, and I ever hoped that you would school out before you got a notion like that in your head." Angie admits to Arvay she wants to date Hatton Howland, but Arvay does not approve of him since he's from the North and doesn't have a good job. Angie says she danced with him once, and they shared a kiss; she cries at her mother's disapproval. Her mother continues working on the dress and ultimately makes the dress longer to give her daughter a more mature look.

Chapter Seventeen

Arvay and Jim talk about Angeline dating. Jim believes it's appropriate for her to date, and Arvay agrees on the condition that she succeed in getting her degree. This leads them to think about what love means to them, and they wonder why this northerner would be in love with their daughter. Jim wonders about Angie's motivations—maybe the man's age, or the joy at winning out over other women. For Arvay, love "meant to possess as she was possessed." Arvay thinks about her own romantic past, for "She had been in Hell's kitchen and licked out all the pots. She had stood for moments on the right hand side of God." Once they agree to let Angie date him, Hatton spends a lot of time in their home. Angie grows attached to him and cares more about the flowers he brings than about her studies.

One evening Arvay overhears Angie and Hatton discuss the issue of rape, which scares Arvay. Arvay tells Jim about it, but he is not concerned, although he agrees to find out more about Hatton. He says Angie's decision to be with Hatton should be respected. Jim finds out about Hatton's job at the gas station and his plans to marry and support a wife in the future; he sees ambition in the young man, and he allows Hatton to take care of his car. Jim tells Arvay that Hatton works hard and can make money, even though sometimes by gambling. Angie and Hatton elope, and Kenny breaks this news to his mother, stunning her. Still, she cooks them a wedding meal and acknowledges the marriage. The couple talk about their plans to live at the Howland home, although they could spend time at the Meserves', as well. Jim suggests Hatton buy property in a swamp with his gambling money, and he does. Hatton says he'll tell Angie later on why this was so important.

Chapter Eighteen

Arvay feels mixed emotions about her life, which has seen much change. Jim has purchased a boat, which he uses to catch shrimp as means of making money. The Corregios have moved to the sea to oversee the business, leaving Arvay and her husband on the property alone. Kenny has left for college, where he plays for the band. Hatton and Angie seem to have a good marriage and are economically comfortable. Hatton has developed his swampland into a successful, expensive neighborhood, and they enjoy social status as a result. And yet Arvay feels sad at the clearing and the loss of the swamp area; in fact she "had hated and feared the swamp, but long association had changed her without her realizing it."

Arvay also feels alienated from her own family, feeling she may not be of much use anymore; her children have grown up and moved on. Jim, for his part, is pleased with Hatton's progress and realizes that their own property value has increased because of the development. Arvay expresses her continued disbelief that her daughter could get a marriage license at such a young age all alone, but Jim admits he spoke for her at the wedding. Arvay is not surprised that the wedding was kept a secret and becomes angry. She wants to be alone, going into her daughter's bedroom to read the Bible. She feels alienated from her family, including Jim, Kenny, and Angeline, seeing herself a "handmaiden like Hagar, who had found favor in the master's sight." She cries, and Jim takes her back to their bedroom.

Chapter Nineteen

Jim sees himself as a product of the "New South" of commercial development and industry, as he has been energized by his fish business, which allows him to travel and enjoy the ocean. He encourages Arvay to spend time on the boat with him to learn about shrimping. Kenny wants to support himself with music, and Jim points out that whites can use black music to make money.

Jim says the Corregios are prospering living by the sea, but Arvay does not want to move. Arvay fears Jim no longer wants their house, as she wants to keep it to pass down to Kenny one day. Jim becomes closer with the Corregios, and he arranges for Felicia to attend a football game at Kenny's college.

Kenny's band performs during the game, and he proudly claims Felicia as his "date for the day" when others notice her presence. Arvay sees Felicia at the game, Arvay noticing her outfit and wondering how she managed to get to the game. Later, Arvay, Jim, Angie, and Hatton attend a dinner and dance with Kenny and Felicia. Felicia's presence continues to bother Arvay, so Arvay quickly convinces Jim to leave. Jim speeds angrily home; there, they argue. Jim says he should have beaten her when they got married; he pushes Arvay and she yells. He tells her to get ready for bed and makes her embrace him. She explains her conflicting emotions, and Jim kisses her.

Chapter Twenty

Rough weather gives Alfredo and Jim pause as they prepare to head out on a shrimping trip, but they head out nevertheless. Jim sails his new boat, which he called *Angeline,* while Alfredo sails the *Arvay Henson.* The fishing trip lasts several days, and upon returning they sell the shrimp and pay their crew. Afterward, they go to a bar, where Jim speaks with a woman. Jim felt such a sense of happiness as he commanded the ship and caught the shrimp, that he desires to work as a fisherman full-time.

Chapter Twenty-one

Arvay marvels at renovations to her home, including a new porch, which "built Arvay up and made her feel more inside of things. It was a kind of throne room, and out there, Arvay felt that she could measure arms and cope." Arvay is reminded that in her life with Jim she has grown socially and economically. One evening Arvay and Jim discuss their son Kenny, who calls to tell Jim that he has the chance to perform at a club in New York. Jim says that's fine, and if things don't work out in New York he can always return to college in Florida. Arvay feels sad, even abandoned, that her son is leaving, and heads to her bedroom.

Chapter Twenty-two

Jim joins Arvay in the bedroom. He undresses her and she puts on her nightclothes. They go to the porch area, where Arvay reflects on Kenny's life. He must have made the right choices, she thinks, although she senses Felicia probably encouraged Kenny to leave for New York so they could marry without Arvay's intervention. While Arvay sees herself as "a soldier in the army of her Lord," she thinks of Felicia and her mother as godless people trying to lead Kenny astray. Hurston writes, "They were no different from that awful Herodias and her daughter Salome who had got John the Baptist killed for nothing." As she thinks ill thoughts of the Corregios, she empathizes with missionaries who convert people to Christianity. She thinks God is on her side, and suddenly feels pity for the Corregios, for she feels God will act to avenge Felicia and her mother.

Chapter Twenty-three

Arvay still feels uncomfortable about her son's departure to New York and has trouble sleeping. She makes breakfast for Joe and his son, Jeff, and Joe speaks fondly of Kenny's childhood and the music lessons he gave him. Jim calls for Arvay as a dangerous snake is about to attack him. He asks for her help, but Arvay is in shock and can't move. Jeff rescues Jim and prepares to kill the snake. Jim objects, saying the snake acted honorably when confronted. Jim gives Jeff some money as a thank-you before he departs. Later Jim admonishes Arvay for not jumping to his aid earlier. He says that Arvay seems unappreciative of him despite what he has done for her. When he met her, years ago, he saw her as "a king's daughter out of a story-book with your long, soft golden hair." Arvay tells Jim she loves him.

Chapter Twenty-four

Arvay copes with Jim's departure, feeling alienated and powerless, especially since now she has "no control over either" of her children. Jim regularly sends money to her for survival. Although Jeff and his wife live on the property, Arvay still feels alone and uncomfortable, as she feels Jeff does not respect her. One day Arvay receives a message notifying her that her mother has fallen ill. She notifies her children and prepares to return to Sawley. When she arrives, she notices a major transformation. The taxi driver informs her that the turpentine business is gone and that peanuts, tobacco, and tourism have become the drivers of the economy. At her old house, she sees that "Henson place was too awful to contemplate." Her sister looks unkempt; her brother-in-law disheveled. Inside the house, the conditions are unsanitary. Her sick mother tells her that she has signed over the home to Arvay, to be inherited after she dies. Her mother also says that Carl fails to adequately support his wife and children. Arvay also discovers that Kenny sent money to his grandmother. She tells Arvay that she wants a formal funeral with church service and flowers.

Soon after, her mother dies, and the daughters and grandchildren mourn. Arvay says she will take care of the funeral arrangements, and she gives Larraine money for food. She speaks with a banker, who will take care of the financial arrangements and who reserves a hotel room for Arvay. The funeral home staff comes to collect her mother's body, and Arvay gives them instructions. Carl says he cannot pay the funeral bills. The next day Carl visits Arvay at her hotel saying he was injured on the property and wanting to collect money. The hotel manager advises Arvay that he was thus a trespasser and she should not pay him, and she does not give him any money. The hotel manager reveals that Carl claims to have tried to date Arvay years ago. Arvay is happy that her sister ended up with Carl and not her.

Chapter Twenty-five

Maria Henson is treated as a distinguished woman at her funeral. The funeral also brings attention to the banker, who eventually runs for state governor and wins. Arvay recognizes that her marriage to Jim has given her a higher status and more opportunities than many of the other women in the community.

Chapter Twenty-six

Arvay buys food to give to her sister and brother-in-law, then takes a taxi back to her childhood home. She sees that it has been vacated, with trash scattered on the property and evidence that her sister and brother-in-law wanted to set the property on fire. A neighbor informs her about the attempted fire, and offers to cook her a meal with the food she bought. Arvay surveys the property, pausing before the mulberry tree, "her memory-thing" and "a sacred symbol" of the early part of her life. She glances at the house and realizes it was a blessing that they left the house; Arvay herself then decides to set the house on fire. She goes to the neighbor's house and they eat. Arvay tells her neighbor it would be a nice recreation area for the community.

Chapter Twenty-seven

Arvay returns to her house in Citrabelle and offers Jim and his wife the rest of the food. She tells Jeff she's planning to visit Jim by the sea, and Jeff offers to drive her there. Upon arrival, Arvay and Jim reunite, and Jeff and his wife return to Citrabelle. Jim shows Arvay his boats, including the *Arvay Henson, Angeline,* and *Kenny.* He wants other boats in honor of Hatton Howland and Angeline's grandchild. He also wants a boat called *Big Jim.* They enter the *Arvay Henson,* and Arvay says she wants to take a voyage by sea. Jim buys her the proper clothing and introduces her to people there, giving her a sense of life in the area.

They sleep on the boat named for her and set sail the following day, catching shrimp and hitting one rough patch during which Arvay helps Jim, thus showing her devotion to him. She acknowledges the beauty of the sea, and he calls it the "[b]iggest thing that God ever made." During the voyage, Arvay realizes the importance of her marriage to Jim. They have a discussion and reconcile their differences, and she kisses him. She acknowledges her identity as a mother, recognizing that "God had made her a mother to give peace and comfort" and comparing the births of Kenny and Angie to a type of resurrection. "Her job was mothering," Hurston writes. The next morning, Arvay realizes that she "was serving and meant to serve." At the end, Arvay feels complete and confident in her identity.

CRITICAL COMMENTARY

Hurston's final published novel, *Seraph on the Suwanee* touches upon a variety of themes, such as identity, marriage, gender, religion, nature, race, and class. While *Seraph on the Suwanee* is not among Hurston's more famous texts, it nevertheless reveals the author's sophisticated use of plot, characterization, and imagery in a sustained narrative. By focusing on the lives of white people, the novel shows Hurston's versatility as a writer and her ability to cross color lines in her presentation of unifying themes, many of which connect with those of her other novels and short fiction.

Primarily, the text may be seen as a meditation on the complexities of identity within the melting-pot culture of the United States in the early 20th century. Many of the main characters in the story—including Arvay and Jim, Kenny and Angie, Larraine and Carl, and Joe—undergo a series of changes in their lives. As these changes occur, the characters cope and try to assimilate their evolving lives into a stabilizing identity. The quest for identity is thus among the chief challenges for the characters in the novel; Hurston's characters show how the idea of self constantly evolves. Characters embrace and reject identities, sometimes finding resolutions that negotiate different aspects of many different identities. While some resolve their conflicts and reach a sense of self, others remain unfulfilled. This is a theme that Hurston has dealt with primarily focusing on African Americans; by framing the question of identity in relation to white characters, Hurston shows that the struggle for identity cuts across racial lines, but affects people differently, based on a variety of social, historical, and economic factors.

The character of Arvay Henson Meserve is clearly the most striking example of a person in search of identity, as her situation constantly changes throughout the novel. The contrasts and insecurities that mark the early part of her life continue, and it is not until the end of the novel that she feels content. In the beginning, her identity focuses around her family, her church, and her status as a single woman without children. She is a dutiful daughter first, then devotes herself to music and the church, aspiring to do missionary work. She initially rejects the ideas of being a wife and mother in favor of her devotion to God, but she also secretly identifies as a sinner in coveting her sister's husband and wishes he would leave her sister for her. The community views her as an oddball, and she is seen as sickly because of her seizures. Upon meeting Jim Meserve, she transforms her life and her outward identity, playing a role that she and others wanted for her. But inside she feels many of the same tensions and doubts that have characterized her life so far. In fact, she "is a woman who does not think much of herself," a fact that frames her relationships with other people and her concept of self, thus complicating her identity (Howard 269).

The novel covers a lot of ground, spanning from Arvay's childhood to old age, describing the many changes that would frame her search. As a young woman, she has her first sexual encounter with Jim at the mulberry tree, gets married, and has children. Arvay and Jim leave Sawley and move to Citrabelle, where they begin anew, living on their own property, working in a different industry, and meeting new people. The adjustment to life in Citrabelle is difficult for Arvay, and she thinks fondly about her old home. As her husband rises in prominence from his work, she must adapt to a new life of comfort and leisure; slowly but surely, she realizes how different she becomes in this respect in comparison to Larraine and Carl.

Arvay's role as mother frames her experience throughout her life. Her relationship with her afflicted son, Earl, is especially traumatic. While Jim and the other children do not seem to understand Earl, Arvay values her maternal relationship with him: She protects him and loves him, and when the rest of the family does not understand, Arvay feels alone. The more she feels alone, the closer she becomes to Earl, as evidenced by the trip they take to Sawley; in this, we see the two outsiders fleeing, and wishing for escape. In Sawley, Arvay even considers leaving her husband but realizes how much he has given her. Arvay assumes the role of grieving mother after the tragic death of Earl. However, Arvay's emotions are in conflict, reflecting both sadness and relief at his death, which further indicates the tense, complex relationships within the family. His death symbolizes the end of one stage of her life and the beginning of a new one. We can see Arvay's evolving relationship with Angie, as well, as she moves from protecting her to allowing her to be her own person.

Arvay can be seen as a class-conscious woman in her disapproval of Hatton Howland based on his background and job at the gas station. Because of her disapproval, Hatton and Angie wed in secret, showing the practical impact of her mother's protective attentions. In Arvay's relationship with the Corregios, we can see fear and prejudice as other traits of Arvay's. She views the Corregios as inferior and does not view them as American, or even white. Again, these views probably are based in Arvay's insecurity about who she is as an individual; her dislike of the Corregios can be traced to jealousy or competitiveness She notices that Felicia Corregio has fuller hair than her own daughter, and she does not appreciate that Jim likes spending time with them or, especially, that he likes Mrs. Corregio's food.

After Jim decides to be a shrimper and relocate to the coast, Arvay finds herself feeling even more isolated. At her mother's death, she finds herself back home in Sawley, a major life event that actually helps her to come to terms with the many contradictions she has experienced in her life so far. She thinks about her life now in comparison to her earlier life in Sawley, realizing that Jim may have saved her from a life of poverty and pain in Sawley, as symbolized by her sister and brother-in-law. Her epiphany in Sawley changes her self-conception, and she heads back to Citrabelle, and then to the coast, where she reunites with Jim. While on a shrimping trip with him, they resolve their differences and Arvay decides, in her old age, to embrace her identity as a wife and mother. Only through the context of comparison—of seeing what she used to have and what she now has, what others have and what she has—can Arvay come to terms with her life as it is.

Hurston's characterization of Jim Meserve also reveals a person in search of an identity. Unlike most of the other Sawley residents, Jim comes from an affluent family, once part of the southern aristocracy, but financially ruined after the Civil War. So he possesses a higher status in the community but does not have the money to show for it, as he is poor too. As a result, he spends much of his life trying to gain land (for himself or others) and to devise various means of making money. As a young turpentine worker in Sawley, he impresses others with his work ethic and intelligence, and with these qualities he pursues Arvay Henson. Later, Jim becomes a father, first to Earl, then to Angie and Kenny, and this is a role he relishes. While he remains a distant father to Earl due to his mental and physical problems, he functions as the devoted father to Angie and Kenny. He dotes on the daughter, and seems to Arvay to exhibit more love and favoritism to her. When he relocates the family to Citrabelle, he assumes a new identity as entrepreneur, fruit grower, bootlegger, and ultimately shrimper in his quest for money.

Jim asserts his identity as a man throughout the text. In his courtship rituals with Arvay, he shows a level of power and possession over her by escorting her to and from church, the social center of the community. He holds traditional views about gender roles for men and women, thinking that all females should be married and have children; thus he scoffs at Arvay's missionary plans. He even learns from his friend and coworker Joe that he should dominate women, advice that he takes to heart. Jim continues to demonstrate this power over Arvay prior to their wedding when they make love. By this act, he considers them to be wed and tells her that she should not devote her life to God after their act of sexual intimacy. He desires her to serve him and not God. (His name, Meserve, even suggests that other people, such as his employees, wife, and children, should serve him.)

Jim also uses physical and verbal power to assert his manliness. At one point, Jim engages in a fight with a man in the community, but later reconciles with him. His manliness is especially on display when he tries to handle a dangerous snake, believing he can overpower it. But his plan backfires, and the snake almost kills him. When Arvay failed to rescue him, he feels she was not performing her wifely duties; however, his anger after the snake incident can be read more as his own disappointment for having failed in his test of manliness.

He sees himself as the primary breadwinner and his identity derives from his providing for his family well. He teases his wife that she should have another male child; although it is a joke, it frightens Arvay to such an extent that she prays to lose the child if it is not a male. That child turns out to be a male, Kenny, and Jim encourages him throughout to grow up as a strong young man, even setting up a meeting with Felicia Corregio. With his daughter, Angie, he plays the role of strong father by being present for her wedding, unbeknownst to Arvay. Finally, when things fall apart between him and Arvay, Jim sets off and does his own thing, under the pretense that he does not need the support of others. This is later contradicted, when he and Arvay get back together, both of them ultimately accepting their identities as intertwined, even though this acceptance occurs late in life.

Other characters experience similar tensions concerning life change and identity, each one attempting to integrate the raw material of life into some substantial sense of self. Joe Kelsey, for one, rises from his folk roots and becomes a middle-class landowner; his wife, Dessie, is affected by these changes as well. Angie Meserve breaks free from her parents' protection, goes to college, and marries the highly successful Hatton Howland, whose development schemes bring prosperity to the Meserve-Howland family. Kenny transforms his life through music, specifically black expression like jazz and the blues, with the help of Joe Kelsey. He breaks out of the mold too, moving to New York to give his music career a try. On the other hand, Larraine and Carl Middleton experience downward mobility, victims of spiraling poverty and a work ethic that is not like that of Jim, Joe, or Hatton.

Religion

While Hurston explores religion throughout her works, in *Seraph on the Suwanee* she departs from her discussion of its role in African-American communities and looks at how it affects whites in Florida. The seraph, or angel, referred to in the novel's title is Arvay Henson Meserve. She symbolizes the seraph because she possesses a special relationship with God and has the ability to save other people, notably her husband, Jim. Hurston also shows her at times using religious language.

For people in Sawley, the Day Spring Baptist Church functions not only as a religious place but also as a social center. For Arvay Henson, the institution becomes a focal part of her life early on. As a young girl, she enjoys attending church and playing the organ, and she even desires to be a missionary. She declares herself uninterested in being a wife or mother, wanting to focus on her religious devotion instead. Given this background, it is ironic, then, that Hurston situates the courtship between Jim Meserve and Arvay Henson in the church setting. Jim courts the young woman by walking her to and from church, and by talking to her while there. People are surprised and thus attend one Sunday in large numbers to watch the romance unfolding at the church. They are especially interested because of Arvay's early public announcement that she would withdraw from worldly concerns and serve God as a missionary.

Carl Middleton, a preacher at the church, plays an important role in the story. As a young girl, Arvay desired him, and in fact she felt that Carl was in love with her as well. Since Carl marries her sister instead, Arvay must quietly deal with her continuing desire for him, which now means that she covets her sister's husband. In fact, her desire to be a missionary may be totally based on this first major romantic disappointment, as she hopes he will join her as a missionary in a faraway place. In a way, her missionary dream is an escape fantasy that would put her together with the man she desires, however unlikely that may be. Of course, by marrying Jim, she ends the possibility of both missionary work and a life with Carl, and later she is quite happy that she didn't end up with Carl, seeing his poverty. At that point, she interprets her childhood love for him as an irrational youthful infatuation.

Jim Meserve, unlike Arvay, is far more interested in worldly concerns, although he does recognize how much value she and the community place on the church. This is evidenced by his courtship, which takes place in church or involved the church, and for him church is a pleasure because of her. At one service, he touches Arvay and even gives her money for the collection plate, suggesting a certain possession of her. Jim is ultimately able to convince Arvay that her spiritual concerns are less than her worldly ones, and that instead of serving God she should serve Jim. His name, Meserve, suggests that it is he who is to be served. After their marriage, religion takes on less importance, though a contrast can be seen between Jim and Arvay. For example, she gets upset when Jim mocks the biblical story of Cain and Abel; for Arvay, however, it is serious, as she dreams about her sister getting attacked. At the birth of each of their children, they inscribe the name in their family Bible. The name Angeline is a form of *angel,* which suggests spiritual qualities for their only daughter, the next-born child after their disabled Earl.

For Arvay, religion and the Bible serve as her frame of reference for creating an identity in the world, but Arvay has some complicated religious positions, suggesting her thoughts are not quite as pure as she may like them to seem. Most significantly, Earl functions as a "burden" for Arvay, the way sin might; ultimately, when he is killed off, Arvay feels both sadness and relief. At one point, in an angry encounter with Mary, Arvay tells her that God does not want to hear her prayers; this is a self-righteous way to deal with a stranger who has caused only mild offense. Arvay then displaces some of her feelings for God onto her husband, later calling him a "miracle" and saying that she feels "blessed" to be with him; this is evidence of her confusing spiritual and worldly affairs. When her daughter secretly gets married to Hatton Howland, Arvay seeks comfort in the Bible and begins to think she is a misfit in the family due to her humble roots. She compares herself to the enslaved biblical figure of Hagar, a handmaiden, and she sees Jim as the master figure.

In addition, Arvay views the Corregios as godless, and this impression is based on their ethnic background as a Portuguese family. Felicia and her mother are of particular concern, as Arvay thinks they are trying to prey on Kenny, and she compares them to Herodias and Salome, who caused the death of John the Baptist. In fact, those two biblical figures "had been put in the Bible to warn folks against just such sluts as Felicia and her Mama." Her anger later turns to pity as she decides that God will punish Felicia and her mother for their sinful ways. For Arvay, whiteness symbolizes divinity and salvation; her theology has thus racist and xenophobic elements in it. Arvay's association of whiteness with divinity mirrors that of Mrs. Turner in *Their Eyes Were Watching God,* who views Janie as divine because of her white traits.

At the novel's close, Arvay returns to a purer sense of religion as she nears the acceptance of a sense of self. When she is on the boat with Jim, she discovers the beauty of the ocean and attributes that greatness to God. Jim, usually the worldly one, tells her that God formed this ocean and it was his biggest work. At this point Arvay begins to rediscover the divinity in herself and in her relationship with her husband; she compares her marriage to the relationship between Rebecca and Isaac in the Bible. As Arvay contemplates her experience and wonders about the meaning of life, she frames her life in the context of Moses, seeing herself as "Moses before his burning bush." In the end, Arvay decides that God desired her to be wife and mother, and this is the role she must fulfill in the world. Earl symbolizes her sin, for "[s]omebody had to pay off the debt so that the rest of the pages could be clean." Thus she begins to see meaning in his death, that he "had served his purpose and was happily removed from his sufferings." Her other children, Kenny and Angie, then become a form of "Resurrection"; in a sense, they redeem her for her past sins. Arvay finally convinces herself that motherhood is its own divine purpose. Hurston writes, "Holy Mary, who had been blessed to mother Jesus had been no better off than she was. She had been poor and unlearnt too."

Nature

Adept at her use of local color, Hurston captures the natural setting of rural Florida in the early 20th century in *Seraph on the Suwanee.* Nature influences the lives of the characters in the novel in different ways. Hurston alternately presents nature as a malevolent and a benevolent force, as both giving and taking life. Characters who manage to accept their connection to the natural world ultimately emerge stronger than those whose identities are marked by estrangement from nature. Hurston captures a culture in transition from an agrarian to an industrial society, documenting the effects that economics would have on nature and ultimately on people.

The novel begins with a description of the town of Sawley, its geographical features, and the relationship between that landscape and the people. At this time, residents of Sawley live primarily from the profits generated by the lumber and turpentine industries. They tend to be the descendents of white settlers who immigrated to the area, displacing the Native Americans. The Suwanee River functions as the major body of water in the area, providing irrigation, food, and transportation, but also mosquitoes and malaria. The seraph of the title refers to the character Arvay, who comes to have a special relationship with the swampy area near the Suwanee River.

Arvay's relationship with nature is particularly symbolized by her connection to turpentine, the mulberry tree, the swamp, and the sea. Turpentine, which is the main product made in Sawley, is used on Arvay as a natural remedy for her seizures in the early part of her life. The mulberry tree is of notable importance. In fact, Arvay's "image of herself centers around a tree, in this case a mulberry tree that grows behind her home in Sawley" (Morris and Dunn 9). Originally the place where Arvay would go to fantasize about a romance with Carl Middleton, the mulberry later serves to erase that former longing when she and Jim go to the tree and engage in their first physical encounter. She takes Jim to the tree as a means of trying to rid herself of those memories, which she deems sinful since she was coveting her sister's husband. When she has the sexual experience with Jim there, the tree takes on a new meaning for Arvay. She even places her underwear on the tree, a symbol of the loss of her innocence or virginity. She realizes later her mixed feelings about the encounter, but in any case the tree episode reveals the beginning of a new life and the end of an older one. For Jim, the encounter under the tree suggests a type of marriage bond between the two of them. After her mother's death, upon returning to Sawley after many years, Arvay spots the mulberry tree and is reminded of her past. It was, for her, "a sacred symbol," and she wants it to be preserved for the enjoyment of the rest of the community.

Land functions as an important symbol of identity for the characters. Ownership of land often leads to wealth, while lack of land suggests poverty and degradation. It is not always true that land leads to wealth; Arvay Henson's family owns land but continues to be burdened by meager economic resources. Here Hurston suggests that nature on its own will not provide for humans, but humans must work hard in their use of, and respect for, the land in order to flourish. When the couple relocates to Citrabelle, the couple continues to share an intimate connection with nature. The name of the town is suggestive, *Citra* calling to mind citrus, and *belle* meaning beautiful. Jim's job as supervisor of fruitpickers shows the connection between the land and economic prosperity. He acquires land in an area near a swamp, which he sees as lucrative but Arvay views as dark and dangerous. He builds a house there and cultivates fruit trees on the property, which brings in a good deal of income. Jim employs the Kelseys and then the Corregios to live and work on the property; for these people too, their livelihoods are based on farming.

Thus the land also becomes a source of economic success for Joe Kelsey, who himself makes able use of his own land in order to rise from his poor roots. But the swamp also plays a sinister role in the story, ultimately becoming the place that Earl will die. Even after Earl's death, Jim still thinks the swamp may bring profits, and he encourages Hatton Howland to develop the swampland adjacent for real estate use. In this sense, Jim exploits the land for his own benefit and gain; his economic success is intimately tied to the earth. Hurston also uses the sea as an important symbol of nature, particularly for Jim, Arvay, and Corregio. Jim ultimately purchases a boat to conquer the sea after he conquers the land.

Hurston uses elements of nature as a means of testing the relationship between Jim and Arvay. When Jim tries to show his manhood by wrestling a snake, his wife fails to come to his aid. This is a pivotal moment, as it causes tension in their relationship: Arvay reveals that she does love him, and Jim moves to the sea. Later, after they are reunited and go on the shrimping expedition, they save their marriage by reconciling their differences. There is a bad storm at sea, and this time Arvay proves her mettle by helping Jim. He realizes she loves him and has courage. Arvay sees power and freedom in the sea. Jim says that the sea is God's work, and yet it parallels human behavior. Ultimately, it is the sea that brings Arvay and Jim back together both physically and emotionally.

Marriage

Hurston treats the theme of marriage in many of her other works, including *Jonah's Gourd Vine, Their Eyes Were Watching God,* "The Gilded Six-Bits," and "Sweat." Here, too, in *Seraph on the Suwanee,* Hurston takes a close look at marriage, but in a different way. The marriages in this novel suffer many tensions and problems, but the individuals manage to reconcile and remain together; in the other novels, adultery, betrayal, deception, and death bring an end to the marriages. *Seraph on the Suwanee* chronicles several prominent marriages, such as Maria and Brock Henson, Carl and Larraine Middleton, Arvay and Jim Meserve, Joe and Dessie Kelsey, Mr. and Mrs. Corregio, and Jeff Kelsey and his wife; these marriages are diverse in ethnicity, race, and age, but similarities are revealed. Hurston comments on socially expected gender roles and the significance of family in relation to identity.

The most significant marital relationship is that of Arvay Henson and Jim Meserve. Arvay initially resists societal expectations that she marry and start a family. She desires to commit herself to religion, especially after the minister Carl Middleton marries her sister rather than her. By defying social conventions, she becomes an odd specimen in the eyes of her family and peers; this is emphasized all the more by Arvay's quiet, shy personality. Jim Meserve defies Arvay's wishes and attempts to court her before the people in town. He insists he will be a good spouse for her, and that women should marry and start families and settle down. His efforts ultimately prove fruitful. His name, Meserve, suggests domination and possession, and he tends to have traditional attitudes about love and marriage. He views a wife as someone who should serve her husband.

Arvay's family also holds traditional ideas about marriage, and they encourage her to marry Jim, her father, Brock, even telling old Arkansas tales about what married people should do. Brock acquiesces to Jim's request to have Arvay's hand in marriage, showing the ownership both husband and father exert over Arvay. When they do marry, Arvay wants a traditional church wedding, but Jim suggests a nontraditional celebration of union, when they meet at the mulberry tree. For him, the union was sealed during a sexual act, rather than in the religious act in a church. As Susan Meisenhelder comments, "Ultimately reduced to a sexual object in her relationship with Jim, Arvay leaves the mulberry tree to begin a life of passive sexual availability, her underwear left hanging on its branches" (101). He claims that their symbolic tryst there represents a kind of salvation for him; later he prefers to officially marry in a courthouse and not in a church. Arvay's adjustment from religious solitude to marriage proves difficult as she continues to be plagued by self-doubt. She questions if she is worthy of Jim due to her humble background; she also questions her love for him and has lingering thoughts about Carl.

Her identity then emerges in her roles of wife and mother, but in the context of her marriage, Arvay feels like a slave and an outcast. Even as a mother, things are complicated, as her firstborn son, Earl, possesses serious physical and behavioral defects. She views Earl as a symbol of her sin for coveting her sister's husband, and she spends much of her life trying to relieve herself of that guilt through her attentions to Earl. Other family tensions arise when Jim gives more attention to their second child, Angeline, and Arvay accuses Jim of neglecting Earl. Jim and Arvay have very different personalities, and he often retreats from home and drinks alcohol, which causes even more problems. When Arvay gets pregnant again, he teases her that she must have a male child, upsetting her. The misunderstanding shows the strains in their relationship, and may reflect Arvay's mixed feelings about her marriage. This is seen again in their argument about how to raise Earl, as Jim wants to institutionalize him and Arvay refuses. When Arvay takes him for a break in Sawley, she realizes she would have a hard time supporting herself there without Jim. After Earl's death, Arvay, like Jim, comes to believe a burden has been lifted in their relationship. The new sense of reality affects their marriage; at the same time, Arvay still views the marriage as tenuous, for she feels threatened when Jim speaks to a woman named Mary.

Their daughter, Angie, chooses a marital path that stands in stark contrast to her mother's. Instead of shunning marriage initially, Angie is eager to marry young. Arvay tries to stop her from dating before she has a college degree, and she disapproves of her daughter's boyfriend, but this episode causes Arvay to open up her mind to differing views of marriage. She is shocked by the secrecy of the elopement, and she feels trapped and enslaved when she learns that Jim was complicit in it. But she ultimately comes to accept her daughter's decision. Angie's marriage experience serves as a counterpoint to her mother's past, an evolution even if Angie is choosing the more socially acceptable path. The marriage between Hatton and Angie brings the family higher status due to Hatton's financial success, but it also increases Arvay's sense of estrangement from her daughter; her daughter enjoys comforts that she never knew at the same age. Witnessing Angie's marriage to Hatton compounds her class consciousness and feelings of anxiety about it.

Arvay finds much of her identity in her role as a wife and mother. As her marriage becomes shaky and her children grow older, her sense of self diminishes; Angie's marriage and Kenny's departure to New York City leave her with new questions of identity and doubt. Her failure to save Jim from a snake causes emotions in both of them to rise to the surface, and they separate from each other for a time. With her marriage in ruins, she feels alienated and powerless. Only when she returns home to tend to her dying mother does she make the comparison that brings her back to herself: She realizes that her life with Jim has been bearable in comparison to the sad lives of those back in Sawley. Unlike Janie in *Their Eyes Were Watching God* and John Pearson in *Jonah's Gourd Vine,* the primary married couple in this text reunite and maintain their marriage. Before the humbling beauty of the sea, Arvay and Jim resolve their differences. She decides that God meant for her to be a wife and mother, and she accepts this as her identity.

Hurston reflects on marriage through other couples as well. Joe and Dessie Kelsey, for example, serve the important function of representing interracial friendships between blacks and whites; the two families are quite close, and Joe passes along black culture to Kenny by teaching him about jazz and the blues. The Corregio marriage is between a hardworking but poor Portuguese man and an American woman; Arvay's disapproval is based on ethnic prejudice and jealousy. Hatton Howland and Angeline's marriage comes to represent the rising middle-class family. Like Jim, they achieve success by making use of the land, but they do so in a very different way, one which would alter the southern landscape and put an end to agrarian life as it was known. Larraine and Carl Middleton, by contrast, show the harsh realities that a transforming society can impose on those who cannot adapt to economic changes.

CHARACTERS

Corregio, Felicia The daughter of a working-class family of mixed ethnic heritage, Felicia Corregio comes to Citrabelle as an outsider, but she is striking in looks and personality to others in the community. Kenny has a date with her at a football game and Arvay fears she will woo him into marriage. Arvay sees Felicia and her mother as godless, comparing them unfavorably to Herodias and Salome from the Bible.

Corregio, Lucy Ann Another daughter of the Corregios, she is attacked by Earl Meserve, leading to his pursuit in the swamp and his death. Lucy Ann is also a beautiful young girl popular with young men.

Henson, Brock Arvay's father, Brock works in the turpentine industry and helps Jim Meserve get a job in it. He is a fairly poor but caring father, and he encourages the match between Arvay Henson and Jim Meserve. During Jim's courtship of Arvay, Brock tells stories of Arkansas customs obligating men to ask fathers for permission to marry their daughters; he subsequently gives this permission to Jim.

Henson, Maria Arvay's mother, she is a devout, religious woman who serves as a role model for her daughter. She is protective of her daughter and has initial fears about Jim. As the novel progresses, she shows favor to Arvay since Larraine and her husband try to take advantage of her. She dies, leaving her land to Arvay. She is given a proper burial to show her significance to the community.

Howland, Hatton Hatton marries Angie Meserve in an elopement kept secret from Arvay but attended by Jim. From humble northern roots, working initially in a gas station, he achieves much success by investing his gambling money into real estate. He capitalizes on the real estate rush in Florida by clearing swampland and turning it into viable property. Jim is a mentor of his, and Arvay eventually accepts their marriage.

Kelsey, Dessie The wife of Joe Kelsey and a close friend of the Meserves, she also assists

Arvay in the birth of her first child. She is African American.

Kelsey, Jeff The son of Dessie and Joe, he works for Jim Meserve on the fruit harvests. He saves Jim's life when Jim is almost killed by a vicious snake. He is African-American.

Kelsey, Joe He initially works in the turpentine industry with Jim in Sawley and later moves to Citrabelle to work on Jim's fruit harvest. He is an African American, married to Dessie, and a very close friend of Jim's. He later starts his own business and rises economically. He also teaches Kenny about jazz and the blues. Arvay possesses mixed feelings toward him, alternately thinking he may have a positive or negative influence on her husband.

Meserve, Angeline Angeline, or Angie, is the second child of Jim and Arvay, born after Earl and before Kenny. Her desires contrast with those of her mother: She wants to go to college and date men. She marries Hatton in a ceremony attended by her father but kept secret from her mother. With Hatton Howland, she has a comfortable middle-class life.

Meserve, Arvay Henson Arvay is the central character, and her identity changes throughout the novel. She is the daughter of Brock and Maria Henson; the wife of Jim Meserve; the mother of Earl, Angeline, and Kenny. Born in Sawley, she moves with her husband to Citrabelle to begin a prosperous new life. Arvay is the seraph, or angel, of the Suwanee described in the novel's title.

She begins the novel as an immature young woman who turns to the church after having her heart broken by the pastor Carl Middleton, who marries her sister. She is an outsider who shuns marriage and faints at the slightest attention made by a male, but ultimately she is won over by Jim Meserve. Throughout her marriage she feels ambivalence and self-doubt about her family life. Her first child, Earl, who is seriously disabled, is killed after he attacks a girl and then shoots his father; his death incites both trauma and relief in Arvay. Her two other children, Angie and Kenny, are bright and successful, but she has strained relations with them at times too. Her attitudes toward other people range widely, from warmth and love toward the Kelseys to cold skepticism toward a stranger named Mary and xenophobia and racism toward the Corregios.

Arvay's most complex relationship is with her husband, Jim. From the moment they consummate their love sexually, Arvay has mixed feelings about her life with him. They have many differences, and she often retreats to solitude and to her Bible during rough times. They have communication difficulties and often misunderstand each other. After she fails to rescue Jim from a snake attack he flees to the coast to work on a shrimper, and she heads to Sawley to tend to her dying mother. When she sees the decay of the lives of her family back in Sawley, she returns to her fine life with Jim. During their sail on the sea, she returns to spirituality and accepts her identity as a wife and mother.

Meserve, Earl Earl is the first child of Arvay and Jim, born with major physical and mental disabilities, which cause problems for his parents. Arvay sees Earl as a symbol of her sin for coveting her sister's husband, Carl. Still, Earl holds a special place in Arvay's heart, and she refuses to institutionalize him, against Jim's wishes. He assaults Lucy Ann Corregio and flees to a swamp area, where he shoots his father and is then shot dead by other men. His death sparks feelings of both sorrow and relief in Arvay.

Meserve, Jim Jim is Arvay's husband and the father of Earl, Angeline, and Kenny. Coming from a formerly wealthy plantation-owning family, Jim aspires high even if he begins humbly as a man working in turpentine. He courts Arvay at church, insisting that she wants the life of a wife and mother, effectively turning her away from her missionary ambitions. In this sense, he has fixed views about the roles of men and women, and he expects Arvay to serve him rather than God; his name, Meserve, underlines this fact. He marries her with the permission of her father; they consummate their love under the mulberry tree and he claims she is his salvation.

Jim and Arvay move to Citrabelle to begin life anew, setting up on their own swampland property and growing fruit trees as well. There, he provides well for his wife and three children and contributes to the prosperity of others who work for him, notably the Kelseys and the Corregios. He has a close relationship with his children, with the exception of Earl, who is killed in the swamp; he also serves as a mentor to his son-in-law, Hatton, helping him with financial matters. After the snake incident, he leaves his wife and heads to the sea to work as a shrimper; at sea, he senses freedom, autonomy, and adventure. Arvay eventually comes back to him, they reconcile their differences, and he introduces her to the joys of the open ocean.

Meserve, Kenny Kenny is the third and youngest child of Jim and Arvay Meserve. Enterprising and intelligent as a child, he later grows passionate about music, especially jazz and the blues, taught to him by Joe Kelsey. In college, he joins the jazz band and has a date with Felicia Corregio during a football game, incensing his mother. He moves to New York City for a chance to work as a musician. His appropriation of black music is representative of white patronage of blacks during the HARLEM RENAISSANCE.

Middleton, Carl The pastor of Day Spring Baptist Church, he is the source of Arvay's secret sin. She falls in love with him as a youth playing the organ at the church, but ultimately he marries Arvay's sister, Larraine, breaking Arvay's heart. Carl and Larraine decline financially and socially over the course of the novel; they are poor, sick, and desperate by the time Arvay returns to Sawley for her mother's funeral. Carl attempts to extort money from Arvay, but she does not give in. Arvay finds it hard to believe she ever loved him, but it is revealed that maybe he initially loved Arvay too.

Middleton, Larraine Arvay's sister, Larraine is married to Carl Middleton. In the beginning, her future looks bright with him, and she is envied by Arvay for her popularity and social grace. Arvay secretly covets her husband and desires harm to befall Larraine so she can wed him. Larraine and Carl experience a downfall during their lives, and in the end they are poor and desperate. Her condition serves as an impetus for Arvay to appreciate her life and return to her husband.

BIBLIOGRAPHY

Howard, Lillie. "Seraph on the Suwanee." In *Zora Neale Hurston: Critical Perspectives Past and Present,* edited by Henry Louis Gates, Jr., and K. A. Appiah, 267–279. New York: Amistad, 1993.

Hurston, Zora Neale. *Seraph on the Suwanee.* In her *Novels and Stories,* 597–920. New York: Library of America, 1995.

Meisenhelder, Susan Edward. *Hitting a Straight Lick with a Crooked Stick: Race and Gender in the Work of Zora Neale Hurston.* Tuscaloosa: University of Alabama Press, 1999.

Morris, Ann R., and Margaret M. Dunn. "Flora and Fauna in Hurston's Florida Novels." In *Zora in Florida,* edited by Steve Glassman and Kathryn Lee Seidel, 1–12. Orlando: University of Central Florida Press, 1991.

"Spunk" (1925)

This story chronicles a deadly love triangle involving the protagonist, Spunk, and is notable for its use of DIALECT, which lends a sense of gritty realism. "Spunk" appeared in a 1925 issue of *OPPORTUNITY* magazine, a publication by the National Urban League that spotlighted African-American culture. The story was published early in Hurston's career and helped to give her exposure as a rising author.

SYNOPSIS

I

Spunk is walking with Lena, an attractive married woman in the Village. Joe, Lena's husband, walks into a store and asks for something to drink. Elijah (or Lige) asks him about his wife, Lena, and Joe says he knows she is with Spunk, but he plans to win back her affection. After Joe leaves, Walter and Elijah discuss the romantic triangle involving Joe, Lena, and Spunk, making speculation and joking around. Lige says that Spunk denies that Lena is Joe's wife, seeing her as his lover and his lover only.

II

The men in the village store hear gunshots. Spunk and Lena enter the store; Lena cries because Spunk has killed Joe. Spunk admits killing Joe but claims it was in self-defense, since Joe tried to kill him first. Lena leaves and Spunk leads the townspeople to Joe's body. Spunk is acquitted of the murder and does not immediately face consequences for his actions.

III

Elijah says that Spunk and Lena now live together and plan to marry. He remarks on the presence of a bobcat by their house. Spunk fears the cat, thinking it is the ghost of Joe Kanty.

IV

Elijah tells Walter that he watched Spunk die after he was cut by a saw. As he was dying, Spunk claimed that the accident occurred because Joe shoved him into it. When the men arrive at Lena's home, she mourns the loss of Spunk.

CRITICAL COMMENTARY

The structure of the story, divided into four parts, presents the tale in a fragmented manner. It is essentially a series of vignettes that connect thematically. Hurston uses dialect to convey a sense of realism in this tale.

The characters, who are black working-class southerners, use a variety of nonstandard English. This enables Hurston to present the voices of the black folk while, at the same time, filtering their perspectives through a voice in standard English—that of the narrator—which would match the discourse community of readers of the story. In any case, the townspeople serve an important narrative function, framing the story and action. Much of what the reader knows comes directly from the mouths of the townspeople, gossiping about Joe, Lena, and Spunk, rather than from the narrator.

The character of Joe stands in stark contrast to Spunk. Spunk symbolizes male aggression, sexuality, power, and authority. He possesses a strong sense of himself as a man, and he openly spends time with Lena. Other people know about their affair, but he considers himself the superior man and thus worthy of Lena's attention. He respects no law, disregarding her marriage contract with Joe and then killing him. After the murder, he does not seem to experience remorse and is relieved when exonerated of the crime. Lena is a rather passive character, succumbing to Spunk's charms and openly betraying her husband, then marrying the man who killed her husband. The reader does not get much of a glimpse into her character, aside from that given by the town gossip, but from that and her actions we get a sense that Lena is a vulnerable character, easily swayed by men. By pushing against societal norms of respecting marriage vows, Lena and Spunk ultimately face punishment.

The black cat—a traditional symbol of doom and death—lends a sense of the supernatural to the story, as Spunk believes that Joe's soul has been reincarnated into the body of the black bobcat. This bobcat skulks around Spunk and Lena's home. Ultimately, Spunk is killed when he falls onto a saw. The men at the store think "Joe's spirit pushed him" into the saw (Patterson 92). The cat may also be considered a manifestation of Spunk's guilty conscience for killing Joe.

Through the depiction of the love triangle between Joe, Lena, and Spunk, Hurston touches on a variety of themes that she deals with in her other work as well, including marriage, adultery, aggression, and power. The theme of adultery in particular anticipates short fiction such as "The Gilded Six-Bits," in which Missie Mae has an affair with Otis Slemmons, and the novel *Jonah's Gourd Vine,* in which John Pearson repeatedly carries on affairs with other women.

CHARACTERS

Elijah **Elijah (or Lige)** is a townsman who reveals to the reader gossip about Joe, Lena, and Spunk, often by speaking with Walter or other people in the story. He claims to have seen Spunk die.

Joe Joe is the cuckolded husband of Lena, and while he knows about her affair and intends to get her back, he is killed by Spunk. He reappears later in the story in the form of the black cat, haunting their home and later pushing Spunk onto a circular saw.

Lena Lena is at the center of the affair. She is married to Joe but in a relationship with Spunk as well, and her identity remains defined by others in the story. After Joe's death, she marries Spunk. In the end she loses both of her husbands.

Spunk The protagonist of this story encapsulates power, authority, sexuality, masculinity, and identity—and yet he is brought down ultimately for his actions. Initially boldly open about his relationship with the married Lena, he claims he is the better man for her. He then kills Joe, supposedly in self-defense, and is acquitted of the crime. He marries Lena, but they are terrorized by a black bobcat representing Joe's soul. In death as in life his persona takes on legendary airs.

Walter Another townsman, he gossips about Joe, Lena, and Spunk, often in the store with Lige Walter.

BIBLIOGRAPHY

Headon, David. "'*Beginning To See Things Really*': *The Politics of Zora Neale Hurston.*" In *Zora in Florida,* edited by Steve Glassman and Kathryn Lee Seidel, 28–37. Orlando: University of Central Florida Press, 1991.

Hurston, Zora Neale. "Spunk." In her *The Complete Stories,* 26–32. New York: HarperCollins, 1995.

Patterson, Tiffany Ruby. *Zora Neale Hurston and a History of Southern Life.* Philadelphia: Temple University Press, 2005.

"Story in Harlem Slang" (1942)

In "Story in Harlem Slang," Hurston makes use of varieties of nonstandard English as a means of documenting the real language spoken by African Americans in Harlem. Hurston also includes a useful "Glossary of Harlem Slang," providing definitions for terms used in the story; this suggests that her original audience included readers outside of the black community and thus unfamiliar with the way of speaking. The story, telling the tale of Jelly and Sweet Back, is significant for its setting in HARLEM, NEW YORK, its presentation of the slang used there, and Hurston's characterization of the GREAT MIGRATION. "Story in Harlem Slang" appeared in *The American Mercury* in 1942.

SYNOPSIS

A first-person narrator tells the story of an African-American man in Harlem and the people he encounters there. The narrator describes the protagonist of the story, Marvel, who adopted the name Jelly after being in Harlem for a while, since he needed a name that would fit the image he wanted to project: "Well, he put it in the street that when it came to filling that long-felt need, sugar-curing the ladies' feelings, he was in a class by himself and nobody knew his name, so he had to tell 'em." Jelly is "a sealskin brown and papa-tree-top-tall"; he is skinny and likes to wear his hair in waves, a popular style.

Jelly sometimes spends the afternoons on the street, dressed up in a "zoot suit," a popular 1940s style for black men. One day Jelly sees his friend Sweet Back and goes over to say hi, hoping Sweet Back might have something to give him. The two greet each other by slapping each other's hands. Jelly says he has no money, and Sweet Back asks him why not. Jelly says he was just joking, that in fact he does have money and a woman who provides him with it. Sweet Back counters that he saw Jelly with an ugly woman the night before. Jelly disputes the claim, saying he went out drinking the night before with a light-skinned beauty, chauffeured by taxi. Sweet Back counters back, saying the woman "was one of them coal-scuttle blondes with hair just as close to her head as ninety-nine is to a hundred." Jelly insists he attracts pretty women, and in fact he left Alabama to run away from a woman who wanted to date him. He expresses his preference for light-skinned black women, saying, "Man, I don't deal in no coal." Jelly and Sweet Back pretend to gear up for a fight, but then start laughing.

A woman passes by, and the two men speak with her, hoping she will have some love or money to offer. The woman, who is from Georgia, says she has seen them in the past and knows that they exploit women. Sweet Back performs a "gesture" that makes the woman think they may try to rob her, so she threatens to scream and call the police. She leaves. Sweet Back says he did not want to rob her, since he has plenty of funds; he glances toward Jelly in hopes he sounds credible. Jelly expresses his nostalgia for Alabama and especially for southern food. A glossary of slang terms follows the story.

CRITICAL COMMENTARY

Hurston's portrayal of Jelly reveals the significance of the GREAT MIGRATION, the dreams that the move from South to North would translate to a move from poverty to success. During this period, Harlem was a center of the black diaspora, with a large population of black migrants from all over the United States as well as from Africa, the Caribbean, and South America. (This is well documented by an Alain Locke essay in *The New Negro.*) Many black southerners had idealized views of the North, and specifically Harlem, before moving there. The characters in this short story are all products of this migration of blacks. Once in Harlem, however, the continuing reality of poverty causes Jelly to long for the South. Hurston writes, "He was remembering those full, hot meals he had left back in Alabama to seek wealth and splendor in Harlem without working." Ironically, for Jelly, the South is associated with nourishment while the North generates hunger. Hurston depicts a complicated assessment of the differences between the North and the South and illustrates that "the North was no utopia, just as the South was not necessarily hell" (Hemenway 291).

Despite his moves north from Alabama in search of more social and economic opportunities, Jelly evidently does not achieve much prosperity. Hurston characterizes him as poor, relying on women to financially support him. Hurston sets up a connection between money and pride, whereby those who have money also have comforts of luxury and the attentions of others. Jelly says, "How can I be broke when I got de best woman in Harlem? If I ask her for a dime, she'll give me a ten dollar bill: ask her for drink of likker, and she'll buy me a whiskey still." His bragging, clearly just wishful thinking, is a playful way of connecting with his friend Sweet Back, who appears to be in a similar situation to his. Beneath the joking, the status marker connecting money and sexuality is evident. In the same conversation, Hurston reveals how poor, and hungry, he actually is: "It had to be late afternoon, or he would not have been out of bed. All you did by rolling out early was to stir your stomach up." Poor and hungry, Jelly focuses on the hope of finding a woman who can take care of him emotionally, sexually, and financially. This runs counter to standard gender roles, since it is often the man who is considered the provider for the woman.

By moving north, Jelly appears to be in a state of flux; his migration mirrors his search for identity. This can be seen in his name change, suggesting a break from his early life to his later life. Jelly's real name, Marvel, suggests the word *marvelous,* yet he renames himself Jelly, suggesting sweetness; the name also has a sexual connotation, since *jelly* or *jelly roll* was a slang term for sex in that era. In this way, he seeks to present an identity of being a romantic man eager to please women. Indeed, the theme of sexuality is also very present in this story, especially in the exchanges between Sweet Back, Jelly, and the young woman. Sweet Back and Jelly take predatory positions toward this woman as a means of earning friendship and money. Hurston presents "two uptown hipsters who while away a day playing the dozens as they stalk out their next meal" (Boyd 352). The woman Jelly and Sweet Back talk to is also from the South, having migrated from Georgia. She draws a connection to the South by noting they speak using southern expressions. Despite their common background, she refuses to humor them, saying, "Nobody ain't pimping on me. You dig me?" This woman knows their reputation, which is confirmed by their actions, and she refuses to be exploited.

Hurston, like the characters, came from the South and relocated to Harlem. The emphasis on slang and the use of a first-person narrator reinforces the importance of the oral tradition to African-American culture.

CHARACTERS

Marvel (Jelly) A migrant from Alabama who moves north to Harlem, he is a symbol of the Great Migration. Jelly comes to New York searching for opportunity, but he finds himself impoverished, hungry, and desperate. He changes his birth name of Marvel to Jelly as part of his new identity, hoping to entice women. He spends the day talking with his friend Sweet Back and trying to get the attention of women, but his days are ultimately vacant and hungry, and he longs for the South.

Sweet Back This character is Jelly's friend, with whom he speaks on the street about money and women. The two trade barbs in a playful exchange that reveals a rich nonstandard version of English. His name suggests the idea of sweetness, and he too attempts to exploit women for sex and money. He is portrayed as uneducated when he asks the passing woman if Georgia is in Delaware.

BIBLIOGRAPHY

Boyd, Valerie. *Wrapped in Rainbows: The Life of Zora Neale Hurston.* New York: Scribner, 2003.

Hemenway, Robert E. *Zora Neale Hurston: A Literary Biography.* Urbana: University of Illinois Press, 1980.

Hurston, Zora Neale. "Story in Harlem Slang." In her *The Complete Stories,* 127–138. New York: HarperCollins, 1995.

"Sweat" (1926)

This short story focuses on the relationship between Delia Jones and Sykes Jones, an African-American couple. The title, "Sweat," refers to Delia's hard work and labor as she tries to support her family as a washerwoman. The interrelation of marriage, economics, and gender roles frame the story. "Sweat" appeared in the sole issue of *FIRE!!*, in 1926, along with Hurston's play *Color Struck*. While the magazine published only one edition, it included important pieces that contributed to African-American literature. George Hutchinson writes, "The short-lived *Fire!!* and *Harlem* were declarations of independence from the established black periodicals as much as from the white magazines, which came in wider variety" (129).

SYNOPSIS

A third-person narrator recounts the story of Delia Jones, a married black woman who works as a launderer for white families in the state of Florida. She has been married 15 years to her husband, Sykes, but she is the only person in their family who works and makes an income. On a Sunday, as she washes, she is confronted by something that reminds her of a snake, which scares her. It is actually her husband's whip. In response, her husband tells her she shouldn't work on Sunday, because it's a holy day. He messes up her laundry, and she gets mad. "Sweat, sweat, sweat!" she cries, and angrily threatens to hit him with a pan. This is a turning point for her, as she stands up to her husband, recalling his abuse and violence in the household. They then go to bed.

It's summer, and people are gathered on the porch of Joe Clarke's store; they see Delia Jones walk by. Elijah Moseley and Walter Thomas comment on the couple; Joe Clarke talks about how men treat women in general. Bertha and Sykes Jones are there together, clearly in an extramarital affair; in fact, Sykes pays Bertha's rent so he can have his mistress nearby. Delia and Sykes fight about their marital problems.

Later in the summer, Sykes tries to get his wife to abandon their marriage and leave their home. He points Delia to a box with a snake in it; as she fears snakes, she protests and asks him to remove it. Sykes does not, but instead leaves and does not return in the evening. The next day, Delia goes to church, and upon returning home finds the snake still in the box. The snake then crawls into bed, where Sykes is headed. As he confronts the snake in the bedroom, he cries out for Delia, but for once he is the vulnerable one.

CRITICAL COMMENTARY

In the story, Delia Jones is a black woman living in the South during the early 1900s, working in a traditional role as a domestic, doing laundry for white families. She supports herself and her husband, and represents the hardworking woman who is often underappreciated for what she does. The title, based on what Delia cries out in an important scene, is reflective of the labor Delia does, which others take for granted. By crying out "Sweat, sweat, sweat!" Delia acknowledges her own work and expresses frustration at her husband, who does not work. Delia has a strong work ethic, even working on Sunday, the day of rest and Sabbath for the community; even in this, Sykes find a reason to fault her.

Hurston characterizes Sykes Jones as a man emasculated by his wife's role as a breadwinner. She has the financial and the domestic power, while he is revealed to be powerless in these affairs. In other words, it may be said that Delia's "work makes him feel like less than a man" (Howard 67). As a result, he finds alternate means of expressing his manhood and identity, particularly through his expression of sexuality. His affair with Bertha becomes his means of controlling their relationship. Hurston uses some phallic imagery as a way of emphasizing his attempts to assert his manhood. The whip he carries in the beginning functions primarily as a symbol of power and aggression, but it can be seen as a phallic image as well. The real snake that Sykes puts in the box in the kitchen can also be interpreted as a phallic image, another means of asserting his masculine control over his wife. In reality, it's all a show: Sykes may have some physical prowess, but he has no actual power. Delia does all the work and makes all the money, and she is in charge of their domestic sphere. His snake plan reveals this, as he is left helplessly calling after his wife to come help him. In this way, Hurston suggests that masculinity and male power are artificial forms of authority, or are at least highly constrained.

As throughout her work, in "Sweat" Hurston depicts marriage as an institution fraught with adultery, deception, and violence. Sykes is in this way emblematic of the many dangers of marriage: He represents adultery and violence, and he is ungrateful yet dependent upon Delia. He makes no attempt to hide his affair with Bertha, and the townspeople all know about it. Delia knows it too, but she remains faithful to him. Sykes is also aggressive and antagonistic toward his wife, but Delia Jones finally rebels against him by threatening to hit him with a skillet. The use of a skillet is symbolic, for it symbolizes female domesticity, it being a kitchen device for cooking. Sykes's attempt to overpower his wife backfires in the end, as he becomes submissive to Delia. When in the bedroom with the snake alone, he realizes that he needs her for his survival, but she is not there to help. In fact, she watches from outside the domestic sphere of the house, while he is being threatened by a snake within the very sphere that she is in control of.

There are important connections to adulterous characters in other Hurston texts, notably Mitchell Potts and Laura Crooms's husband in "The Eatonville Anthology" and John Pearson in *Jonah's Gourd Vine.* More generally, the interconnected themes of marriage, economics, and gender can be compared to their treatment in "The Eatonville Anthology," *Jonah's Gourd Vine, Seraph on the Suwanee,* and *Their Eyes Were Watching God.*

CHARACTERS

Bertha Bertha carries on an open extramarital affair with Sykes Jones; she does not conceal this, and can be seen spending time with him at Joe Clarke's store. Sykes pays her rent so she can live close to him. Comparisons can be drawn to Hattie Tyson and Ora Patton in *Jonah's Gourd Vine,* as well as to Delphine and Daisy in "The Eatonville Anthology."

Clarke, Joe Joe Clarke is a recurring character throughout Hurston's work, notably in "The Eatonville Anthology" and *Mules and Men.* His store serves as a community gathering place, where people gossip and trade stories. In "Sweat," there is a scene where Bertha and Sykes are there together, carrying on their affair, when Delia walks by. Joe Clarke comments on the complexity of male-female relationships.

Jones, Delia Delia is a devoted and hardworking woman who earns money by doing laundry for white families. Married 15 years to Sykes, Delia is responsible for all domestic work in her own household as well. She has a fear of snakes and is terrorized in her own home by her husband, who plays on her phobia and abuses her. Her emphasis on "Sweat, sweat, sweat!" illustrates the hard work she does. By the end of the story, Delia has transformed herself from powerless to powerful.

Jones, Sykes Sykes Jones is the do-nothing husband of Delia. He criticizes Delia's hard work and is aggressive toward her. Despite her devotion, Sykes has a public affair with Bertha and pays her rent so she can be nearby. Sykes may feel threatened by Delia's role as breadwinner, and his assertions of sexuality and violence may be manifestations of his desire to reassert his masculinity. He is ultimately brought down by his sloth and must face the snake that he has put in the house to scare Delia. Hurston attributes phallic symbols to him in the form of the whip and the snake.

BIBLIOGRAPHY

Howard, Lillie P. *Zora Neale Hurston.* Boston: Twayne Publishers, 1980.

Hurston, Zora Neale. "Sweat." In her *The Complete Stories,* 73–85. New York: HarperCollins, 1995.

Hutchinson, George. *The Harlem Renaissance in Black and White.* Cambridge, Mass.: Belknap Press, 1995.

Seidel, Kathryn Lee. "The Artist in the Kitchen: The Economics of Creativity in Hurston's 'Sweat'." In *Zora in Florida,* edited by Steve Glassman and Kathryn Lee Seidel, 110–120. Orlando: University of Central Florida Press, 1991.

Their Eyes Were Watching God

Published in 1937, *Their Eyes Were Watching God* is Hurston's most widely read and discussed book, considered by many to be her masterwork. The novel, which takes place in the South, chronicles the lives of the protagonist, Janie, her three husbands, her grandmother Nanny, and others she comes in contact with during her life. Through these characters, Hurston presents African-American cultural expression in a complex and nuanced manner that reveals and celebrates the diversity of black experience. When the novel first appeared, it received a mixed review by Alain Locke in *OPPORTUNITY,* and Richard Wright in *New Masses* found much

Dust jacket of *Their Eyes Were Watching God,* ca. 1937 *(Yale Collection of American Literature, Beinecke Rare Book and Manuscript Library)*

to disparage. Later critical commentary situated the text among the most significant of 20th-century American novels, especially for its insightful exploration of race, class, and gender.

The story is told through two primary narrative voices: a third-person omniscient narrator, and the protagonist, Janie; however, Hurston presents a story-within-a-story in the section narrated by Janie; this is a story from the grandmother, narrated from Janie's perspective. Through these narrative voices, the reader witnesses different perspectives on the action, both as an outsider and as an insider privy to the thoughts of the characters. This gives the novel a complex, nonlinear narrative that begins in the present, shifts to the past, and then returns to the present at the end. By avoiding a strictly sequential ordering for the narrative, Hurston conveys how the past and the present influence each other; time and our perceptions of it are dynamic rather than static phenomena. The story takes place in the early 20th century, although it reaches back to other eras, including the Civil War and Reconstruction. This sociohistorical context frames the narrative and shapes Hurston's representation of African-American life and culture. By presenting the Civil War and its aftermath alongside her modern-day narrative, Hurston examines the continued legacy that slavery would have for Americans, across racial lines, showing how social, political, and economic tensions frame the reality of the day. Into her narrative, Hurston also weaves elements of the folklore that she documents heavily throughout her work, paying homage to the great oral tradition in African-American culture.

Hurston's writing, certainly a product of the HARLEM RENAISSANCE, is nevertheless informed by a number of other literary movements—past and contemporary with Hurston—including romanticism, realism, naturalism, and modernism. As Hurston was well read in American literature, her own writing calls upon her predecessors as she synthesizes various literary elements. What sets *Their Eyes Were Watching God* apart is Hurston's focus on a black woman in early 20th-century America, a time and place in which the black female experience was marginalized. The story also is especially notable for putting a black female on center stage; whereas elsewhere during her era black women were marginalized in fiction as well as in life, this text validates the black woman's experience by focusing directly on Janie Crawford, her family, and her life.

Richard Wright, 1943 *(Library of Congress)*

Hurston began work on the novel in 1936 while living in Haiti and finished it in December of that year. *Their Eyes Were Watching God* was adapted for network television in 2005, with Halle Berry playing the lead role of Janie Crawford. This televised event of Hurston's most famous novel was, for many Americans, their first exposure to a once little known but now increasingly relevant 20th-century writer.

SYNOPSIS

Chapter 1

Janie Crawford returns to EATONVILLE, FLORIDA, following the death of her husband, Tea Cake. As she returns under the setting sun, others in the town watch her and consider their conflicting feelings about her. "They made burning statements with questions, and killing tools out of laughs," Hurston writes. They remark on how she is shabbily dressed, wearing overalls rather than the fine outfit she wore when she left town, and some of them wish for her downfall; they talk about her age, her appearance, her hair, and especially Tea Cake—there is an assumption that he must have abandoned her. Janie greets them but does not stop to chat. Pheoby Watson, Janie's old friend, defends Janie and leaves to bring her food.

Pheoby finds Janie and they talk. Pheoby compliments her appearance and offers her "mulatto rice," which Janie eats. Pheoby wants to know what has happened to her. Janie responds that she knows what the other folk in town are saying about her, so she won't speak to them, but she will confide in Pheoby, because they are "kissin'-friends." She reveals that Tea Cake is gone but had been good to her and did not take her money. She and Pheoby thus begin a long conversation, which constitutes the main narrative of the novel.

Chapter II

Janie views her life in the context of a tree as she recounts her past to Pheoby, who listens intently. Janie did not know her mother or father; her mother had left home, so she was raised by her grandmother, Nanny, who worked for a white family. The family was Washburn, and they lived in western Florida. Janie would play with all the other Washburn grandchildren, and they were frequently disciplined by Nanny. Janie says that as a child she had no awareness of her race until seeing a picture of herself. When she looked at a photo taken of her, she noticed that one girl had darker skin than the others, but she did not realize it was her. She asked about it, and thus realized she was black; others found this amusing. At this time, when she was called Alphabet, her family did not have their own home and she wore secondhand clothing. Other children teased her about her parents, saying her father had done something bad to her mother. Nanny wanted Janie to feel proud, so they would eventually get their own home.

Janie explains that her self-awareness stems from a particular incident that took place near her grandmother's home one day when she was laying under a pear tree. She was curious about the pear blossoms, and as she watched a bee pollinate a flower, a sensual excitement was aroused within her: "She saw a dust-bearing bee sink into the sanctum of a bloom; the thousand sister-calyxes arch to meet the love embrace and the ecstatic shiver of the tree from root to tiniest branch creaming in every blossom and frothing with delight." It stirred something inside her emotionally and physically, and she viewed it as a type of wedding. Janie wished she were a "tree" in the world. Trying to make sense of what she just saw, she went inside, where her grandmother was asleep, then headed to the gate to look down the road. She noticed Johnny Taylor ambling up the road, but he seemed different to her now. They then had a physical encounter, and Nanny caught them kissing. Nanny told her she was maturing and would need a man, but not someone like Johnny Taylor. Janie wondered when she could marry, and Nanny says she will try to find a husband for her; even though she wanted Janie to get an education, she now thinks marriage is acceptable. Nanny said that Logan Killicks was interested in being her husband, but Janie found him ugly and unexciting.

Nanny told Janie how she was different, without parents, and in need of "protection," causing Janie to cry. Her grandmother said that "colored folks is branches without roots." Being a slave affected her perspective, Nanny explained to Janie. As a slave she could not fulfill her dreams. She had a relationship with the plantation owner where she was a slave and bore a child to him. When he left to fight in the Civil War, his wife demanded to see the baby, angry at what she saw and demanding that Nanny be beaten. Nanny managed to avoid the beatings, and one day, after the sound of gunshots and the sight of a ship in port, she learned that the slaves were freed, but the Civil War would yet continue for a period. Nanny decided not to marry, and she moved to western Florida to raise her daughter, Leafy, and try to give her a chance in life. Leafy attended school, where one day, as a teenager, she was raped by her teacher. She thus became pregnant, but after the birth of Janie she drank alcohol and ran off, leaving Janie in the care of her grandmother.

Chapter III

Janie decides to marry Logan Killicks, according to her grandmother's wishes. After some time, Janie visits her grandmother, concerned about that marriage. Janie reveals that she does not love her husband, though Nanny thinks she is being silly, and Nanny reminds her that Logan owns land and a home, but Janie says she has no attachment to his property or to him. She repeats that she finds him ugly. She wants to return to the feeling "lak when you sit under a pear tree and think." African-American women shouldn't worry so much about love, Nanny says, because it means a life of labor. Nanny tells her that her views on marriage will evolve and become more practical. Nanny dies.

Chapter IV

Janie realizes that Logan treats her differently than when they first married. One morning Logan leaves to look at a mule and tells Janie to slice potatoes while he's away. While he's gone, Janie spots a finely dressed man walking down the road; his appearance is fancier than most of the rural folk in the area. She pumps water, and this man takes a sip of the water. Jody Starks introduces himself and tells about his history: born in Georgia, he moved to Florida to find more opportunity, and he plans to move to an all-black community there. He is surprised that her husband would have her do this sort of farm labor. He calls her a "pretty doll-baby" and reveals he wants to marry her, telling her to meet him the following morning. At night, Janie reflects on her situation, thinking he represents "change and chance," and she remembers what Nanny told her. The following morning as she prepares breakfast, she tells Logan she has been contemplating their relationship, and she says he doesn't need her on the farm. She leaves home and meets Jody; together, they head to Green Cove Springs, where they marry.

Chapter V

Jody and Janie arrive in Eatonville, where Janie is mistaken for Jody's daughter. Jody inquires about buying land, wanting to speak to the mayor, but there is no mayor in the town. The couple are directed to a place to stay, and there they meet townspeople on the porch. Jody makes an impression on the people in town and decides to buy land from Captain Eaton, who has much property in the area. Jody decides to build a store, which the town needs. He calls the townspeople together to talk about building the store. When the store is complete, a special opening event is held; Janie wears a nice dress and serves food. Jody makes a speech to the town, recommending they elect a mayor and incorporate the town in the state. Jody is nominated to be mayor, and he does not want Janie to air her opinion on the subject. As mayor, Jody erects a lamp in town, for which he holds a big ceremony, and he undertakes other projects such as ditches and roads. Jody proves to be a smart businessman and powerful local politician, but Janie expresses frustration at being the mayor's wife, feeling alienated from the community. Their white home, fitted with fancy spittoons, resembles a plantation house, setting it apart from the other homes. Other townspeople look up to Jody, but they are resentful that this black man has so much wealth and power. However, they are unwilling to confront Jody or rebel against his authority.

Chapter VI

Janie works in their store, where people gather and tell stories about the mule owned by Matt Bonner, who is teased for often losing track of the mule. Janie enjoys these stories, but her husband does not allow her to participate in the storytelling. Because of her position as the wife of a prominent man, she should not be engaging in that sort of behavior, he says. Janie dislikes working in the store, as well as at the post office, finding the tasks difficult and tedious. Jody also insists that she wear a scarf to hide her beauty, after an incident in which he notices a man touching Janie's hair. One afternoon Matt loses his mule, and people mock the animal when it later shows up at the store. Janie gets upset at them for treating the mule that way. Jody hears her and agrees, so he buys the mule, making Janie happy. She says Jody is like Abraham Lincoln or George Washington for his "power tuh free things." The mule becomes part of the community life and gossip, living at the store, but eventually it dies. A funeral is held for the mule, at which Jody makes an impressive speech, but he prohibits Janie from attending due to her status. After the people leave, buzzards gather around the carcass to eat it. The main buzzard, Parson, looks at the mule, and asks repeatedly, "What killed this man?" and the response is always, "Bare, bare fat."

Jody returns to the store after the funeral and notices that Janie is unhappy, which he interprets as ingratitude. He talks about the funeral and laments that other people have so few expectations in life. Later, with the arrival of Daisy Blunt, a group gathers outside his store. She is a striking presence, and men surround her. Daisy acts nonchalant. Dave tells her he cares more for her than Jim, which Jim denies, and the two continue competing for her attention. A woman arrives and asks Jody for documentation of the food stock, causing a dispute between Jody and Janie over its location. After decades of marriage, Janie realizes she "wasn't petal-open anymore with him." Over time, Janie's feelings for Jody change. On another occasion, Mrs. Tony Robbins arrives at the store, claiming she needs food since her husband will not provide it. Jody gives her some meat, but she then complains that the portion is too small. People gossip about her, and Jody says that her husband knows about her behavior. Janie has an outburst of frustration about their conversation, for which Jody admonishes her.

Chapter VII

Janie begins to feel torn about her life. She notices that her husband's body is changing; at the same time he criticizes her own appearance. Jody frequently shouts at Janie for her job at the store, even publicly critiquing her when she does not correctly complete a sale with a customer. He tries to joke about it, calling her old. People chuckle, but the incident turns serious when Janie confronts Jody. She remarks that he is older than she, and that "[w]hen you pull down yo' britches, you look lak de change uh life." Jody is in such disbelief that he is silenced. Failing to verbalize a response, Jody violently hits Janie.

Chapter VIII

Jody dozes at home. He and Janie converse very little anymore. Jody stops eating Janie's food and starts to keep company with other people. He continues to decline physically, and he does not allow Janie to enter his bedroom. Still, he has others check up on Janie and give him reports on the job she does at the store. Janie finally has a doctor come to see Jody, determining that he has kidney failure. Jody, however, is convinced that someone conjured against him. He does not believe he will die. Jody wants Janie to leave the room, but she decides to speak to him. She says he has become a different man, ungrateful and selfish. Jody dies. Janie sees herself in a mirror and removes her head scarf, noticing her physical transformation as well. She puts her scarf on again, and tells the other folks that her husband has died.

Chapter IX

A funeral is held for Jody Starks. The ceremony is lavish and well attended, reflecting his wealth and status. Janie continues to work at the store, but she destroys the head scarves he made her wear. Janie enjoys her solitude and feels liberated; men start paying her more attention. One man cautions her about remarrying, but she assures him that she's not considering it. He continues, saying she is still young and needs a man to take care of her. She is bothered by this commentary and heads home. Several months later, Janie still feels Jody's presence in her store. Hezekiah, who helps out in the store, tries to act like Jody, which amuses her. Despite attempts at courting her, men do not prove successful in gaining her affections. Janie spends time with her good friend Pheoby, to whom she reveals she likes her liberty.

Chapter X

Janie works alone at the store while Hezekiah plays baseball. A man, who looks familiar, comes in. He buys cigarettes and asks her for a light; they chuckle. He explains that he mistakenly thought the ball game would take place in Hungerford, even though it is actually at Winter Park. He asks her if she wants to play checkers, but she claims she doesn't know how to play. He says he'll teach her, even making her a "good player," and Janie appreciates that he wants to spend time with her this way. She finds him attractive. He introduces himself as Vergible Woods, nicknamed Tea Cake. He helps her close the store and then walks her home.

Chapter XI

Janie contemplates her relationship with Tea Cake, especially the age gap between the two. He seems to be in his twenties while Janie is "around forty." She notices that he seems poor, and she wonders if he's trying to get money out of her. He spends a good amount of time at her store, passing the time and even convincing Janie to play checkers, which surprises people. One day Janie leaves Hezekiah to shut down the store so she can spend time with Tea Cake. They stay on her front porch, eating cake and drinking lemonade. They then go fishing at night, which extends past midnight. Hezekiah cautions Janie about Tea Cake's attentions the following day, but Janie sees Tea Cake back at her house with fish the following night.

There, Janie and Tea Cake cook the fish in her kitchen, and he plays on her piano. She falls asleep and awakens to Tea Cake combing her hair. They talk about their age difference, and he leaves. For Janie, Tea Cake was a "a glance from God," who "looked like the love thoughts of women." In fact, she wonders if he might represent the "pear tree blossom in the spring." One day he brings her strawberries, and they end up spending the night together. Another day he suggests they prepare for a picnic, and Janie agrees. Tea Cake tells her, "You got de keys to de kingdom."

Chapter XII

People in the community disapprove of Janie's relationship with Tea Cake, first because of his low status but also because her husband has only recently died. They notice that Janie doesn't go to church, and they object as well to her clothing and the things she does with Tea Cake, such as fishing, hunting, and attending films. Pheoby confides in Janie about the community's commentary, suggesting Tea Cake doesn't understand Janie's status in town. She suggests he is trying to get her money, and notes, by the way, that people don't like the color blue she's been wearing. Janie responds, first, that Jody had "classed me off" during their marriage. Tea Cake doesn't ask for money, she says, and she admits to wearing blue because Tea Cake likes it.

In fact, she reveals to Pheoby that they plan to marry. Pheoby is disappointed, and it is risky. Janie retorts that she has risked her life in the past. Janie plans to put the store up for sale, not needing it for her relationship with Tea Cake. Unlike with Jody, with Tea Cake it's "uh love game," and Janie no longer wants to follow her grandmother's rules. Her grandmother's past as a slave, she clarifies, caused her to value money and stability above all else. Pheoby wonders what it's like to have status and warns her friend to be cautious. She recalls the story of Annie Tyler, who had a relationship with Who Flung; the two were not at all right for each other. Janie says she has learned from Tea Cake, and she points out that she will be leaving the town eventually.

Chapter XIII
Janie takes the train to Jacksonville, Florida, to meet Tea Cake. There, they marry at a minister's home. Out of caution, Janie has not revealed that she has brought money with her, remembering her friend's advice. One morning Tea Cake leaves to shop for food. Janie has coffee with the landlady, and as she gets dressed she realizes that her money is gone. She looks all over for it and thinks about the story of Who Flung and Annie Tyler. Annie, a wealthy older woman, has romances with younger men, whom she treated well. One of these men, Who Flung, convinced her to sell her home and move to Tampa, and he then proceeded to exploit her and take her money. He never married her, and Annie later had to be taken care of by her daughter. Janie does not want to experience what Annie Tyler did.

Tea Cake returns and explains what happened. He explains that he saw the money as he was dressing, and he took it to buy fish. On his way to buy fish, he saw a man he knew, who invited him to join a feast. Tea Cake agreed, and bought fish for it. The party was full of people, and Tea Cake got in a fight. He didn't invite Janie, he says, because they were all poor people and she would have been uncomfortable. Janie says she will kill him if he ever does something like that again. Tea Cake agrees to gain back her money by gambling. He prepares and Janie prays. He wins the money back, but is beaten up afterward. Janie cries, learning that he won several hundred dollars. She then reveals the truth about her finances, and Tea Cake says he will take care of her financially. They plan to move to an area referred to by Hurston as "the muck," in the Everglades, where they will establish their home. As Tea Cake dozes, Janie's emotions mount, feeling that "her soul crawled out from its hiding place."

Chapter XIV
Janie adjusts to life on the "muck," a large area where cane, beans, and weeds grow. Tea Cake stresses the importance of planting early and being ready when it is time to pick the crop. Others wanting to make money from crop-picking continue to come there, including Native Americans. Tea Cake wants to go hunting and teaches Janie how to shoot; she proves to be a skilled shooter, better even than Tea Cake. People are surprised when she helps out with the work in the field, considering her wealth and status. Tea Cake himself does not want Janie to feel pressured to do that work, and she assures him she wants to do it. Their new home has a lively atmosphere, with people working by day and having a good time at night. People gather there, with Tea Cake playing the guitar and Janie cooking the food, sometimes that she has hunted herself. Their home is a social center, with gambling, music, and storytelling. Here she enjoys participating in the storytelling, and she "got so she could tell big stories herself from listening to the rest."

Chapter XV
Janie begins to feel jealous. She suspects a woman named Nunkie of desiring Tea Cake, as this woman has been affectionate with him over a period of several weeks, and Tea Cake does not seem to ignore her attention. Others notice their interaction as well. One day, Janie discovers Tea Cake and Nunkie together in a sugarcane field, and she

demands to know what they are doing. He claims she had his work tickets (which can be transferred into money) from the pocket of his shirt, and he needed to go retrieve them. Janie tries to grab Nunkie, but the woman runs away. Janie returns home. They later get in a fight, and Janie accuses Tea Cake of infidelity, but he denies having any feelings for Nunkie.

Chapter XVI

The planting and picking period ends, but Janie and Tea Cake remain in the area. Janie becomes acquainted with a woman named Mrs. Turner, who has a light complexion and Caucasian-like features. She is quite pleased with her physique, although Tea Cake ridicules her for it, and thus Mrs. Turner despises him in kind. Mrs. Turner admires Janie's skin color and hair, and she notes her disapproval that Janie married a darker black man such as Tea Cake, mentioning a brother who she thinks would be more suitable for her. The two have a disagreement over the contributions made by Booker T. Washington when Mrs. Turner suggests he was unimportant to black society. Mrs. Turner says the problem with blacks is their appearance, including their outward behavior and their skin color, and she resents being grouped with them since she looks different.

Janie does not know how to respond, but eventually says the issue of skin color does not really concern her. Mrs. Turner wonders how Janie can stand all the blacks spending so much time at her home, and she expresses surprise when Janie tells her that Tea Cake does not have much money. Janie says that Tea Cake makes her happy. Mrs. Turner points out that she is very different from Janie. Mrs. Turner continues to see Janie and tells her she can visit her when she wants; she reveres Janie's white characteristics and thus wants to transform herself through association with her. She hopes to one day reach a "heaven of straight-haired, thin-lipped, high-nose boned white seraphs." Tea Cake and Janie remain fairly indifferent to Mrs. Turner's behavior. People eventually return to the "muck."

Chapter XVII

In response to Mrs. Turner's suggestion that Janie meet her brother, Tea Cake assaults his wife to show that he is "in possession." Tea Cake boasts about being able to control how his wife spends time, and he explains why he hit her. Another man suggests confronting Mr. Turner, or assaulting Mrs. Turner herself, but Tea Cake doesn't think that would be effective. They agree that Mrs. Turner is prejudiced and should be made to leave the area, as she probably wants Janie's money. The men buy alcohol and get drunk, and go to Mrs. Turner's restaurant. A fight breaks out between two of the men in the restaurant, which leads to a bigger fight among people in the restaurant. After the fight, Mrs. Turner decides that she and her family should leave town because she considers the people on the "muck" to be uncivilized and uncouth.

Chapter XVIII

On the "muck," celebrations continue, now with some Caribbean people who perform. Janie notices a good deal of movement and is informed that a hurricane is coming. At night, the animals stir and make noise; some people become scared and leave, though many stay. Tea Cake and Janie are invited to leave with another man, but Tea Cake refuses, saying he needs to stay on the "muck" to make money. The man says he will regret this. As the weather worsens, they pass the time at their home, telling Big John de Conquer stories and playing dice games. People are not concerned, because there are levees blocking the lake; they say the rich aren't worried, so they shouldn't be either. Janie sees signs of the hurricane; suddenly Tea Cake and his friend Motor Boat stop playing dice. They realize that the "time was past for asking the white folks what to look for through that door." Tea Cake asks Janie if she regrets leaving with him and moving to the "muck". She says no. The weather rages on as "their eyes were watching God."

The storm worsens. Tea Cake decides they must flee, even though Janie wonders if they shouldn't just stay put. They retrieve their important documents and their money, but they realize there are no cars to leave in. They leave along with Motor Boat, finding another house to rest and take shelter in before continuing on. Janie and Tea Cake struggle as they alternately swim and wade through water, heading for an area called "the fill," which appears to be dry; here they see many white people. Janie reaches for a piece of a roof, hoping it would provide protection for Tea Cake, who has become overwhelmed. She ends up getting blown into the water, and yells for Tea Cake. He points her to a cow in the water, where there is also a dog. She hangs on to the cow's tail, and Tea Cake swims over to her. The dog bites Tea Cake, and Tea Cake kills the dog with a knife. Janie and Tea Cake arrive with the cow at "the fill" and they survive. They end up in Palm Beach, where she tries to convince Tea Cake to see a doctor, but he refuses. They sleep, and Janie expresses her gratitude for being alive.

Chapter XIX

Janie wants Tea Cake to rest, but he says they need to leave. Men are needed to dig graves and handle the dead bodies of those killed by the hurricane, but since Tea Cake has money, he does not think he will have to do that work. As he leaves to find the other men from his farm, he is stopped by some men with weapons. Despite his protests, he is told that he must help deal with the dead bodies, or else they will kill him. He helps out along with the others; both black and white men do this work, and yet the grave sites are segregated. Tea Cake comments about God and color prejudice. Afterward, he sees Janie sobbing, and he decides they should return to the Everglades, as he knows the white people there. They arrive back at the farm the next day, where Motor Boat had stayed and survived the hurricane, working for several weeks in storm clean-up. Tea Cake eventually falls ill, and Janie calls for a doctor. She explains about the dog bite during the hurricane, and the doctor provides medication. He suspects Tea Cake has rabies and recommends that he be hospitalized. He warns Janie that Tea Cake may bite her, infecting her as well. Janie is distraught. Tea Cake continues to suffer due to the rabies. The following day, Tea Cake confronts her in the kitchen and asks why she hasn't been sleeping in bed with him. He aims his gun at her and tries to shoot her, but the gun shoots a blank. She loads the rifle with a bullet and tells him to lay down his gun. They both shoot their weapons; this time Tea Cake's gun releases a bullet, but it misses. Janie has shot him, however, and he then bites her in the arm.

Janie is in prison on the day of her trial. The jury is made up of all white men; Janie sees both whites and blacks in the courtroom, but the blacks do not support Janie. The doctor and the sheriff testify in the case; another black man tries to testify against Janie, but the prosecutor, Mr. Prescott, quiets him. Janie testifies in her own defense, explaining her relationship with her husband and what happened during the shooting. The judge tells the jury to determine if Janie's actions constitute homicide or compassion. The jury deliberates and quickly decides to acquit Janie. White women sob in the courtroom; the black people leave. Janie is released from prison. In one conversation, it is suggested that black women are free to murder.

Janie buries Tea Cake in Palm Beach. At his funeral, Tea Cake's friends come desiring Janie to forget about the past. Janie has worn her work clothes to the ceremony.

Chapter XX

Some speculated that Mrs. Turner's brother was what caused Janie to kill her husband, but others said it was mere self-defense. Janie stayed in that area for some time, eventually leaving with seeds.

The action returns to the present as Janie goes back to Eatonville and finishes telling Pheoby her story. She tells her friend that she feels content, that she has "been tuh de horizon and back." Love is dynamic and not static, she explains. Pheoby expresses that she feels transformed as a result of this story; she reflects on her own relationship and decides to behave differently with her husband. Pheoby then leaves. Janie goes up to her room, feeling a sense of "peace," for she "pulled in her horizon like a great fish-net" and "called in her soul to come and see."

CRITICAL COMMENTARY

This novel functions as a story within a story, one narrative being used to frame another. The primary story focuses on Janie's return to Eatonville after burying her third husband and telling her friend Pheoby her life story; her life story is the secondary narrative, constituting the bulk of the text, framed by the first plot line. The beginning and the end of the book are told by a third-person omniscient narrator, whose voice tells the tale in standard English. Janie's tale, framed by that third-person narrative, is told in the first person and presents her own point of view, as does Nanny's tale. In the first-person narration, Hurston employs colloquial black English to achieve a realistic dialogue. By weaving a rich and complex tale about one individual's quest for identity, Hurston treats various themes, such as nature, race, class, gender, and religion. An exploration of Hurston's literary technique and thematic concerns in *Their Eyes Were Watching God* can help us better understand the text.

Hurston opens and closes the novel with metaphors of the horizon and the open ocean, and in so doing frames the human narrative in relationship to the natural world. This framework puts human experience in deep contact with nature, although Hurston achieves this in a far subtler way than in many of the folktales, in which the connection between humans and nature is very explicit. The novel begins with an image of the horizon and calls to mind a metaphorical use of the horizon as a means of referring to an individual's future, dreams, and desires. The sun meets the sky at the horizon, and as a person advances toward the horizon, it recedes farther back at the same time. It serves as a visual reference point, but it is not ever reachable. Thus horizon, literal or figurative, suggests possibility, but also limitation. In *Their Eyes Were Watching God,* Janie's dreams and ambitions are symbolized by horizons: Though she tries to near them, they seem always to retreat.

Hurston characterizes Janie as a romantic person, someone seeking a pure form of love rather than simple marriage for convenience or prestige, and the horizon imagery comes into play here. At her grandmother's urging, Janie marries Logan Killicks, because he has money and property. Janie finds herself stifled and unhappy in this marriage, as it was not based on love but on material reasons; she also finds herself angry at her grandmother. The horizon imagery is used to describe Janie's relationship with her grandmother, whom she blames for that marriage and sees as a limiting force. Janie realizes that "Nanny had taken the biggest thing God ever made, the horizon—for no matter how far a person can go the horizon is still way beyond you—and pinched it in to such a little bit of a thing that she could tie it about her granddaughter's neck tight enough to choke her."

Even later in life, Janie still feels constrained by her past, which makes her all the more susceptible to fall in love with Jody Starks and Tea Cake. When she meets Jody Starks, she sees a different man from her husband, one who appears more cosmopolitan, who dresses well, and who might offer the life Janie has been looking for. In fact, Jody "spoke for far horizon." She sees him as her best opportunity, and thus she leaves Logan for Jody. But Jody, too, proves to be a problematic husband, oppressive and controlling. He quiets her, excludes her from community events, and degrades her appearance. After Jody dies, Janie feels free. Her relationship with Tea Cake, once again, is an attempt for Janie to realize her desires to live in a truly loving relationship. When Janie finishes telling her life story to her friend Pheoby, she says she has "been tuh de horizon and back," suggesting she has completed her life journey. "She pulled in her horizon like a great fish-net," Hurston writes, signifying the many accomplishments of Janie as well as the unrealized dreams that she comes back to. The image of her pulling in the horizon may also symbolize the end of her life.

In tandem with her metaphor of the horizon, Hurston uses the symbol of water, and more specifically the sea, to represent the close relationship between human destiny and nature. Water functions as both a nourishing and a dangerous force, freeing and constraining the fate of humans. In fact, Hurston begins the novel with a paragraph that uses the sea as a metaphor for humans' lives. Hurston writes, "Ships at a distance have every man's wish on board. For some they come in with the tide. For others they sail forever on the horizon, never out of sight, never landing until the Watcher turns his eyes away in resignation, his dreams mocked to death by Time. That is the life of men." The characterization of human desires and experiences as being fluid, even arbitrary or elusive, is an important framework for the novel, which deals with human ambition, goals, and identity. The evocative opening statement illustrates the flowing, cyclical nature of an individual's wishes and desires in the world.

Water as freedom can be seen in the character of Nanny as well. For Nanny, water is important because she escaped to a river or swamp when she fled her plantation "and made it to de swamp by de river"; this area, despite its dangerous reptiles, is preferable to the life of slavery. When she learns about the emancipation of slaves, it is at port, with "uh big ship at a distance and a great stirrin' round." In this sense, then, water functions as a force of life, as a means of giving opportunity; water flows freely, and humans' lives should too.

Water is also seen as a force for danger and destruction. The hurricane is perhaps the clearest such example of the power of water, or more generally of nature, over people. The hurricane episode plunges Janie and Tea Cake into a flooded mess and totally uproots their lives. Initially, no one seems to be worried about the coming storm, and people continue to play games and tell stories at their home, but ultimately they realize that they will have to fight for their lives. Hurston describes the hurricane as if it were a living creature when she writes, "The sea was walking the earth with a heavy heel." Here she shows that the storm is not a totally chaotic, isolated event, but rather an organism that adheres to its own order. As they struggle through the "water full of things living and dead," Janie and Tea Cake grow closer together in their fight against nature. And yet it is also at this point that the dog bites Tea Cake, infecting him with rabies, which would ultimately bring him down and change their lives forever. Janie and Tea Cake prove to be powerless against the wrath of nature in the form of the hurricane.

The depiction of water proves important again in the end of the novel. One of the final images shows Janie with "her strong feet in the pan of water," while she finishes telling her life story to Pheoby. Hurston returns to the sea imagery, as Janie tells Pheoby, "Love is lak de sea. It's uh movin' thing, but still and all, it takes its shape from de shore it meets, and it's different with every shore." Love changes and alters course over time; love is a journey, dynamic, active, evolving. This reflection deeply inspires Pheoby, who feels she will make changes in her life and will confront the busybody townspeople. Hurston ends the novel with more sea imagery, writing, "She pulled in her horizon like a great fish-net." As with a net for collecting fish, Janie is able to pull together the experiences of her life: She can now account for her dreams and experiences.

Hurston draws connections between the natural world and human destiny in many other ways throughout the novel. One of the pivotal moments in Janie's life occurs when she views a pear tree as a teenager; this is one of several occasions where Hurston uses tree imagery to enrich the scene. Watching the bee pollinate a pear blossom stimulates Janie, and it produces in her a desire to engage in a similar natural union, which she pursues with Johnny Taylor. Hurston uses sexual language to describe the activity of the bee entering the bloom, such as her description of the reaction of the calyxes and the "creaming" that occurs. Hurston subtly refers to this episode when she notes that, for Janie, Jody Starks "did not represent sun-up and pollen." Hurston scholars have emphasized the role that the tree plays, noting that this "real pear tree in Nanny's yard acquires transcendent significance" (Kubitschek 22), and that "the central symbol is a pear tree" (Morris and Dunn 8). For one thing, the episode "reflects her immature consciousness" (Kubitschek 22). It also shows, more practically, that "Janie longs to find a bee for her blossom" (Morris and Dunn 8).

Hurston uses tree imagery to describe Nanny's life, possibly suggesting that she is the source of Janie's experiences. Nanny says "colored folks is branches without roots and that makes things come round in queer ways." Due to the horrifying experiences of blacks during slavery, and after, during Reconstruction, Nanny sees her people as being without roots. Lacking roots, then, Nanny sees no real structure ordering family and society for blacks. Interestingly, Nanny names her daughter Leafy; Leafy was fathered by Nanny's owner. When Nanny flees the plantation, she heads to a swamp area with Leafy, where she sees owls, cypresses, and snakes. One day she puts her daughter "in moss and fixed her good in a tree." In this way, the tree functions as a source of refuge. Later, when Nanny sees Janie kiss Johnny, Hurston writes, "Nanny's head and face looked like the standing roots of some old tree that had been torn away by storm." The use of tree imagery to describe Nanny connects her to Janie, due to her moment with the pear tree. More generally, it shows the importance that nature plays in human affairs in Hurston novels.

Janie's third husband, Tea Cake, also is depicted as connected to nature through trees. Janie and Tea Cake's relationship "is associated with nature and springtime" (Morris and Dunn 8). To begin with, his birth name is Vergible Woods, calling to mind a forest. This surname can be viewed as "an organic metaphor related to the pear tree metaphor" (Fannin 51). As Janie begins to fall in love with him, she believes he is the only man who could evoke that feeling she experienced under the pear tree. Hurston uses other, similar imagery to describe Janie's relationship with Tea Cake. For example, people get upset about "Tea Cake making flower beds in Janie's yard," which could be seen as having sexual connotations, the planting of seeds symbolizing sexual intercourse. The couple's happiest times together are in the wilderness of the Everglades, and after Tea Cake's death, Janie heads back to Eatonville with seeds bought by Tea Cake. The seeds suggest the memory of him and of their relationship together. These symbolic "seeds fit into the pattern of springtime" as well as "new growth carried throughout the novel" (Morris and Dunn 9). Janie's involvement with Tea Cake provides her with a sense of renewal and rejuvenation, and this is reflected in the various tree and seed imagery.

The mule is another important symbol of nature in the novel. The mule functioned as an important animal to black communities in the rural South; it was considered lowly but vital to the work of a farm. For Nanny, the mule symbolizes the plight of the black woman, as she notes that the black female "is de mule uh de world so fur as Ah can see." The burden of this animal, hard-working and often unappreciated, is paralleled in the situation of black women. We can also see the mule as symbolizing, for Janie, the difference between Jody Starks and Logan Killicks.

On the day Janie meets Jody Starks, Logan has ordered her to work while he goes to look at a mule for sale. A stark contrast is drawn between these two men, Jody exuding urban sophistication with his fine clothing, while Logan is the old rural hick buying a mule. Jody is even surprised to see Janie doing the work she is doing. The mule symbolizes the difference between the rural, plainspoken farmer Logan Killicks and the urban and sophisticated Jody Starks. The mule is also significant to Jody and Janie's marriage, since the mule stories told at their store represent a sort of escape—and alienation—for Janie. It is escape for her to listen to the stories because with Jody, she is not allowed to engage in such joking. But it is alienation since she cannot truly partake; Jody silences her and prevents her from storytelling, one of her passions.

People enjoy telling stories about the mule owned by Matt Bonner, using the mule as a means to explain what is going on in the community; it also functions to expose the power relationship between Janie and Jody. This mule talk becomes a daily ritual, and "the introduction of Matt Bonner's skinny yellow mule into the narrative provides great fun, initially through a whole series of jokes played on Bonner" (Lowe 169). For example, some people tell Matt that women use the mule's protruding bones to hang laundry on. On one occasion, the storytelling goes too far, and some men start harassing the mule, touching it and bothering it. Janie gets very upset and screams at the men. Janie's outrage over the cruel physical torture of the old mule is "one of the clearest demonstrations in the book that human humor can sometimes be despicable" (Lowe 170). Jody, who sees the commotion, then buys the mule from Matt to allow it to rest before its death. Janie is happy for having liberated the old mule, but Jody's action becomes another means of his assertion of power: Jody "buys the animal and pastures him just outside his store, as a gesture of largesse, but we realize this ironically creates more of a display of power" (Lowe 170–171).

Janie's empathy toward the mule can be seen as her identification with the oppressed animal; like the mule, she feels exploited and objectified. And yet, despite her attachment to the mule, when the mule dies, Janie is excluded from the funeral service for it, for Jody does not want her to attend a low-class event of that nature. Jody attends himself, however, so he can get more attention from the community. At the funeral, Jody gives a speech about the mule, and while he does so he stands on top of the mule as a means of establishing his authority. Again, Jody's actions are meant to assert his power while keeping his wife out of the picture. Later, he tells Janie that he was mocking the funeral, laughing at the people there; he says blacks should be more serious and not spend time on such trivial things. Sam says the mule is going to heaven, where it will not experience what it experienced in life. This is ironic, because the mule had a difficult life because of how the people treated it, a fact noted afterward by the buzzards.

Hurston uses much personification in this scene, drawing many different connections between animals and humans. In addition to the strangeness of holding an actual funeral for a mule, Hurston describes what happens after all the people leave, and only some buzzards are left. The buzzards wait until the people are gone, and then the head buzzard leads the others. The head buzzard acts like a human preacher and asks, "What killed this man?" and the other birds, acting like a congregation, respond, "Bare, bare fat." The buzzards' actions reflect the relationship between preacher and congregation, leader and followers; it is also a humorous juxtaposition as the head buzzard functions in the same role as Jody. While the town symbolically consumed the mule by maltreating it and using it for storytelling, the birds literally consume the mule by eating and using it as nourishment. In this scene, Hurston employs a sort of magical realism, intermixing the real-seeming human affairs with fantastical, unrealistic animal behavior. In essence, Hurston is employing a oral folktale technique, but she is weaving it seamlessly into her narrative. It lends a sense of confusion between what is real and what is not, and suggests that humans and the natural world are not so far apart in reality.

Marriage

Hurston clearly presents marriage as a central—and highly problematic—theme in this novel. Janie's marriages to Logan Killicks, Jody Starks, and Tea Cake Woods each provide her with rich, varied, and finally unhappy life experiences. In her marriage to Logan Killicks, Janie feels trapped, since she was never in love; with Jody Starks, she feels stifled, silenced, and unappreciated. With Tea Cake, Janie feels happy and fulfilled, but the relationship ends in tragedy after the hurricane, the rabid dog bite, and the shooting of her husband in self-defense.

Janie's marriage choices stand in tension with the wishes of her grandmother, Nanny, who wants Janie to marry for practicality and money instead of for love. This is perhaps natural, as Nanny, a former slave, wants to make sure that her granddaughter enjoys life the way her generation was not able to. Nanny's domestic life was itself a chaotic, tragic situation, as she was exploited by her master, then abused by that master's wife. Then, after gaining freedom, her own daughter is raped and abandons her child. Having been denied a traditional family life, she tries to correct that path for her daughter and granddaughter. It is Nanny who tells Janie when it is time for a relationship, and it is Nanny who chooses the mate. While she does not force Janie into the marriage—it is a marriage of consent—the pressures of her grandmother and of the past convince Janie to make the mistake that is her first marriage. It proves to be a mistake because Janie devalues materialism and places a premium on idealized love. Her lifelong search for a true love is rooted in her experience laying under the pear tree, when she is moved by the sight of the bee pollinating the blossom. Throughout her life, this is the ideal of natural union that she seeks to achieve.

Janie's first marriage occurs at Nanny's home, and when she leaves for Logan's house, Janie is not happy. She hopes that one day she will learn to love him, and she even seeks advice from her grandmother about how to get by in her unhappy marriage. She's not pregnant nor abused, and in fact she works for Logan, but she is simply not happy. Nanny dismisses her complaints and tries to point out how fortunate she is. Janie continues to try to force herself to be more practical about marriage, especially after Nanny dies. Hurston presents Janie's marriage to Logan as an evolving one, but not in a good way. The change for the better comes in the form of Jody Starks, in a chance meeting outside. He impresses her with his manner and dress, and he has ambitions of moving to an all-black town and being a successful entrepreneur. He is also disconcerted to see Janie doing manual labor, and he reveals he would not treat his wife this way. The episode stirs Janie, and she thinks he will provide the life she is looking for, or at least something fuller than the bland life she has with Logan.

Hurston does not reveal, through Janie's narrative, what happens to Logan after Janie leaves him, suggesting how minimally important that relationship was to her. Janie's subsequent marriage to Jody—in Green Cove Springs, whose name suggest springtime or rebirth—is fraught with power issues, leading her to be once again unhappy. The couple live in Eatonville, and with Jody's success as a store-owner and mayor, they achieve high status and wealth. But Jody's desire for power is not limited to the town: He desires to control Janie, too. He tells her how to dress, when she can speak, what events she can attend; he even denies her the pleasure of storytelling with the other community members on the porch of the store. He possesses a patriarchal view of marriage, their home being the domestic, female space to which he wants her expression to be confined. Janie also feels alienated in their nice home, as she is viewed as an outsider by the people, even though she does not care about the material items.

Janie feels a surprising connection to Matt Bonner's mule, defending it against attacks by some men. Here Janie may be circling back to her grandmother's statement that black women are treated as mules. Once again, her husband tries to sanction her affinity for the mule, refusing to allow her even to attend the ceremony for the mule when it dies. At one point, after Mrs. Tony Robbins comes begging for food, Janie expresses herself publicly, asserting that men think they are smart and try to control everything. Jody is taken aback at her expressing herself like this, which may only increase his desire to control his wife. When Jody falls ill, Janie confronts him publicly again, essentially emasculating him when she says, "When you pull down yo' britches, you look lak de change uh life." Starks feels humiliated and shamed before the other men, and he reacts by hitting Janie. Soon after, he dies, and Janie symbolically pulls off the scarf he'd made her wear to cover her beauty; while she puts it on once more, it's to play the role of the grieving widow, a social expectation. Through two marriages in a row, Janie is given stability and material comfort, but neither time is she happy or fulfilled; at Jody's death, in fact, Hurston portrays Janie as a freed woman.

Tea Cake Woods is different. He is working class, and comes from humble folk roots. Even though Janie as a widow is wealthy and has social status, she enjoys spending time with him doing things that would be unconventional for a woman with her stature, like fishing or playing checkers. He surprises her with strawberries, and plans a picnic. Janie enjoys their time together, but the townspeople are scandalized by the disconnect between their two social statuses, and that she's involved with a man so soon after her husband's death. Janie is even warned about dating him, for he could be seeking her money, but she does not judge him. Another reversal of dynamics, as compared to her other marriages, is that Janie is older than Tea Cake, further fueling speculation that the younger Tea Cake wants her money, and

Pheoby reminds her of the infamous story of Annie and Who Flung. Janie has a moment of doubt, when he spends her money at a party, but he redeems himself by winning the money back by gambling.

Their move to the "muck" can be seen as the pivotal transformation of their marriage. They have isolated themselves from their old community, leaving behind many bad memories. They come closer together as Tea Cake teaches her how to hunt and pick crops; her new activities also contribute to a sense of identity, as well as a oneness with the community and the land. There are problems, of course, notably caused by the possible fling with Nunkie and the speculation about Mrs. Turner's brother, which is especially troublesome as it causes Tea Cake to hit Janie. The hurricane is another obvious turning point, and it is what leads to the tragic ending of the tale. They ignore warnings to evacuate, inadvisably leaving only at the last minute. Together, Janie and Tea Cake make it through the natural disaster, but the rabid dog that bites Tea Cake leaves its mark, and the couple cannot recover. Demented from the rabies, he tries to kill Janie, but she is prepared, and shoots him dead in self-defense.

At the end of the novel, Hurston portrays Janie as a single woman. All told, Janie abandons her first husband, struggles against her second and feels freed upon his death, and kills her third husband to protect herself: "Marriage, Hurston seems to say, is a deadly proposition: someone has to give up his or her life" (Boyd 304). The text does not put marriage into a positive light, nor does it reject it outright; the novel is far too complex to reduce it to a simple morality tale. There are many varied experiences here, but the author is not necessarily asking her readers to judge them. Hurston depicts marriage as highly complex, the intersection of many factors, of personality, background, history, race, gender, class, politics, and also luck. The conclusion, in which the action is brought back to the present, may provide some insight into a "message" of the novel. Pheoby, entirely moved by her friend's narrative, wants to change. She, as a woman, feels empowered by Janie's lessons to transform her relationship with Sam. Even if Janie's experiences have led to tragedy, by expressing them through the tale she has told, she attempts to change others.

Race

In *Their Eyes Were Watching God,* Hurston presents a great deal of commentary on race relations. The novel seems to ask if race is not, after all, socially constructed—that is to say, categories not based on biology but on concepts thought up by humans. Hurston's depiction of race in this novel bears affinity with her other texts, including, notably, *Jonah's Gourd Vine* and *Seraph on the Suwanee.* Her representation of intraracial racism and intrarace consciousness parallels her treatment in *Color Struck,* as well as texts by other writers of her day, including Jessie Fauset's *Comedy, American Style* and *Plum Bum* and Wallace Thurman's *The Blacker the Berry.*

Hurston's characterization of Nanny allows the novel to pay specific attention to the history of blacks in America. While the story is ostensibly about Janie, her history is extremely relevant, for Hurston shows that, as regards race, what is past is still in many ways present. Thus the character of Nanny,

Janie's grandmother, plays a very important role. She represents the slave past, the liberation, but also the disorder that accompanied emancipation. As a slave, she has a typical experience of terror and oppression, and she is sexually exploited by the master, bearing his child. Since the child, Leafy, bears his white features, the mistress of the plantation knows what happened, and threatens to beat Nanny, causing her to flee with her child. Nanny's status as a slave on a plantation is passed down culturally to Janie. Many of Nanny's fears and preoccupations, which affect Janie, were born during her time as a slave. "Her horrible experiences have led her to see the domestic pedestal as the safest escape from the dangers of racial/sexual oppression" (Bethel 15).

Jessie Redmon Fauset *(Library of Congress)*

Nanny points out to Janie that the black woman is like the mule, bearing the burdens of labor and work for others and not being appreciated. The way to avoid that type of life, she thinks, is to marry a man with money and status. Thus after Nanny views Janie kissing Johnny Taylor, she becomes nervous about the future of her granddaughter. She is concerned that Janie spends time with young men who would not be able to provide social and financial security. And so she encourages Janie to marry Logan Killicks, a black man with money and property, because she feels that black women cannot get by without being married to a stable man. Her fears may lead Janie to make unhappy choices, but Nanny's intentions are based in her own history. She says, "And Ah can't die easy thinkin' maybe de menfolks white or black is makin' a spit cup outa you."

Nanny's experience with race also frames the way Janie sees herself as a young child. In fact, early in her life, Janie does not view herself in racial terms. When she plays with the Washburn family, for whom her grandmother works as a domestic, she sees herself as no different. As a child, she does not recognize race classifications. She "spends so much time with these children that she doesn't even know she's black until she sees a picture of herself, when she's about six years old" (Boyd 301). Only when she sees a picture of herself along with her friends does she realize the difference. While it may not be unusual for a young child not to recognize his or her own race, the larger point is that Nanny has not addressed this sensitive issue with her.

Valerie Boyd points out that the event shows the grandmother trying "to shield her granddaughter from the real world" (Boyd 301).

Race comes into play in Janie's relationship with her husbands, and with them she comes to understand more closely her relationship to the black community. Jody Starks is an example of a successful, powerful black entrepreneur who is able to provide Janie with social and financial stability, even if not emotional security or simple love. Unlike many of the other rural folk, he is worldly and cosmopolitan, and models his business after those he saw being run by white people. The complicated nature of early black success and power is seen, however, when the other people in Eatonville grow to resent him more and more as his power and stature continue to rise. One offense is his home, which he modeled after white slave plantation homes; he even paints the house white and enjoys typically white bourgeois comforts, such as cigars, furniture, and fancy spittoons. Tea Cake serves as a contrast to Jody Starks. Unlike Jody, Tea Cake expresses no desire to imitate the white bourgeoisie. A blues man and gambler, he relates well to other black people. He appears genuine and presents no threat to other African Americans as he does not seek power over them.

Hurston uses the character of Mrs. Turner to comment on intrarace relations, even intraracial color prejudice. In doing so, she shows the dangers of racial categorizing. Mrs. Turner symbolizes racial self-hatred, as she holds great contempt for darker-skinned blacks. This means that she is prejudiced against the darker-skinned Tea Cake while she idolizes the lighter-skinned Janie; she even suggests Janie might be interested in her brother, who is also light-skinned. While in the eyes of everyone else she is black like them, Mrs. Turner sees herself as having the different, superior features of a light-skinned black. As she holds Janie in very high esteem, Mrs. Turner enjoys visiting her, but Janie objects to Mrs. Turner's racism. Janie realizes that blackness is not a singular concept, and that African Americans have very diverse backgrounds. When Mrs. Turner suggests that Booker T. Washington was no hero, Janie objects and defends him. While she disagrees with Mrs. Turner, Janie is characterized as indifferent to or unaffected by this insecure, fearful woman; Tea Cake, for his part, is dismissively mocking of her.

That dynamic changes, however, after there has been suggestion that Janie is indeed interested in Mrs. Turner's brother. This rumor ends up affecting the relationship between Tea Cake and Janie, as he assaults her to show his possession. This episode has been the subject of much debate among Hurston scholars and readers. John Lowe points out the social and historical atmosphere at the time when the novel takes place, which was marked by frequent domestic violence, noting that Janie herself reacts violently when she suspects Tea Cake of having an affair with Nunkie. In addition, Lowe explains, "Critics who complain about his sense of male possessiveness miss Hurston's frequent demonstration that love, if genuine, is possessive by definition, no matter which sex is involved." Tea Cake may fear losing Janie precisely because of his skin color (Lowe 187). For race or even class reasons, Tea Cake may feel insecure about his relationship to Janie, thus leading him to make a show of his control and ownership of his wife. His anger about Mrs. Turner's meddling continues until he makes her decide to leave town by the problems he causes in her restaurant.

The hurricane reveals deep racial divisions, in various respects. According to Valerie Boyd, Hurston's representation of this hurricane and the subsequent discrimination was based on historical events, explaining that "Hurston borrowed this brutal scene from actual events following the 1928 Lake Okeechobee hurricane, which killed nearly two thousand people in the Florida Everglades" (Boyd 305). Hurston's "reconstruction of the mass burial is a devastating yet subtle indictment of the racism that formed the backdrop for her" text (Boyd 305). After the storm has passed, the clean-up involves different procedures for burying blacks and whites: Even after death, there is not equality between the races, as the graves must be segregated and only the whites are buried in coffins. The storm has so ravaged the bodies that it is difficult to tell the difference between the races, and bogus methods were used to determine race, such as those based on hair type. The confusion regarding the race of the dead bodies calls into question the idea of racial differences. After all, if it's impossible to tell who is black and who is white, then why does the color of one's skin matter? Hurston also points out the irony that while nature makes no distinction in its death and destructions, the people do. In addition, the disparity in survival between black and white is seen, as whites are more readily able to get to dry land.

After the hurricane, Tea Cake notes that he wants to quickly return to the Everglades, since the white people know him well there. This is interesting, because he is not basing his desire on black or white, but on experience: Those whites who know him trust him, while those who do not may treat him differently. Again, Hurston's text gives a critique of racial prejudice. But Tea Cake otherwise makes ethnic distinctions too, notably in his frank dismissal of the Native Americans, who encouraged him to leave before the storm. Having recognized the signs of the coming hurricane, these indigenous people take the care needed to evacuate and try to help the others by telling them to do the same, but Tea Cake's arrogance and prejudice ultimately cause him to be trapped in the storm, leading to his downfall.

In the trial scene for Janie, race is portrayed as an important factor. While Janie is found not guilty, she is judged by a jury consisting of all white men. Both whites and blacks attend the trial, although these groups are described as being separate. Ironically, the black people act more negatively to Janie, suggesting that they would have judged her more harshly than the white men. The white women, on the other hand, applaud when the prosecutor silences a man who wants to testify against Janie; these women sob in joy when the verdict is handed down.

After the trial, some suggest that the white male jury ruled in Janie's favor because of her Caucasian features and light skin color; others note that killing is seen as acceptable when it involves black people, and that white men and black women are the most free people. Hurston does not necessarily advocate any of the positions taken by the blacks during the trial, but her inclusion of them points to the simple fact that justice is not color blind, neither in effect nor in intent. Even where justice is served, as may be the case with Janie, people will view justice through the lens of race. Also, the sheer disproportionate power of whiteness in the justice system, where whites judge a black woman in a black community, can be seen as a commentary on injustice in the judicial system. Hurston depicts the white women as being sympathetic to Janie's situation, but she also raises the question of whether these women were actually exploiting her situation simply to make themselves feel good. As was often seen during the Harlem Renaissance, white people appropriated black causes and culture for their own consumption.

Class

When Janie returns to Eatonville, she is wearing overalls, the type of clothing workers or farmers would wear. The women watching notice how this is quite a change from the fine satin dress she sported when she left town years earlier. Indeed, this scene aptly reflects Janie's fluid economic status throughout the novel. The daughter of a runaway alcoholic mother, the granddaughter of a freed slave, Janie shifts from working class to middle class and even to upper class, but it also falls over the course of the novel. Through multiple characters and across several generations, Hurston presents a range of socioeconomic situations in *Their Eyes Were Watching God.* Janie's class is fluid throughout the novel, and her views on finances stand in contrast to her grandmother's and, in some cases, her husbands'. Others find themselves in different financial situations.

Nanny's status as a slave shaped her worldview. After her escape and then subsequent freedom, Nanny works hard, as a domestic for the white Washburn family. She wants to make a new life for herself and her daughter and bring them out of the destitute situation of the free slave. She also has high expectations for her daughter, Leafy, to get educated, become a teacher, and move upward socially. The rape by her teacher ends those hopes, as Leafy later runs off, but Nanny then focuses her economic hopes and expectations on her granddaughter, Janie, whom she take cares of. Because of her background and her expectations, she is able to convince Janie to accept a marriage based not on love but on stability and practicality.

When Janie later complains about not loving Logan Killicks, Nanny defends him on the basis of his class status. He owns a home, with an organ, and he has no mortgage, she says; for her, he is the new, rising black middle class. Nanny complains that black women focus too much on love. For Janie, Jody Starks comes to represent a new class of man. He too is comfortable, and owns a home and land; he seems more refined than many of the other rural folk. By working hard and saving money, Jody is able to bring himself to a new level of wealth. In contrast to Logan, who makes Janie work, Jody tells Janie she should not be doing manual labor but living well while others get paid to do work. Jody Starks proves to be a model entrepreneur, opening a store in Eatonville that proves a major success. But Jody wants power and prestige even more than he wants wealth. He quickly rises in prominence in the town, becoming mayor even though a newcomer.

With Jody, Janie's life changes, and she has a newfound class status because of her husband's position; at the opening day of their store, for example, she wears a garment that shows her wealth. Their home also speaks to their wealth and status. It is a large house resembling an antebellum plantation home, and it is white, outfitted with fancy spittoons. People in the town begin to resent their lifestyle, and in this way Hurston exposes the complexities of wealth and status in this southern black community. While many of those townspeople may wish for the same things, they do not appreciate other blacks flaunting their success. In addition, in the eyes of the others in Eatonville, Jody is seen as imitating *white* men, another reason for the tensions between them. He is part of the black community, but somehow he is apart.

Jody's purchase of the mule after Janie confronts the men about their harassment becomes a show of his wealth and power as well. Jody quickly settles a dispute by laying down cash for the mule—a means of negotiation not many people would have. He seems compassionate, both to his wife and to the mule, but his later actions—prohibiting Janie from attending the creature's funeral, then grandstanding with an ovation at the ceremony itself—reveal that his motivations were not quite as pure as he would have them seem. However, no one ever confronts Jody about the tensions felt by the community. When Jody dies, his status is reflected in the funeral given to him. Hurston characterizes it as "the finest thing Orange County had ever seen with Negro eyes." Janie, in turn, inherits the role of widow of a prominent man, and she keeps her status, remaining comfortably wealthy.

When Janie meets Tea Cake, he seems to be the epitome of the working class, in clear contrast to her. He is a gambler, a blues man, a laborer. Even his name suggests lowly roots, for "tea cakes" are generally an inexpensive sugary treat rather than an expensive or gourmet food. Janie does not judge him for this, but she also does not initially reveal just how much money she actually has. Pheoby also comments on the disconnect between Janie and Tea Cake, saying that other people talk about how she gets dragged down socially by being seen with him. Janie objects, saying she likes what they do together and is comfortable with their situation. Here Janie's class-consciousness becomes explicit: she explains that her ambitions are not the materialistic ones taught to her by her grandmother.

In fact, Janie does eventually grow concerned about his true nature, and wonders if he is not trying to get her money. Echoing similar advice from Hezekiah, her friend Pheoby warns her that he might be a gold digger, reminding her of one such relationship between Annie Tyler and Who Flung. After they move and marry, Tea Cake takes some of her cash and spends it on a party. She worries that her fears have come true, but he tells her the truth and apologizes. Overall, Tea Cake serves as a counterpoint to Janie's other husbands, Logan Killicks and Joe Starks, both of whom had money and status, but who could not make Janie happy. Tea Cake's honesty and folkways are, in contrast, appealing.

When Janie and Tea Cake move to the "muck" of the Florida Everglades, Janie experiences a reentry into the working-class world, which she knew as a child. While other people expect Janie to act superior and not work in the fields, picking crops or hunting, Janie actually assumes her new role quite readily. She is working hard, independently but for a common cause, and for once she does not feel exploited by her husband. Janie becomes a product and part of the muck; she begins wearing work clothes and enjoys keeping the company of the many workers who pass the evenings in their home. Whereas she was alienated from the Eatonville community with Jody, here she interacts with others in a meaningful way, and is ultimately treated as one of them, without regard to social class. This setting transforms Janie and enables her to develop her sense of self and relationship to the surrounding world.

Still, social class is a factor on the "muck," especially during the hurricane. While the Native Americans are properly leaving, Tea Cake chooses to follow the lead of the wealthy white people, assuming that they would do what is right. Tea Cake makes a value judgment for the wealthy whites over the Native Americans that ultimately proves to be fatal. In addition, Mrs. Turner represents a highly class-conscious individual, although in her case her bias is more based on skin color than on money. Still, Mrs. Turner is keenly attentive to others' social situations, and only light-skinned blacks or white people receive her respect. For Mrs. Turner, her insecurity with her own social situation determines how she treats others.

Religion

While this novel deals less directly with religion than some of Hurston's other novels, the theme of religion is interconnected with the characters and events. During the hurricane, in the sentence that gives the title to the book, Hurston writes "They seemed to be staring at the dark, but their eyes were watching God." In other words, God's power manifests itself in the hurricane; at the same time, they are at God's mercy, rather helpless and vulnerable. The title of the novel proves symbolic: Here they are insignificant in the face of the hurricane, a turning point in the novel. There is a sense that amid all of Janie's many life choices, ultimately God—or more generally the natural world—determines one's fate or destiny. Again, this supports the notion that Hurston does not mean to moralize in this tale, but to present the multiple, and at times unexpected, facets that make up an individual's life.

Hurston uses religious language or imagery to frame some of the characters. For example, Nanny represents a spiritual figure whose main goal in life is to set her granddaughter on the right track. She functions as a sort of genesis for the rest of the narrative, even if her role is minimal, confined to a small part of Janie's story. Her constant advice to Janie on how to act is her means of expressing herself, her sermon, since as a former slave she was never able to achieve what she wanted and fulfill her potential. Hurston frames this using religious language, as Nanny says, "Ah wanted to preach a great sermon about colored women sittin' on high, but they wasn't no pulpit for me." She was a preacher without a place to preach her word, but Janie became her audience. She declared she would "save de text" for Janie, meaning she would preach her ideas and values to Janie. Her "text" consists of her story about life on the plantation, her escape, and the path to freedom. In context, her "sermon" to Janie serves as a commentary on the mistakes of the past and how to correct them for the future. Ironically, the advice, meant to liberate Janie, ends up entrapping her in the marriage to Logan Killicks.

Hurston characterizes Jody Starks as a sort of preacher in his role as community leader;

he is portrayed, as well, as seeing himself as a sort of god or savior for the town. To begin with, Hurston presents Jody as a transformative figure when Janie meets him, by chance, outside; it is as if they were destined to meet. As mayor and businessman of Eatonville, Jody is portrayed as a natural leader; in fact it is he who proposes incorporating the town, and his role is, in a sense, depicted as godlike. Jody is prone to exclaim the phrase "I god," which is a corruption of "oh, God," but the suggestion that he is saying "I am God" is too strong to ignore. Even after Jody's death, Hezekiah starts using the phrase "I god" as a means of imitating him and trying to invoke the strength of Jody. So, Jody sets himself up as a godlike figure with power and dominion over the town; his lavish life, cut off from the other townspeople, is additional evidence that he views himself as exceptional. People even refer to him as "Our beloved Mayor," which reminds them of the phrase "God is everywhere."

One of Jody's major projects, to erect a light post in town, is a major event. He gives a speech for it, which functions as a type of sermon, as he talks about the "Sun-maker," or God, who brings light in the morning. By analogy, by erecting the lamp, Jody portrays himself as another "sun-maker," one who brings light after it is dark. Afterward, he asks a man to pray and invoke God for a blessing for their town. The importance he accords to this rather banal event shows how he sees himself in inflated terms; he confers a sense of the spiritual to the everyday as a means of projecting power. Jody gives another speech at the funeral for Matt Bonner's mule, at which he literally perches upon the dead animal to give an oration. Once again, he is making use of the occasion to project his image of power in a surreal, detached way. The response of the buzzards provides an amusing juxtaposition, as they are repeating, more or less, the spectacle that Jody has just created; the scene, now acted by a bunch of large birds, points out the strangeness of the human actions. The main bird is Parson, a reference to a preacher or religious leader, who acts like Jody, inspecting the mule and making a speech. The other buzzards reply to his invocations as would a congregation. The scene emphasizes the role of ceremony in the community.

Hurston portrays Janie herself as a sort of godlike character on several occasions as well. Mrs. Turner, for one, is shown as a follower in search of a leader, which she finds in Janie. Mrs. Turner symbolically worships Janie, seeing her Caucasian features as praiseworthy. For Mrs. Turner, Janie is a transformative figure, suggesting a higher power. It should also be noted that her idea of heaven is one filled with white angels. More significantly, Pheoby's reaction to Janie's story, at the end of the novel, suggests awe and reverence. After hearing Janie's tale, Pheoby exclaims, "Lawd!" This outburst expresses Pheoby's amazement at the story, but it also subtly suggests that she is calling Janie herself by that name.

Hurston also connects Janie's husbands to God, describing Tea Cake as "a glance from God." Later, during the hurricane, Tea Cake asks Janie if she regrets not being back at Eatonville, and she responds, "Ah wuz fumblin' round and God opened de door." This is further suggestion that Tea Cake serves as a sort of savior for Janie. This is also in direct contrast to the portrayal of

Jody: While Jody saw himself as a sort of god, here it is Janie who sees Tea Cake as a gift from God. All these examples, finally, figure into Janie's larger life story—which is about her, not about God. That is to say, her story is about her own life, which is nevertheless informed by spirituality. However, the connections Hurston makes to religion are subtle; the larger conceptual framework, as already described, is the relation between the natural world and human destiny.

Gender

Janie's quest for identity is marked by her attempt to negotiate her role as a woman. Hurston incorporates into Janie's life story many elements that comment upon socially expected roles for men and women. As Lillie P. Howard points out, the novel "has universal implications for women in that it protests against the restrictions and limitations imposed upon women by a masculine society" (93). By focusing this text on a black woman, Hurston brings to the fore the condition of women as they faced the struggle to find their identities in a male-dominated society.

Janie's notions of gender roles can be seen as generating first from her grandmother. While Nanny seems to have intentionally not created a race consciousness in Janie, evidenced by Janie's ignorance early on that her skin color was different, Nanny is very careful to instill in Janie her notions about the role of women. Nanny dismisses Janie's romantic ideal of love, feeling that marriage serves a strictly pragmatic purpose, one in which the woman is passive and taken care of by the man. In a sense, she views marriage as a one-time event, wherein the woman is sold to the man so he can possess her and take care of her for life. Considering Nanny's experience as a slave, this is certainly an ironic take, since she was treated as an object. In fact, Nanny admits that, after freedom, she had the opportunity to wed, but she did not, for she felt that that would not be the best way to protect Leafy. But Nanny's experience as a slave and her struggles afterward also exposed Nanny's vulnerabilities to the world and shaped her pragmatic sense; since Nanny was denied the opportunity to live a full, free life as wife and mother, she has very specific ideas about what her offspring ought to do. She believes that Janie has a chance to move beyond the mistakes that she herself made, and the way to do this is by submitting to a male in marriage. Nanny also desires her daughter to become a schoolteacher, a standard role for a female at the time.

Janie's own views of her gender role are in constant tension with those of her grandmother. On the one hand, she accepts them, using them as a sort of restraining force, but she also rejects them and wants to break free, carving out her own place in society and constructing her own gender identity. Janie's incident with the pear tree shows that, from a young age, she was aware of divisions, and how men and women play different roles just as the bee and the flower played different roles in that union. By marrying Logan, despite her better instincts, she succumbs to her grandmother's insistence about gender roles, which would mirror society's expectations as well. Logan is the male provider, with property and a home. When Janie complains about not being in love with him after the wedding, Nanny notes how Janie will command respect from others in the community.

Once married to Janie, Logan is happy to put Janie to work, even asking her to do tasks that others may view as a man's work, such as cutting wood or plowing with a mule. As she works, she recalls Nanny's statement that black women are treated like mules. In a sense, Janie is thus caught between two standard roles for women: the hardworking laborer, or mule, and the submissive wife.

Jody Starks tries to rescue her from the one role—that of the mule, as he expresses surprise that Janie would be made to do such labor for Logan—but he will do so by confining her to the other role, of wife. He says she should be sitting on a porch, while rocking and fanning herself. He recreates the picture of a traditional upper-class woman, too delicate to deal with the farm labor and deserving of a leisurely life. Once married, he tries to prove his manliness and increases the amount of control he exerts over his wife. He views himself not only as the patriarch and provider, but also the leader and voice of the couple. At Jody's inauguration speech as mayor, he silences his wife when she wants to say a few words, saying, "She's uh woman and her place is in de home." He makes it clear that, as the wife of the most prominent man in Eatonville, she must comport herself in a particular way, dressing finely and not getting involved in petty or low-class affairs. He has her wear nice clothing and refuses to allow her to attend the mule's funeral. A symbol of his possession of his wife can be seen in the floral spittoon he buys her—while the spittoon is a markedly masculine symbol, he buys her a floral one, showing both his masculine power and his view of femininity.

The more he overpowers or silences Janie, the more Janie retreats into herself, becoming alienated from the community and feeling powerless and passive. However, this also causes Janie to want to break out, and challenge his assumptions. After Mrs. Tony Robbins has come begging for food, Janie responds by saying that men are not as smart as they think they are. This act surprises Jody, since he has tried hard to silence her.

The biggest challenge to Jody comes when he mocks Janie for being an old, feeble woman when she incorrectly cuts a slice of tobacco. At this point, Jody "tries to draw attention away from himself by publicly ridiculing Janie" (Lowe 176). Janie, finally, responds with a bold and public insult: "When you pull down yo' britches, you look lak de change uh life." Not only is she challenging her husband by speaking out against him in public, she is also challenging his very masculinity and sexual vitality. By analogizing her husband's situation to that of a woman during menopause, she feminizes him. Janie "effectively emasculated him" (Lowe 177). Jody is so stunned that, for once, he is the silenced one. He cannot come up with a retort to his wife, so he resorts to violence, hitting her. In this pivotal scene, Janie transcends her role as a woman and alters the power dynamics in her relationship with her husband. His response reflects a reassertion of his manliness and power, but the damage has been done; others in the town see a change, and Jody's sense of power deflates.

After Jody's death, Janie continues to play the standard gender role of grieving wife, by putting on her scarf, but she feels freed, which is evident in her next relationship, with Tea Cake. Janie's marriage to Tea Cake exhibits her rebellion against the gender role ideas instilled by Nanny. Janie has more money than Tea Cake, and she is also older than he is, which represents a reversal of gender roles. Hurston depicts their relationship as one with more equitable gender roles, as she engages in activities like fishing and playing games. In fact, others in the community see her actions as questionable, considering her status and wealth. However, Janie, finally freed from Jody's grip, doesn't concern herself with what others think; she does what she does because it makes her happy. By joining Tea Cake in the fields, Janie is achieving an equality with her husband; his acceptance of this shows that gender roles do not play a major role in their relationship. However, Tea Cake shows that ultimately, when threatened, he will play the male role of possessor. When there is speculation about Janie and Mrs. Turner's brother, he hits her to show his control and manhood. Hurston writes, "Being able to whip her reassured him in possession." In addition, the other people react in agreement with Tea Cake, expressing their approval that he would show his ownership of Janie in that way.

On the "muck" in the Everglades, Janie transcends her role as a woman even further, getting her hands dirty in the fields and spending time with the common folk. She stops wearing her urban finery and puts on overalls. While she worked before—doing chores for Killicks and working in the store for Starks—here she is on equal footing with the others; she feels freed by her work rather than taken for granted. Janie also learns to perfect her art as a storyteller, which is generally depicted as a man's domain in the African-American folktale tradition. This is a means for Janie to express herself and break out of her gender role, and this also lays the foundation for her later recounting of her life story to Pheoby. As a woman, she is in control of her own narrative: She crafts and tells her own life. By transcending standard gender roles and breaking free from the expectations of her grandmother and her husbands, Janie has been able to construct an identity that affirms self-awareness, self-discovery, and self-respect. The tale ends in tragedy, but Janie emerges strong, a free woman who determines her own life and, by telling the story to Pheoby, inspires others.

CHARACTERS

Bonner, Matt He is the owner of the mule that is the source of much attention and amusement. Bonner is reputed not to take very good care of the mule.

Crawford, Janie Janie is one of Hurston's most memorable characters in all her fiction; the novel is Janie's life story, as told by Janie to her friend Pheoby. Janie is brought up by her grandmother, Nanny, after her mother, Leafy, abandons her. Her grandmother was a slave, and her mother was the product of a slave-master relationship. Janie's father was a teacher, who raped Leafy. As a child, Janie has little race consciousness, as she spends time with the white Washburn family but does not make a color distinction. She has two important realizations as a youth. One is when she realizes the black-white color distinction, by looking at a photo of her and her white friends; the other is when she experiences a sensual bliss while watching a bee pollinate a pear blossom.

Hurston presents Janie's life as a quest to find fulfillment, and the journey involves many life experiences. She marries Logan

Killicks at her grandmother's urging, but the marriage is loveless even though he can provide for her materially and socially. Jody Starks, her second husband, appeals to Janie's sense of romance. He seems genteel and cosmopolitan, and promises to rescue her from her life of desperation. They begin their lives in Eatonville, where Starks becomes a mayor and wealthy businessman, the owner of the main store in town where people gather as a meeting place. Once again, Janie begins to feel oppressed, as Jody exerts too much power over her, controlling her actions and silencing her voice. They live in a large white home, but she feels alienated in it, cut off from black society as if in a plantation home. As a result, Janie feels sympathy for Matt Bonner's mule, feeling as lowly and unappreciated as that common work animal. She ultimately stands up to her husband but only shortly before his death, and he assaults her for it. When he dies, Janie feels a sense of relief, symbolically pulling off the scarf he had made her wear.

With Tea Cake, her third husband, Janie feels freed, as they have a more equal relationship, and she enjoys doing many of the same things that he does. She is older than he is and has more money, which makes others worry he is a gold digger. They move to the Everglades and work on the fields together, along with many others in the community. The rural experience is a happy one for Janie, but there are problems, notably caused by Mrs. Turner, a self-hating black woman. Concern about Mrs. Turner's brother and Janie cause Tea Cake to hit Janie. The novel's downturn begins with a hurricane that Janie and Tea Cake survive together, despite not having evacuated in time. During the storm, Tea Cake is bitten by a rabid dog, and the resulting infection causes him to change irreversibly. Janie shoots him dead in self-defense, although he bites her before he dies, possibly infecting her too. She is acquitted at her trial by an all-white-male jury, but the black community is not pleased.

Janie returns to Eatonville, where she recounts her story to Pheoby, inspiring her with her tale of love and female power. At the novel's end, Hurston portrays Janie as a transformative woman entering yet another stage of her life. Hurston ends the novel on an ambiguous note; when she heads upstairs, Janie may be symbolically heading to her death, but Hurston does not reveal this explicitly.

Daisy, Jim, and Dave These three characters are Eatonville townspeople who try to gain each other's affections and are seen at the store in town.

Hezekiah He helps in the store after Jody dies, attempting to mimic the old storekeeper. He also warns Janie about Tea Cake, fearing he is after Janie's money.

Killicks, Logan Logan Killicks is Janie's first husband, the choice of her grandmother as he owns a home and property and can provide materially for Janie. Nanny believes he can offer her granddaughter security and prevent her from having a harsh life. Hurston presents Logan as a pragmatic and plainspoken male who does not excite Janie's love. In fact, Janie says he is ugly and smells. He puts Janie to work on the farm. Logan's character plays a minor role, but he proves to be of major importance, as he provides the major impetus for Janie to want to free herself. Her relationship to him is a learning experience, standing in contrast to her desires sparked in the pear tree. Hurston does not provide details about what happened to Logan after Janie left him, further suggesting Janie's ambivalence toward him.

'Lias He tries to get Tea Cake to leave the "muck" due to the impending hurricane.

Matt Bonner's mule The mule owned by Matt Bonner is one of the central characters in the novel. The mule, an animal used for work purposes and important to rural black communities in the South, represents a hardworking but unappreciated figure. Matt Bonner's mule is ill fed, old, and overworked, and it becomes the source of many jokes and tales; it is a beast of burden and the butt of many jokes. When the jokes go too far and men mistreat the animal, Janie screams at them, revealing her empathy with this lowly, dejected animal. Jody buys the mule from Matt and puts it to pasture. When the mule dies, it is given a funeral at which Jody stands atop the mule to give an oration, but Janie is excluded from the event. A bunch of buzzards then repeats the spectacle and eats the dead animal. The mule also shows the centrality of the natural world and its impact on the lives of humans.

Motor Boat Motor Boat is a friend of Janie and Tea Cake's. He initially flees the hurricane with them, but later decides to stay in a house during the storm.

Nanny Nanny is Janie's grandmother, who raises Janie. As a slave, she had a relationship with her white master and bore his child, which she names Leafy. When the slave master's wife sees her baby with white features, she threatens her, spurring Nanny to flee the plantation. She takes cover in a swampy area and hides out. Nanny has the opportunity to marry, but does not. She has high hopes for her daughter to become a teacher, but when Leafy is raped by a teacher, her life changes. Leafy gives birth to Janie, then becomes an alcoholic and runs off, leaving Janie in Nanny's care. Nanny works as a domestic for the white Washburn family, exposing Janie to the family as a young child and not instilling a sense of race consciousness. As a result of her past, Nanny has pragmatic, traditional notions of gender roles and wants Janie to have a secure life. She is surprised when she catches Janie kissing Johnny Taylor and she disapproves of Janie's idealized notions of romance. Janie, in turn, often thinks back in anger to her grandmother's influence. Nanny's character serves as the genesis for the story; while it is Janie's story that Hurston tells here, the action is grounded in Nanny's life story and propelled forward by her character.

Nunkie Nunkie is a woman on the muck who Janie suspects of having an affair with Tea Cake. She finds the two together, but Tea Cake denies having any affections for her.

Prescott, Mr. He is the white prosecuting attorney during Janie's trial for killing Tea Cake.

Starks, Jody (Joe) Janie's second husband, Jody Starks is presented as being both similar to and different from her first husband, Logan Killicks. They meet while Janie is doing manual labor, and he suggests they run off together. He is characterized as being worldly and fashionable in his sense of dress and in his habits. He becomes mayor of the town of Eatonville, opens the main store there, and increases both his wealth and his influence in the community. He has a forceful, charismatic nature, but he enjoys his power too much; he sees himself as a godlike individual, a savior for this black community. Jody sees himself as a liberator when he purchases Matt Bonner's mule, but that too becomes a means for him to show his power, ultimately perching atop the deceased creature to give a speech, which is mimicked afterward by some buzzards.

Jody has traditional patriarchal ideas about marriage, and he wants Janie to submit to him. He tells her how to dress, and he controls what events she may attend; for example, he refuses to allow her to attend the mule's funeral, considering it too lowly an affair for his wife. He silences Janie's voice, refusing to let her speak at his mayoral inauguration, and he suppresses her desire to take part in storytelling at the store. Jody is an oppressive force in Janie's life, but she stands up to him ultimately, even feminizing him toward the end, when he gets older. When she humiliates Jody publicly, he becomes the silenced one, but exhibits his power even more forcefully by hitting her. Jody dies from kidney failure soon after, and a funeral is held that reflects his wealth and status. At his death, Janie removes the scarf he had made her wear to hide her beauty from other men, and his death is characterized as a freeing moment for Janie.

Robbins, Mrs. Tony She comes to the store to beg for food. After she leaves, people gossip about her, and Janie makes a comment about men.

Turner, Mrs. Mrs. Turner lives on the "muck" and operates a restaurant for the African-American laborers. She has middle-class status and sees herself as superior to the other blacks, especially because of her lighter skin and Caucasian-like features. She believes dark-skinned blacks are different from light-skinned blacks, and she wishes there were two categories. Mrs. Turner worships Janie because of her features and is prejudiced against Tea Cake because of his dark skin. She encourages Janie to leave him and have a relationship with her brother, who proudly criticized Booker T. Washington, disputing his status as a black leader and role model. Mrs. Turner reflects extreme colorism, class elitism, and snobbery, and Hurston uses this character to present the problem of intraracial prejudice, a theme she visits in some of her other work, notably her play *Color Struck* and her novel *Jonah's Gourd Vine.*

Tyler, Annie While this character is not directly involved in the action, the memory of her plays an important role. She was a wealthy widow who was taken advantage of by younger men who wanted her money, most notably Who Flung. Pheoby reminds Janie of this example in her warnings about Tea Cake, and Janie herself thinks about it when Tea Cake takes some of her money.

Watson, Pheoby Pheoby plays a dual role in the novel, both serving as a character in Janie's narrative and being the character that

Janie tells the story to. She is a nurturing listener, and the reader follows in her role, hearing Janie's tale at the same time as Pheoby. She is Janie's closest friend in Eatonville when Janie returns after Tea Cake's death, and she is transformed by Janie's inspiring narrative. She serves as a sort of mediator between Janie and the community, both revealing to Janie how the community feels about her and defending Janie against their gossip and accusations. After hearing Janie's tale, she expresses her amazement and her plans to change her relationship with Sam. When others talk about Janie, Pheoby tells them they need to live their own lives and plans to reveal to them the insights Janie has expressed. Unlike many of Janie's other female acquaintances, Pheoby proves to be a reliable and loyal friend through time. She reflects the importance of female companionship as a means of expressing female identity and empowerment. Janie is an empowered woman as she tells her story, but she needs Pheoby as a listener in order to achieve that goal. Unlike her husbands' shows of power, Janie shares her power and identity.

Who Flung Also not a direct character, he is the man who took advantage of Annie Tyler, exploiting this older woman for her money. He is used to caution Janie about the possibility that Tea Cake is after her money.

Woods, Vergible (Tea Cake) Vergible Woods, known as Tea Cake, is Janie's third husband and the man with whom Janie experiences a more fulfilling life. He is a man from humble roots, as he is working class and does not have the status Janie has. He is younger than Janie and has less money, and as a gambler and blues man, he is seen by the Eatonville community as a mismatch for Janie. Tea Cake charms Janie with small pleasures. Despite warnings that he wants Janie's money, they leave Eatonville and marry; there is an incident right after their wedding in which he takes some of Janie's money and she doubts him, but he apologizes and gambles the money back. Ultimately they move to the "muck" in the Everglades, where Janie returns to her folk roots, which makes her happy. Working together, the couple share an equality that Janie was not able to attain in her other marriages. Tea Cake does not show much interest in traditional gender roles, but he does hit his wife on one occasion, to show his possession of her.

Tea Cake ignores warnings about a coming hurricane, which ultimately leads to his downfall. He and Janie eventually flee to save themselves from the storm, but as they wade and swim through the flooded area he becomes weak. Tea Cake is bitten by a dog and infected with rabies, changing the man irreversibly. Janie gets him medical care but knows he has been changed; in the end he tries to shoot Janie, but Janie shoots him dead in self-defense. However, he bites Janie, possibly infecting her with rabies, before he dies. Hurston presents Tea Cake as an important force in the novel, closing it with a vision of Tea Cake. Despite his death, he was part of Janie's climb out of oppression toward identity, and with him Janie experienced a humble, if brief, happiness. Tea Cake's memory lives on for Janie.

FILM ADAPTATION

A television film version of *Their Eyes Were Watching God* was made for network television, playing on ABC in 2005. For more information, see FILM ADAPTATION OF *THEIR EYES WERE WATCHING GOD*, in Part III.

BIBLIOGRAPHY

Abrams, M. H., and Geoffrey Galt Harpham. *A Glossary of Literary Terms.* Boston: Thomson Wadworth, 2005.

Bethel, Lorraine. "'This Infinity of Conscious Pain': Zora Neale Hurston and the Black Female Literary Tradition." In *Zora Neale Hurston's Their Eyes Were Watching God,* edited by Harold Bloom, 9–17. New York: Chelsea House Publishers, 1987.

Carby, Hazel V. *Reconstructing Womanhood: The Emergence of the Afro-American Woman Novelist.* New York: Oxford University Press, 1987.

Fannin, Alice. "A Sense of Wonder: The Pattern for Psychic Survival in *Their Eyes Were Watching God* and *The Color Purple.*" In *Alice Walker and Zora Neale Hurston: The Common Bond,* edited by Lillie P. Howard, 45–56. Westport, Conn.: Greenwood Press, 1993.

Howard, Lillie P. *Zora Neale Hurston.* Boston: Twayne Publishers, 1980.

Hurston, Zora Neale. *Their Eyes Were Watching God.* In her *Novels and Stories,* 173–333. New York: Library of America, 1995.

Kubitschek, Missy Dehn. "'Tuh de Horizon and Back': The Female Quest in *Their Eyes Were Watching God.*" In *Zora Neale Hurston's Their Eyes Were Watching God,* edited by Harold Bloom, 19–33. New York: Chelsea House Publishers, 1987.

Jones, Sharon L. *Rereading the Harlem Renaissance: Race, Class, and Gender in the Fiction of Jessie Fauset, Zora Neale Hurston, and Dorothy West.* Westport, Conn.: Greenwood Press, 2002.

Locke, Alain. Review of *Their Eyes Were Watching God.* In *Zora Neale Hurston: Critical Perspectives Past and Present,* edited by Henry Louis Gates, Jr., and K. A. Appiah, 18. New York: Amistad, 1993.

Lowe, John. *Jump at the Sun: Zora Neale Hurston's Cosmic Comedy.* Urbana: University of Illinois Press, 1994.

Morris, Ann R., and Margaret M. Dunn, "Flora and Fauna in Hurston's Florida Novels." In *Zora in Florida,* edited by Steve Glassman and Kathryn Lee Seidel, 1–12. Orlando: University of Central Florida Press, 1991.

Wright, Richard. Review of *Their Eyes Were Watching God.* In *Zora Neale Hurston: Critical Perspectives Past and Present,* edited by Henry Louis Gates, Jr., and K. A. Appiah, 16–17. New York: Amistad, 1993.

"Uncle Monday" (1934)

"Uncle Monday" is another of Hurston's reporting pieces, presenting a nonfiction account of her experience with a conjure doctor who claims to walk on water and transform himself into an alligator. Along with "Mother Catherine," the story appeared in *Negro: An Anthology* (1934), edited by Nancy Cunard, which was a landmark anthology devoted to publishing black cultural expression. Comparison can be drawn between the character of Uncle Monday and the conjurers that Hurston apprenticed with in *Mules and Men.* Like that text, this piece emphasizes the interconnected roles that spirituality, nature, and folklore play in the African-American experience.

SYNOPSIS

Uncle Monday is said to possess special powers, such as the ability to walk on water and the ability to transform himself into something that appears to be an alligator. He also knows details about people that no one else knows about, suggesting he has special knowledge.

Hurston gives a detailed sketch of Uncle Monday through stories that others tell about him. For example, Joe Lindsay watched Uncle Monday emerge from a lake, realizing that his clothes were not wet and that he had walked on water. Another time Emma Lou Pittman saw Uncle Monday injured in his home, but later he came to town completely healed, with no evidence of injuries. Two men who had gone hunting claimed to have had a mysterious encounter with an alligator in a lake, which was purported to be Uncle Monday. Joe Clarke, one of the first to discover the man's identity, asked Uncle Monday if he feared being alone. Uncle Monday replied that he has not lived for very long and that he has risen from the dead; he tells Joe that he has come from the place Joe will eventually rest.

While there are many stories surrounding this man, Uncle Monday's reputation is ultimately as a conjurer, and people go to him for help. Another conjurer, Ant Judy Bickerstaff, is a rival conjurer. She explains that one day she went fishing. While fishing, she sensed evil and suddenly saw Uncle Monday, who threatened her and then vanished. This episode made her not feel like a real conjure woman anymore.

CRITICAL COMMENTARY

Hurston presents a memorable portrait of a conjurer in this story, chronicling Uncle Monday's unusual abilities—in fiction or in fact—to affect the destiny of other individuals. By her choice of language and details, Hurston depicts his abilities as realistic rather than unrealistic—regardless of what the truth is behind them—and he is portrayed as a sort of legend in the community. Those who inform Hurston about Uncle Monday have grown to respect his powers, and his presence has apparently worked to inform these individuals' worldviews. In some cases, the reverence may be rooted in fear or intimidation, such as with Ant Judy Bickerstaff, an expert conjure woman who has nevertheless been changed by Uncle Monday.

Uncle Monday's name is suggestive, for a couple of reasons. The fact that he is called uncle indicates a sort of spiritual, if not genetic, kinship with the community. Hurston employs religious imagery to describe Joe Lindsay's version of what happens when Uncle Monday walks on water, depicting a sort of Christ figure who has the characteristics of men but can perform superhuman feats. Hurston writes, "For there was an old man walking out of the lake between two cypress knees. The water there was too deep for any wading, and besides, he says the man was not wading, he was walking vigorously as if he were on dry land." In all his various experiences, Uncle Monday is portrayed as having a unique connection with nature. This is especially evident in the story about how he has obtained his powers, by connecting with a serpent who vomits out a magical stone. Through his knowledge of and bond with the natural world, he ultimately comes to be able to manipulate it.

Uncle Monday's conjuring forms an important part of the African-American folk tradition. Folktales, of course, are another important part of that tradition, and the story of Uncle Monday itself demonstrates the importance of the oral storytelling tradition, as Hurston is gathering in this text a number of oral histories related by members of the community. Each of their stories, in a sense, is an oral tale being fixed on the page by Hurston. This orality is marked in the text by the language Hurston uses and the spontaneous details she provides, making readers feel privy to unique information, as if the story is unfolding in front of them.

Uncle Monday possesses many similarities to the conjurers presented by Hurston in part II of *Mules and Men,* such as Turner, Marie Laveau, Anatol Pierre, Father Watson, and Dr. Duke. The attention paid to these conjurors both here and in that text shows Hurston's keen interest in the subject and her devotion to preserving these fragile histories.

CHARACTERS

Bickerstaff, Ant Judy She is a conjurer and a sort of foil for Uncle Monday. Ant Judy sees herself as a challenge or rival to his powers, believing she can counteract them. Still, her experience with him strengthens her reverence for his abilities, even if she thinks he is a force for evil.

Clarke, Joe Joe discovers Uncle Monday's identity and reveals it to other people. He also asks the man about fear and old age. Joe Clarke is a character in many of Hurston's texts, lending a continuity across her various texts.

Lindsay, Joe Joe Lindsay is one of the people who claims to have witnessed Uncle Monday walking on water, as he emerged from the lake without being wet.

Monday, Uncle Uncle Monday, an "out-and-out conjure doctor," possesses special powers and has a mystical presence in his community. He is said to walk on water, to transform himself into something that looks like an alligator, to recover miraculously from injuries, and to be able to manipulate nature. His abilities are derived from a stone that has been vomited by a serpent. Although not necessarily related to the individuals in his community, he seems to possess special, mystical bonds both with other people and with the natural world. In fact, his origins are shrouded in mystery: "Nobody knows where he came from nor who his folks might be. Nobody knows for certain just when he did come to town." He can be compared most notably to the conjurers described in *Mules and Men.*

Pittman, Emma Lou She witnessed Uncle Monday at his home, injured and making animal sounds; despite her attempts to call for help, others are unable to enter his home during the episode. Later that same day, she sees him in town without the injuries.

BIBLIOGRAPHY

Hassall, Kathleen. "*Text and Personality in Disguise and in the Open: Zora Neale Hurston's* Dust Tracks on a Road." In *Zora in Florida,* edited by Steve Glassman and Kathryn Lee Seidel, 159–173. Orlando: University of Central Florida Press, 1991.

Howard, Lillie P. *Zora Neale Hurston.* Boston: Twayne Publishers, 1980.

Hurston, Zora Neale. "Uncle Monday." In her *The Complete Stories,* 106–116. New York: HarperCollins, 1995.

Part III

Related People, Places, and Topics

Barnard College A prestigious women's college in New York, Barnard College is one of the institutions of higher learning that impacted Hurston's life and work, particularly her field research on African American folklore, music, and culture. Hurston's experience as a student at Barnard provided her with the means of better understanding her heritage, enabling her to develop the research, writing, and critical thinking skills she would use throughout her literary and anthropological career.

The impetus for Hurston's attending Barnard College occurred at the *Opportunity* awards ceremony on May 1, 1925, where Hurston met a number of prominent people as she received her award for "Drenched in Light." Among them was Annie Nathan Meyer, who had established Barnard College in 1889 as an offshoot of Columbia University to create a space in which women could learn and be challenged equally to men. Funded by Meyer's husband, Dr. Alfred Meyer, as well as other prominent backers, like John D. Rockefeller, Barnard soon established a reputation for excellence in women's education and produced many leaders. Meyer, taking an interest in African-American affairs and having donated money to civil rights groups, decided to integrate Barnard in the 1920s. At that

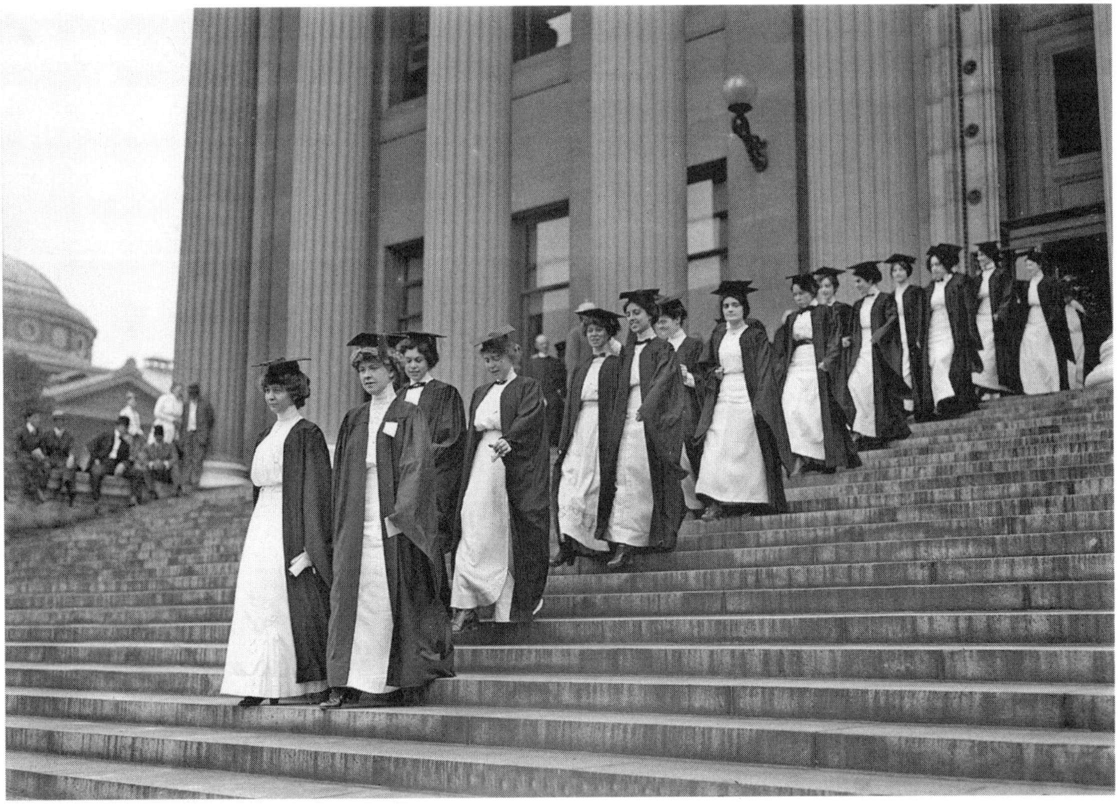

Barnard College graduates, 1913 *(Library of Congress)*

time, most African Americans who attended universities went to specifically black institutions. Impressed by Hurston, Meyer encouraged her to attend. Hurston provided her Howard University records and was accepted by the dean, Virginia Gildersleeve; however, her academic record was not strong enough for a scholarship, so Hurston and Meyer sought funding elsewhere. Hurston would later receive a scholarship, in 1926, allowing her to focus on her studies, and she would receive her degree in 1928. On an entrance form to the school, Hurston indicated her interest in drama and, while not revealing her work as a domestic, she did list her writing accomplishments and dreams to be a writer (Boyd 103). In the year she began at Barnard, she would have already published several pieces, including "Spunk," "Magnolia Flower," and "The Hue and Cry about Howard University." While at Barnard, she studied a number of fields, including French, and performed well academically. When Hurston began classes at Barnard in 1925, she lied about her age, claiming she'd been born in 1899 so that she would fit in better; in fact, she was in her mid-thirties, a fact she would later admit to in her correspondence with Annie Nathan Meyer.

Money problems posed a particular challenge. In October 1925, Hurston became employed by FANNIE HURST, who paid her to do secretarial and other administrative tasks; Hurston also was offered lodging by Hurst. This would allow her to support herself as she studied, and she had a warm relationship with Fannie Hurst. Hurst, who was interested in African-American issues, functioned "as older, wiser mentor," and Hurston herself was aware how much she could help her career (Boyd 107). Hurst would assist her protégé by bringing writing by Hurston "to the magazine editors with whom she was so well-connected"; she met Charles Norris and Vilhajalmur Stefansson through Hurst (Boyd 109). The relationship with this famous writer also endeared Hurston to her classmates. However, the work Hurston had to do to support herself prevented her from spending an appropriate amount of time on her studies. The dean, Gildersleeve, decided that Hurston would be better off spending more time on her studies, so she found a way for her to obtain a scholarship. In all, Hurston was funded by many different sources during her time at Barnard.

Bibliography

Boyd, Valerie. *Wrapped in Rainbows: The Life of Zora Neale Hurston.* New York: Scribner, 2003.

Howard, Lillie P. *Zora Neale Hurston.* Boston: Twayne, 1980.

Wall, Cheryl A. *Women of the Harlem Renaissance.* Bloomington: Indiana University Press, 1995.

Boas, Franz (1858–1942) A noted anthropologist, Franz Boas was at the forefront of creating and promoting this developing field of study. More important to the discussion here, he served as a mentor for Zora Neale Hurston and inspired her to pursue her interest in social science and anthropology. Having lost her own father while a young woman, Hurston may have seen Boas as a sort of "father figure" (Boyd 114). His approach and methodology profoundly influenced Hurston, enabling her to view African-American culture in a deeper, more complex way. This field provided her with a methodology for analyzing her heritage, as she began to see complexity in the relationships between race, culture, and geography, both in her own home town of Eatonville and in Harlem. She began to see individuals as "phenomena who should be studied as closely as any textbook" (Boyd 115).

Needing more variety in her coursework, she took a class with Franz Boas, on faculty at Columbia University, Barnard's affiliate. In fact, Boaz had established the anthropology program at Columbia, in 1899, which was considered "the most influential anthropology department" in America (Boyd 114). He was known to be a tough professor, requiring students to adhere to a strict methodology and support all claims with evidence. Hurston was Boas's sole black pupil, and Boas saw her cultural background as a benefit to her research and understanding of anthropological work. Boas was an advocate of equality among different races and cultures, holding that any one was not superior to any other. One of her early projects with him was a study in Harlem in which they measured the skulls of blacks in Harlem to show that they were not inferior to whites'.

In February 1927, Hurston traveled to Florida on a fellowship to study the black oral tradition in the South, which Boas had helped her secure. He had been communicating with Carter G. Woodson at the Association for the Study of Negro Life and History, as well as with the American Folklore Society, both of which agreed to fund Hurston's trip. Her research grant amounted to more than a thousand dollars for use while collecting folktales. In Florida, she bought a car to use while researching, journeying throughout Florida and then Louisiana; she also bought a gun for protection (Boyd 144–145). During her trip throughout the South, she experienced discrimination, with public restrooms and hotels being segregated.

Franz Boas *(Library of Congress)*

While on her research excursion in the South, Hurston traveled widely. When she arrived in EATONVILLE, FLORIDA, people were "happy to see that Lucy Hurston's baby girl had turned out to be a fine young woman" (Boyd 144). However, her educational background, now separating her so much from the people she grew up with, made it extremely difficult for her to obtain information. Eatonville may not, in fact, have produced any new material during the research trip, but that can also be attributed to the fact that Hurston knew many of their stories already (Boyd 144). In Mobile,

Alabama, she encountered Cudjo Lewis, the man "believed to be the sole survivor of the last slave ship to land in the United States" (Boyd 150). Hurston also spent time with her family in Memphis, got married to Herbert Sheen (a fact she did not divulge to her research adviser), and met LANGSTON HUGHES. She and Hughes decided to travel north together, first stopping at the Tuskegee Institute, in Alabama, where they gave lectures and met JESSIE FAUSET. They paid homage to Booker T. Washington in a visit to his grave, then spent time in Georgia, South Carolina, and Pennsylvania before arriving back in New York.

Hurston composed her research findings into a report for Boas; both Hurston and Boas were disappointed with some of her results, a fact noted in this report (Boyd 154). In addition, she also completed work for Woodson, publishing an account about Fort Moosa in the *Journal of Negro History.* Woodson also published Hurston's piece "Cudjo's Own Story of the Last African Slaver," which, it was later realized, was plagiarized. Unbeknownst to Boas, Hurston "culled the bulk of the material for her 'original' paper from" another source (Howard 21–22). In 1934, with the help of Boas, the Julius Rosenwald Foundation proposed several thousand dollars' worth of funds so she can pursue research at Columbia University. Hurston and Boas agree on studying general ethnology through fieldwork in Haiti, but the foundation is not supportive of the idea. The funding is reduced, and ultimately Hurston does not attend graduate school at Columbia.

Bibliography

Boyd, Valerie. *Wrapped in Rainbows: The Life of Zora Neale Hurston.* New York: Scribner, 2003.

Howard, Lillie P. *Zora Neale Hurston.* Boston: Twayne, 1980.

dialect Zora Neale Hurston's novels, short stories, folklore, and drama reflect some of the best examples of dialect in the American literary tradition. The dialect Hurston presents is a form of nonstandard English, a black vernacular specific to a particular region or community. While it differs from the English taught in grammar books, black vernacular English is a complex language in its own right, adhering to syntactical rules just as any other language. By presenting black dialects, Hurston realistically depicted black cultural expression and life in the early 20th-century South. By using this language, she implicitly validates it, showing it as a valuable and relevant part of the culture, and not inferior to white versions of English.

Early reviews of Hurston's books made particular note of her use of dialect, and it was not always an object of praise. While Lucille Tompkins found it accessible and appealing in her *New York Times Book Review* article, ALAIN LOCKE, himself an influential African-American writer, chided Hurston, claiming it was overly simple. The style also distinguished Hurston from other of her contemporaries, like JESSIE FAUSET and Nella Larsen. Hurston had a "sensitivity to the rhythms of southern black" language and she "drew from the repository of African-American oral" expression in writing (Wall 141). Her texts are "suffused with the similes, the metaphors, and the rhythms that are the poetry of black vernacular expression" (Wall 142).

Although Hurston employed dialect in many of her texts, *Their Eyes Were Watching God* provides many of the most important examples. The juxtaposition between the black vernacular used in Janie's narrative or the characters' dialogue stands in contrast to standard English that frames the story in the opening and ending of the work. Hurston shifts between voices, showing the different ways in which blacks use language to express themselves. One good example is when Janie insults her husband, Jody Starks, by saying, "Humph! Talkin' bout *me* lookin' old! When you pull down yo' britches, you look lak de change uh life." Hurston spells words phonetically as they are spoken, dropping the final "g" from words such as *talking* and *looking,* and alters other words as well: "yo'" for *you* and "lak" instead of *like,* and "uh" instead of the word *of.* This comes at a crucial moment in the novel, when Janie is confronting her oppressive husband, and the outburst represents an expressive moment of honesty. Hurston shows how powerful dialect can be in empowering individuals to assert a sense of self.

Portrait of Nella Larsen inscribed to Carl Van Vechten and his wife, Fania Marinoff *(Yale Collection of American Literature, Beinecke Rare Book and Manuscript Library)*

One of Hurston's lasting legacies is her ability to show how sophisticated African-American English is. Rather than presenting dialect in a condescending or patronizing manner, she shows its richness and complexity. (Some of her critics, however, argued just the opposite: that her use of it was to portray blacks as simple or uneducated.) The vivid and dynamic quality of the dialect reveals the innovative and creative ways in which people used language to express themselves. By using black southern dialect, Hurston emphasizes the importance of presenting realistic language in representing African-American life and culture.

While it is a rich and realistic presentation of speech, it can be challenging to readers, particularly to those who are encountering this type of speech for the first time. One useful method is to read out loud, slowly sounding the words out. By hearing the words, it can be easier to decipher what is being said than by simply reading them. As Hurston's use of dialect reveals her desire to present a realistic portrayal of African-American cultural expression, understanding the language used as well as the meaning of that language is important when approaching her texts.

Bibliography

Hurston, Zora Neale. *Their Eyes Were Watching God.* In her *Novels and Stories,* 173–333. New York: Library of America, 1995.

Zora Neale Hurston, Rochelle French, and Gabriel Brown, Eatonville, Florida, June 1935 *(Library of Congress)*

Locke, Alain. Review of *Their Eyes Were Watching God.* In *Zora Neale Hurston: Critical Perspectives Past and Present,* edited by Henry Louis Gates, Jr., and K. A. Appiah, 18. New York: Amistad, 1993.

Tompkins, Lucille. Review of *Their Eyes Were Watching God,* in *Zora Neale Hurston: Critical Perspectives Past and Present,* edited by Henry Louis Gates, Jr., and K. A. Appiah, 18–19. New York: Amistad, 1993.

Wall, Cheryl A. *Women of the Harlem Renaissance.* Bloomington: Indiana University Press, 1995.

Eatonville, Florida Hurston spent much of her youth in Eatonville, living there with her family from 1894 to 1904 and returning many times during her life. In *Dust Tracks on a Road,* her memoir, Hurston claims that Eatonville is her birthplace, although she was actually born, in 1891, in NOTASULGA, ALABAMA. Eatonville was founded, in 1886, as a uniquely African-American town, and it is considered to be the first all-black town incorporated in the United States. Because of this history, Hurston may have wanted to claim even closer ties to the proudly black community by saying she was born there.

Hurston uses Eatonville as a setting in much of her work, using real people as inspirations for fictional characters, most notably in the novels *Their Eyes Were Watching God* and *Jonah's Gourd Vine* and the story cycle "The Eatonville Anthology." This reveals the importance that the all-black environment had on her development. Significantly, many of the folktales that she would weave into her narratives were those she heard while at Joe Clarke's store in the real Eatonville, and her passion for storytelling was sparked during those early conversations in town. Hurston's comments about Eatonville in her nonfiction show her allegiance to the town where she grew up and began to formulate an identity. In the opening chapter of *Dust Tracks on a Road,* entitled "My Birthplace," Hurston writes: "I was born in a Negro town. I do not mean by that the black back-side of an average town. Eatonville, Florida, is, and was at the time of my birth, a pure Negro town—charter, mayor, council, town marshal and all. It was not the first Negro community in America, but it was the first to be incorporated, the first attempt at organized self-government on the part of Negroes in America." In the essay "How It Feels to Be Colored Me," Hurston explains that the only whites in town were those in transit, passing through to travel elsewhere. She writes: "Up to my thirteenth year I lived in the little Negro town of Eatonville, Florida. It is exclusively a colored town." Throughout her works, the town serves as an important site of racial identity, community, and history.

Today, Eatonville is still on the map, located several miles north of Orlando. Its small population is primarily but not exclusively African American, and the town remains a source of pride among African Americans due to its history. Many tourists are drawn there to experience the place that played such a significant role in Hurston's life and works, especially during an annual arts festival celebrating Hurston's contributions to literature.

Bibliography

Hurston, Zora Neale. "How It Feels to Be Colored Me." In her *Folklore, Memoirs, and Other Writings,* 826–829. New York: Library of America, 1995.

———. *Dust Tracks on a Road.* In *Folklore, Memoirs, and Other Writings,* 557–808. New York: Library of America, 1995.

Jones, Sharon L. *Rereading the Harlem Renaissance: Race, Class, and Gender in the Fiction of Jessie Fauset, Zora Neale Hurston, and Dorothy West.* Westport, Conn.: Greenwood Press, 2002.

Wall, Cheryl A. *Women of the Harlem Renaissance.* Bloomington: Indiana University Press, 1995.

Fauset, Jessie (1882–1961) In a picture taken in Tuskegee, Alabama, Zora Neale Hurston stands in a dignified pose by the grave of Booker T. Washington, along with LANGSTON HUGHES and Jessie Fauset (Jones 69). The picture illustrates Hurston's connection with other authors during the Harlem Renaissance period and the extent to which other African-American intellectuals influenced her worldview and writings. Connected to Hurston by this symbolic photo, Jessie Fauset herself was a prolific poet, short story writer, essayist, novelist, and editor who helped shape the Harlem Renaissance and explored the lives of black women in her work. Although critics have paid less attention to Fauset's contributions than they have to Hurston's, she was an important force in the 1920s and 1930s.

Jessie Fauset, Langston Hughes, and Zora Neale Hurston at the Tuskegee Institute, Tuskegee, Alabama, gravesite of Booker T. Washington, 1927 *(Yale Collection of American Literature, Beinecke Rare Book and Manuscript Library)*

A native of Camden, New Jersey, Fauset spent much of her life in the Northeast, unlike many other Harlem Renaissance writers, who migrated there later in life. Like Hurston, she was the daughter of a minister, her father, Redmon Fauset, having served as preacher at an African Methodist Episcopal church, a still popular denomination (Jones 20). Her father's role as reverend provided the family with respect and status in their community; the family believed in education, sending Fauset to an integrated public high school in Philadelphia in which Fauset was nevertheless the only African-American student in her classes. She was an excellent and ambitious student, earning a scholarship to Cornell University, where she studied languages and social sciences. Again, she was one of the few African Americans in attendance at Cornell at this time. She contacted W. E. B. DuBois, a black scholar, in regard to a teaching position and obtained one at Fisk University (Jones 21). This was a great change for Fauset, who in her past educational experiences had become used to being in a tiny black minority. However, she would return to another elite northern school, the University of Pennsylvania, where she would achieve a master's degree in 1919.

Like many other African-American writers, including Hurston, Fauset supported herself through teaching, working in Baltimore

W. E. B. DuBois, author, scholar, public intellectual, civil rights leader, and editor of *The Crisis* *(Yale Collection of American Literature, Beinecke Rare Book and Manuscript Library)*

and Washington, D.C., public high schools. Fauset entered and influenced the Harlem Renaissance intelligentsia in her role as an editor of *Crisis,* the magazine published by the NAACP. Along with OPPORTUNITY, *Crisis* was one of the leading outlets for black writers in America. As an editor, she helped to determine which African-American writers would gain national and international exposure through the magazine; she also influenced the representation of African Americans through her editorial decisions during her tenure there, from 1912 to 1919.

Her first novel, *There Is Confusion,* was celebrated by other Harlem Renaissance writers, as it fit in with the goal of providing a more realistic, more complex view of black experience than had been previously accomplished (Jones 23). In *There Is Confusion,* Fauset profiles the development of a black female dancer who seeks to express her creativity. In her second novel, *Plum Bun,* Fauset chronicles the life of another artist figure, Angela Murray, who pretends to be white in order to achieve success as a visual artist. Seeing greater opportunity for whites, she tries to pass as a white woman in New York as she studies art; however, she ultimately cannot deal with the psychological and emotional demands of denying her heritage, and she reveals her real racial background. The novel illustrates the concept of passing, a common theme in Harlem Renaissance literature to show the social, rather than biological, construction of race. Her third novel, *The Chinaberry Tree,* focuses on a character named Laurentine Strange, a seamstress who struggles to express her creativity amid the racial and economic tensions in her life. Fauset's final novel *Comedy, American Style,* is a scathing attack against black

Dust jacket cover of *Comedy, American Style* (1933), the last of four novels by Jessie Fauset *(Yale Collection of American Literature, Beinecke Rare Book and Manuscript Library)*

intraracial color prejudice, in which Olivia Blanchard Cary favors her lighter-skinned daughter over her darker-skinned son.

Fauset's oeuvre, in sum, deals with many of the subjects that Hurston does, and their acquaintance suggests some degree of mutual influence. As two very prolific writers of the period, their texts engaged in a literary dialogue. Although Hurston is often categorized as a writer of the folk and Fauset a writer of the bourgeois, both writers deal with similar themes, focusing on characters from all economic and social backgrounds.

Bibliography

Jones, Sharon L. *Rereading the Harlem Renaissance: Race, Class, and Gender in the Fiction of Jessie Fauset, Zora Neale Hurston, and Dorothy West.* Westport, Conn.: Greenwood Press, 2002.

Wall, Cheryl A. *Women of the Harlem Renaissance.* Bloomington: Indiana University Press, 1995.

film adaptation of *Their Eyes Were Watching God* (2005) A television film version of *Their Eyes Were Watching God* was made for network television, playing on ABC in 2005. Hurston's 1937 novel was adapted for the screen by Misan Sagay, Bobby Smith, Jr., and Suzan-Lori Parks; the film was directed by Darnell Martin; the lead role of Janie Starks was played by Halle Berry. Oprah Winfrey, serving as an executive producer, generated much attention for the film. While the film remained true to some aspects of the plot, major omissions involving characters and events caused the film to ignore much of Hurston's social and political commentary in the novel. As a result, while the film introduced Hurston's landmark text to a wide audience for the first time, the film version does not come close to illustrating the complexity and innovation of *Their Eyes Were Watching God.*

SYNOPSIS

The movie begins with Janie walking down the road toward Eatonville, wearing coveralls. She enters her home and plays the piano. Women talk about her as Pheoby approaches in the house. Pheoby compliments Janie on her appearance, then criticizes Tea Cake; Janie defends him and their relationship and indicates she is not interested in how other people view her. The action flashes back to Janie's childhood as she proceeds to tell Pheoby her life story.

Janie feels transformed as she watches a bee pollinate a blossom in a pear tree; she then runs to Johnny Taylor. The two kiss. Nanny sees it and yells, berating Janie for being with him. Nanny insists on marriage and education for Janie, and she wants her to marry Logan Killicks, who has land. Nanny hits Janie; Janie goes into water and resurfaces, claiming to be "watching God."

Logan arrives, and they marry, but Janie cries as she feels no romance in marriage. She has to work on the farm. Logan leaves one day to get his plow, and soon after, Jody Starks arrives. They talk, and she says she is married. He compliments her and tells her about EATONVILLE, FLORIDA, encouraging her to go there. Later, in bed with Logan, she talks about leaving; he calls her ungrateful for his support, mentioning his property, which she will inherit. Janie leaves, meets Jody on the road, and they go to Eatonville on a buggy.

Janie and Jody arrive in Eatonville after being married—which is not shown in the film—and they look at the place, discussing the idea of purchasing land there. Jody buys land from Captain Eaton and becomes the mayor; the town continues to be developed. Janie comments on her condition, kissing him and noting how Nanny would be happy for her. She tries on a nice dress that the townswomen made for her, but Jody gives her a fancier dress that she must wear to a special event in town. At the street lighting ceremony, Jody speaks about his plans for Eatonville, wanting to incorporate the town;

however, he does not allow Janie to speak during the event. He and Janie talk afterward, and she is concerned about their life. He kisses her back, which reveals markings from the dress.

When Jody sees a man touching Janie's beautiful hair, he gives her a scarf to cover her head. Janie throws it and runs out of the store; back at the house, they argue, and she eventually puts the cloth on her head. Two decades pass, and Janie is shown once again in the store. She clumsily slices a piece of tobacco, causing Jody to yell at her and berate her aging appearance in public. Janie responds with a retort about his own appearance, and Jody hits her, causing blood to streak down her face. Janie moves out of the house. At their home, Jody is near death and they discuss their life; he says he wants her to die. He dies, and there is a funeral; afterward, Janie removes her head covering. Suddenly we see Janie in water again, suggesting liberation.

Later, back in the store, Tea Cake comes in to order tobacco. He and Janie talk, then play checkers. There is another man, Amos, who wants to marry Janie. Tea Cake offers her a soda, and when he bids her good night, he touches her cheek. Tea Cake offers to walk Janie home, where they go to cook a fish dinner, relax on the porch, and dance. He plays the piano, with her next to him, and they kiss. They talk about their relationship and about romance, and he leaves. The next time he returns, he brings her strawberries. They later drive off together, leaving from the store. Tea Cake teaches Janie to shoot and touches her with a flower.

Janie and Pheoby talk about Tea Cake. Pheoby expresses concern about the relationship between Tea Cake and Janie, reminding her of the story of Annie Tyler, who was exploited by a man for her money. Janie reveals her affection for Tea Cake in response to Pheoby's concerns. Later, Janie and Tea Cake are together, dressed nicely and dancing. The two become intimate. When Janie awakes, Tea Cake is missing and her wallet is empty. She waits, thinking about Annie Tyler and worrying if Pheoby was right. He returns, injured and without the money, but they talk about what happened and reconcile. She tells him about her money, but he says he doesn't care.

They travel to the "muck," where they live and work. Janie starts wearing work clothing, and she expresses being content there. They kiss. There is a storm coming, and they end up deluged in a flood during the hurricane. As they fight through the storm, Tea Cake stabs a barking dog and gets bitten, but they survive. Tea Cake falls ill, and a doctor reports that he has rabies. Paranoid, Janie takes Tea Cake's gun from under his pillow and removes the bullets; later, he confronts her with the gun, and she pulls out a rifle and kills him. She cries and holds him.

The film cuts back to the present day. Janie expresses her feelings to Pheoby; Pheoby feels sad, but empowered. Pheoby leaves. Janie goes out to the porch. She runs, again ending up in water, and she says, "I'm watching God."

CRITICAL COMMENTARY

The film adaptation is a dramatic rendering of the novel, featuring music, a high-profile cast, and powerful cinematography; the music captures the atmosphere, and viewers gain a sense of African-American culture and community in the early 1900s. As does the novel, the film adaptation focuses on Janie's growth as a human being in relationship to her grandmother Nanny, her friend Pheoby, and her husbands Logan, Jody, and Tea Cake. This film adaptation emphasizes the primary theme of love and marriage, but it seems to have less to say about race, class, and gender. Neither the character of Mrs. Turner nor the courtroom scene at Janie's trial is addressed in the film adaptation; both of these are extremely important elements in the novel. By emphasizing the romance element, the film proves to be less interesting than the novel in its representation of social issues. However, the film adaptation of *Their Eyes Were Watching God* reflects this important writer's continuing legacy.

The primary theme in this film version is love and marriage. Through the primary flashback, the reader learns of Janie's journey in finding a mate and feeling a sense of unity with another person. While younger, Janie experiences a transformative event when she sees the bee pollinating a tree blossom. That act symbolizes sexuality and procreation. Stirred by this event, Janie kisses Johnny Taylor, engaging in an act of intimacy that her grandmother deems inappropriate. As a means of containing her granddaughter's sexuality and offering her security and respectability, Nanny encourages Janie to wed Logan Killicks. Logan possesses money and can provide her with stability. For Nanny, marriage functions as an economic arrangement and can be a vehicle for upward mobility. However, Janie finds herself in a loveless marriage with him. It does not prove to be fulfilling or satisfying for her, because she married him for money, not love. When she meets Jody Starks, he seems like an escape, as he encourages her to move to Eatonville. When Janie talks to Logan about leaving, the man calls her ungrateful and he even speaks about his land and the promise of her obtaining his possessions. However, for Janie, happiness is more important than material items.

Her second marriage, with Jody, represents her attempt to reach happiness. Jody quickly becomes a prominent man; he purchases real estate and becomes mayor and a successful businessman. Due to Jody's hard work and vision, the town becomes developed. Janie admits that her grandmother would be happy to see her in this position; however, Jody proves to be oppressive and controlling. For example, he does not believe that the dress that the women made for her is good enough for the lamp-lighting event, so he makes her wear a fancier one. This symbolizes his penchant for control over his wife. He also gets jealous of another male who is attracted to her hair, thus making Janie wear a cloth on her head. The material serves to bind her, constrict her, and contain her sexuality—and it lets him be in control. He sees her as property and a commodity; he does not view her as an equal. Janie asserts herself and uses her voice when he berates her appearance and she speaks back. His reaction is to assault her, causing her to bleed: Janie is an abused wife. When Jody becomes ill, she comments to him on their relationship and her disappointments. His death ultimately liberates her, and she takes the material off her head. Thus, the relationship and marriage with Jody prove even more confining than the one with Logan Killicks. She still fails to find the happiness she has spent her life looking for.

The relationship between Tea Cake and Janie is shown to be the most equal. They play checkers, cook fish together, and dance, and Tea Cake shows himself to have a playful and spontaneous side. She is excited by this different man, and despite objections from Pheoby and other townspeople, she leaves town with Tea Cake in an attempt to achieve happiness. Problems are revealed, such as when he takes her money, but overall it is a happier situation than her other marriages. On the "muck" with Tea Cake, Janie dons overalls and labors like the others, feeling freedom and contentment. Although Tea Cake does not possess the money that Jody Starks and Logan Killicks had, she feels that the relationship has something more important. However, the bliss remains short-lived, as the hurricane and the dog bite bring an end to their relationship. He symbolizes, finally, an attainable love and affection, yet he dies. Janie's story empowers Pheoby, suggesting that the memory of Tea Cake lives on; her happiness and tragedies inspire another person.

While the novel *Their Eyes Were Watching God* presents an in-depth and thoughtful critique of interracial and intraracial relationships, the film version does not address these issues with the same depth. For example, even though the film, through its portrayal of Eatonville in particular, shows a vibrant black community, this adaptation does not reveal the complexity of race. Hurston's depiction of Mrs. Turner and the courtroom scene are the two major missing elements. In the novel, Mrs. Turner is a light-skinned black woman who dislikes darker-skinned blacks, believing lighter-skinned blacks are superior; her colorism and attitudes contribute to problems on the muck. Hurston uses the figure of Mrs. Turner as a means of critiquing the dangers of color prejudice. As for the omitted trial scene, this crucial passage in the novel pits a black woman against an all-white-male jury, showing that blacks do not have an equal voice in the justice system. That scene also shows the complex differences between blacks' and whites' views toward justice, with the blacks angered at Janie's acquittal and the whites moved to tears. The glaring absence of these elements from the film suggests that in the modern adaptation romance takes precedence over race.

As in the novel, social and economic class function as important themes in the film version of *Their Eyes Were Watching God.* Janie achieves a middle-class existence with Logan, but the class standing does not make her happy. When married to Jody, she finds herself with an even more successful mate. But his money and social standing mean that Janie must act in the role of an upper-class woman. The social and economic advantages of being his wife may initially appeal to her, but as the relationship progresses, she becomes very unhappy. While Logan and Jody symbolize upward social mobility, her relationship with Tea Cake represents a step down, since he has much less money than either of them or Janie herself. However, the relationship with him proves to be the most egalitarian, and on the "muck" she takes on a working-class identity. Thus she goes from being a middle-class farmer's wife and upper-class mayor's wife to being in a more or less equal relationship with a laborer. Yet as a laborer she is happy; when she returns to Eatonville, she wears coveralls, quite a change from her past. The film adaptation, like the novel, reveals the fluidity of class.

Despite its flaws, the film may ultimately be a useful tool in examining the novel.

Comparing and contrasting the film version with the novel is a useful way of considering how Hurston's text is packaged and presented to a contemporary audience, making it accessible and palatable to modern tastes. Interrogating the inclusion and exclusion of aspects of the novel in relationship to the film can ultimately lead to a deeper and better understanding of *Their Eyes Were Watching God* and the relevancy of Zora Neale Hurston in contemporary times.

Bibliography

Boyd, Valerie. "Our Eyes Are Watching Halle." *Essence.* March 2005, 132.

Johnson, Sharon D. "All Eyes on 'Eyes': Oprah's adaptation of Zora's classic novel, starring Halle as Janie, is a historical moment for the worlds of television and literature." *Black Issue Book Review.* March–April 2005, 42–44.

Their Eyes Were Watching God. 2005 DVD release. Directed by Darnell Martin. A Harpo Films production. Script written by Suzan-Lori Parks, Misan Sagay, and Bobby Smith, Jr.

Fire!! *Fire!!* was an important publication during the HARLEM RENAISSANCE. Although only one issue was published, in November 1926, this magazine features many significant African-American writers of the day. Its subtitle, "A Quarterly Devoted to the Younger Negro Artists," suggests that its creators sought to offer a different and fresher perspective than other African-American publications. George Hutchinson points out its historical importance: "The short-lived *Fire!!* and *Harlem* were declarations of independence from the established black periodicals as much as from the white magazines, which came in a wider variety" (Hutchinson 129).

Wallace Thurman served as the publication's editor-in-chief, and his coeditors included LANGSTON HUGHES, Gwendolyn Bennett, Richard Bruce, Zora Neale Hurston, Aaron Douglas, and John Davis. Other contributors included artists such as Aaron Douglas and Richard Bruce, and writers such as Countee Cullen, Edward Silvera, Helene Johnson, Waring Cuney, Arna Bontemps, Lewis Alexander, and Arthur Huff Fauset. Patrons involved in funding it are listed in it, and include: Maurine Boie, Nellie R. Bright, Arthur Huff Fauset, Dorothy Hunt Harris, Arthur P. Moor, Dorothy R. Peterson, Mr. and Mrs. John Peterson, E. B. Taylor, and Carl Van Vechten. The issue cost one dollar per copy.

Cost presented the biggest obstacle to the continuation of the magazine. David Levering Lewis notes, "To succeed, Thurman's magazine would have had to run for a year, gain loyal readers among curious whites, and attract a critical mass among the Talented Tenth." Generational tastes and preferences were also a factor in the magazine's failure to continue: Some "Afro-American notables and their allies found the quarterly distinctly not to their liking" (Lewis 197). In an ironic twist on the publication's name, many copies of the magazine were "destroyed in a basement fire" (Lewis 197).

Hurston's appearance in the magazine and her connection with others involved with it show her prominence in African-American literature at an early stage of her career. Hurston published two pieces in *Fire!!*: the play *Color Struck* and the story "Sweat." Hurston's play *Color Struck* chronicles the relationship between John and Emmaline, through which she exposes black intraracial color consciousness and prejudice. Emmaline accuses John of favoring light-skinned blacks, but it is ultimately Emmaline who bears a child, out of wedlock, to a light-skinned man. Hurston's story "Sweat" focuses on the tumultuous relationship between Delia Jones and Sykes Jones. The other selections in *Fire!!* illustrate the diversity of voices within the Harlem Renaissance circle. Thurman's "Cordelia the Crude" is about a woman who migrates from the South to Harlem. Gwendolyn Bennett's story "Wedding Day" is set in France, and Richard Bruce's "Smoke, Lilies and Jade" features a highly experimental narrative style with a fragmented structure. The poetry in the issue of *Fire!!* deals with a variety of themes including oppression, lynching, race, gender, nature, death, religion, and employment. In the piece "Intelligentsia," Arthur Huff Fauset describes the characteristics of the intellectual set, and Wallace Thurman contributes an essay about Carl Van Vechten's novel *Nigger Heaven.*

Wallace Thurman *(Yale Collection of American Literature, Beinecke Rare Boook and Manuscript Library)*

Bibliography

Fire!!.: A Quarterly Devoted to the Younger Negro Artists 1, no. 1 (November 1926).

Hutchinson, George. The *Harlem Renaissance in Black and White.* Cambridge, Mass.: Belknap Press, 1995.

Lewis, David Levering. *When Harlem Was in Vogue.* New York: Oxford University Press, 1981.

Great Migration The Great Migration, spanning the early to mid 1900s, was a massive but gradual movement of African Americans from the South to the North and Midwest, from rural areas to urban areas, in search of better lives and more opportunities. It is one of the central, definitive elements in African-American history and culture; its impact on jazz, blues, literature, and popular culture continues to be felt today. The Great Migration changed the social, economic, and political makeup of the United States as the African-American population concentrated into southern and northern urban centers. It transformed demographics, not only bringing blacks out of the South, but also redistributing them, mostly to urban centers, within the South itself. The ramifications were major. This migration also influenced various aspects of popular culture, including jazz and blues, which suddenly enjoyed new audiences, as well as new inspirations.

The migration of African Americans to the North stemmed from a variety of factors, but was mostly based on jobs and the economy. Many African Americans had worked in agriculture, earning very little for their labor and often being exploited in sharecropping systems. Blacks working in other types of jobs also found themselves underpaid and unable to move up the ranks. Pest invasions decimated crops; migrant work was unstable and low-paid. For women, the attraction for social mobility was especially great, as they often worked in menial domestic jobs, being exploited economically or sexually. In the North and West, and in cities in general, commerce was dynamic and offered higher pay and more opportunities. Additionally, businesses in the North put measures in place to attempt to attract African-American employees to move up. Meanwhile, southern areas put policies in place to try to counteract the trend. People "discussed, debated, and decided the merits and demerits of migration" (Trotter 384). Many southern blacks were against migration, as it would tear apart communities and economies.

Robert S. Abbott, founder of the *Chicago Defender* *(Yale Collection of American Literature, Beinecke Rare Book and Manuscript Library)*

According to Joe William Trotter's *The African American Experience,* "conditions in southern agriculture and the lure of higher wages in northern industries stood at the forefront of these forces" (Trotter 380). World War I created jobs in the North, so people moved in search of these jobs (Trotter 378). Trotter claims that as a result "of World War I, an estimated 700,000 to 1 million blacks left the South for northern and western cities" (378). Sometimes men would relocate first, the rest of the family following when stability was achieved; however, women "shared decision making and sometimes determined the destination," as both men and women were eager to change their conditions (Trotter 385). Migrants were often innovative and enterprising, generating a sense of community and commonality. People would pool their resources to purchase tickets at discounted prices, thus creating "migration clubs" (Trotter 385). A newspaper called *Chicago Defender* was an instrumental force in recruiting blacks to the North, specifically to Chicago, with promises of social and economic opportunity. David Levering Lewis, in *When Harlem Was in Vogue,* acknowledges the role of this newspaper, noting that the *Defender* praised "the milk and honey up North" (Lewis 21). According to Lewis, more than 1 million blacks "were reading or having read to them" this publication, and he argues that "its powerful reinforcement of the lure of high wages in the North" was beyond question (Lewis 21).

This migration also helped give rise to the HARLEM RENAISSANCE. HARLEM, NEW YORK, became home to many blacks who had migrated there from the South, the Midwest, and the West. Caribbean and African blacks also moved to Harlem. Harlem thus became the American center for the black diaspora. In addition to affordable housing and the promise of jobs, the concentration of writers, musicians, and artists made the city a popular draw for people like LANGSTON HUGHES, Zora Neale Hurston, and DOROTHY WEST, all of whom migrated to New York City for education or for their writing careers. For ALAIN LOCKE in *The NEW NEGRO,* Harlem symbolized the epitome of black migration and the confluence of diverse peoples from around the world.

Hurston herself was a migrant throughout her life; born in NOTASULGA, ALABAMA, she relocated to EATONVILLE, FLORIDA, as a youth. She moved north, to Baltimore and Washington, D.C., and then to Harlem. While she would later travel back to Florida, the Caribbean, and California, it was here, in Harlem, that much of her influence would be felt. Hurston deals with black migration throughout her works. She presents her own tendency to migrate in her self-portrait in *Dust Tracks on a Road*; the drama *Color Struck* describes characters that return from the North. She alludes to it in *Jonah's Gourd Vine,* notably when Reverend John Pearson, the protagonist, comments on black people migrating north. Hurston details the lives of other southern transplants to the North in "Story in Harlem Slang," showing poverty and destitution often followed blacks even when they moved; opportunity did not necessarily present itself by virtue of a geographical change. "Muttsy" is another example, one which seems to have parallels to Hurston's experience.

Bibliography

Hurston, Zora Neale. *Novels and Stories.* New York: Library of America, 1995.

Lewis, David Levering. *When Harlem Was in Vogue.* New York: Oxford University Press, 1981.

Locke, Alain, ed. *The New Negro.* New York: Johnson Reprint, 1968.

Trotter, Joe William. *The African American Experience.* Boston: Houghton Mifflin, 2001.

Harlem, New York Harlem is a vibrant, culturally diverse area in New York City that drew many African-American artists, writers, and musicians during a sort of "renaissance," which occurred roughly from 1900 to 1940, coinciding with the migration of blacks to the North and to cities. The Harlem Renaissance celebrated African-American music (including jazz and the blues), literature, visual arts, and it also championed civil rights and social justice issues. During the heyday of this movement, many African-American writers wrote about or lived in Harlem. The area symbolized black identity and cultural heritage, as well as a renewed appreciation of the contributions of blacks to American society. Hurston connected with Harlem, the place and the culture, having moved there during the heyday of the Renaissance. Harlem's effect upon Hurston's life proved to be very powerful: It influenced how she saw herself and the world, and even more significantly, it enabled her to engage with the African-American community in a setting of pride and diversity.

Harlem was an African-American neighborhood for some time, as blacks arriving in the area needed housing, and Harlem presented a decent amount of dwellings or room for housing development. This made Harlem "the cultural capital" for blacks, while giving this place "youthful exuberance and promise" (Hemenway 29). As more and more African Americans arrived in New York, they wanted to move where others had built up a black community. As of 1930, it is estimated that 200,000 people resided within "this racial metropolis" (Hemenway 30). While Harlem experienced later urban decay, the neighborhood has seen a resurgence recently.

Bibliography

Hemenway, Robert E. *Zora Neale Hurston: A Literary Biography.* Urbana: University of Illinois Press, 1980.

Jones, Sharon L. *Rereading the Harlem Renaissance: Race, Class, and Gender in the Fiction of Jessie Fauset, Zora Neale Hurston, and Dorothy West.* Westport, Conn.: Greenwood Press, 2002.

Street in Harlem, New York, June 1943 *(Library of Congress)*

Harlem Renaissance The Harlem Renaissance, also known as the New Negro Movement, began in the early 1900s and ended around 1940. Coinciding with modernist trends, the Harlem Renaissance was an interdisciplinary cultural movement that reflected literary, musical, dance, artistic, and dramatic developments in African-American expression. Additionally, the civil rights movement and the rise of organizations for social justice also brought much to bear upon the Harlem Renaissance. This movement would have a wide-ranging impact on American literature, changing the growth and direction of what was valued and what was not. An exploration of race, class, and gender also helped to foster dialogue on these important issues.

One of the main and central causes of the Harlem Renaissance was the phenomenon known as the GREAT MIGRATION, when many African Americans relocated from the South to the North in search of a better life. Wanting to leave behind rural poverty, people saw promise in jobs in the North in industry and business. In addition to the search for jobs, many people left vying for more opportunities in education, as unequal funding and segregated school systems created major education inequality in the South. Civil rights was another issue, as many African Americans wanted to leave behind the culture and places that had permitted slavery and segregation for so long. The reality was often different from the dreams, and poverty remained a problem. Blacks moved to many northern cities, but the greatest concentration of artists, writers, musicians, and civil rights leaders was found in HARLEM, NEW YORK. While originally a movement based in Harlem, the name *Harlem Renaissance* refers broadly to the work and the artists producing that work during the time period, not only to work produced in that particular area.

Many of the writers of the Harlem Renaissance originated from other parts of the country, migrating to New York for employment, education, and opportunity. Such writers include Zora Neale Hurston, LANGSTON HUGHES, DOROTHY WEST, and Wallace Thurman. Thurman, for example, was from Utah, Hughes from Missouri, and Dorothy West from Boston. They brought their experiences from afar to a new home, where they could work together and inspire each other in a united community.

The Harlem Renaissance writers and artists heavily relied on patronage from wealthy individuals devoted to promoting the arts, especially those interested in African-American culture. Many of these patrons were wealthy whites, such as CHARLOTTE OSGOOD MASON, Hurston's patron, whom she affectionately would call "Godmother." Mason provided her with funds for her writing, research, and travel. However, relationships between patrons and writers could be complicated, as patrons often sought to control the content of a writer's work, forcing the scope or vision of a writer to be compromised. In *When Harlem Was in Vogue,* David Levering Lewis discusses the connection between race and economics, arguing that "motives of WASP philanthropy were an amalgam of inherited abolitionism, Christian charity and guilt, social manipulation, political eccentricity, and a certain amount of persiflage" (99). In other words, the motives were not necessarily always pure, and in many cases patrons had stereotypical or even backward views of blacks. Still, for those who chose to take part,

Claude McKay. Photograph by Carl Van Vechten. Permission granted by Van Vechten Trust *(Yale Collection of American Literature, Beinecke Rare Book and Manuscript Library)*

the patronage was an important means of allowing writers to practice their craft.

The Harlem Renaissance showcased the talents of numerous novelists, poets, and essayists. These writers focused on themes such as race, class, gender, history, identity, sexuality, marriage, nature, migration, and slavery versus freedom. The idea of utilizing African-American literature as a means of promoting social justice and equality often framed these texts, allowing them both to entertain and to offer commentary. Notable texts include: *The Souls of Black Folk* by W. E. B. DuBois; *Up From Slavery* by Booker T. Washington; *The Autobiography of an Ex Colored Man* by James Weldon Johnson; *Rachel* by Angelina Weld Grimke; *Plum Bun* by Jessie Redmon Fauset; stories, like "The Typewriter," by Dorothy West; *Passing* and *Quicksand* by Nella Larsen; *The New Negro* by Alain Locke; *The Blacker the Berry* by Wallace Thurman; *The Purple Flower* by Marita Bonner; and poetry by Langston Hughes, Countee Cullen, Sterling Brown, Anne Spencer, Claude McKay, Alice Ruth Moore Dunbar Nelson, or Arna Bontemps. Some white writers also played a role, like Carl Van Vechten, who penned the controversial novel *Nigger Heaven.*

Literature of the Harlem Renaissance focuses on three primary aesthetics: folk, bourgeois, and proletarian; elements of each can be combined in the same narrative. The folk aesthetic features working-class characters in a rural setting, with an emphasis on the oral tradition or dialect (Jones 6). Many of Hurston's writings fall within this model. Her novel *Their Eyes Were Watching God,* for instance, relies on the oral tradition as Janie tells her life story to her friend Pheoby using black vernacular; additionally, many characters represent folk characters, such as Nanny, a former slave, and the townspeople in Eatonville. *Mules and Men* also exemplifies a folk aesthetic, as Hurston presents tales within rural African-American communities. Other Harlem Renaissance–era writers also presented this aesthetic. A folk aesthetic can be seen in those of Langston Hughes's poems that make use of nonstandard English and dialect; his poetry styled on blues or jazz, two musical forms themselves growing out of the folk tradition, demonstrates this as well. The characters, setting, and theme in Hughes and Hurston's play *Mule Bone,* also reflects a folk aesthetic.

The bourgeois aesthetic features middle-class characters who have achieved social and economic success, perhaps even symbolizing an "American dream" of wealth or prosperity (Jones 7). These texts often feature characters who speak in standard American English and have professional, nonagricultural careers. African-American writers employing this mode are Jessie Fauset and Dorothy West, whose fiction documents the experiences of the black middle class. Countee Cullen modeled his poems after 19th-century British romantic writers such as Keats and Shelley, in contrast to the folk elements in the poetry of Hughes. Hurston also employs this aesthetic in her representations of the black middle class, notably in the character of Jody Starks in *Their Eyes Were Watching God* as he becomes mayor and a successful businessman in the Eatonville community. His analogue in other of Hurston's texts, Joe Clarke, also represents this aesthetic.

The "proletarian" aesthetic focuses on "the protest element" (Jones 7). Proletarian texts seek to offer political and economic commentary, looking to raise awareness about urgent problems with the objective of trying to fix them. The goal of such texts is to inform, explain, and incite rather than to entertain. Proletarian literature often examines class, gender, and race, and not from a neutral perspective: It has the goal of effecting change, or changing minds. It is important to note that "these texts may feature characters from the folk and/or bourgeois classes as a means to meditate on power dynamics and relations in American society" (Jones 8). Richard Wright was a proponent of such a literature, and while he criticized Hurston's *Their Eyes Were Watching God,* the social awareness informing that novel and Hurston's critiques within it may be seen as having a "proletarian" function. Other writers who made use of a proletarian aesthetic include Hughes, Cullen, Fauset, and West.

The blues, jazz, and dance were also an important component of the culture of the Harlem Renaissance. These forms of cultural expression held both national and international appeal, launching into the spotlight artists like Cab Calloway, Bessie Smith, and Duke Ellington. Blues and jazz as musical forms migrated from the South to the North and beyond, evidenced by the popularity of Josephine Baker in France. These musicians helped to shape the direction of 20th-century American music and culture. Some writers, such as Langston Hughes, even incorporated blues influences into their writing style, either thematically or structurally. Visual arts were another important aspect of the Harlem Renaissance. Artists like Laura Wheeler Waring, Augusta Savage, and Aaron Douglas expressed black culture through various media; their talents received attention on a national and international scale. However, many black visual artists faced discrimination in the larger art world, but their contributions were nonetheless remarkable.

The NAACP, or the National Association for the Advancement of Colored People, was a major factor in the Harlem Renaissance. This civil rights organization promoted the ideas of equality and fair treatment for all Americans. It also published a journal, called *Crisis,* which highlighted the contributions of blacks to American culture and society. *Crisis* helped to provide a forum for African-American voices within the American literary tradition as an alternative

Cover of the March 1920 issue of *The Crisis* featuring poet Georgia Douglas Johnson. New York National Association for the Advancement of Colored People *(Yale Collection of American Literature, Beinecke Rare Book and Manuscript Library)*

to mainstream magazines aimed at mostly white audiences. As George Hutchinson notes, "Among its most important accomplishments in the early years was the publication of *Crisis* magazine, which surely ranks as one of the great journalistic enterprises in American history" (Hutchinson 141–142). W. E. B. DuBois was one figure who would work with *Crisis* and the NAACP to help shape the direction of the movement; another was JESSIE FAUSET, an acquaintance of Hurston's, who served as editor for *Crisis*.

There were magazines and books that profoundly affected the movement, in addition to those coming out of the NAACP. *OPPORTUNITY* magazine, published by the Urban League, was "the premier journal of African American cultural criticism and performance" (Hutchinson 170). It took a different approach than NAACP. While "the NAACP undertook direct action and immediatism, the Urban League tended toward diplomacy and gradualism" (Hutchinson 171). The Urban League also helped African-American migrants integrate and settle into their new environments.

It was also in *Opportunity* that Hurston first received national attention, winning a writing contest for "Drenched in Light" in 1924. At the awards banquet the following year, she would encounter other luminaries such as Countee Cullen, Langston Hughes, Carl Van Vechten, and FANNIE HURST, as well as Annie Nathan Meyer; meeting these people would prove an important step in Hurston's career, as she began to assemble a network of influential peers. With Langston Hughes, she would coauthor a play, *Mule Bone*; Annie Nathan Meyer would help her go to Barnard College; Fannie Hurst would employ her and prove a longtime friend. Thus, Hurston's involvement with *Opportunity* helped to propel her career as a writer, as well as expand her educational opportunities. Hurston's novels also received coverage in *Opportunity* in the form of reviews.

FIRE!! is another magazine that was crucial to the era, especially as it tried to offer an alternative to the other African-American magazines. Although only one issue was published, this journal features many of the most prominent figures from the Harlem Renaissance, including Aaron Douglas, Richard Bruce, Wallace Thurman, Zora Neale Hurston, Countee Cullen, Edward Silvera, Langston Hughes, Helene Johnson, Waring Cuney, Arna Bontemps, Lewis Alexander, Gwendolyn Bennett, and Arthur Huff Fauset. The eclectic selections range from short fiction to drama to poetry and nonfiction. Hurston's pieces included were "Sweat" and *Color Struck.*

The NEW NEGRO, which was edited by Alain Locke, was another powerful text. This anthology featured up-and-coming African-American writers and represents an attempt to bring together a variety of fresh new perspectives on African-American issues. In *The New Negro,* Locke writes about the new identity of African Americans, casting this identity in both a social and a historical context. The anthology features writers such as Jean Toomer, Zora Neale Hurston, Countee Cullen, Claude McKay, Langston Hughes, and Georgia Douglas Johnson. The text presents material that was originally published in *Opportunity* and *Survey Graphic.*

Certain economic factors led to the demise of the Harlem Renaissance movement, including the stock market crash and the Great Depression. With severely limited resources, publications folded and patrons stopped funding work. People had less money to spend on cultural production, thus decreasing the demand for artists' and writers' works. However, while the artistic output may have decreased and the vibe may have dimmed, many devoted writers continued in their tradition—including Hurston, Hughes, West, DuBois, and others—and they also influenced a future generation that would come after World War II.

Bibliography

Hutchinson, George. *The Harlem Renaissance in Black and White.* Cambridge, Mass.: Belknap Press, 1995.

Jones, Sharon L. *Rereading the Harlem Renaissance: Race, Class, and Gender in the Fiction of Jessie Fauset, Zora Neale Hurston, and Dorothy West.* Westport, Conn.: Greenwood Press, 2002.

Lewis, David Levering. *When Harlem Was in Vogue.* New York: Oxford University Press, 1981.

Locke, Alain, ed. *The New Negro.* New York: Johnson Reprint, 1968.

Smith, Rochelle, and Sharon L. Jones, eds. *The Prentice Hall Anthology of African American Literature.* Upper Saddle River, N.J.: Prentice Hall, 2000.

Wall, Cheryl A. *Women of the Harlem Renaissance.* Bloomington: Indiana University Press, 1995.

Howard University Howard University is a respected black university located in Washington, D.C., founded in 1866. Howard was founded with the intention to prepare blacks in the same way that Ivy League schools had prepared whites in the past; it emulated these in several respects, mandating a classical education in Greek and Latin. During Hurston's life, not many of the college-educated professional African Americans had attended Howard University, as only the most fortunate had the opportunity to do so. In the period after emancipation, a number of black colleges opened their doors, including Fisk, Morehouse, Atlanta, and Hampton Institute.

Hurston's decision to attend Howard University was prompted by her friend May

Howard University, Washington, D.C. *(Library of Congress)*

Miller, a student there who was related to a Howard administrator. Though Hurston thought her academic record wasn't strong enough, she was accepted (Boyd 79). She transferred to Howard from Morgan Academy in 1918, moving to the capital and seeking work to pay for school. She found a job at the Cosmos Club, "a social headquarters for Washington's intellectual aristocracy, which meant its membership was open exclusively to white males" (Boyd 80). She later worked for a barbershop that was open only to white people; since it was visited by prominent members of the city and the government, Hurston learned a lot about the inner workings of society.

At registration, Hurston realized that she needed more schooling to bring her up to the necessary level; she was encouraged to begin at the Howard Academy, the preparatory academy associated with the university, which she did for a year (Boyd 80). Zora began attending Howard University courses later, in 1919. Hurston's academic record varied considerably, but mostly she did well. Hurston majored in English. While at Howard, Hurston composed a good deal of poetry, some of it appearing in *The Stylus*, the university's literary magazine, published by the literary society of the same name. *The Stylus* was established in 1915, and admission was granted by competition. Alain Locke was one of the main sponsors of the society. "John Redding Goes to Sea" was published in the magazine. Hurston also joined the Zeta Phi Beta sorority and met her future husband, Herbert Sheen, while at Howard.

Bibliography

Boyd, Valerie. *Wrapped in Rainbows: The Life of Zora Neale Hurston.* New York: Scribner, 2003.

Trotter, Joe William, Jr. *The African American Experience.* Boston: Houghton Mifflin, 2001.

Hughes, Langston (1902–1967) Born James Mercer Langston in Joplin, Missouri, Langston Hughes was one of the leading figures of the HARLEM RENAISSANCE. Like Hurston, he wrote in a variety of genres, including nonfiction, fiction, drama, and poetry. His poems, which use simple and direct language, contain a sophisticated understanding of human experience. Hughes's valorization of the black folk experience, his use of dialect, his incorporation of musical elements, and his keen awareness of the power of literature to cause change all contributed to Hughes's reputation as a formidable force during the Harlem Renaissance.

Hughes grew up in Missouri, in the household of a prominent black family who exposed him to the Bible and *Crisis* magazine. His great-uncle held a number of important positions, including being dean of Howard University's law school and a congressman from Virginia. This uncle was a graduate of Oberlin College, one of the first colleges in the United States to admit blacks. One of Hughes's grandmothers had also gone to Oberlin. Hughes's mother was a strong female role model, but he did not get along well with his father, an attorney. His parents divorced, creating an upset in Hughes's life. After living in several states, Hughes would later move to Cleveland, Ohio, with his mother and stepfather. While at Central High School there, he developed his skills as a writer and read poets such as Walt Whitman, Vachel Lindsey, and Amy Lowell. By the early 1920s, he had published in *The Brownie's Book,* a magazine aimed at children.

Hughes later moved to New York City, where he became a Columbia University student, one of only a few African Americans there. Hughes left the university without a degree to pursue his literary work. A scholar points out, "He was twenty, free, and a poet in Harlem, adored by Jessie Fauset, literary editor of *The Crisis,* and encouraged by DuBois" (Lewis 80). After working odd

Langston Hughes, 1943 *(Library of Congress)*

jobs to make money, Hughes got a kitchen job on a ship sailing to Africa. The voyage to Africa gave him an opportunity to connect with the land of his ancestors, but he did not spend much time on the continent. Hughes traveled widely, heading by ship to Paris, where he would be inspired for his jazz poems, as well as to Spain.

Hughes shared a number of experiences with Hurston. Hurston traveled through the South with Hughes before returning to New York while on her research trip; the two visited Booker T. Washington's grave in Tuskegee, Alabama. Both had as their patron CHARLOTTE OSGOOD MASON, a wealthy white socialite with an interest in African-American and Native American culture, although Hughes let her funding go when he felt compromised by her pressures. Hurston and Hughes collaborated on the drama *Mule Bone,* which caused a rupture in their friendship. During the collaboration on *Mule Bone,* inspired by Hurston's story "The Bone of Contention," Hurston worked on dialogue and characterization while Hughes worked more on structure. After tensions during the writing, most having to do with a lack of money, Hurston tried to get sole copyright credit. This episode created a rift between the two and ultimately their friendship ended.

Bibliography

"Langston Hughes." In *The Prentice Hall Anthology of African American Literature,* edited by Rochelle Smith and Sharon L. Jones, 444–447. Upper Saddle River, N.J.: Prentice Hall, 2000.

Lewis, David Levering. *When Harlem Was in Vogue.* New York: Oxford University Press, 1981.

Hurston, John (1861–1918) Zora Neale Hurston's father, John Hurston, a native of NOTASULGA, ALABAMA, held a variety of jobs during his life, including minister and mayor, as well as farming and carpentry work. He is the model for the character John Pearson in *Jonah's Gourd Vine.*

Hurston's father wed her mother, Lucy Ann Potts, and the couple had several children. While John came from a family of sharecroppers, Lucy Ann Potts came from a more affluent, landowning family, a source of tension for Lucy's mother. John relocated his family to the area of EATONVILLE, FLORIDA, in 1894, where he rose to prominence. He worked as a preacher at Zion Hope Baptist Church and the Macedonia Baptist Church and later directed the South Florida Baptist Association. He was known in Eatonville for being a strong, brave leader and an inspiring preacher. John's wife Lucy passed away in 1904, and he married another woman. He was later killed in a car accident, similar to the one in *Jonah's Gourd Vine.*

Bibliography

Hemenway, Robert E. *Zora Neale Hurston: A Literary Biography.* Urbana: University of Illinois Press, 1980.

Hurston, Lucy (1865–1904) Born Lucy Ann Potts in NOTASULGA, ALABAMA, Zora Neale Hurston's mother married John Hurston. Unlike John's family, Lucy's family were landowners. With John, she had several children and moved to EATONVILLE, FLORIDA. She died in 1904, when Zora was still young. She serves as the inspiration for Lucy Ann Pearson in *Jonah's Gourd Vine* and may have inspired elements of Janie Crawford in *Their Eyes Were Watching God.*

Lucy "made Zora her special child and had the most influence on her early life" (Hemenway 15). Hurston writes of her lovingly in *Dust Tracks on a Road,* noting she was a strong, inspiring, nurturing figure: "Mama exhorted her children at every opportunity to 'jump at de sun.' We might not land on the sun, but at least we would get off the ground. Papa did not feel so hopeful. Let well enough alone. It did not do for Negroes to have too much spirit." Lucy Hurston recognized her daughter's independent nature and expected her to be a strong woman.

Bibliography

Hemenway, Robert E. *Zora Neale Hurston: A Literary Biography.* Urbana: University of Illinois Press, 1980.

Hurston, Zora Neale. *Dust Tracks on a Road.* In her *Folklore, Memoirs, and Other Writings,* 557–808. New York: Library of America, 1995.

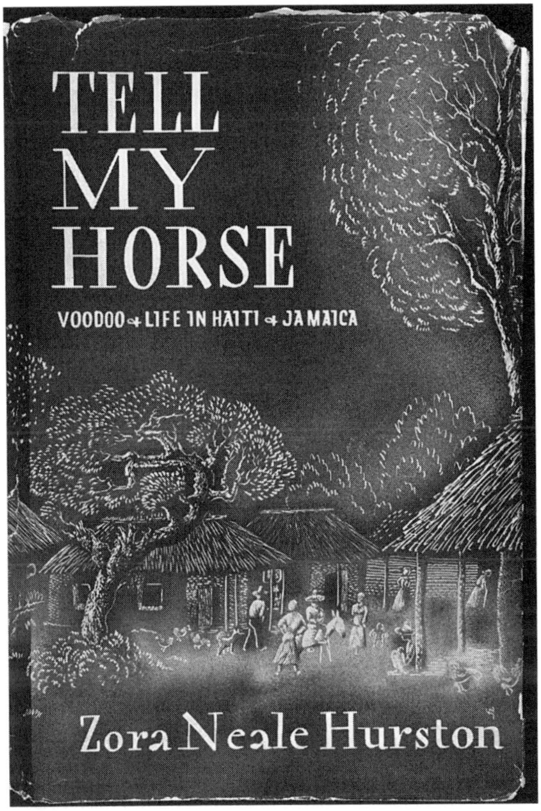

Dust jacket of *Tell My Horse: Voodoo and Life in Haiti and Jamaica,* ca. 1938 *(Yale Collection of American Literature, Beinecke Rare Book and Manuscript Library)*

Jamaica and Haiti Zora Neale Hurston's research trips carried her throughout the United States, but her interest in the African diaspora extended beyond American shores. Hurston spent time in Jamaica and Haiti learning about rituals and customs that would enrich her own writing and enhance her perspective on culture, particularly concerning folk customs. While in Haiti, Hurston wrote *Their Eyes Were Watching God,* but the point of the trips was to research culture there. Most notably, her time in the Caribbean resulted in *Tell My Horse,* a text about voodoo and zombies in Haiti.

Hurston received funding from the Guggenheim Foundation for her research trip to the Caribbean in 1936, and she subsequently left for her research in Haiti and Jamaica. Hurston portrays Jamaica as a patriarchal place obsessed with color and where females were seen as second-class citizens. In Port-au-Prince, Haiti, Hurston studied Creole skills, learned about voodoo, and documented zombie culture. She returned to the United States in 1937. She completed *Tell My Horse* while she was back in Florida. However, *Tell My Horse* failed to sell many copies. According to one critic, this text, which was "less interesting than *Mules and Men,*" may not have been much of a success because of Hurston's discussion of "politics" (Howard 38).

Kingston, Jamaica ca. 1900 *(Library of Congress)*

Bibliography

Hemenway, Robert E. *Zora Neale Hurston: A Literary Biography.* Urbana: University of Illinois Press, 1980.

Howard, Lillie P. *Zora Neale Hurston.* Boston: Twayne, 1980.

Locke, Alain (1886–1954) A native of Philadelphia, Alain Locke played a pivotal role in the HARLEM RENAISSANCE by promoting and mentoring aspiring African-American writers, including LANGSTON HUGHES, JESSIE FAUSET, and Zora Neale Hurston. He edited *The* NEW NEGRO, an important Harlem Renaissance anthology. Locke considered Harlem to be the epitome of black culture. He argued that Harlem deserved a central place in the psyche of the New Negro because blacks from all over the world migrated there in search of opportunity (Smith and Jones 423–424).

Locke came from a well-educated, middle-class black family, whose father, an alumnus of Howard University, was an educator. Locke was an excellent student, and he attended Harvard University at a time when few African Americans had that opportunity. He then became the first African American to win a Rhodes scholarship, studying at Oxford, as well as universities in Berlin and Paris. Locke taught philosophy at Howard University and sponsored a literary society, which published a magazine called *The Stylus.* While at Howard University, Zora Neale Hurston contributed to *The Stylus.* Locke cultivated a relationship with CHARLOTTE OSGOOD MASON, who would later fund other artists and writers of the Harlem Renaissance, including Hurston. Although Locke did encourage Hurston earlier in her career, he also wrote a scathing review of *Their Eyes Were Watching God,* claiming the novel lacked depth and complexity. In the review, which appeared in a 1938 issue of *Opportunity,* Locke notes that Hurston's "gift for poetic phrase, for rare dialect, and folk humor keep her flashing on the surface of her community and her characters and from diving down deep either to the inner psychology of characterization or to sharp analysis of the social background."

Locke is probably best known for the anthology *The New Negro,* published in 1925 which grew out of a special issue of *Survey Graphic* magazine. In this book, he published a number of notable African-American authors and included a groundbreaking essay in which he outlined his philosophy of the New Negro Concept. He suggests that "the Old Negro" was dependent, weak, and one-dimensional, a stereotypical concept created by others in order to promote the idea that blacks were weak, underpowered, and unequal (Smith and Jones 422). The New Negro, according to Alain Locke, represents a newfound identity, one involving independence, power, authority, and even flair; this new generation will contribute leaders to society in all aspects of life. The New Negro projects black pride and black power, and he cares about his heritage.

The New Negro showcased the talents of black writers and included art, poetry, drama, nonfiction, and fiction. This anthology thus helped to usher in a new appreciation of black artistic expression; it helped open doors for emerging black poets, dramatists, essayists, and painters by drawing on a multiracial audience. Some have argued that Locke's book privileged an intellectual or aristocratic readership. George Hutchinson notes: "He tried to further a cultural realization based on a racially proud yet cosmopolitan sensibility, drawing confidence from 'classical' African and African American folk culture and from a belief that important sectors of white America were prepared for an interracial and

1926 portrait of Alain Locke inscribed to James Weldon Johnson "in esteem and cordial regard." *(Yale Collection of American Literature, Beinecke Rare Book and Manuscript Library)*

cultural pluralist future. Framing all was his, shall we say, Negrocentric vision of American culture" (397).

Bibliography

Hutchinson, George. *The Harlem Renaissance in Black and White.* Cambridge, Mass.: Belknap Press, 1995.

Lewis, David Levering. *When Harlem Was in Vogue.* New York: Oxford University Press, 1981.

Locke, Alain. "From *The New Negro.*" In *The Prentice Hall Anthology Of African American Literature,* edited by Rochelle Smith and Sharon L. Jones, 422–430. Upper Saddle River, N.J.: Prentice Hall, 2000.

———. Review of *Their Eyes Were Watching God,* in *Zora Neale Hurston: Critical Perspectives Past and Present,* edited by Henry Louis Gates Jr. and K. A. Appiah, 18. New York: Amistad, 1993.

Mason, Charlotte Osgood (1854–1946)
A patron of the arts, Charlotte Osgood Mason provided economic support for various African-American writers and artists during the HARLEM RENAISSANCE. The Harlem Renaissance relied heavily on patronage by wealthy individuals interested in fostering the contributions of African Americans. However, sometimes the benefactors exerted control over the artist's work, trying to have it conform to their own ideas, especially about African Americans. Mason, known at times as "Godmother," wielded much influence upon African-American writers such as ALAIN LOCKE, Zora Neale Hurston, and LANGSTON HUGHES in the early 1900s. Her funding contributed greatly to these writers' output, but her views on blacks and the control she tried to exert put the patron-artist relationship in tension.

Charlotte Osgood Mason's birth name was Charlotte van der Veer Quick; she died in 1946 in New York. She was a widow; her husband, Rufus Osgood Mason, had died, leaving her his money. Mason's interests included Native American culture as well as African-American culture. She had given money to a number of other interests, including black schools and universities in the South. After meeting Alain Locke in 1927 at an art talk he gave, Mason funded some of his work. She also funded Aaron Douglas, Hall Johnson, Richmond Barthe, Langston Hughes, as well as Claude McKay. In addition to funding projects, Mason was known for lavishing her subjects with gifts. For writers like Hughes, it has been speculated that she provided "between $50,000 and $75,000" (Boyd 158). She dictated a rule to those she funded that her sponsorship was subject to absolute anonymity, and if anyone divulged their sources of funds, they would be instantly dropped. However, Hurston and Hughes were aware of each other's funding by Mason.

Hurston met Mason in 1927 at the wealthy woman's home on Park Avenue in New York City (Boyd 156). Mason appreciated "the young woman's effulgent intellect and absolute lack of pretension," particularly in contrast to Alain Locke (Boyd 157). Hurston, for her part, felt an affinity with Charlotte Osgood Mason and thought her interest was genuine. Without the necessary funding Mason provided, Hurston might not have been able to travel so extensively and collect folklore. However, the authority and power Mason wished to exert in framing her vision of black culture would ultimately compromise the sanctity of the artist's project. Their financial arrangement put Mason in control, with a yearlong contract stipulating the terms. It should be noted that Mason viewed herself as the owner of Hurston's research, restricting how she could use the information without her permission, and she expected Hurston "to do research *on her behalf*" (Boyd 159). Mason also could decide "what material Zora might display in her revues or what she might publish in her books" (Howard 23).

Bibliography

Boyd, Valerie. *Wrapped in Rainbows: The Life of Zora Neale Hurston.* New York: Scribner, 2003.

Howard, Lillie P. *Zora Neale Hurston.* Boston: Twayne, 1980.

Wall, Cheryl A. *Women of the Harlem Renaissance.* Bloomington: Indiana University Press, 1995.

Morgan Academy Morgan Academy is the preparatory academy affiliated with Morgan State University, a historically black university in Baltimore, Maryland. Hurston studied at Morgan Academy in 1917 and 1918, which helped her develop academic skills she would later use at HOWARD UNIVERSITY and BARNARD COLLEGE. Additionally, Hurston's time in Baltimore served as a chance for her to grow intellectually, socially, and emotionally.

After leaving Florida, Hurston worked for a musical company, Gilbert and Sullivan, traveling through the United States. Hurston became sick, however, and had appendix surgery at the Maryland General Hospital in Baltimore, where she settled afterward. She began working and took evening classes at Morgan Academy, later enrolling as a student there. Hurston worked hard at Morgan, performing especially well in English, but she felt somewhat at odds there, as most of the other students had come from wealthy families and were far younger than she. Overall, the experience was a good one, and Hurston felt much personal growth. She earned her high school diploma, and two decades later she was awarded an honorary doctorate from Morgan State.

While Hurston was studying at Morgan, her father died in a car wreck in Memphis, Tennessee, an event she would fictionalize in *Jonah's Gourd Vine.* Hurston chose not to attend her father's funeral, as she had become estranged from him when he married another woman following her mother's death. Hurston later moved to Washington, D.C., and enrolled at Howard University.

Bibliography

Boyd, Valerie. *Wrapped in Rainbows: The Life of Zora Neale Hurston.* New York: Scribner, 2003.

Hemenway, Robert E. *Zora Neale Hurston: A Literary Biography.* Urbana: University of Illinois Press, 1980.

Howard, Lillie P. *Zora Neale Hurston.* Boston: Twayne, 1980.

National Urban League The National Urban League is a civil rights organization established in 1910 with the goal of promoting social justice, equality, and opportunity for African Americans. The Urban League, like the NAACP, became a key player during the Harlem Renaissance. It was founded by Ruth Standish Baldwin and Dr. George E. Haynes.

Charles Spurgeon Johnson, editor of *Opportunity.* Photograph by Carl Van Vechten. Permission granted by the Van Vechten Trust. *(Yale Collection of American Literature, Beinecke Rare Book and Manuscript Library)*

The organization became especially influential with its publication, OPPORTUNITY. Under the leadership of Charles Johnson from 1922 to 1928, *Opportunity* became a vehicle for introducing African-American writers to national and international audiences. Johnson's vision and ambition made the magazine an important force within American literature; he believed it could be used to advance crucial social justice and civil rights concerns. To honor JESSIE FAUSET's book *There Is Confusion,* Johnson invited a number of black authors, including LANGSTON HUGHES, Jean Toomer, Countee Cullen, and Gwendolyn Bennett, to a banquet in New York. Other notables included ALAIN LOCKE, W. E. B. DuBois, and James Weldon Johnson. Zora Neale Hurston was not, however, present at the event, but she would benefit from some business that occurred there. Paul Kellogg, the editor of *Survey Graphic,* proposed to Johnson that he publish a compendium of black writers; this was the idea that grew into Alain Locke's *The New Negro,* the reference anthology of the HARLEM RENAISSANCE.

Hurston's first major exposure to large audiences began through *Opportunity,* which published "Drenched in Light," "Muttsy," and "Spunk" between 1924 and 1926. In 1925, Hurston moved to New York at Johnson's urging, after she had won an *Opportunity* writing competition for "Drenched in Light." Johnson was highly impressed with Hurston's work and his early support for Hurston catapulted her to the top ranks of the Harlem Renaissance writers. At the awards banquet, Hurston came in contact with other notables, including Countee Cullen, Langston Hughes, Carl Van Vechten, FANNIE HURST, and Annie Nathan Meyer. The following year, she won another *Opportunity* prize for "Muttsy." With these honors, the National Urban League actively promoted the works of African-American authors, and the effects these events and the publication had were widespread.

Bibliography

Boyd, Valerie. *Wrapped in Rainbows: The Life of Zora Neale Hurston.* New York: Scribner, 2003.

Hemenway, Robert E. *Zora Neale Hurston: A Literary Biography.* Urbana: University of Illinois Press, 1980.

Trotter, Joe William. *The African American Experience.* Boston: Houghton Mifflin, 2001.

The New Negro Published during the 1920s, *The New Negro* was a landmark text of African-American literature. Its editor, ALAIN LOCKE, like other leaders in the African-American community, believed in using writing as a means of achieving social justice, equality, and opportunity; he also believed in actively promoting authors, with the goal of introducing them to a wide audience and thus creating opportunity for advancement. With *The New Negro,* Locke created a canon of HARLEM RENAISSANCE literature. His exclusions and inclusions have had long-lasting effects on what texts are valued in African-American literature. Hurston's contribution to this text, which was her short story "Spunk," helped to solidify her position as an important member of the movement.

In *The New Negro,* Locke presents a multifaceted view of African-American cultural expression through essays, fiction, poems, drama, and art. Writers featured in the anthology represent a diverse mix. Among the notable writers included are Alain Locke, William Stanley Braithwaite, Rudolph Fisher, Jean Toomer, Eric Walrond, Countee Cullen, Claude McKay, James Weldon Johnson, LANGSTON HUGHES, Georgia Douglas Johnson, Anne Spencer, Angelina Grimké, Lewis Alexander, JESSIE FAUSET, and Zora Neale Hurston.

The textual work in the anthology is rich and diverse. Countee Cullen writes about

Angelina Grimké in Middle Eastern costume and Tuareg tribe headdress, ca. 1897 *(Library of Congress)*

race relationships in his poem "Tableau," while in "Harlem Wine," he captures the mood and atmosphere of a particular place. Claude McKay's "The Tropics in New York" reflects upon the present versus the past; his poem "White Houses" is a strong critique of racial oppression. Langston Hughes's powerful and well-known poem, "The Negro Speaks of Rivers," examines race, identity, and nature, and "Dream Variation" serves as a celebration of African-American heritage. His poignant "I Too" meditates on what it means to be an African American in the early 20th century, recognizing his status but hoping for equality someday. Anne Spencer's "Lady, Lady" reflects on gender, while Angelina Grimké's "The Black Finger" deals with questions of race and nature. The text also features visual art, with contributions by Winold Reiss, Aaron Douglas, and Miguel Covarrubias; this was another important art form during the Harlem Renaissance, engaging in dialogue with the other forms of expression.

Bibliography

Boyd, Valerie. *Wrapped in Rainbows: The Life of Zora Neale Hurston.* New York: Scribner, 2003.

Hutchinson, George. *The Harlem Renaissance in Black and White.* Cambridge, Mass.: Belknap Press, 1995.

Locke, Alain, ed. *The New Negro.* New York: Johnson Reprint, 1968.

New Orleans Hurston traveled to New Orleans, Louisiana, to research African-American culture, specifically relating to conjuring and voodoo. She spent much of 1928 and 1929 engaged in this research there, interspersing it with other similar work in Florida and the Bahamas. While there, Hurston established relationships with many conjurers, including the protégés of the famous conjure woman Marie Laveau. The research she conducted there is presented in the second part of *Mules and Men.* In that major anthropological work, Hurston calls New Orleans "the hoodoo capital of America."

Bibliography

Hurston, Zora Neale. *Mules and Men.* In *Folklore, Memoirs, and Other Writings,* 1–267. New York: Library of America, 1995.

Notasulga, Alabama Zora Neale Hurston was born in Notasulga, Alabama, even though she claims in some texts (notably *Dust Tracks on a Road*) that she was born in EATONVILLE, FLORIDA. Notasulga is a tiny town near Tuskegee. Hurston's parents, JOHN and LUCY HURSTON, were both born in Notasulga, Alabama, and they began their family there. The Hurstons relocated to Eatonville between 1893 and 1895, when Zora was very young.

Bibliography

Boyd, Valerie. *Wrapped in Rainbows: The Life of Zora Neale Hurston.* New York: Scribner, 2003.

Wall, Cheryl A. *Women of the Harlem Renaissance.* Bloomington: Indiana University Press, 1995.

Opportunity The National Urban League published this magazine as a means of promoting African-American authors, as well as political and cultural commentary. It served as a mouthpiece for the civil rights and social

French Market in New Orleans *(Library of Congress)*

justice issues advocated by the organization. Other such magazines included *Crisis*, *Messenger*, and *FIRE!!* These too were to be used to advocate for civil rights and social justice, especially by seeking a connection between literature and activism. These publications contributed greatly to providing national recognition for black writers during the HARLEM RENAISSANCE; *Opportunity*, in particular, thrust Hurston into the national limelight.

Initially, *Opportunity* did not focus upon literary contributions but on social and cultural affairs, as Charles S. Johnson, the editor from 1922 to 1928, had studied sociology at the University of Chicago. The transformation of *Opportunity* to a more arts-focused publication stems from a dinner that Johnson organized to honor JESSIE FAUSET's *There Is Confusion*, a fictional book about the African-American experience. Ultimately, this event became a celebration of emerging African-American authors. Many prominent people associated with the Harlem Renaissance were included in the event, including ALAIN LOCKE, W. E. B. DuBois, and James Weldon Johnson. Paul Kellogg, who edited *Survey*

Graphic magazine, was included in the event, and he suggested the idea of a special issue focusing on African Americans (Boyd 89–90). This special issue, which Locke edited, ultimately sold many copies (Boyd 96). Later, Alain Locke would edit the anthology called *The New Negro,* which grew out of this special issue of *Survey Graphic* focusing on black culture. *Opportunity* promoted the works of African-American writers through a writing competition. Hurston's tale "Drenched in Light" appeared in *Opportunity* in 1924. Hurston won awards at the *Opportunity* awards banquet in 1925. Other award winners were Cullen and Hughes, for poetry, and Sterling Brown and E. Franklin Frazier, for essays. Hurston also received awards for "Spunk," (second place in fiction) *Color Struck* (second place for drama), "Spears" (honorable mention), and "Black Death" (honorable mention), in 1925 (Boyd 91–97). Hurston earned money, and Johnson was so impressed that he urged Hurston to move to New York. The following year, Hurston won an *Opportunity* award for "Muttsy." *Opportunity* also later published reviews of her works. These awards and the exposure she got from them proved immensely important in Hurston's writing career.

A. Philip Randolph, cofounder and coeditor of *The Messenger* *(Yale Collection of American Literature, Beinecke Rare Book and Manuscript Library)*

Bibliography

Boyd, Valerie. *Wrapped in Rainbows: The Life of Zora Neale Hurston.* New York: Scribner, 2003.

Trotter, Joe William. *The African American Experience.* Boston: Houghton Mifflin, 2001.

St. Lucie County Welfare Home This is the facility, located in St. Lucie County, Florida, where Hurston died. In 1959, Hurston was ill and needed public assistance in order to purchase her necessary medication. She did not reveal to her relatives that she was sick. Having had a stroke and gotten progressively worse during the fall of 1959, she was admitted to this facility in October. She died from hypertensive heart disease in 1960. Hurston was buried at the Genesee Memorial Gardens.

The last years of Zora Neale Hurston's life were marked by anonymity and decline. This highly accomplished woman, who had contributed so much to American culture, spent the end of her life fighting against poverty, working odd jobs, and struggling to pay her rent. After such a rich life lived, the conditions surrounding Hurston's death—in obscurity, in a public welfare facility—were not worthy of the woman who suffered them.

Bibliography

Boyd, Valerie. *Wrapped in Rainbows: The Life of Zora Neale Hurston.* New York: Scribner, 2003.

Hemenway, Robert E. *Zora Neale Hurston: A Literary Biography.* Urbana: University of Illinois Press, 1980.

Walker, Alice An important contemporary writer, Alice Walker is among the many African-American writers deeply influenced by Zora Neale Hurston. Her works are widely read by the general public and in universities, and their engaging subject matters provoke emotion and debate. Walker's most famous text, *The Color Purple,* received the Pulitzer Prize, the American Book Award, and the National Book Award and was made into a film. The work is an epistolary novel, told through letters, that chronicles a moving and tragic tale of Celie and her family's life.

Alice Walker was born in Eatonton, Georgia, to parents who were farm laborers. When wounded in her eye as a child, Walker began to observe and record the world around her. She left Eatonton in 1961, heading first to Spelman College, in Atlanta, then to Sarah Lawrence, in Bronxville, New York. During her time as a student at Sarah Lawrence, Alice Walker got pregnant, resulting in emotional turmoil. Walker also has a long career as a social activist, beginning with her activities during the civil rights movement in the 1960s. She married a white attorney, Melvyn Levanthal, in 1967, and they lived in Mississippi despite miscegenation legislation. The couple had a child, Rebecca, and they divorced in 1977.

In the 1970s, Walker's focus on black women writers from the South prompted a rush of creative production that has been sustained to this day. In her works, the influence of Hurston is evident in both subtle and glaring ways. Like Hurston, Walker is a product of the South and moved around the country. Walker writes about the lives of southern black women with sensitivity and complexity. Stylistically, she has experimented with different narrative techniques and has used dialects and nonstandard Englishes. Thematically, she also deals with issues of race, class, and gender in a very thoughtful and insightful way. Both authors translate the power of black culture in their texts.

Aside from her own work, one of Walker's most important goals was to resurrect Hurston's memory and to bring new attention to her works. In "Zora Neale Hurston: A Cautionary Tale and Partisan View," Alice Walker explores the legacy of Zora Neale Hurston. Walker describes first hearing about Hurston in a class at Jackson State College, in which emphasized male authors. Still, Walker read *Mules and Men* and was astonished. She shared the text with her family, and it resonated, due to their oral storytelling heritage. She depicts this HARLEM RENAISSANCE author as an innovative and rebellious individual, a Harlem Renaissance trailblazer. "Looking for Zora" contains an account of Hurston's death, as Walker sought to find out about the end of Hurston's life, and where she was buried. She pretends to be a Hurston relative in order to get information about the location of the cemetery where Hurston is buried; she then prepares a commemorating marker on her grave that lists her many accomplishments. When she arrived, Walker was shocked at the decaying condition of the cemetery.

In *In Search of Our Mothers' Gardens: Womanist Prose,* published in 1983, Walker coined the term *womanism* to refer to feminism from the minority perspective, though the definition is multiple, referring to many aspects of the female minority condition (xi). Walker's conceptualization of womanism as an ideology, philosophy, and approach to life influenced African-American literary criticism. It provided an alternative, more inclusive approach to traditional feminist theory, which had incorporated perspectives of minority women. This text is informed by Hurston's work, and it also provides a new lens with which to view Hurston's work. Alice Walker's own work emerges from a neorealist movement that began in the 1970s and continues today. This movement features authors who create literary works influenced by historical events in the past, such as slavery, which have influenced the present-day lives of African-American writers. Additionally, these writers attempt to present a realistic depiction of African-American life. Writers including Gloria Naylor, Alice Walker, Octavia Butler, and others have engaged in the same conversation that Hurston was so instrumental in starting about the influence of the past upon the present lives of African Americans. The unprecedented acceptance and popularity of African-American literature today highlights the opportunities for contemporary black female writers and the debts owed to those who cleared the way.

Bibliography

"Alice Walker," in *The Norton Anthology of African American Literature,* edited by Henry Louis Gates, et al., 2375–2377. New York: W.W. Norton, 1997.

Boyd, Valerie. *Wrapped in Rainbows: The Life of Zora Neale Hurston.* New York: Scribner, 2003.

Smith, Rochelle, and Sharon L. Jones, eds. *The Prentice Hall Anthology of African American Literature.* Upper Saddle River, N.J.: Prentice Hall, 2000.

Trotter, Joe William. *The African American Experience.* Boston: Houghton Mifflin, 2001.

Walker, Alice. *In Search of Our Mothers' Gardens: Womanist Prose.* San Diego: Harcourt Brace Jovanovich, 1983.

West, Dorothy (1907–1998) Dorothy West was a writer and editor also greatly influenced by Hurston, and she contributed to African-American culture and literature during a long and distinguished career. As a colleague and fellow writer of the HARLEM RENAISSANCE, Dorothy West was connected to Zora Neale Hurston in many ways. Their careers shared much in common, both authors exploring similar topics in relation to gender, race, and class.

A native of Boston, she migrated to New York in pursuit of a career as a writer. Her background in Massachusetts heavily influenced her writing and experience. She was born to an affluent family, though both her parents, Christopher West and Rachel Pease Benson, were originally southerners (Jones 119). Christopher was an ex-slave from Virginia who moved to Massachusetts and made money from an ice cream parlor and fruit imports; his wife was from South Carolina, and the two wed in Boston. (Like Hurston, West was inspired by her parents' life and wrote a story using her father as the source of a character, Bart Judson in *The Living Is Easy*.) Dorothy West obtained an outstanding education, beginning school very young, and attending the prestigious Martin School and Boston Girl's Latin School; at Boston Latin, she was the only black girl. From there she went on to Columbia. She had begun writing young, having won an award from the *Boston Post*.

At age 17, West submitted work to the OPPORTUNITY magazine contest, as did Hurston. West won a prize for her short story "The Typewriter," and the prize won her national exposure as well, as it did for Hurston. This tale was also reprinted in *The Best Short Stories of 1926*. West helped to found the publication *Challenge*, which received submissions from many, including Zora Neale Hurston, Arna Bontemps, Helene Johnson, Langston Hughes, and Claude McKay. Hurston's "The Fire and the Cloud" appeared in this publication. *Challenge* lasted from 1934 to 1937. West also edited *New Challenge*, worked for the Federal Writers Project, and contributed to the *New York Daily News* from 1940 to 1960. She moved to Martha's Vineyard in 1945, where she wrote for the *Vineyard Gazette*. One of her most famous works is *The Wedding*, which was made into a television movie.

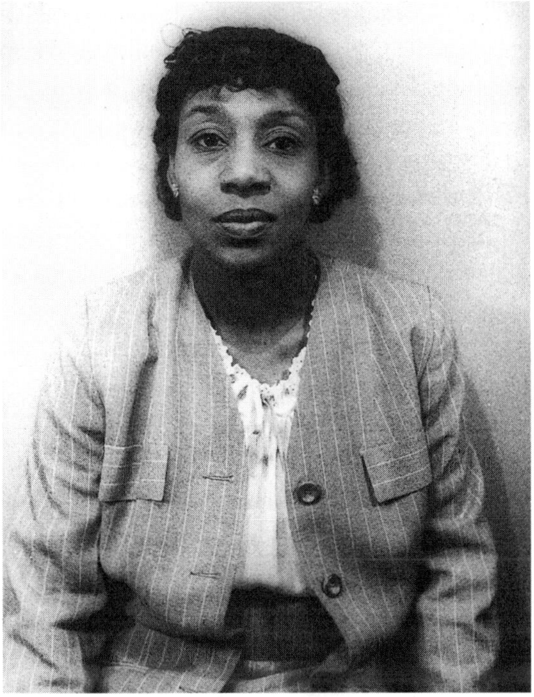

Novelist, editor, and essayist Dorothy West, 1948. Photograph by Carl Van Vechten. Permission granted by Van Vechten Trust *(Yale Collection of American Literature, Beinecke Rare Book and Manuscript Library)*

Bibliography

Boyd, Valerie. *Wrapped in Rainbows: The Life of Zora Neale Hurston*. New York: Scribner, 2003.

Jones, Sharon L. *Rereading the Harlem Renaissance: Race, Class, and Gender in the Fiction of Jessie Fauset, Zora Neale Hurston, and Dorothy West*. Westport, Conn.: Greenwood Press, 2002.

Wright, Richard (1908–1960) Richard Wright engaged in a sometimes antagonistic literary relationship with Hurston, presenting an ideological counterpoint to Hurston's realistic presentations and folk projects.

Wright came from a poor background in the South, living with other relatives when his mother could not take care of him. In 1927, at the age of nineteen, Wright moved to Chicago, following the tradition of the GREAT MIGRATION. He became disenchanted with life in the North and turned to communist ideology, like many blacks who were drawn to the equality it promised. Ultimately he renounced his communist activities and found his expression in writing. Wright contributed to *New Masses* and *Partisan Review,* publications promoting communism. Wright published many works employing his ideology, such as *Uncle Tom's Children* and *Native Son,* which was among his most influential books. *Black Boy,* an autobiographical text, appeared in 1945. After this text appeared, he relocated to Paris, France, where he lived the life of an American expatriate, interacting with Simone de Beauvoir, Jean-Paul Sartre, and Albert Camus. He subsequently traveled widely in Europe in the 1950s.

Richard Wright. Photograph by Carl Van Vechten. Permission granted by Van Vechten Trust *(Yale Collection of American Literature, Beinecke Rare Book and Manuscript Library)*

Wright was interested in issues of aesthetics and theory, and he contributed to the definition of a "proletarian" aesthetic for African-American literature. Wright's connection to Zora Neale Hurston may be best known through his scathing review of *Their Eyes Were Watching God* in *New Masses* in 1937. In this famous indictment, he argues that it "carries no theme, no message, no thought." The problem was that it did not adhere to his proletarian aesthetic of literature: In his view, it did not call for any change, argue for any cause, or shout for justice. However, the novel arguably does contain these elements, but it does so in a subtler way.

Following on his theories about proletarian literature, Wright became an important voice during the period of African-American literature known as the protest period, which ranged from roughly 1940 to 1960. Authors such as Gwendolyn Brooks, Ralph Ellison, Ann Petry, Lorraine Hansberry, and Wright himself examined social and economic injustice in a very direct and forthright manner. They believed that literature should not function solely to entertain, but also to inform, educate, and inspire—and specifically regarding civil rights and equality. The efforts of such writers coincided with major events in the civil rights movement. While writers of the HARLEM RENAISSANCE paved the way,

Wright and others in the 1940s pushed a social and political agenda that would help to awaken the consciousness of their readers.

Bibliography

Boyd, Valerie. *Wrapped in Rainbows: The Life of Zora Neale Hurston.* New York: Scribner, 2003.

"Richard Wright." In *The Norton Anthology of African American Literature,* edited by Henry Louis Gates, et al., 1376–1380. New York: W.W. Norton, 1997.

Smith, Rochelle, and Sharon L. Jones, eds. *The Prentice Hall Anthology of African American Literature.* Upper Saddle River, N.J.: Prentice Hall, 2000.

Trotter, Joe William. *The African American Experience.* Boston: Houghton Mifflin, 2001.

Wright, Richard. Review of *Their Eyes Were Watching God.* In *Zora Neale Hurston: Critical Perspectives Past and Present,* edited by Henry Louis Gates, Jr., and K. A. Appiah, 16–17. New York: Amistad, 1993.

PART IV

Appendixes

Bibliography of Zora Neale Hurston's Works

Novels

Jonah's Gourd Vine. Philadelphia: J.B. Lippincott, 1934.

Moses, Man of the Mountain. Philadelphia: J.B. Lippincott, 1939.

Novels and Stories. New York: Library of America, 1995.

Seraph on the Suwanee. New York: Charles Scribner's Sons, 1948.

Their Eyes Were Watching God. Philadelphia: J.B. Lippincott, 1937.

Memoir/Autobiography

Dust Tracks on a Road. Philadelphia: J.B. Lippincott, 1942.

Anthologies

The Complete Stories. New York: HarperCollins, 1995.

I Love Myself When I Am Laughing . . . and Then Again When I Am Looking Mean and Impressive: A Zora Neale Hurston Reader. Edited by Alice Walker. Old Westbury, N.Y.: Feminist Press, 1979.

Spunk: The Selected Stories of Zora Neale Hurston. Berkeley, Calif.: Turtle Island Foundation, 1985.

Nonfiction Books

Every Tongue Got to Confess: Negro Folk-tales from the Gulf States. New York: HarperCollins, 2001.

Folklore, Memoirs, and Other Writings. New York: Library of America, 1995.

Go Gator and Muddy the Water: Writings by Zora Neale Hurston from the Federal Writers' Project. New York: W.W. Norton, 1999.

Mules and Men. Philadelphia: J.B. Lippincott, 1935.

The Sanctified Church. Berkeley, Calif.: Turtle Island Foundation, 1981.

Tell My Horse. Philadelphia: J.B. Lippincott, 1938.

Plays

Color Struck: A Play in Four Scenes. In *Fire!!* 1, no. 1 (November 1926): 7–14.

The First One: A Play, in *Ebony and Topaz.* Edited by Charles S. Johnson, 53–57. New York: National Urban League, 1927.

Mule Bone: A Comedy of Negro Life (play coauthored with Langston Hughes), 41–153. New York: HarperPerennial, 1991.

Spears: A Play. In *X Ray: Journal of the Zeta Phi Beta Sorority* (December 1926).

Poetry

"O Night." *The Stylus* 1 (May 1921): 42.

"Poem." *Howard University Record* 16 (February 1922): 236.

"Night," "Journey's End," "Passion." *Negro World,* 1922.

Short Stories

"Black Death." In *The Complete Stories,* 202–208. New York: HarperCollins, 1995.

"The Bone of Contention." In *Mule Bone: A Comedy of Negro Life.* Edited by George Houston Bass and Henry Louis Gates, 25–39. New York: HarperPerennial, 1991.

"Book of Harlem." In *The Complete Stories,* 221–227. New York: HarperCollins, 1995.

"Cock Robin Beale Street." *Southern Literary Messenger* 3 (July 1941): 321–323.

"Conscience of the Court." *Saturday Evening Post* (March 18, 1950): 22–23, 112–122.

"Drenched in Light." *Opportunity* 2 (December 1924): 371–374.

"The Eatonville Anthology." *The Messenger* 8 (September, October, November 1926): 261–262, 297, 319, 332.

"The Fire and the Cloud." *Challenge* 1 (September 1934): 10–14.

"The Gilded Six-Bits." *Story* 3 (August 1933): 60–70.

"Harlem Slanguage." In *The Complete Stories,* 227–232. New York: HarperCollins, 1995.

"John Redding Goes to Sea." *The Stylus* 1 (May 1921): 11–22.

"Magnolia Flower." *Spokesman* (July 1925): 26–29.

"Muttsy." *Opportunity* 4 (August 1926): 246–250.

"Now You Cookin' with Gas" In *The Complete Stories,* 233–241. New York: HarperCollins, 1995.

"Possum or Pig." *Forum* 76 (September 1926): 465.

"The Seventh Veil." In *The Complete Stories,* 242–260. New York: HarperCollins, 1995.

"Spunk." *Opportunity* 3 (June 1925): 171–173.

"Sweat." *Fire!!* 1 (November 1926): 40–45.

"Story in Harlem Slang." *American Mercury* 55 (July 1942): 84–96.

"Under the Bridge." *X-Ray: Journal of the Zeta Phi Beta Sorority* (December 1925).

"The Woman in Gaul." In *The Complete Stories,* 261–283. New York: HarperCollins, 1995.

Essays

"Art and Such." In *Reading Black, Reading Feminist: A Critical Anthology.* Edited by Henry Louis Gates, 21–26. New York: Meridian, 1990.

"Characteristics of Negro Expression." In *Negro: An Anthology.* Edited by Nancy Cunard, 39–46. London: Wishart, 1934.

"Conversions and Visions." In *Negro: An Anthology.* Edited by Nancy Cunard, 47–49. London: Wishart, 1934.

"Crazy for Democracy." *Negro Digest* 4 (December 1945): 45–48.

"Cudjo's Own Story of the Last African Slaver." *Journal of Negro History* 12 (October 1927): 648–663.

"Dance Songs and Tales from the Bahamas." *Journal of American Folklore* 43 (July–September 1930): 294–312.

"Fannie Hurst." *Saturday Review* (October 9, 1937): 15–16.

"High John de Conquer." *American Mercury* 57 (October 1943): 450–458.

"Hoodoo in America." *Journal of American Folklore* 44 (October–December 1931): 317–418.

"How It Feels to Be Colored Me." *World Tomorrow* 11 (May 1928): 215–216.

"The Hue and Cry about Howard University," *Messenger* 7 (September 1925): 315–319, 338.

"I Saw Negro Votes Peddled." *American Legion Magazine* 49 (November 1950): 12–13, 54–57, 59–60.

"The Last Slave Ship." *American Mercury* 58 (March 1944): 351–358.

"Lawrence of the River." *Saturday Evening Post* (September 5, 1942): 18, 55–57.

"Mother Catherine." In *Negro: An Anthology*. Edited by Nancy Cunard, 54–57. London: Wishart, 1934.

"Mourner's Bench, Communist Line: Why the Negro Won't Buy Communism," *American Legion Magazine* 50 (June 1951): 14–15, 55–60.

"My Most Humiliating Jim Crow Experience." *Negro Digest* 2 (June 1944): 25–26.

"Negroes without Self-Pity." *American Mercury* 57 (November 1943): 601–603.

"A Negro Voter Sizes Up Taft." *Saturday Evening Post* (December 8, 1951): 29, 150.

"Now Take Noses." In *Cordially Yours*, 25–27. Philadelphia: Lippincott, 1939.

"The 'Pet Negro' System." *American Mercury* 56 (March 1943): 593–600.

"The Rise of the Begging Joints." *American Mercury* 60 (March 1945): 288–294.

"The Sermon." In *Negro: An Anthology*. Edited by Nancy Cunard, 50–54. London: Wishart, 1934.

"Shouting." In *Negro: An Anthology*. Edited by Nancy Cunard, 49–50. London: Wishart, 1934.

"Spirituals and Neo-Spirituals." In *Negro: An Anthology*. Edited by Nancy Cunard, 359–361. London: Wishart, 1934.

"The Ten Commandments of Charm." *X-Ray: Journal of the Zeta Phi Beta Sorority* (1925).

"The Trial of Ruby McCollum." In *Ruby McCollum: Woman in the Suwanee Jail*, by William Bradford Huie, 89–101. New York: Dutton, 1956.

"Uncle Monday." In *Negro: An Anthology*. Edited by Nancy Cunard, 57–61. London: Wishart, 1934.

"What White Publishers Won't Print." *Negro Digest* 8 (April 1950): 85–89.

Book Reviews

"At the Sound of the Conch Shell." Review of *New Day* by Victor Stafford Reid. *New York Herald Tribune Weekly Book Review*, March 20, 1949, 4.

"Bible, Played by Ear in Africa." Review of *How God Fix Jonah* by Lorenz Graham. *New York Herald Tribune Weekly Book Review*, November 24, 1946, 5.

"Full of Mud, Sweat and Blood." Review of *God Shakes Creation* by David M. Cohn. *New York Herald Tribune Books*, November 3, 1935, 8.

"Jazz Regarded as Social Achievement." Review of *Shining Trumpets* by Rudi Blesh. *New York Herald Tribune Weekly Book Review*, December 22, 1946, 8.

Review of *Voodoo in New Orleans* by Robert Tallant. *Journal of American Folklore* 60 (October–December 1947): 436–438.

"Rural Schools for Negroes." Review of *The Jeanes Teacher in the United States* by Lance G. E. Jones. *New York Herald Tribune Books*, February 20, 1938, 24.

"Some Fabulous Caribbean Riches Revealed." Review of *The Pencil of God* by Pierre Marcelin and Philippe Thoby Marcelin. *New York Herald Tribune Weekly Book Review*, February 4, 1951, 5.

"Star-Wrassling Sons-of-the-Universe." Review of *The Hurricane's Children* by Carl Carmer. *New York Herald Tribune Books*, December 26, 1937, 4.

"Stories of Conflict." Review of *Uncle Tom's Children* by Richard Wright. *Saturday Review* (April 2, 1938): 32.

"Thirty Days among Maroons." Review of *Journey to Accompong* by Katharine Dunham. *New York Herald Tribune Weekly Book Review,* January 12, 1947, 8.

"The Transplanted Negro." Review of *Trinidad Village* by Melville Herskovits and Frances Herskovits. *New York Herald Tribune Weekly Book Review,* March 9, 1947, 20.

Newspaper Publications

"Bare Plot against Ruby." *Pittsburgh Courier,* November 29, 1952.

"Court Order Can't Make Races Mix." *Orlando Sentinel,* August 11, 1955.

"The Farm Laborer at Home." *Fort Pierce Chronicle,* February 27, 1959.

Hoodoo and Black Magic. Column in *Fort Pierce Chronicle,* July 11, 1958–August, 7 1959.

"The Life Story of Mrs. Ruby J. McCollum!" *Pittsburgh Courier* (February 28, 1953; March 7, 1953; March 14, 1953; March 21, 1953; March 28, 1953; April 4, 1953; April 11, 1953; April 18, 1953; April 25, 1953; May 2, 1953).

"McCollum–Adams Trial Highlights." *Pittsburgh Courier,* December 27, 1952.

"Ruby Bares Her Love." *Pittsburgh Courier,* January 3, 1953.

"Ruby McCollum Fights for Life." *Pittsburgh Courier,* November 22, 1952.

"Doctor's Threats, Tussle over Gun Led to Slaying." *Pittsburgh Courier,* January 10, 1953.

"Ruby's Troubles Mount." *Pittsburgh Courier,* January 17, 1953.

"This Juvenile Delinquency." *Fort Pierce Chronicle,* December 12, 1958.

"The Tripson Story." *Fort Pierce Chronicle,* February 6, 1959.

"Victim of Fate." *Pittsburgh Courier,* October 11, 1952.

"Zora's Revealing Story of Ruby's First Day in Court." *Pittsburgh Courier,* October 11, 1952.

The bibliography was compiled by consulting the following sources in addition to original sources:

Boyd, Valerie. *Wrapped in Rainbows: The Life of Zora Neale Hurston.* New York: Scribner, 2003.

Croft, Robert W. *A Zora Neale Hurston Companion.* Westport, Conn.: Greenwood Press, 2002.

Hall, Blaine L. "Writings by Zora Neale Hurston." In *Critical Essays on Zora Neale Hurston.* Edited by Gloria L. Cronin, 257–262. New York: G.K. Hall, 1998.

Hemenway, Robert. *Zora Neale Hurston: A Literary Biography.* Urbana: University of Illinois Press, 1980.

Hurston, Zora Neale. *Folklore, Memoirs, and Other Writings.* New York: Library of America, 1995.

Kaplan, Carla, ed. *Zora Neale Hurston: A Life in Letters.* New York: Doubleday, 2002.

Wall, Cheryl A. *Women of the Harlem Renaissance,* 235–237. Bloomington: Indiana University Press, 1995.

Selected Bibliography of Secondary Sources

The following texts were consulted by the author in the creation of this extensive selected bibliography: *Zora Neale Hurston: An Annotated Bibliography and Reference Guide* (1997), compiled by Rose Parkman Davis; Robert W. Croft's *A Zora Neale Hurston Companion* (2002); *Zora Neale Hurston: Critical Perspectives Past and Present,* edited by Henry Louis Gates Jr. and K. A. Appiah (1993); the MLA International Bibliography; the Wright State University Library catalogue; and original sources.

Notable Books about Zora Neale Hurston (biography)

Boyd, Valerie. *Wrapped in Rainbows: The Life of Zora Neale Hurston.* New York: Scribner, 2003.

Hemenway, Robert E. *Zora Neale Hurston: A Literary Biography.* Urbana: University of Illinois Press, 1980.

Hurston, Lucy Anne. *Speak, So You Can Speak Again: The Life of Zora Neale Hurston.* New York: Doubleday, 2004.

Kaplan, Carla, ed. *Zora Neale Hurston: A Life in Letters.* New York: Doubleday, 2002.

Nathiri, N. Y., ed. *Zora! Zora Neale Hurston: A Woman and Her Community.* Orlando, Fla.: Orlando Sentinel/Sentinel Communications, 1991.

Notable Books about Zora Neale Hurston (General Criticism)

Campbell, Joseph P. *Student Companion to Zora Neale Hurston.* Westport, Conn: Greenwood Press, 2001.

Croft, Robert W. *A Zora Neale Hurston Companion.* Westport, Conn.: Greenwood Press, 2002.

Davis, Rose Parkman, comp. *Zora Neale Hurston: An Annotated Bibliography and Reference Guide.* Westport, Conn.: Greenwood Press, 1997.

Gates, Henry Louis, Jr., and K. A. Appiah, eds. *Zora Neale Hurston: Critical Perspectives Past and Present.* New York: Amistad, 1993.

Holloway, Karla F. C. *The Character of the Word: The Texts of Zora Neale Hurston.* New York: Greenwood Press, 1987.

Howard, Lillie P. *Zora Neale Hurston.* Boston: Twayne, 1980.

Jones, Sharon L. *Rereading the Harlem Renaissance: Race, Class, and Gender in the Fiction of Jessie Fauset, Zora Neale Hurston, and Dorothy West.* Westport, Conn.: Greenwood Press, 2002.

Meisenhelder, Susan Edwards. *Hitting a Straight Lick with a Crooked Stick: Race and Gender in the Work of Zora Neale Hurston.* Tuscaloosa: University of Alabama Press, 1999.

Patterson, Tiffany Ruby. *Zora Neale Hurston and a History of Southern Life.* Philadelphia: Temple University Press, 2005.

Plant, Deborah G. *Every Tub Must Sit on Its Own Bottom: The Philosophy and Politics of Zora Neale Hurston.* Urbana: University of Illinois Press, 1995.

Walker, Alice. *In Search of Our Mothers' Gardens: Womanist Prose.* San Diego: Harvest/HBJ, 1983.

Notable Books about the Harlem Renaissance

Brown, Lois. *Encyclopedia of the Harlem Literary Renaissance.* New York: Facts On File: 2005.

Hutchinson, George. *The Harlem Renaissance in Black and White.* Cambridge, Mass.: Belknap Press, 1995.

Jones, Sharon L. *Rereading the Harlem Renaissance: Race, Class, and Gender in the Fiction of Jessie Fauset, Zora Neale Hurston, and Dorothy West.* Westport, Conn.: Greenwood Press, 2002.

Lewis, David Levering. *When Harlem Was in Vogue.* New York: Oxford University Press, 1981.

Smith, Rochelle, and Sharon L. Jones, eds. *The Prentice Hall Anthology of African American Literature.* Upper Saddle River, N.J.: Prentice Hall, 2000.

Trotter, Joe William. *The African American Experience.* Boston: Houghton Mifflin, 2001.

Notable Books and Book Chapters about Hurston's Works

"The Gilded Six-Bits"

Baum, Rosalie Murphy. "The Shape of Hurston's Fiction." In *Zora in Florida,* edited by Steve Glassman and Kathryn Lee Seidel, 94–109. Orlando: University of Central Florida Press, 1991.

Jones, Sharon L. *Rereading the Harlem Renaissance: Race, Class, and Gender in the Fiction of Jessie Fauset, Zora Neale Hurston, and Dorothy West.* Westport, Conn.: Greenwood Press, 2002.

"The Bone of Contention"

Jones, Sharon L. *Rereading the Harlem Renaissance: Race, Class, and Gender in the Fiction of Jessie Fauset, Zora Neale Hurston, and Dorothy West.* Westport, Conn.: Greenwood Press, 2002.

Jonah's Gourd Vine

Cronin, Gloria L., ed. *Critical Essays on Zora Neale Hurston.* New York: G.K. Hall, 1998.

Gates, Henry Louis, Jr., and K. A. Appiah, eds. *Zora Neale Hurston: Critical Perspectives Past and Present.* New York: Amistad, 1993.

Glassman, Steve, and Kathryn Lee Seidel, eds. *Zora in Florida.* Orlando: University of Central Florida Press, 1991.

Holloway, Karla. "The Emergent Voice: The Word within Its Texts." In *Zora Neale Hurston: Critical Perspectives Past and Present.* Edited by Henry Louis Gates, Jr., and K. A. Appiah, 67–75. New York: Amistad, 1993.

Howard, Lillie P, ed. *Alice Walker and Zora Neale Hurston: The Common Bond.* Westport, Conn.: Greenwood Press, 1993.

Wall, Cheryl A. "Zora Neale Hurston: Changing Her Own Words." In *Zora Neale Hurston: Critical Perspectives Past and Present.* Edited by Henry Louis Gates, Jr., and K. A. Appiah, 76–97. New York: Amistad, 1993.

Washington, Mary Helen. "'I Love the Way Janie Crawford Left Her Husbands': Emergent Female Hero." In *Zora Neale Hurston: Critical Perspectives Past and Present.* Edited by Henry Louis Gates, Jr., and K. A. Appiah, 98–109. New York: Amistad, 1993.

Dust Tracks on a Road

Birch, Eva Lennox. "Autobiography: The Art of Self-Definition." In *Black Women's Writing.* Edited by Gina Wisker, 127–145. New York: St. Martin's, 1993.

Boi, Paola. "Zora Neale Hurston's *Autobiographie Fictive*: Dark Tracks on the Canon of a Female Writer." In *The Black Columbiad: Defining Moments in African American Literature and Culture.* Edited by Werner Sollors and Maria Diedrich, 191–200. Cambridge, Mass.: Harvard University Press, 1994.

Cronin, Gloria L., ed. *Critical Essays on Zora Neale Hurston.* New York: G.K. Hall, 1998.

Feracho, Lesley. *Linking the Americas: Race, Hybrid Discourses, and the Reformulation of Feminine Identity.* Albany: State University of New York Press, 2005.

Glassman, Steve, and Kathryn Lee Seidel, eds. *Zora in Florida.* Orlando: University of Central Florida Press, 1991.

Kawash, Samira. *Dislocating the Color Line: Identity, Hybridity, and Singularity in African–American Narrative.* Stanford, Calif.: Stanford University Press, 1997.

Lowe, John. "Humor and Identity in Ethnic Autobiography: Zora Neale Hurston and Jerre Mangione." In *Cultural Difference and the Literary Text: Pluralism and the Limits of Authenticity in North American Literatures,* edited by Winfried Siemerling and Katrin Schwenk, 75–99. Iowa City: University of Iowa Press, 1996.

Raynaud, Claudine. "'Rubbing a Paragraph with a Soft Cloth'? Muted Voices and Editorial Constraints in *Dust Tracks on a Road.*" In *De/Colonizing the Subject: The Politics of Gender in Women's Autobiography.* Edited by Sidonie Smith and Julia Watson, 34–64. Minneapolis: University of Minnesota Press, 1992.

Rodriguez, Barbara. "On the Gatepost: Literal and Metaphorical Journeys in Zora Neale Hurston's *Dust Tracks on a Road.*" In *Women, America, and Movement: Narratives of Relocation,* 235–257. Columbia: University of Missouri Press, 1998.

Wall, Cheryl A. *Women of the Harlem Renaissance.* Bloomington: Indiana University Press, 1995.

Moses, Man of the Mountain

Gates, Henry Louis, Jr., and K. A. Appiah, eds. *Zora Neale Hurston: Critical Perspectives Past and Present.* New York: Amistad, 1993.

Grant, Nathan. *Masculinist Impulses: Toomer, Hurston, Black Writing and Modernity.* Columbia: University of Missouri Press, 2004.

Jones, Sharon L. *Rereading the Harlem Renaissance: Race, Class, and Gender in the Fiction of Jessie Fauset, Zora Neale Hurston, and Dorothy West.* Westport, Conn.: Greenwood Press, 2002.

Konzett, Delia Caparoso. *Ethnic Modernisms: Anzia Yezierska, Zora Neale Hurston, Jean Rhys, and the Aesthetics of Dislocation.* New York: Palgrave Macmillan, 2002.

Lowe, John. *Jump at the Sun: Zora Neale Hurston's Cosmic Comedy.* Urbana: University of Illinois Press, 1994.

McDowell, Deborah E. "Lines of Descent/Dissenting Lines." In *Zora Neale Hurston: Critical Perspectives Past and Present.* Edited by Henry Louis Gates, Jr., and K. A. Appiah, 230–240. New York: Amistad, 1993.

Mule Bone

Carson, Warren J. "Hurston as Dramatist: The Florida Connection," In *Zora in Florida.* Edited by Steve Glassman and Kathryn Lee Seidel, 121–129. Orlando: University of Central Florida Press, 1991.

Hill, Lynda Marion. *Social Rituals and the Verbal Art of Zora Neale Hurston.* Washington, D.C.: Howard University Press, 1996.

Mules and Men

Andrews, Adrianne R. "Of Mules and Men and Men and Women: The Ritual of Talking B(l)ack." In *Language, Rhythm, and Sound: Black Popular Cultures into the Twenty-First Century.* Edited by Joseph Adjaye and Adrienne R. Andrews, 109–120. Pittsburgh, Pa.: University of Pittsburg Press, 1997.

Baker, Houston A., Jr. "Workings of the Spirit: Conjure and the Space of Black Women's Creativity." In *Zora Neale Hurston: Critical Perspectives Past and Present.* Edited by Henry Louis Gates, Jr., and K. A. Appiah, 280–308. New York: Amistad, 1993.

Cronin, Gloria L., ed. *Critical Essays on Zora Neale Hurston.* New York: G.K. Hall, 1998.

Duck, Leigh Anne. *The Nation's Region: Southern Modernism, Segregation, and U.S. Nationalism.* Athens: University of Georgia Press, 2006.

Gates, Henry Louis, Jr., and K. A. Appiah, eds. *Zora Neale Hurston: Critical Perspectives Past and Present.* New York: Amistad, 1993.

Glassman, Steve, and Kathryn Lee Seidel, eds. *Zora in Florida.* Orlando: University of Central Florida Press, 1991.

Harris, Trudier. *The Power of the Porch: The Storyteller's Craft in Zora Neale Hurston, Gloria Naylor, and Randall Kenan.* Athens: University of Georgia Press, 1996.

Pavoloska, Susanna. *Modern Primitives: Race and Language in Gertrude Stein, Ernest Hemingway, and Zora Neale Hurston.* New York: Garland Publishing, 2000.

Wall, Cheryl A. *Women of the Harlem Renaissance.* Bloomington: Indiana University Press, 1995.

Seraph on the Suwanee

Cronin, Gloria L., ed. *Critical Essays on Zora Neale Hurston.* New York: G.K. Hall, 1998.

Gates, Henry Louis, Jr., and K. A. Appiah, eds. *Zora Neale Hurston: Critical Perspectives Past and Present.* New York: Amistad, 1993.

Grant, Nathan. *Masculinist Impulses: Toomer, Hurston, Black Writing, and Modernity.* Columbia: University of Missouri Press, 2004.

Jones, Sharon L. *Rereading the Harlem Renaissance: Race, Class, and Gender in the Fiction of Jessie Fauset, Zora Neale Hurston, and Dorothy West.* Westport, Conn.: Greenwood Press, 2002.

Lowe, John. *Jump at the Sun: Zora Neale Hurston's Cosmic Comedy.* Urbana: University of Illinois Press, 1994.

Howard, Lillie. "Seraph on the Suwanee." In *Zora Neale Hurston: Critical Perspectives Past and Present.* Edited by Henry Louis Gates, Jr., and K. A. Appiah, 267–279. New York: Amistad, 1993.

Marsh-Lockett, Carol P. "What Ever Happened to Jochebed? Motherhood as Marginality in Zora Neale Hurston's *Seraph on the Suwanee.*" In *Southern Mothers: Fact and Fictions in Southern Women's Writing.* Edited by Nagueyalti Warren and Sally Wolff, 100–110. Baton Rouge: Louisiana State University Press, 1999.

Tate, Claudia. "Hitting 'A Straight Lick with a Crooked Stick': *Seraph on the Suwanee,* Zora

Neale Hurston's Whiteface Novel," in *The Psychoanalysis of Race*. Edited by Christopher Lane, 380–394. New York: Columbia University Press, 1998.

"Spunk"

Jones, Sharon L. *Rereading the Harlem Renaissance: Race, Class, and Gender in the Fiction of Jessie Fauset, Zora Neale Hurston, and Dorothy West.* Westport, Conn.: Greenwood Press, 2002.

"Sweat"

Glassman, Steve, and Kathryn Lee Seidel, eds. *Zora in Florida.* Orlando: University of Central Florida Press, 1991.

Jones, Sharon L. *Rereading the Harlem Renaissance: Race, Class, and Gender in the Fiction of Jessie Fauset, Zora Neale Hurston, and Dorothy West.* Westport, Conn.: Greenwood Press, 2002.

Wall, Cheryl A. *Women of the Harlem Renaissance.* Bloomington: Indiana University Press, 1995.

Their Eyes Were Watching God

Awkward, Michael, ed. *New Essays on Their Eyes Were Watching God.* New York: Cambridge University Press, 1990.

Baker, Houston A., Jr. "Ideology and Narrative Form." In *Zora Neale Hurston's Their Eyes Were Watching God.* Edited by Harold Bloom, 35–39. New York: Chelsea House, 1987.

Bethel, Lorraine. "'This Infinity of Conscious Pain': Zora Neale Hurston and the Black Female Literary Tradition." In *Zora Neale Hurston's Their Eyes Were Watching God.* Edited by Harold Bloom, 9–17. New York: Chelsea House, 1987.

Bloom, Harold, ed. *Zora Neale Hurston's Their Eyes Were Watching God.* New York: Chelsea House, 1987.

Bond, Cynthia. "Language, Speech, and Difference in *Their Eyes Were Watching God.*" In *Zora Neale Hurston: Critical Perspectives Past and Present.* Edited by Henry Louis Gates, Jr., and K. A. Appiah, 204–217. New York: Amistad, 1993.

Cronin, Gloria L., ed. *Critical Essays on Zora Neale Hurston.* New York: G.K. Hall, 1998.

Duck, Leigh Anne. *The Nation's Region: Southern Modernism, Segregation, and U.S. Nationalism.* Athens: University of Georgia Press, 2006.

Gates, Henry Louis, Jr. "Zora Neale Hurston and the Speakerly Text." In *Zora Neale Hurston's Their Eyes Were Watching God: A Casebook.* Edited by Cheryl A. Wall, 59–116. New York: Oxford University Press, 2000.

Gates, Henry Louis, Jr., and K. A. Appiah, eds. *Zora Neale Hurston: Critical Perspectives Past and Present.* New York: Amistad, 1993.

Grant, Nathan. *Masculinist Impulses: Toomer, Hurston, Black Writing, and Modernity.* Columbia: University of Missouri Press, 2004.

Howard, Lillie P, ed. *Alice Walker and Zora Neale Hurston: The Common Bond.* Westport, Conn.: Greenwood Press, 1993.

Johnson, Barbara. "Metaphor, Metonymy, and Voice in *Their Eyes Were Watching God.*" In *Zora Neale Hurston's Their Eyes Were Watching God: A Casebook.* Edited by Cheryl A. Wall, 41–58. Oxford: Oxford University Press, 2000.

Johnson, Barbara, and Henry Louis Gates, Jr. "A Black and Idiomatic Free Indirect Discourse." In *Zora Neale Hurston's Their Eyes Were Watching God.* Edited by Harold

Bloom, 73–85. New York: Chelsea House, 1987.

Jones, Sharon L. *Rereading the Harlem Renaissance: Race, Class, and Gender in the Fiction of Jessie Fauset, Zora Neale Hurston, and Dorothy West.* Westport, Conn.: Greenwood Press, 2002.

Kawash, Samira. *Dislocating the Color Line: Identity, Hybridity, and Singularity in African-American Narrative.* Stanford, Calif.: Stanford University Press, 1997.

Kubitschek, Missy Dehn. "'Tuh de Horizon and Back': The Female Quest in *Their Eyes Were Watching God.*" In *Zora Neale Hurston's Their Eyes Were Watching God.* Edited by Harold Bloom, 19–33. New York: Chelsea House, 1987.

Lamothe, Daphne. "Voudou Imagery, African American Tradition, and Cultural Transformation in Zora Neale Hurston's *Their Eyes Were Watching God.*" In *Zora Neale Hurston's Their Eyes Were Watching God: A Casebook.* Edited by Cheryl A. Wall, 165–187. Oxford: Oxford University Press, 2000.

Lowe, John. *Jump at the Sun: Zora Neale Hurston's Cosmic Comedy.* Urbana: University of Illinois Press, 1994.

McGlamery, Tom. *Protest and the Body in Melville, Dos Passos, and Hurston.* New York: Routledge, 2004.

Meese, Elizabeth. "Orality and Textuality in *Their Eyes Were Watching God.*" In *Zora Neale Hurston's Their Eyes Were Watching God.* Edited by Harold Bloom, 59–71. New York: Chelsea House, 1987.

Stein, Rachel. *Shifting the Ground: American Women Writers' Revisions of Nature, Gender, and Race.* Charlottesville: University Press of Virginia, 1997.

Wall, Cheryl A. *Women of the Harlem Renaissance.* Bloomington: Indiana University Press, 1995.

Washington, Mary Helen. "'I Love the Way Janie Crawford Left her Husbands': Zora Neale Hurston's Emergent Female Hero." In *Zora Neale Hurston's Their Eyes Were Watching God: A Casebook.* Edited by Cheryl A. Wall, 27–40. Oxford: Oxford University Press, 2000.

Willis, Susan. "Wandering: Hurston's Search for Self and Method." In *Zora Neale Hurston: Critical Perspectives Past and Present.* Edited by Henry Louis Gates, Jr., and K. A. Appiah, 110–129. New York: Amistad, 1993.

Wolff, Maria Tai. "Listening and Living: Reading and Experience in *Their Eyes Were Watching God.*" In *Zora Neale Hurston: Critical Perspectives Past and Present.* Edited by Henry Louis Gates, Jr., and K. A. Appiah, 218–229. New York: Amistad, 1993.

Notable Articles on Hurston's Works

"The Bone of Contention"

Rosenberg, Rachel A. "Looking for Zora's *Mule Bone*: The Battle for Artistic Authority in the Hurston-Hughes Collaboration." *Modernism/Modernity* 6, no. 2 (1999): 79–105.

Dust Tracks on a Road

Trefzer, Annette. "Floating Homes and Signifiers in Hurston's and Rawlings's Autobiographies." *Southern Quarterly* 36, no. 3 (1998): 68–76.

———. "'Let Us All Be Kissing Friends?'": Zora Neale Hurston and Race Politics in Dixie." *Journal of American Studies* 31, no. 1 (1997): 69–78.

Walker, Pierre A. "Zora Neale Hurston and the Post-Modern Self in *Dust Tracks on a Road.*"

African American Review 32, no. 3 (1998): 387–399.

"The Eatonville Anthology"

Crosland, Andrew. "The Text of Zora Neale Hurston: A Caution." *CLA Journal* 37, no. 4 (1994): 420–424.

"The Gilded Six-Bits"

Eisen, Kurt. "Blues Speaking Women: Performing Cultural Change in *Spunk* and *Ma Rainey's Black Bottom*." *Text & Presentation* 14 (1993): 21–26.

Hoeller, Hildegard. "Racial Currency: Zora Neale Hurston's 'The Gilded Six-Bits' and the Gold-Standard Debate." *American Literature* 77, no. 4 (2005): 761–785.

Jones, Evora W. "The Pastoral and Picaresque in Zora Neale Hurston's 'The Gilded Six-Bits'." *CLA Journal* 35, no. 3 (1992): 316–324.

Jonah's Gourd Vine

Beilke, Debra. "'Yowin' and Jawin': Humor and the Performance of Identity in Zora Neale Hurston's *Jonah's Gourd Vine*." *Southern Quarterly* 36, no. 3 (1998): 21–33.

Cartwright, Keith. "'To Walk with the Storm': Oya as the Transformative 'I' of Zora Neale Hurston's Afro-Atlantic Callings." *American Literature* 78, no. 4 (2005): 741–767.

Ciuba, Gary. "The Worm against the Word: The Hermeneutical Challenge in Hurston's *Jonah's Gourd Vine*." *African American Review* 34, no. 1 (2000): 119–133.

Jones, Kirkland C. "Folk Humor as Comic Relief in Hurston's *Jonah's Gourd Vine*." *Zora Neale Hurston Forum* 1, no. 1 (1986): 26–31.

Philip, Joseph. "The Verdict from the Porch: Zora Neale Hurston and Reparative Justice." *American Literature* 74, no. 3 (2002): 455–483.

Plant, Deborah G. "Cultural Collision, Africanity, and the Black Baptist Preacher in *Jonah's Gourd Vine* and *In My Father's House*." *Griot* 14, no. 1 (1995): 10–17.

Spencer, Stephen. "The Value of Lived Experience: Zora Neale Hurston and the Complexity of Race." *Studies in American Culture* 27, no. 2 (2004): 17–33.

West, Genevieve. "Feminist Subversion in Zora Neale Hurston's *Jonah's Gourd Vine*." *Women's Studies* 31, no. 4 (2002): 499–515.

Moses, Man of the Mountain

Caron, Timothy P. "'Tell Ole Pharaoh to Let My People Go': Communal Deliverance in Zora Neale Hurston's *Moses, Man of the Mountain*." *Southern Quarterly* 36, no. 3 (1998): 47–60.

Morris, Robert J. "Zora Neale Hurston's Ambitious Enigma: *Moses, Man of the Mountain*." *CLA Journal* 40, no. 3 (1997): 305–335.

Sheffey, Ruthe T. "Zora Neale Hurston's *Moses, Man of the Mountain*: A Fictionalized Manifesto on the Imperatives of Black Leadership." *CLA Journal* 29, no. 2 (1985): 206–220.

Thompson, Mark Christian. "National Socialism and Blood-Sacrifice in Zora Neale Hurston's *Moses, Man of the Mountain*." *African American Review* 38, no. 3 (2004): 395–415.

Wallerstein, Nicholas. "Feminist/Womanist Liberation Hermeneutics and the Kyriologic of Zora Neale Hurston." *Literary Griot* 11, no. 2 (1999): 97–115.

Mule Bone

Boyd, Lisa. "The Folk, the Blues, and the Problems of Mule Bone," *Langston Hughes Review* 13, no. 1 (Fall–Spring 1995): 33–44.

Kraut, Anthea. "Reclaiming the Body: Representations of Black Dance in Three Plays by Zora Neale Hurston." *Theatre Studies* 43 (1998): 23–36.

Lowe, John. "From Mule Bones to Funny Bones: The Plays of Zora Neale Hurston," *Southern Quarterly* 33, nos. 2–3 (1995): 65–78.

Rosenberg, Rachel A. "Looking for Zora's *Mule Bone*: The Battle for Artistic Authority in the Hurston-Hughes Collaboration," *Modernism/Modernity* 6, no. 2 (1999): 79–105.

Mules and Men

Cartwright, Keith. "'To Walk with the Storm': Oya as the Transformative 'I' of Zora Neale Hurston's Afro-Atlantic Callings." *American Literature* 78, no. 4 (2006): 741–767.

Domina, Lynn. "'Protection in My Mouf': Self, Voice, and Community in Zora Neale Hurston's *Dust Tracks on a Road* and *Mules and Men*." *African American Review* 31, no. 2 (1997): 197–209.

Hoffman-Jeep, Lynda. "Creating Ethnography: Zora Neale Hurston and Lydia Cabrera." *African American Review* 39, no. 3 (2005): 337–353.

Jirousek, Lori. "'That Commonality of Feeling': Hurston, Hybridity and Ethnography." *African American Review* 38, no. 3 (2004): 417–427.

Landun, John. "Reading Hurston Writing." *African American Review* 38, no. 1 (2004): 45–60.

Nicholls, David G. "Migrant Labor, Folklore, and Resistance in Hurston's Polk County: Reframing *Mules and Men*." *African American Review* 33, no. 3 (1999): 467–479.

Sorensen, Leif. "Modernity on a Global Stage: Hurston's Alternative Modernism." *MELUS* 30, no. 4 (2005): 3–24.

Spencer, Stephen. "The Value of Lived Experience: Zora Neale Hurston and the Complexity of Race." *Studies in American Culture* 27, no. 2 (2004): 17–33.

Walters, Keith. "'He Can Read My Writing but He Sho' Can't Read My Mind': Zora Neale Hurston's Revenge in *Mules and Men*." *Journal of American Folklore* 112, no. 445 (1999): 343–371.

Seraph on the Suwanee

Coleman, Ancilla. "Mythological Structure and Psychological Significance in Hurston's *Seraph on the Suwanee*." *Publications of the Mississippi Philological Association* 1988: 21–27.

Dubek, Laura. "The Social Geography of Race in Hurston's *Seraph on the Suwanee*." *African American Review* 30, no. 3 (1996): 341–351.

Jackson, Chuck. "Waste and Whiteness: Zora Neale Hurston and the Politics of Eugenics." *African American Review* 34, no. 4 (2000): 639–660.

Ward, Cynthia. "From the Suwanee to Egypt, There's No Place Like Home." *PMLA* 115, no. 1 (2000): 75–88.

"Story in Harlem Slang"

Eisen, Kurt. "Blues Speaking Women: Performing Cultural Change in *Spunk* and *Ma Rainey's Black Bottom*." *Text & Presentation* 14 (1993): 21–26.

Lester, Neal A. "Sounds of Silent Performances: Homoeroticism in Zora Neale Hurston's 'Story in Harlem Slang: Jelly's Tale.'" *Southern Quarterly* 36, no. 3 (1998): 10–20.

"Spunk"

Eisen, Kurt. "Blues Speaking Women: Performing Cultural Change in *Spunk* and *Ma*

Rainey's Black Bottom." *Text & Presentation* 14 (1993): 21–26.

"Sweat"

Eisen, Kurt. "Blues Speaking Women: Performing Cultural Change in *Spunk* and *Ma Rainey's Black Bottom.*" *Text & Presentation* 14 (1993): 21–26.

Green, Suzanne D. "Fear, Freedom and the Perils of Ethnicity: Otherness in Kate Chopin's 'Beyond the Bayou' and Zora Neale Hurston's 'Sweat'." *Southern Studies* 5, nos. 3–4 (1994): 105–124.

Hurd, Myles Raymond. "What Goes Around Comes Around: Characterization, Climax, and Closure in Hurston's 'Sweat'." *Langston Hughes Review* 12, no. 2 (1993): 7–15.

Lupton, Mary Jane. "Zora Neale Hurston and the Survival of the Female." *Southern Literary Journal* 15, no. 1 (1982): 45–54.

Meisenhelder, Suzanne. "'Eating Cane' in Gloria Naylor's *The Women of Brewster Place* and Zora Neale Hurston's 'Sweat'." *Notes on Contemporary Literature* 23, no. 2 (1993): 5–7.

Seidel, Kathryn Lee. "The Artist in the Kitchen: The Economics of Creativity in Hurston's 'Sweat'." In *Zora in Florida*. Edited by Steve Glassman and Kathryn Lee Seidel, 110–120. Orlando: University of Central Florida Press, 1991.

Their Eyes Were Watching God

Ashe, Bertram. "'Why Don't He Like My Hair?'": Constructing African-American Standards of Beauty in Toni Morrison's *Song of Solomon* and Zora Neale Hurston's *Their Eyes Were Watching God.*" *African American Review* 29, no. 4 (1995): 579–592.

Basu, Biman. "'Oral Tutelage' and the Figure of Literacy: Paule Marshall's *Brown Girl, Brownstones* and Zora Neale Hurston's *Their Eyes Were Watching God. MELUS* 24, no. 1 (Spring 1999): 161–176.

Cartwright, Keith. "'To Walk with the Storm': Oya as the Transformative 'I' of Zora Neale Hurston's Afro-Atlantic Callings." *American Literature* 78, no. 4 (2006): 741–767.

Chinn, Nancy. "Like Love, 'A Moving Thing': Janie's Search for Self and God in *Their Eyes Were Watching God.*" *South Atlantic Review* 60, no. 1 (1995): 77–95.

Curren, Erik D. "Should Their Eyes Have Been Watching God?: Hurston's Use of Religious Experience and Gothic Horror." *African American Review* 29, no. 1 (1995): 17–25.

Donlon, Joyce Hazelwood. "Porches: Stories: Power: Spatial and Racial Intersections in Faulkner and Hurston." *Journal of American Culture* 19, no. 4 (1996): 95–110.

Ford, Sarah. "Necessary Chaos in Hurston's *Their Eyes Were Watching God.*" *CLA Journal* 43, no. 4 (2000): 407–419.

Haas, Robert. "Might Zora Neale Hurston's Janie Woods Be Dying of Rabies?: Considerations from Historical Medicine." *Literature and Medicine* 19, no. 2 (Fall 2000): 205–228.

Jones, Evora. "Ascent and Immersion: Narrative Expression in *Their Eyes Were Watching God.*" *CLA Journal* 39, no. 3 (1996): 369–379.

Jones, Sharon L. "Reclaiming a Legacy: The Dialectic of Race, Class, and Gender in Jessie Fauset, Zora Neale Hurston, and Dorothy West." *Hecate: A Women's Interdisciplinary Journal* XXIV/i (1998): 155–164.

Jones, Tayari A. "Beyond the Privilege of the Vernacular: A Textual Comparison of the Characterization of Bondswomen in *Their Eyes Were Watching God* and 'Father to

Son'." *Langston Hughes Review* 16, nos. 1–2 (1999–2001): 71–80.

Kaplan, Carla. "The Erotics of Talk: 'That Oldest Human Longing' in *Their Eyes Were Watching God*." *American Literature* 67, no. 1 (1995): 115–142.

Knudson, Janice L. "The Tapestry of Living: A Journey of the Self-Discovery in Hurston's *Their Eyes Were Watching God*." *CLA Journal* 40, no. 2 (1996): 214–229.

McGowan, Todd. "Liberation and Domination: *Their Eyes Were Watching God* and the Evolution of Capitalism." *MELUS* 24, no. 1 (1999): 109–128.

Oxindine, Annette. "Pear Trees beyond Eden: Women's Knowing Reconfigured in Woolf's *To the Lighthouse* and Hurston's *Their Eyes Were Watching God*." In *Approaches to Teaching Woolf's* To the Lighthouse. Edited by Beth Rigel Daugherty and Mary Beth Pringle, 163–168. New York: Modern Language Association, 2001.

Philip, Joseph. "The Verdict from the Porch: Zora Neale Hurston and Reparative Justice." *American Literature* 74, no. 3 (2002): 455–483.

Racine, Maria J. "Voice and Interiority in Zora Neale *Hurston's Their Eyes Were Watching God*." *African American Review* 28, no. 2 (1994): 283–292.

Ramsey, William M. "The Compelling Ambivalence of Zora Neale Hurston's *Their Eyes Were Watching God*." *Southern Literary Journal* 27, no. 1 (1994): 36–50.

Shroeder, Patricia R. "Rootwork: Arthur Flowers, Zora Neale Hurston, and the 'Literary Hoodoo' Tradition." *African American Review* 36, no. 2 (2002): 263–272.

Simmons, Ryan. "'The Hierarchy Itself': Hurston's *Their Eyes Were Watching God* and the Sacrifice of Narrative Authority." *African American Review* 36, no. 2 (2002): 181–193.

Sorensen, Leif. "Modernity on a Global Stage: Hurston's Alternative Modernism." *MELUS* 30, no. 4 (2005): 3–24.

Spencer, Stephen. "The Value of Lived Experience: Zora Neale Hurston and the Complexity of Race." *Studies in American Culture* 27, no. 2 (2004): 17–33.

Watson, Reginald. "Mulatto as Object in Zora Neale Hurston's *Their Eyes Were Watching God* and John O Killen's *The Cotillion*." *CLA Journal* 43, no. 4 (2000): 383–406.

Weathers, Glenda B. "Biblical Trees, Biblical Deliverance: Literary Landscapes of Zora Hurston and Toni Morrison." *African American Review* 39, nos. 1–2 (2005): 201–212.

Film version of *Their Eyes Were Watching God*

Boyd, Valerie. "Our Eyes Are Watching Halle." *Essence,* March 2005, 132.

Johnson, Sharon D. "All Eyes on 'Eyes': Oprah's adaptation of Zora's classic novel, starring Halle as Janie, is a historical moment for the worlds of television and literature." *black issues book review.* March–April 2005, 42–44.

Zora Neale Hurston Chronology

This chronology is indebted to the following sources:

"Chronology," in *Novels and Stories,* 1013–1032. New York: Library of America, 1995.

Wall, Cheryl A. *Women of the Harlem Renaissance.* Bloomington: Indiana University Press, 1995.

1891
Zora Neale Hurston is born in Notasulga, Alabama, to Lucy Ann Potts and John Hurston.

1894
The Hurstons move to Eatonville, Florida.

1904
Lucy Hurston dies. Zora moves to Jacksonville, Florida.

1905
Hurston attends school in Jacksonville. Her father meets another woman.

1906–1911
This period of Hurston's life is not well documented, but it is understood that Hurston moves around and holds various jobs.

1912
Hurston lives with her brother Dick and his wife in Sanford, Florida. She returns to Eatonville at her father's request, but she leaves after getting in a fight with his new wife.

1914–1915
Hurston lives with her brother Bob, a physician in Memphis.

1915–1916
Hurston works for Gilbert and Sullivan, a music company, but stops when she falls ill. She gets appendicitis and receives surgery in Baltimore, Maryland.

1917
John Hurston dies in a car accident in August. Hurston begins studying at Morgan Academy the following month, while working in Baltimore.

1918
Hurston earns her diploma in June and moves to Washington, D.C., where she works at the Cosmos Club. She begins preparations for study at Howard University in September.

1919–1920

Hurston meets Herbert Sheen at Howard University, whom she will later wed. She completes her Howard degree, having concentrated in English.

1921

Hurston's short story "John Redding Goes to Sea" is published in *The Stylus,* a literary magazine at Howard University. Hurston meets Jean Toomer, Alain Locke, W. E. B DuBois, Jessie Fauset, and Alice Dunbar-Nelson, all important writers during the Harlem Renaissance.

1924

Hurston publishes the short story "Drenched in Light" in *Opportunity* magazine, a National Urban League publication, which gained her attention.

1925

Hurston moves to New York City. At the *Opportunity* prize ceremony, she meets Countee Cullen, Carl Van Vechten, Langston Hughes, Fannie Hurst, and Annie Nathan Meyer. She gets a job working for Hurst. Hurston's tale "Spunk" appears in *Opportunity.* She enrolls at Barnard College, where she is the only black student, and she is a student of anthropology expert Franz Boas ("Chronology" 1016).

1926

Hurston moves close to her employer, Fannie Hurst. She wins another prize from *Opportunity* for "Muttsy." She writes *Color Struck* and "Sweat" for *Fire!!* magazine, publishing alongside writers such as Wallace Thurman and Gwendolyn Bennett.

1927

Hurston obtains funding for researching folktales from Charlotte Osgood Mason, a wealthy white patron from New York. She leaves New York and goes to Florida to conduct the research. She also marries Herbert Sheen and spends time with Langston Hughes in Tuskegee, Alabama, where they visit Booker T. Washington's grave. Hurston publishes essays in the *Journal of Negro History.*

1928

Hurston conducts research on folktales and music in Florida, meeting Big Sweet, and then goes to New Orleans to study conjuring. She earns her Barnard College degree in May.

1930

Hurston composes *Mule Bone* with Langston Hughes.

1931

Hughes and Hurston get into a conflict about *Mule Bone,* and their friendship ends. Hurston divorces her husband.

1933

Hurston publishes "The Gilded Six-Bits" in *Story.* The publisher Bertram Lippincott contacts Hurston about publishing a novel, and she then composes *Jonah's Gourd Vine.*

1934

Hurston publishes *Jonah's Gourd Vine,* her first novel. She begins work on *Moses, Man of the Mountain,* but sets it aside while she continues her anthropology research.

1935
Hurston publishes *Mules and Men,* the result of her research in Florida and Louisiana.

1936
Hurston earns a Guggenheim fellowship and travels to the Caribbean to conduct research. While in Haiti, Hurston writes *Their Eyes Were Watching God.*

1937
Hurston travels between Haiti, New York, and Florida. *Their Eyes Were Watching God* is published.

1938
Her account of her Caribbean research, *Tell My Horse,* is published. Hurston begins working for the Federal Writers Project in Florida, working in supervisory roles and researching for the text "The Florida Negro."

1939
She marries Albert Price, whom she meets during her work recording oral tales for the Federal Writers Project. She publishes *Moses, Man of the Mountain.*

1940
Hurston wants to divorce Albert Price, but they stay together and go to Beaufort, South Carolina. She researches religion and gets involved with a movie production. She goes back to New York.

1941
Hurston relocates to Los Angeles. She works "as story consultant" for Paramount. She writes *Dust Tracks on a Road,* her memoir ("Chronology" 1025).

1942
She returns to Florida, teaching on faculty at Florida Normal. *Dust Tracks on a Road* is published.

1943
Dust Tracks on a Road wins the Anisfield-Wolf Book Award and Hurston is honored by Howard University as an outstanding alumna. She divorces Albert Price and works for a civil rights organization.

1944
She is engaged to James Howell Pitts, but they do not end up marrying.

1947
Hurston spends time in Honduras, composing *Seraph on the Suwanee.*

1948
Hurston is accused of molesting a child; she is arrested and faces indictment. She moves to the Bronx. She publishes *Seraph on the Suwanee.*

1949
The molestation charges are dropped.

1950
Hurston works as a domestic in Florida, living with friends in Belle Glade. She works on "The Lives of Barney Turk," which is not published. She also gets involved with a political campaign.

1951
Hurston works on "The Golden Bench of God," which is also not published. She moves to Eau Gallie, Florida, living in the

same place she stayed while working on *Mules and Men.*

1952
Hurston suffers medical problems.

1953–1954
Hurston works on a book about Herod the Great.

1955
Hurston has a letter published in which she registers complaints about the *Brown v. Board of Education* decision.

1956
Hurston is evicted from her home and finds work on a military base in Florida.

1957
She loses her job at the base and relocates to Merritt Island, then to Fort Pierce. She writes essays for a local African-American newspaper, the *Fort Pierce Chronicle.*

1958
Hurston works at the Lincoln Park Academy.

1959
Hurston suffers a stroke and moves to the Saint Lucie County Welfare Home.

1960
Hurston dies from hypertensive heart disease. She is buried at Genesee Memorial Gardens in Fort Pierce, Florida.

INDEX

Note: Page numbers in **boldface** refer to main articles. Page numbers in *italic* refer to illustrations.

A

G

I

Q

R